BMW R1200 liquid-cooled Twins
Service and Repair Manual

by Matthew Coombs

Models covered

(6281-288-5AP1)

R1200GS. 1170cc. 2013 to 2016
R1200GS Adventure. 1170cc. 2013 to 2016
R1200RT. 1170cc. 2014 to 2016
R1200RS. 1170cc. 2015 to 2016
R1200R. 1170cc. 2015 to 2016

© Haynes Publishing 2016

A book in the **Haynes Service and Repair Manual Series**

ISBN 978 1 78521 281 9

British Library Cataloguing in Publication Data
A catalogue record for this book is available from the British Library

Library of Congress Control Number 2015958620

Printed in Malaysia

Haynes Publishing
Sparkford, Yeovil, Somerset BA22 7JJ, England

Haynes North America, Inc
859 Lawrence Drive, Newbury Park, California 91320, USA

ABCDE
FGHIJ
KLMNO
PQR

Printed using NORBRITE BOOK 48.8gsm (CODE: 40N6533) from NORPAC; procurement system certified under Sustainable Forestry Initiative standard. Paper produced is certified to the SFI Certified Fiber Sourcing Standard (CERT - 0094271)

Contents

LIVING WITH YOUR BMW R1200

Introduction

Pre-ride checks

MAINTENANCE

Routine maintenance and servicing

Contents

REPAIRS AND OVERHAUL

BMW – They did it their way

by Julian Ryder

BMW - Bayerische Motoren Werke

If you were looking for a theme tune for BMW's engineering philosophy you'd have to look no further than Francis Albert Sinatra's best known ditty: 'I did it my way.' The Bayerische Motoren Werke, like their countrymen at Porsche, takes precious little notice of the way anyone else does it, point this out to a factory representative and you will get a reply starting: 'We at BMW... '. The implication is clear.

It was always like that. The first BMW motorcycle, the R32, was, according to motoring sage L J K Setright: 'the first really outstanding post-War design, argued from first principles and uncorrupted by established practice. It founded a new German school of design, it established a BMW tradition destined to survive unbroken from 1923 to the present day.' That tradition was, of course, the boxer twin. The nickname 'boxer' for an opposed twin is thought to derive from the fact that the pistons travel horizontally towards and away from each other like the fists of boxers.

Before this first complete motorcycle, BMW had built a horizontally-opposed fore-and-aft boxer engine for the Victoria company of Nuremburg. It was a close copy of the British Douglas motor which the company's

The roots of the GS range go back to the 2-valve Boxer engine, seen here fitted to the second generation R80GS

chief engineer Max Friz admired, a fact the company's official history confirms despite what some current devotees of the marque will claim. In fact BMW didn't really want to make motorcycles at all, originally it was an aero-engine company - a fact celebrated in the blue-and-white tank badge that is symbolic of a propeller. But in Germany after the Treaty of Versailles such potentially warlike work was forbidden to domestic companies and BMW had to diversify, albeit reluctantly.

Friz was known to have a very low opinion of motorcycles and chose the Douglas to copy simply because he saw it as fundamentally a good solution to the engineering problem of powering a two-wheeler. In the R32 the engine was arranged with the crankshaft in-line with the axis of the bike and the cylinders sticking out into the cooling airflow, giving a very low centre-of-gravity and perfect vibration-free primary balance. It wasn't just the motor's layout that departed from normal practice, the clutch was a single-plate type as used in cars, final drive was by shaft and the rear wheel could be removed quickly. The frame and suspension were equally sophisticated, but the bike was quite heavy. Most of that description could be equally well applied to any of the boxer-engined bikes BMW made in the next 70-plus years.

Development within the surprisingly flexible confines of the boxer concept was quick. The second BMW, the R37 of 1925, retained the 68 x 68 mm Douglas bore and stroke but had overhead valves in place of the side valves. In 1928 two major milestones were passed. First, BMW acquired the car manufacturer Dixi and started manufacturing a left-hand-drive version of the Austin 7 under license. Secondly, the larger engined R62 and R63 appeared, the

With the introduction of the 4-valve engine, the R1100GS and R1150GS models followed . . .

latter being an OHV sportster that would be the basis of BMW's sporting and record-breaking exploits before the Second World War.

The 1930s was the era of speed records on land, on sea and in the air, and the name of Ernst Henne is in the record books no fewer than ten times: eight for two-wheeled exploits, twice for wheel-on-a-stick 'sidecar' world records. At first he was on the R63 with supercharging, but in 1936 he switched to the 500 cc R5, high-pushrod design reminiscent of the latest generation of BMW twins. Chain-driven camshafts operated short pushrods which opened valves with hairpin - not coil - springs. A pure racing version of this motor also appeared, this time with shaft and bevel-gear driven overhead camshafts, but with short rockers operating the valves so the engine can't be called a true DOHC design. Again with the aid of a blower, this was the motor that powered the GP 500s of the late '30s to many wins including the 1939 Senior TT. After the War, this layout would re-emerge in the immortal Rennsport.

From 1939 to 1945 BMW were fully occupied making military machinery, notably the R75 sidecar for the army. The factory didn't restart production until 1948, and then only with a lightweight single. There was a false start in 1950 and a slump in sales in 1953 that endangered the whole company, before the situation was rescued by one of the truly classic boxers. Their first post-War twin had been the R51/2, and naturally it was very close to the pre-War model although simplified to a single-camshaft layout. Nevertheless, it was still a relatively advanced OHV design not a sidevalve sidecar tug which enabled a face-lift for the 1955 models to do the marketing trick.

The 1955 models got a swinging arm - at both ends. The old plunger rear suspension was replaced by a swinging arm while leading-link Earles forks adorned the front. Thus were born the R50, the R60 and the R69. The European market found these new bikes far too expensive compared to British twins but America saved the day, buying most of the company's output. The car side of the company also found a product the market wanted, a small sports-car powered by a modified bike engine, thus BMW's last crisis was averted

In 1960 the Earles fork models were updated and the R69S was launched with more power, closer transmission ratios and those funny little indicators on the ends of the handlebars. Very little changed during the '60s, apart from US export models getting telescopic forks, but in 1970 everything changed...

The move to Spandau and a new line of Boxers

BMW's bike side had outgrown its site in Munich at the company's head-quarters, so, taking advantage of government subsidies for enterprises that located to what was then West Berlin, surrounded by the still Communist

. . . and were superseded by the R1200GS in 2004 . . .

. . . and then by the twin cam R1200GS in 2010 . . .

. . . and finally by the liquid-cooled twin cam GS in 2013

DDR, BMW built a new motorcycle assembly plant at Spandau in Berlin. It opened in 1969, producing a completely new range of boxers, the 5-series, which begat the 6-series, which begat the 7-series.

In 1976, at the same time as the launch of the 7-series the first RS boxer appeared. It's hard to believe now, but it was the only fully faired motorcycle, and it set the pattern for all BMWs, not just boxers, to come. The RS suffix came to mean a wonderfully efficient fairing that didn't spoil a sporty riding position. More sedate types could buy the RT version with a massive but no less efficient fairing that protected a more upright rider. Both bikes could carry luggage in a civilised fashion, too, thanks to purpose-built Krauser panniers. Both the RT and RS were uncommonly civilised motorcycles for their time.

When the boxer got its next major makeover in late 1980 BMW did something no-one thought possible, they made a boxer trail bike, the R80G/S. This wasn't without precedent as various supermen had wrestled 750 cc boxers to honours in the ISDT and in '81 Hubert Auriol won the Paris-Dakar on a factory boxer. Some heretics even dared to suggest the roadgoing G/S was the best boxer ever.

The K-series

By the end of the '70s the boxer was looking more and more dated alongside the opposition, and when the motorcycle division's management was shaken up at the beginning of 1979 the team working on the boxer replacement was doubled in size. The first new bike wasn't launched until late '83, but when it was it was clear that BMW had got as far away from the boxer concept as possible.

The powerplant was an in-line water-cooled DOHC four just like all the Japanese

The R1200GS Adventure is established as one of the best long distance enduro bikes

opposition, but typically BMW did it their way by aligning the motor so its crank was parallel to the axis of the bike and lying the motor on it side. In line with their normal practice, there was a car-type clutch, shaft drive and a single-sided swinging arm. It was totally novel yet oddly familiar. And when RT and RS version were introduced to supplement the basic naked bike, the new K-series 'flying bricks' felt even more familiar.

It was clear that BMW wanted the new four, and the three-cylinder 750 that followed it, to be the mainstay of the company's production - but in a further analogy with Porsche the customers simply wouldn't let go of the old boxer. Just as Porsche were forced to keep the 911 in production so BMW had to keep the old air-cooled boxer going by pressure from their customers. It kept going until 1995,

during which time the K-bikes had debuted four-valve heads and ABS. And when the latest generation of BMWs appeared in 1993 what were they? Boxers. Granted they were four-valve, air/oil-cooled and equipped with non-telescopic fork front ends, but they were still boxers. And that high camshaft, short pushrod layout looked remarkably similar to something that had gone before...

The New 4-valve Boxers

Even by BMW's standards, the new-generation Boxers were a shock. Maybe we shouldn't have been surprised after the lateral thinking that gave us the K-series, but the way in which the men from Munich took the old opposed-twin Boxer concept that launched the company and projected it into the 21st-Century was nothing short of breath-taking in its audacity. About the only design features the old and new Boxers had in common was that they both had two wheels and two cylinders. The 4-valve engine was produced in 850 and 1100 cc version, with the later eventually being upgraded to 1150 cc for GS, R, RS and RT versions, and stretched further to 1200 cc for the C model made famous in the 007 film Golden Eye.

The new bikes mixed old and new technology in a very clever way. Fuel injection and four-valve heads were very cutting edge, high camshafts operating pushrods (for ground clearance) and air cooling (albeit with some substantial help from oil) was not. The really revolutionary stuff was in the chassis department: Telelever at the front and Paralever at the rear bolted to the motor via tubular steel sub-frames and nothing in the way of a conventional frame in the middle. The Telelever front fork is carried on a couple of wishbones with anti-dive built into the linkage. Rear Paralever suspension uses a single-sided swingingarm with a shaft drive

Overall luxury is provided by the fully loaded R1200RT

The R1200 RS

HP2, in which HP stands for high performance. That model used a DOHC engine first seen in the HP2 Sport road bike. This is the engine that has now been put into full production for the R1200 series not confined to the comparatively expensive HP models, so it's not another generational step, more a quantum jump. The only significant changes are the cylinder heads, which have the chain-driven twin camshafts positioned horizontally operating one exhaust and one inlet valve each. The motor is of course 're-tuned' from the sports bike to give a better spread of torque.

A year after the first 1200GS was launched the range was extended with the R1200 ST and RT, These models carried on BMW's tradition of cleverly differentiated sports tourer and full-house tourer, two motorcycles that look quite similar on paper but exhibit very different characters on the road. In another indication that this was an evolution, not a revolution, most of the R1200 range got the upgrade immediately. The GS and the RT tourer plus the GS Adventure all got the new twin-cam heads in 2010. The R1200R roadster, that didn't appear until 2006, didn't get the new heads until 2011.

Most companies trying to sell large-capacity motorcycles since the financial upheavals of 2009 have not had a good time. The market for big sports bikes in particular has shrunk severely. One company that doesn't seem to have noticed the shrinking market is BMW. The mass sales of the GS, in Continental Europe particularly, has given the company the courage to field everything from singles and twins to race winning superbikes with across-the-frame four-cylinder motors. It would be impossible, though, to envisage BMW abandoning their roots. At regular intervals over many years, the death of the Boxer twin has been predicted, but it would appear that reports of its death are exaggerated.

running inside it which forms not quite a parallelogram shaped system with a tie-arm running from just below to the swinging arm pivot to the rear hub. It ensures the rear axle moves in an (almost) straight line and suppresses the old BMW habit of the rear end rising when the throttle is opened. The styling was also anything but safe; the old cliché of the boring BMW was blown out of the water.

The R1200 Models

When the 1200cc version of BMW's GS on/off-road model appeared in 2004 it wasn't just an upgrade of the old 1150, it was a new generation of the Munich company's fabled Boxer twins. Thirty kilograms of weight was shed despite the engine gaining a balance shaft, and the chassis was completely revised, with the Paralever rear suspension's linkage arm moved from below the swinging arm to above it. Among a host of improvements, perhaps the most revolutionary is the Single Wire System using technology borrowed from the car world. This is basically a CAN-bus wiring circuit rather than a wiring loom connecting all control units and power-consuming components. No fuses, no relays (except for the starter motor) and built-in diagnostics make this a contender for the first motorcycle electrical system that looks like it was actually designed in the 21st-Century.

As had become usual, the GS model was the first to be launched, it had become BMW's most popular model. BMW define the GS as an 'Adventure Sports' motorcycle, which sums it up nicely. A GS is a bike that will take you just about anywhere and is equally at home on motorways, mountain hairpins and dusty tracks in the middle of nowhere.

No other manufacturer has had anywhere near this sort of success for a model that can trace its origins back to the Paris-Dakar bikes

of the late 1970s and before that semi-official specials used in the International Six days Trial in the days when that event carried a lot of prestige and competitors had to ride bikes built in their own countries. Of course you'd have to be one of those Paris-Dakar heroes to contemplate taking one of today's GSs off road, but they have become favourites of riders who want to do big distances in comfort without riding a full-on tourer. Perhaps the best publicity a motorcycle has ever had came from Ewan McGregor and Charlie Boorman's TV programme 'The Long Way Round' in which the film star and his friend rode two 1150GS BMWs on their long-distance odyssey. The result was waiting lists at BMW dealers and GS-models also have the benefit of strong residual value.

For the really serious off-road hero, BMW also sold a limited-edition version of the GS, the

The R1200R naked Roadster

Acknowledgements

Our thanks are due to CW Motorcycles of Dorchester who supplied the machines featured in the illustrations throughout this manual. We would also like to thank NGK Spark Plugs (UK) Ltd for supplying the colour spark plug condition photographs, the Avon Rubber Company for supplying information on tyre fitting and Draper Tools Ltd for some of the workshop tools shown.

Thanks are also due to Julian Ryder who wrote the introduction 'BMW – They did it their way' and to BMW (GB) Ltd. who supplied model photographs.

About this Manual

The aim of this manual is to help you get the best value from your motorcycle. It can do so in several ways. It can help you decide what work must be done, even if you choose to have it done by a dealer; it provides information and procedures for routine maintenance and servicing; and it offers diagnostic and repair procedures to follow when trouble occurs.

We hope you use the manual to tackle the work yourself. For many simpler jobs, doing it yourself may be quicker than arranging an appointment to get the motorcycle into a dealer and making the trips to leave it and pick it up. More importantly, a lot of money can be saved by avoiding the expense the shop must pass on to you to cover its labour and overhead costs. An added benefit is the sense of satisfaction and accomplishment that you feel after doing the job yourself.

References to the left or right side of the motorcycle assume you are sitting on the seat, facing forward.

We take great pride in the accuracy of information given in this manual, but motorcycle manufacturers make alterations and design changes during the production run of a particular motorcycle of which they do not inform us. No liability can be accepted by the authors or publishers for loss, damage or injury caused by any errors in, or omissions from, the information given.

Illegal Copying

It is the policy of Haynes Publishing to actively protect its Copyrights and Trade Marks. Legal action will be taken against anyone who unlawfully copies the cover or contents of this Manual. This includes all forms of unauthorised copying including digital, mechanical, and electronic in any form. Authorisation from Haynes Publishing will only be provided expressly and in writing. Illegal copying will also be reported to the appropriate statutory authorities.

Other titles of interest from Haynes Publishing

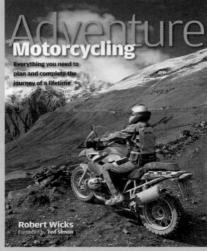

Book No. H4435

Book No. H4572

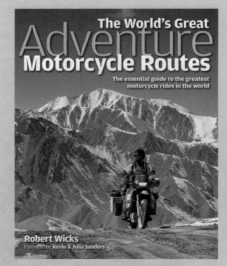

Book No. H4945

Book No. H5059

Frame and engine numbers

The frame VIN (Vehicle Identification Number) is stamped into the frame behind the steering head or directly on the headstock, depending on the model **(see illustrations)**. The engine number is stamped into the back of the crankcase on the right-hand side below the starter motor **(see illustration)**. Both of these numbers should be recorded and kept in a safe place so they can be furnished to law enforcement officials in the event of a theft. There is also a VIN label stuck to the frame or headstock.

The frame VIN and engine number should also be kept in a handy place (such as with your driving licence) so they are always available when purchasing or ordering parts for your machine. The procedures in this manual identify the bikes by model code and, if necessary, also by production year. The model code (e.g. R1200 GS) is used by itself if the information applies to all bikes produced over the life of the model. The production year is added where the information applies only to bikes produced in certain years of the model's life, usually when a component has been changed or upgraded.

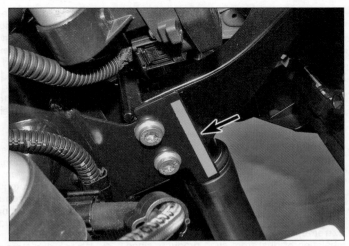

The frame number (arrowed) is stamped into the frame behind the steering head on GS, Adv and RT models . . .

. . . and into the headstock on R and RS models

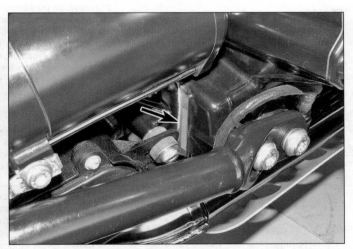

The engine number (arrowed) is stamped into the right-hand side of the crankcase below the starter motor

Buying spare parts

When ordering replacement parts, it is essential to identify exactly the machine for which the parts are required. While in some cases it is sufficient to identify the machine by its title e.g. 'R1200 GS', any modifications made to components mean that it is usually essential to identify the machine by its BMW production or model year e.g. '2014 R1200 GS', and sometimes by its engine and/or frame number as well (see above). The BMW production year starts in September of the previous calendar year, after the annual holiday, and continues until the following August. Therefore a 2014 R1200 GS was produced at some time between September 2013 and August 2014; it may have been sold (to its first owner) at any time from September 2013 onwards.

To identify your own machine, record its full engine and frame numbers and take them to any BMW dealer who should have the necessary information to identify it exactly. Finally, in some cases modifications can be identified only by reference to the machine's engine or frame number; these should be noted and taken with you whenever replacement parts are required.

To be absolutely certain of receiving the correct part, not only is it essential to have the machine's identifying title and engine and frame numbers, but it is also useful to take the old part for comparison (where possible). Note that where a modified component has superseded the original, a careful check must be made that there are no related parts which have also been modified and must be used to enable the replacement to be correctly refitted; where such a situation is found, purchase all the necessary parts and fit them, even if this means replacing apparently unworn items.

Always purchase replacement parts from an authorised BMW dealer who will either have the parts in stock or can order them quickly from the importer, and always use genuine parts to ensure the machine's performance and reliability. Pattern parts are available for certain components (i.e. brake pads and filters); if used, ensure these are of recognised quality brands which will perform as well as the original.

Expendable items such as lubricants, spark plugs, some electrical components, bearings, bulbs and tyres can usually be obtained at lower prices from accessory shops, motor factors or from specialists advertising in the national motorcycle press.

Professional mechanics are trained in safe working procedures. However enthusiastic you may be about getting on with the job at hand, take the time to ensure that your safety is not put at risk. A moment's lack of attention can result in an accident, as can failure to observe simple precautions.

There will always be new ways of having accidents, and the following is not a comprehensive list of all dangers; it is intended rather to make you aware of the risks and to encourage a safe approach to all work you carry out on your bike.

Asbestos

● Certain friction, insulating, sealing and other products - such as brake pads, clutch linings, gaskets, etc. - contain asbestos. Extreme care must be taken to avoid inhalation of dust from such products since it is hazardous to health. If in doubt, assume that they do contain asbestos.

Fire

● Remember at all times that petrol is highly flammable. Never smoke or have any kind of naked flame around, when working on the vehicle. But the risk does not end there - a spark caused by an electrical short-circuit, by two metal surfaces contacting each other, by careless use of tools, or even by static electricity built up in your body under certain conditions, can ignite petrol vapour, which in a confined space is highly explosive. Never use petrol as a cleaning solvent. Use an approved safety solvent.

● Always disconnect the battery earth terminal before working on any part of the fuel or electrical system, and never risk spilling fuel on to a hot engine or exhaust.

● It is recommended that a fire extinguisher of a type suitable for fuel and electrical fires is kept handy in the garage or workplace at all times. Never try to extinguish a fuel or electrical fire with water.

Fumes

● Certain fumes are highly toxic and can quickly cause unconsciousness and even death if inhaled to any extent. Petrol vapour comes into this category, as do the vapours from certain solvents such as trichloro-ethylene. Any draining or pouring of such volatile fluids should be done in a well ventilated area.

● When using cleaning fluids and solvents, read the instructions carefully. Never use materials from unmarked containers - they may give off poisonous vapours.

● Never run the engine of a motor vehicle in an enclosed space such as a garage. Exhaust fumes contain carbon monoxide which is extremely poisonous; if you need to run the engine, always do so in the open air or at least have the rear of the vehicle outside the workplace.

The battery

● Never cause a spark, or allow a naked light near the vehicle's battery. It will normally be giving off a certain amount of hydrogen gas, which is highly explosive.

● Always disconnect the battery ground (earth) terminal before working on the fuel or electrical systems (except where noted).

● If possible, loosen the filler plugs or cover when charging the battery from an external source. Do not charge at an excessive rate or the battery may burst.

● Take care when topping up, cleaning or carrying the battery. The acid electrolyte, evenwhen diluted, is very corrosive and should not be allowed to contact the eyes or skin. Always wear rubber gloves and goggles or a face shield. If you ever need to prepare electrolyte yourself, always add the acid slowly to the water; never add the water to the acid.

Electricity

● When using an electric power tool, inspection light etc., always ensure that the appliance is correctly connected to its plug and that, where necessary, it is properly grounded (earthed). Do not use such appliances in damp conditions and, again, beware of creating a spark or applying excessive heat in the vicinity of fuel or fuel vapour. Also ensure that the appliances meet national safety standards.

● A severe electric shock can result from touching certain parts of the electrical system, such as the spark plug wires (HT leads), when the engine is running or being cranked, particularly if components are damp or the insulation is defective. Where an electronic ignition system is used, the secondary (HT) voltage is much higher and could prove fatal.

Remember...

● **Don't** start the engine without first ascer-taining that the transmission is in neutral.

● **Don't** suddenly remove the pressure cap from a hot cooling system - cover it with a cloth and release the pressure gradually first, or you may get scalded by escaping coolant.

● **Don't** attempt to drain oil until you are sure it has cooled sufficiently to avoid scalding you.

● **Don't** grasp any part of the engine or exhaust system without first ascertaining that it is cool enough not to burn you.

● **Don't** allow brake fluid or antifreeze to contact the machine's paintwork or plastic components.

● **Don't** siphon toxic liquids such as fuel, hydraulic fluid or antifreeze by mouth, or allow them to remain on your skin.

● **Don't** inhale dust - it may be injurious to health (see Asbestos heading).

● **Don't** allow any spilled oil or grease to remain on the floor - wipe it up right away, before someone slips on it.

● **Don't** use ill-fitting spanners or other tools which may slip and cause injury.

● **Don't** lift a heavy component which may be beyond your capability - get assistance.

● **Don't** rush to finish a job or take unverified short cuts.

● **Don't** allow children or animals in or around an unattended vehicle.

● **Don't** inflate a tyre above the recommended pressure. Apart from overstressing the carcass, in extreme cases the tyre may blow off forcibly.

● **Do** ensure that the machine is supported securely at all times. This is especially important when the machine is blocked up to aid wheel or fork removal.

● **Do** take care when attempting to loosen a stubborn nut or bolt. It is generally better to pull on a spanner, rather than push, so that if you slip, you fall away from the machine rather than onto it.

● **Do** wear eye protection when using power tools such as drill, sander, bench grinder etc.

● **Do** use a barrier cream on your hands prior to undertaking dirty jobs - it will protect your skin from infection as well as making the dirt easier to remove afterwards; but make sure your hands aren't left slippery. Note that long-term contact with used engine oil can be a health hazard.

● **Do** keep loose clothing (cuffs, ties etc.

and long hair) well out of the way of moving mechanical parts.

● **Do** remove rings, wristwatch etc., before working on the vehicle - especially the electrical system.

● **Do** keep your work area tidy - it is only too easy to fall over articles left lying around.

● **Do** exercise caution when compressing springs for removal or installation. Ensure that the tension is applied and released in a controlled manner, using suitable tools which preclude the possibility of the spring escaping violently.

● **Do** ensure that any lifting tackle used has a safe working load rating adequate for the job.

● **Do** get someone to check periodically that all is well, when working alone on the vehicle.

● **Do** carry out work in a logical sequence and check that everything is correctly assembled and tightened afterwards.

● **Do** remember that your vehicle's safety affects that of yourself and others. If in doubt on any point, get professional advice.

● If in spite of following these precautions, you are unfortunate enough to injure yourself, seek medical attention as soon as possible.

Note: *The 'Before every journey check list' outlined in your rider's manual covers those items which should be inspected before you ride. These checks should be made with the ignition off. The motorcycle performs a check of the instrument warning functions every time the ignition is turned on.*

Engine oil level

Before you start:

Note: *The oil level varies with engine temperature – BMW stress that an accurate reading will only be obtained after the motorcycle has been ridden to allow it to reach normal operating temperature.*
Caution: Do not run the engine in an enclosed space such as a garage or workshop.

● Start the engine and allow it reach normal operating temperature, then turn it OFF and allow the oil level to stabilise for five minutes before checking it. Check the level with the motorcycle on its centrestand, where fitted, or by holding it or supporting it upright if not, making sure it is on level ground.

● The oil level is viewed through the window in the right-hand side of the engine. Wipe the window clean.

Bike care:

● Some oil usage is normal, but if you have to add oil frequently, you should check whether there are any oil leaks. If there is no sign of oil leakage the engine could be burning oil (see *Fault Finding*).
● Never run the engine with the oil level below the bottom of the circle marked on the window, and do not fill it above the top of the circle.
● Even though all models are equipped with an oil level sensor, this doesn't obviate the need to check the oil level via the inspection window.

The correct oil

● Always top up with a good quality oil of the specified type and viscosity and do not overfill the engine. **Note:** *BMW recommends their own ADVANTEC Ultimate motorcycle oil with the viscosity range 5W-40.*
● To fill the engine from the bottom to the top of the circle on the oil level window requires 0.95 litre of oil.

Oil type	SAE 5W/40, API SL, JASO MA2

1 Check the oil level through the inspection window in the right-hand side of the engine. With the motorcycle upright, the oil level should be within the circle marked on the window as shown.

2 If the level is below the bottom of the circle, use the screwdriver handle and bit from the bike's toolkit as shown to remove the filler cap from the right-hand valve cover.

3 Top the engine up with the recommended type and grade of oil so the level is just below the top of the circle. Take care not to over-fill the engine.

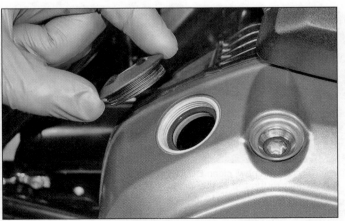

4 If there are any signs of oil leakage from around the cap, fit a new O-ring. Fit and tighten the cap.

Brake fluid levels

Before you start:

● When checking the front brake fluid level, position the bike and handlebars so that the top of the master cylinder is level.
● On RT models, remove the shock absorber right-hand cover to view the fluid level in the rear brake master cylinder reservoir (see Chapter 7).
● Make sure you have the correct brake fluid, DOT 4 is recommended. Wrap a rag around the reservoir being worked on to ensure that any spillage does not come into contact with painted surfaces.

Bike care:

● The fluid level in the front and rear brake master cylinder reservoirs will drop slightly as the brake pads wear down. If either reservoir requires repeated topping-up this is an indication of a fluid leak somewhere in the system, which should be investigated immediately.
● Check for signs of fluid leakage from the brake hoses and components – if found, rectify immediately.
● Check the operation of both brakes before taking the machine on the road. If there is evidence of air in the system (spongy feel to lever or pedal), the system must be bled – follow the procedure as described in Chapter 6.

> ⚠️ *Warning: Brake fluid can harm your eyes and damage painted surfaces, so use extreme caution when handling and pouring it and cover surrounding surfaces with rag. Do not use fluid that has been standing open for some time, as it absorbs moisture from the air which can cause a dangerous loss of braking effectiveness.*

FRONT BRAKE FLUID LEVEL

1 The fluid level is visible through the window in the reservoir body – it must be above the MIN level line (arrowed). Do not allow it to drop below the line.

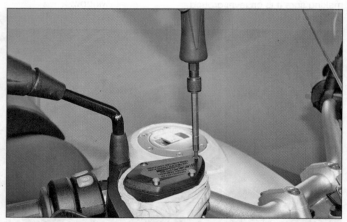

2 To top-up, undo the cover screws and lift off the cover and the diaphragm.

3 Top up with new, clean DOT 4 brake fluid almost to the top of the window. Do not overfill and take care to avoid spills.

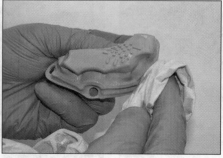

4 Wipe any moisture off the diaphragm using a clean, absorbent and lint-free cloth

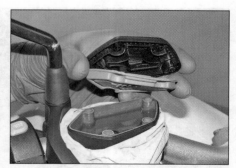

5 Make sure the diaphragm is correctly seated before fitting the cover.

REAR BRAKE FLUID LEVEL

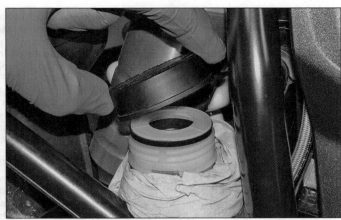

1 The fluid level is visible through the reservoir body – it must be between the MIN and MAX level lines. Do not allow it to drop below the MIN line.

2 To top up, support the reservoir and unscrew the cap, then lift out the plate and diaphragm.

3 Top up with new, clean DOT 4 hydraulic fluid to the MAX level line. Do not overfill and take care to avoid spills (see *Warning* on page 0•12).

4 Wipe any moisture off the diaphragm with a clean, absorbent and lint-free cloth

5 Make sure that the diaphragm is correctly seated. Fit the plate and screw the cap on.

Suspension, steering and final drive

Suspension and Steering:
● Check that the front and rear suspension operate smoothly without binding.
● Check that the suspension is adjusted as required (where applicable).
● Check that the steering moves smoothly from lock-to-lock.

Final drive:
● Check for signs of oil leakage around the final drive housing. If there are any signs of leakage have it checked by a BMW dealer.

Legal and safety

Lighting and signalling:
● Take a minute to check that the headlight, tail light, brake light, instrument lights and turn signals all work correctly.
● Check that the horn sounds when the switch is operated.
● A working speedometer is a statutory requirement in the UK.

Safety:
● Check that the throttle grip rotates smoothly and snaps shut when released, in all steering positions.
● Check that the engine shuts off when the kill switch is operated.
● Check that the sidestand and centrestand return springs hold the stands securely up when retracted.

Fuel:
● This may seem obvious, but check that you have enough fuel to complete your journey. Misfiring due to a low fuel level can damage the catalytic converter in the exhaust system.
● If you notice signs of fuel leakage – rectify the cause immediately.
● Ensure you use the correct grade unleaded fuel (see Chapter 4).

Coolant level

> ⚠️ **Warning: DO NOT remove the radiator pressure cap to add coolant. Topping up is done via the coolant reservoir tank filler. DO NOT leave open containers of coolant about, as it is poisonous.**

Bike care:

● Use only the specified coolant mixture. It is important that the correct proportion of anti-freeze is used in the system all year round, and not just in the winter. Do not top the system up using only water, as the system will become too diluted.

● Do not overfill the reservoir tank. If the coolant is significantly above the MAX level line at any time, the surplus should be siphoned or drained off to prevent the possibility of it being expelled out of the overflow hose.

● If the coolant level falls steadily, check the system for leaks (see Chapter 1). If no leaks are found and the level continues to fall, it is recommended that the machine is taken to a BMW dealer for a pressure test.

Before you start:

● Make sure you have a supply of coolant available. The BMW blue anti-freeze product requires mixing in the ratio 50/50 with equal parts of distilled water. Some products are sold as coolant, ready-mixed with water and can be poured directly into the cooling system. Check carefully which type you are buying.

● Always check the coolant level when the engine is cold.

● Support the motorcycle upright on level ground.

● On GS, GS Adv and RT models the coolant reservoir is on the right-hand side, above the front of the engine – the level lines are visible without removing any bodywork. If topping up is required, on GS models remove the side panel, on GS Adventure models remove the reservoir access panel, and on RT models remove the fairing side panel (see Chapter 7).

● On R and RS models the coolant reservoir is behind the steering head – the level lines are visible without removing any bodywork.

GS, GS ADVENTURE AND RT MODELS

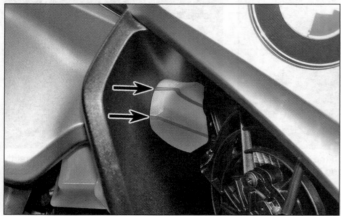

1 The coolant level should lie between the MAX and MIN level lines (arrowed) that are marked on the reservoir.

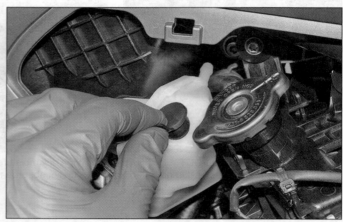

2 If the coolant level is on or below the MIN line, remove the relevant panel (see above), then open the reservoir cap and top up with coolant.

R AND RS MODELS

3 The coolant level should lie between the MAX and MIN level lines (arrowed) that are marked on the reservoir.

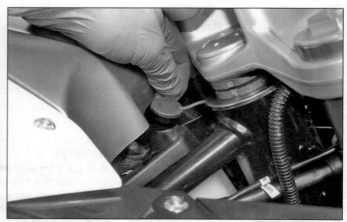

4 If the coolant level is on or below the MIN line open the reservoir filler cap and top up with coolant.

Tyres

The correct pressures:

● The tyres must be checked when cold, not immediately after riding. Note that low tyre pressures may cause the tyre to slip on the rim or come off. High tyre pressures will cause abnormal tread wear and unsafe handling.

● Use an accurate pressure gauge. On machines fitted with the tyre pressure monitoring system (RDC) do not rely on the pressure readout on the instrument display.

● Proper air pressure will increase tyre life and provide maximum stability and ride comfort. Ensure that the pressures are suited to the load the machine is carrying.

● On machines fitted with integrated tyre pressure monitoring, the pressure sensors are activated by centrifugal force once the machine has reached a road speed of approximately 20 mph (30 kph). The pressures are displayed for approximately 15 minutes after the machine has come to a halt. Pressure readings are temperature compensated to indicate the pressure at 20°C irrespective of actual tyre or air temperature. If the tyre pressure drops close to the permitted limit the general warning symbol on the multi-function display illuminates yellow and the tyre symbol is displayed. If the pressure falls to a critical level the general warning symbol flashes red.

Tyre care:

● The need for frequent inflation indicates an air leak, which should be investigated immediately.

● Check the tyres carefully for cuts, tears, embedded nails or other sharp objects and excessive wear. Operation of the motorcycle with excessively worn tyres is extremely hazardous, as traction and handling are directly affected.

● Check the condition of the tyre valve and ensure the dust cap is in place.

● Pick out any stones or nails which may have become embedded in the tyre tread. If left, they will eventually penetrate through the casing and cause a puncture.

● If tyre damage is apparent, or unexplained loss of pressure is experienced, seek the advice of a motorcycle tyre fitting specialist without delay.

Tyre tread depth:

● At the time of writing UK law requires that tread depth must be at least 1 mm over 3/4 of the tread breadth all the way around the tyre, with no bald patches. Many riders, however, consider 2 mm tread depth minimum to be a safer limit.

● Tyres now incorporate wear indicators in the tread. Identify the arrow, triangular pointer, TI or TWI marking on the tyre sidewall to locate the indicator bars and replace the tyre if the tread has worn down level with the bars.

Front	Rear
36 psi (2.5 Bar)	42 psi (2.9 Bar)

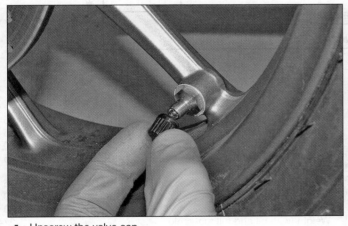

1 Unscrew the valve cap

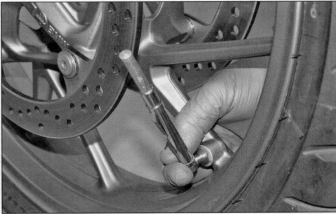

2 Check the tyre pressures when the tyres are cold and keep them properly inflated. Do not forget to refit the cap.

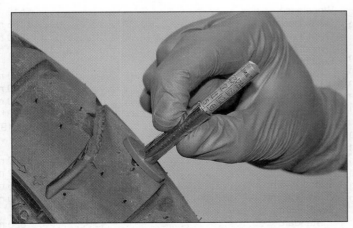

3 Measure tread depth at the centre of the tyre using a tread depth gauge.

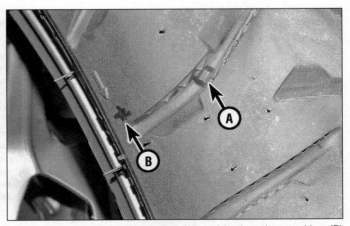

4 Tyre tread wear indicator bar (A) and its location marking (B) – usually a triangle, the letters TI or TWI, or in this case the tyre manufacturer's logo, on the sidewall.

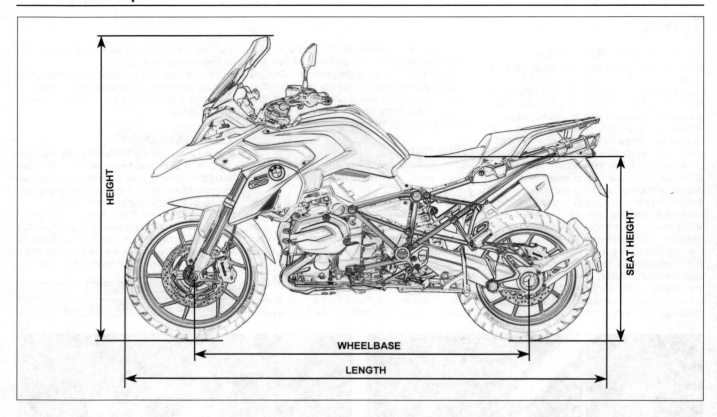

Weights and dimensions

R1200 GS

Wheelbase	.1507 mm
Overall length	.2205 mm
Overall width	.955 mm
Overall height	1430 to 1490 mm
	(1405 to 1465 mm with lowered suspension)

Seat height (rider's)

Standard	850 to 870 mm
Rallye seat	.880 mm
Low rider's seat	820 to 840 mm
Lowered suspension	800 to 820 mm
Weight (with oil and full fuel tank)	.238 kg
Maximum payload	.212 kg

R1200 GS Adventure

Wheelbase	.1510 mm
Overall length	.2255 mm
Overall width	.980 mm
Overall height (windshield raised)	.1450 mm
	(1410 mm with lowered suspension)

Seat height (rider's)

Standard	890 to 910 mm
Rallye seat	.895 mm
Low rider's seat	840 to 860 mm
Lowered suspension	820 to 840 mm
Weight (with oil and full fuel tank)	.260 kg
Maximum payload	.220 kg

R1200 RT

Wheelbase	.1485 mm
Overall length	.2185 mm
Overall width	.980 mm
Overall height (windshield lowered)	.1405 mm

Seat height

Standard	805 to 825 mm
Low seat	760 to 780 mm
High seat	830 to 850 mm
Weight (with oil and full fuel tank)	.274 kg
Maximum payload	.221 kg

R1200 R

Wheelbase	.1515 mm
Overall length	.2165 mm
Overall width	.880 mm
Overall height	.1300 mm

Seat height

Standard	.790 mm
Low seat	.760 mm
High seat	.820 mm
Weight (with oil and full fuel tank)	.231 kg
Maximum payload	.219 kg

R1200 RS

Wheelbase	.1530 mm
Overall length	.2202 mm
Overall width	.925 mm
Overall height	.1260 mm

Seat height

Standard	.820 mm
Low seat	.760 mm
High seat	.840 mm
Weight (with oil and full fuel tank)	.236 kg
Maximum payload	.214 kg

Engine – all models

Type	Four-stroke air/water-cooled horizontal twin
Capacity	1170 cc
Bore and stroke	101 x 73 mm
Compression ratio	12.5: 1
Camshafts	DOHC, chain and gear-driven
Valves	4 valves per cylinder
Fuel system	BMS-X electronic injectors
Clutch	Wet, multi-plate, hydraulically-operated
Transmission	6-speed constant mesh
Final drive	Shaft

Chassis – all models

Type	Tubular steel trellis frame, stress-bearing engine
Rake and trail	
R1200 GS	64.5°, 99.6 mm
R1200 GS Adventure	65.5°, 92.7 mm
R1200 RT	63.6°, 116 mm
R1200 R	62.3°, 125.6 mm
R1200 RS	62.3°, 114.8 mm
Front suspension	
Type	
GS, GS Adv and RT models	BMW Telelever
R and RS models	USD telescopic forks
Travel	
R1200 GS	
Standard suspension	190 mm
Lowered suspension	160 mm
R1200 GS Adventure	210 mm
R1200 RT	120 mm
R1200 R	140 mm
R1200RS	140 mm
Adjustment	
Standard	None
Electronic Suspension Adjustment	
GS, GS Adv and RT models	Rebound and compression damping
R and RS models	None
Rear suspension	
Type	BMW Paralever
Travel	
R1200 GS	
Standard suspension	200 mm
Lowered suspension	170 mm
R1200 GS Adventure	220 mm
R1200 RT	135 mm
R1200 R and RS	140 mm
Adjustment	
Standard	Spring pre-load and rebound damping
Electronic Suspension Adjustment	
GS, GS Adv and RT models	Spring pre-load, rebound and compression damping
R and RS models	Spring pre-load and damping
Wheels	
R1200 GS Adventure	Wire spoked
All other models	Cast aluminium
Wheel size	
R1200 GS and GS Adventure	3.0 x 19 inch (front), 4.5 x 17 inch (rear)
R1200 RT, R and RS	3.5 x 17 inch (front), 5.5 x 17 inch (rear)

Tyre sizes

	Front	Rear
R1200 GS and Adventure	120/70 R 19V	170/60 R 17V
R1200 RT, R and RS	120/70 ZR 17W	180/55 ZR 17W

Front brake	Twin discs with radially-mounted twin opposed-piston calipers
Rear brake	Single disc with two-piston sliding caliper

All models covered in this manual are powered by the same 1170 cc horizontally opposed, twin-cylinder engine. Though derived from the previous generation R1200 series in that it retains the 'boxer twin' characteristics, the engine is in fact all new. The most significant change is that the engine is now cooled by air and water as opposed to air and oil. It also has a hydraulically-actuated conventional wet multi-plate clutch with back-torque limiter, and the six-speed constant mesh transmission is now incorporated within the main crankcase and is lubricated by the engine oil. The shaft drive unit is now on the left-hand side and the exhaust silencer is on the right. The fuel/air intakes are now on the tops of the cylinder heads and the exhausts are on the bottom, and with the horizontal DOHC layout retained this allows the upper camshaft to actuate both intake valves and the lower camshaft to actuate both exhaust valves. The camshafts for the four valves per cylinder are driven by chain and gear, and a balancer shaft keeps things smooth. The cylinders are now integrated into the crankcases.

Throttle body diameter has increased to 52mm and control is now fly-by-wire. The exhaust system retains the electronically operated exhaust flow control valve.

Engine oil is contained within the crankcase and is pressure-fed for lubrication by a chain-driven dual-rotor pump.

Coolant is circulated by a pump via two radiators on GS, Adv and RT models and a single radiator on RS and R models.

The Bosch new digital engine management system (BMS-X) monitors, controls and co-ordinates both the fuel and ignition system functions. The system is operated by the ECU. A second unit, the ground control module is responsible for monitoring and control of all other electrical systems such as lighting, switches and accessories. The two units are linked for such functions as starting and engine immobilisation.

The ECU uses engine speed and throttle valve position as the basis for determining optimum engine operation. Additional data, supplied by temperature, oil level and gear position sensors, and exhaust gas analysers, when combined with control maps and correction values embedded within the ECU, fine tune injection volume and ignition timing to meet the engine's requirements in any given circumstance. In addition, the engine management system has in-built diagnostic functions which record and store all data should a fault occur.

All models utilise Controlled Area Network (CAN)-bus and Local Interconnect Network (LIN)-bus technology to create an electronic information network between the system control units (instrument, ABS, engine control, body control, plus others as fitted according to options selected), sensors and power-consuming components. This allows rapid and reliable data transfer around the network. It also allows comprehensive diagnosis of the entire system from one central point.

Another new feature is the use of a conventional type main frame with rear sub-frame bolted to it. The frame is tubular steel in trellis style and uses the engine as a stressed member.

On GS, Adv and RT models front suspension and steering are again managed separately by BMW's Telelever system. Telelever uses an arrangement of telescopic fork legs to support the front wheel and provide steering, together with a swingarm and shock absorber to provide suspension control. At the top of the Telelever system, the fork tubes are held in a yoke, which is mounted to the frame via the steering head bearing. Midway down the assembly, the fork outer tubes are linked by a bridge which is attached to the front of the Telelever swingarm via a ball joint. The swingarm pivots around a shaft which passes through the front of the engine crankcases, with the shock absorber located between the swingarm and the front sub-frame.

On R and RS models the more conventional set-up of upside-down (USD) telescopic forks mounted in two yokes and pivoting through the steering head is used.

Rear suspension is provided by a single-sided swingarm and centrally mounted shock absorber. The drive shaft to the rear wheel is housed inside the swingarm, but has been moved to the left-hand side of the bike. The joint between the swingarm and the final drive unit is pivoted, with a link arm, BMW's Paralever system, controlling movement between the two. The Paralever system counteracts the adverse effect of the shaft drive on suspension movement.

Both front and rear brakes are hydraulically operated Brembo disc brakes with ABS fitted as standard. The front calipers are now radially mounted and have two pairs of opposed pistons each, and the rear brake has two pistons in a sliding caliper.

R1200 GS (K50)

Launched in 2013, the GS was fitted with either light alloy cast wheels for road and moderate off-road riding, or wire spoked wheels for high speed, rough terrain use. Electronic suspension adjustment (ESA), automatic stability control (ASC), remote tyre pressure monitoring (RDC), cruise control, an anti-theft warning system, lowered suspension and a lowered rider's seat height, and LED headlight and running light, heated grips, a navigation system and various other items are all available as optional extras individually as required or as part of various 'packages' (such as Active, Comfort, Touring, Dynamic). Enduro crash bars and various guards are avaialble individually or as part of a Safety package, and luggage options are available, again individually or in a Storage package.

R1200 GS Adventure (K51)

Launched in 2013, the Adventure model was designed and equipped for long distance and rough terrain use. Standard equipment includes a large capacity (30 litre) fuel tank, large windshield, adjustable seat height, hand protectors, fuel tank and engine protection bars. Dual purpose tyres are fitted to wire spoked wheels and the front and rear suspension has longer travel. Automatic stability control (ASC) and two riding models (rain and road) are fitted as standard, with three further riding models and electronic suspension adjustment (ESA), along with a host of other accessories, available as optional extras.

R1200 RT (K52)

Launched in 2014, the R1200 RT shares the basic engine, transmission, suspension and chassis components of the GS, but as ever is styled and fitted out as a dedicated long distance touring machine, with a selection of comfort and luggage options to suit. Automatic stability control (ASC) and two riding models (rain and road) are fitted as standard, with three further riding models and electronic suspension adjustment (ESA), along with a host of other accessories, available as optional extras.

R1200 R (K53) and R1200 RS (K54)

The R, a naked style roadster, and the RS, basically the R with a sports style half-fairing, were launched in 2015. The R is available in basic form (blue with a black frame), Style 1 (white with a red frame, white belly-pan and stainless centre fuel tank cover), or Style 2 (grey with a grey frame and stainless fuel tank centre cover). Automatic stability control (ASC) and two riding models (rain and road) are fitted as standard, with three further riding models and electronic suspension adjustment (ESA), along with a host of other accessories, available as optional extras.

Chapter 1
Routine maintenance and servicing

Contents

Degrees of difficulty

| **Easy,** suitable for novice with little experience | | **Fairly easy,** suitable for beginner with some experience | | **Fairly difficult,** suitable for competent DIY mechanic | | **Difficult,** suitable for experienced DIY mechanic | | **Very difficult,** suitable for expert DIY or professional | |

Engine

Spark plugs
  Type . . . . NGK LMAR8D-J
  Electrode gap
    Standard . . . . 0.7 to 0.9 mm
    Wear limit . . . . 1.0 mm
Valve clearances (COLD engine)
  Intake valves . . . . 0.10 to 0.17 mm
  Exhaust valves . . . . 0.34 to 0.41 mm

Cycle parts

Brake pad friction material minimum thickness . . . . 1.0 mm
Brake disc minimum thickness
  Front . . . . 4.0 mm
  Rear . . . . 4.5 mm

Lubricants and fluids

Engine oil . . . . SAE 5W/40, API SL, JASO MA2 – BMW Motorrad ADVANTEC
Ultimate oil recommended
Engine oil capacity . . . . max. 4.0 litres
Final drive oil type . . . . Castrol SAF-XO
Final drive oil capacity . . . . 180 cc
Coolant type . . . . 50% distilled water and 50% corrosion inhibited ethylene glycol anti-freeze
Coolant capacity . . . . 1.75 litres (inc. reservoir)
Front fork oil type . . . . BMW telescopic fork oil (10W)
Front fork oil capacity . . . . see Chapter 5 for capacities and levels
Brake fluid . . . . DOT 4
Clutch fluid . . . . Vitamol V10
Miscellaneous
  Front wheel bearings . . . . High melting point lithium grease
  Suspension bearings . . . . High melting point lithium grease
  Lever and stand pivot points . . . . Dry film lubricant
  Throttle twistgrip . . . . Dry film lubricant

Torque settings

Cooling system drain plug – left-hand side . . . . 10 Nm
Cooling system drain plug – right-hand side . . . . 5 Nm
Engine oil drain plug . . . . 42 Nm
Engine oil filter . . . . 11 Nm
Final drive oil drain plug . . . . 20 Nm
Final drive oil filler plug . . . . 20 Nm
Fork clamp bolts in top yoke (R and RS models) . . . . 19 Nm
Spark plugs . . . . 12 Nm
Steering head bearing adjuster nut (R and RS models) –
  using the BMW tool . . . . 15 Nm
Steering stem bolt (R and RS models) . . . . 130 Nm

Note: *All models covered in this manual are fitted with a 'service due' indicator in the instrument display. When the next service is due in less than one month, the service date is displayed momentarily on the multi-function display following the pre-ride check after the ignition has been turned on. If the distance to the odometer reading at which the next service will be due is less than 600 miles (1000 km) the distance is counted down in steps of 60 miles (100 km) and is displayed momentarily on the multi-function display following the pre-ride check. If the service is overdue the general warning symbol lights yellow, and the word SERVICE will be permanently shown, along with the date or odometer reading at which it was due. The service indicator requires resetting by a BMW dealer.*

Pre-ride

Perform the *Pre-ride checks* listed at the beginning of this manual before carrying out any of the following procedures.

After the initial 600 miles (1000 km)

Note: *This check is usually performed by a BMW dealer after the first 600 miles (1000 km) from new. Thereafter, maintenance is carried out according to the following intervals of the schedule.*

Every 6000 miles (10,000 km) or annually

- ☐ Change the engine oil and fit a new filter (Section 1).
- ☐ Check the operation of the brake system, pad and disc wear (Section 8).
- ☐ Check spoke tension – wire spoked wheels (see Section 10).
- ☐ Check and lubricate the stand and lever pivots (Section 3).
- ☐ Check the lights and turn signals.
- ☐ Check the operation of the clutch system (Section 7).

Every 12,000 miles (20,000 km)

- ☐ Check and adjust the valve clearances (Section 2).
- ☐ Fit new spark plugs (Section 4).
- ☐ Fit a new air filter element (Section 5).

Every 12,000 miles (20,000 km) or two years

- ☐ Change the final drive oil (Section 6).

After the first year and every two years thereafter

- ☐ Change the brake fluid (see Chapter 6).

Every 18,000 miles (30,000 km)

- ☐ Change the fork oil (R and RS models) (see Chapter 5).

Non-scheduled maintenance

- ☐ Check the tightness of all nuts and bolts (Section 9).
- ☐ Check battery condition (see Chapter 8).
- ☐ Check the condition of the wheels and wheel bearings (Section 10).
- ☐ Check the front and rear suspension (Section 11).
- ☐ Check the steering head bearings (R and RS models) (Section 12)
- ☐ Check the cooling system (Section 13).
- ☐ Change the coolant (Section 13).

Component locations on the right side – GS (RT positions similar)

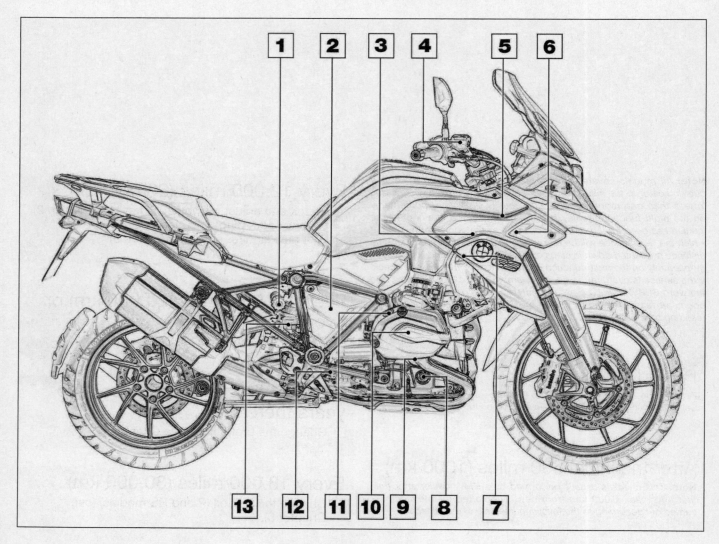

1 Rear shock pre-load adjuster
2 Battery
3 Coolant reservoir
4 Front brake fluid reservoir
5 Frame VIN

6 Front fork oil seal
7 Radiator pressure cap
8 Engine oil level window
9 Coolant drain plug

10 Spark plug
11 Engine oil filler cap
12 Engine number
13 Rear brake fluid reservoir

Component locations on the left side – GS (RT positions similar)

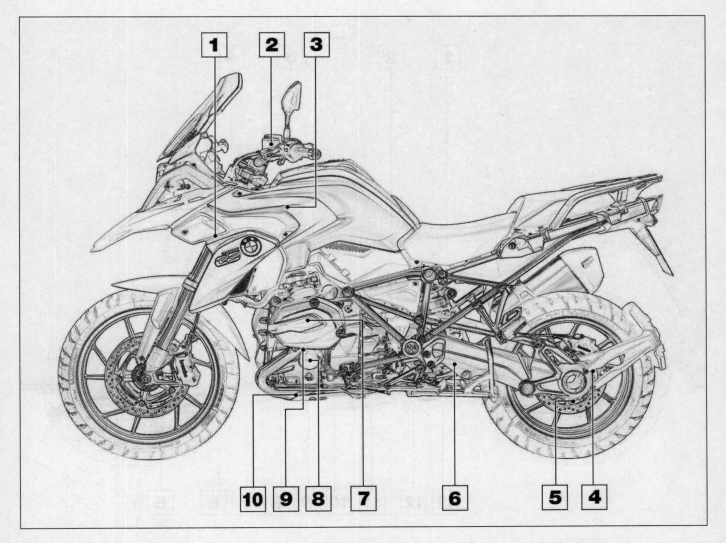

1 Front fork seal
2 Clutch fluid reservoir
3 Air filter
4 Final drive oil filler plug

5 Final drive oil drain plug
6 Rear shock damping adjuster
7 Spark plug

8 Engine oil filter
9 Coolant drain plug
10 Oil drain plug

Component locations on the right side – R and RS models

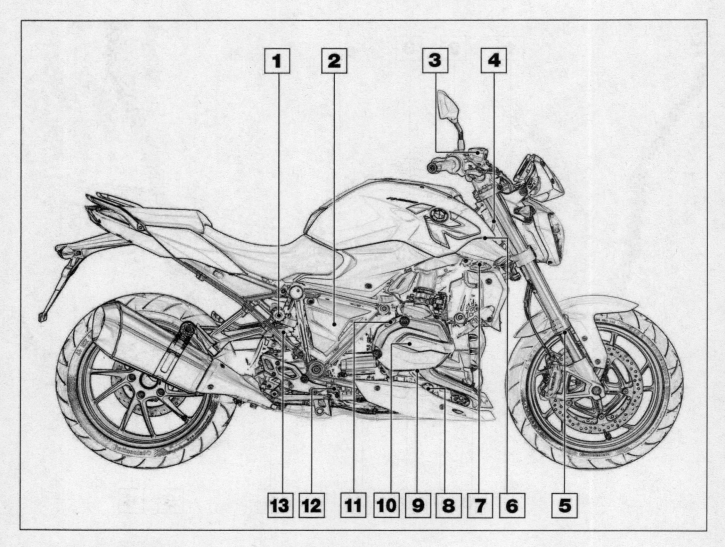

1 Rear shock pre-load adjuster
2 Battery
3 Front brake fluid reservoir
4 Frame VIN
5 Front fork seal

6 Coolant reservoir
7 Radiator pressure cap
8 Engine oil level window
9 Coolant drain plug

10 Spark plug
11 Engine oil filler cap
12 Engine number
13 Rear brake fluid reservoir

Component locations on the left side – R and RS models

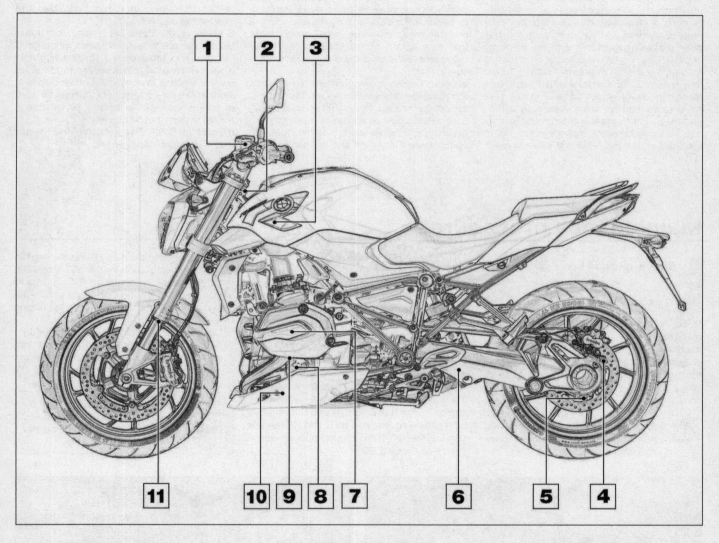

1 Clutch fluid reservoir
2 Steering head bearing adjuster
3 Air filter
4 Final drive oil filler plug

5 Final drive oil drain plug
6 Rear shock damping adjuster
7 Spark plug
8 Engine oil filter

9 Coolant drain plug
10 Engine oil drain plug
11 Fork seal

Introduction

1 This Chapter is designed to help the home mechanic maintain his/her motorcycle for safety, economy, long life and peak performance.

2 Deciding where to start or plug into the maintenance schedule depends on several factors. If the warranty period on your motorcycle has just expired, and if it has been maintained according to the warranty standards, you may want to pick up routine maintenance as it coincides with the next mileage or calendar interval. If you have owned the machine for some time but have never performed any maintenance on it, then you may want to start at the nearest interval and include some additional procedures to ensure that nothing important is overlooked.

If you have just had a major engine overhaul, then you may want to start the maintenance routine from the beginning. If you have a used machine and have no knowledge of its history or maintenance record, you may desire to combine all the checks into one large service initially and then settle into the maintenance schedule prescribed. Note that connection of the bike to the BMW diagnostic tester will show if any recall work is outstanding.

3 Before beginning any maintenance or repair, the machine should be cleaned thoroughly, especially around the oil filter, spark plug covers, valve covers, engine oil drain plug etc. Cleaning will help ensure that dirt does not contaminate the engine and will allow you to

detect wear and damage that could otherwise easily go unnoticed.

4 Certain maintenance information is sometimes printed on labels attached to the motorcycle. If the information on the labels differs from that included here, use the information on the label.

5 Many of the bolts are of the Torx type. Unless you are already equipped with a good range of Torx bits, you are advised to obtain a set – BMW produces a service tools set for owners wishing to carry out extended service work. Make sure you get bits that can be used in conjunction with a socket set so that a torque wrench can be applied.

6 Read the *Safety first!* section of this manual carefully before starting work.

Maintenance procedures

1 Engine oil and filter

Note: Special tool: *A filter wrench is necessary for this procedure* **(see illustration 1.8a).** *BMW can supply the tool (No. 114650), or they are available from good tool suppliers, but note there are many different sizes so take a filter with you to make sure you get the correct one.*

  Warning: Be careful when draining the oil, as the exhaust pipes, the engine, and the oil itself can cause severe burns.

1 Regular oil and filter changes are the single most important maintenance procedure you can perform. The oil not only lubricates the internal parts of the engine, but it also acts as a coolant, a cleaner, a sealant, and a protector. Because of these demands, the oil takes a terrific amount of abuse and should always be changed at the specified interval together with the oil filter.

2 Before changing the oil, warm up the engine so the oil will drain easily. Make sure the bike is on level ground and support it on its centre stand.

3 On GS and GS Adv models remove the engine sump guard, on RT models remove both engine covers, and on R and RS models remove the left-hand engine spoiler where fitted (see Chapter 7).

4 Position a clean drain tray below the engine. Using the special tools in the bike's tool kit, unscrew the oil filler cap on the right-hand valve cover to vent the crankcase and to act as a reminder that there is no oil in the engine **(see illustration)**.

5 Unscrew the oil drain plug from the bottom of the engine and allow the oil to flow into the drain tray **(see illustration)**. Remove the sealing washer – a new one must be used.

 HAYNES HiNT *An oil drain tray can be easily made by cutting away the front or back of an old five litre oil container.*

1.4 Use the tools supplied to unscrew the filler cap

1.5 Unscrew the drain plug and drain the oil

1.6a Clean the magnetic tip (arrowed)

1.6b Fit a new sealing washer

1.7 Fit and tighten the drain plug

6 Clean the drain plug, removing all muck from the magnetic tip **(see illustration)**. Fit a new sealing washer onto the plug **(see illustration)**.

7 When the oil has completely drained, fit the plug using a new sealing washer and tighten it to the torque setting specified at the beginning of this Chapter **(see illustration)**. Do not overtighten the plug as the threads in the sump could be damaged.

8 Now place the drain tray below the oil filter. Unscrew the filter using an end-cap type oil filter wrench and tip any residual out **(see illustrations)**.

9 Smear clean engine oil onto the seal of the new filter, then screw the filter onto the engine until it is finger-tight **(see illustrations)**. Now tighten the filter to the specified torque setting using the filter wrench. Take care not to over-tighten the filter as this may damage the seal. Note that the 'running-in' filter is shown

1.8a Use an end-cap type oil filter wrench to unscrew the filter...

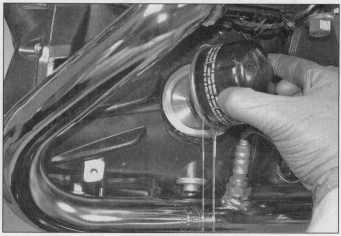

1.8b ...and drain the residual oil

1.9a Lubricate the seal...

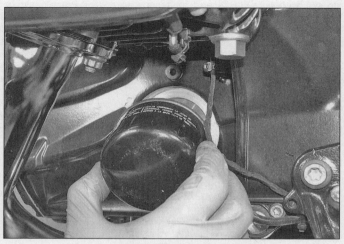

1.9b ...and tighten the filter as described

1.9c Comparison of the two filter types – running-in filter on the left and regular filter on the right

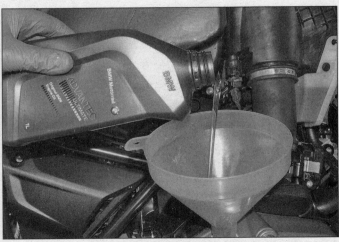

1.10a Add the oil...

1.10b ...to the top of the circle

1.10c Fit the cap

here, as installed from new. The replacement filter (used at subsequent oil changes) is deeper with flats on its end to accept an aftermarket removal tool **(see illustration)**.

10 Add the specified type of oil so the level reaches the top of the circle on the inspection window **(see illustrations)**. Check the filler cap O-ring is in place and in good condition before fitting the cap **(see illustration)**.

11 Start the engine.

> **HAYNES HiNT** *Check the old oil carefully – if it is very metallic coloured, then the engine is experiencing wear from running-in (new engine) or from insufficient lubrication. If there are flakes or chips of metal, or pieces of clutch friction material in the oil, then something is drastically wrong internally and the engine will have to be disassembled for inspection and repair.*

12 Run the engine up to normal operating temperature then re-check the level – it is likely you will have to add a bit more.

13 Check that there are no oil leaks from around the drain plug and the oil filter.

14 If applicable, install the engine sump guard, engine covers or engine spoiler (see Chapter 7).

15 The old oil drained from the engine cannot be re-used and should be disposed of properly. Check with your local refuse disposal company, disposal facility or environmental agency to see whether they will accept the used oil for recycling. Don't pour used oil into drains or onto the ground.

2 Valve clearances

Note: Special tool: *A set of feeler gauges is necessary for this job.*

Check

1 The engine must be cold for this maintenance procedure, so let the machine sit overnight before beginning.

2 Place the motorcycle on its centre stand where fitted, or on an auxiliary stand if not, so the rear wheel is off the ground.

3 Remove the spark plugs (see Section 4).

4 Remove both valve covers (see Chapter 2).

5 Work on one side of the engine, and on one pair of valves (i.e. intake or exhaust), at a time. The intake valves and camshaft are on the top of the cylinder head, and the exhaust valves and camshaft are on the bottom **(see illustration)**. To check the valve clearances, the engine must be turned so the valves being checked are fully closed and seated, so the camshaft lobes that actuate the valves being checked must be pointing away from the valves. To turn the engine to this position, select a high gear and have an assistant turn the rear wheel slowly by hand in the normal direction of rotation (forwards), watching the

2.5a Intake camshaft and valves (A), exhaust camshaft and valves (B)

2.5b Camshaft lobe positions at TDC on the compression stroke

camshafts as they turn until the lobes on the shaft actuating the valves being checked point away from the valves. When the engine is at TDC on its compression stroke all four valves are closed and can be checked at the same time – in this position the intake camshaft lobes will point up and out, and the exhaust camshaft lobes will point down and slightly out **(see illustration)**.

Caution: Be sure to turn the engine in its normal direction of rotation only.

6 Make a chart or sketch of all valve positions so that a note of each clearance can be made against the relevant valve.

7 Check the clearance on each valve by inserting a feeler gauge of the correct thickness (see Specifications – the clearances for the exhaust valves differ from the intake)

between the cam and the cam follower – the gauge should be a firm sliding fit **(see illustration)**. If not, use the feeler gauges to obtain the exact clearance. Record the measured clearances on your chart.

Adjustment

8 When all clearances have been measured and recorded, identify whether the clearance on any valve falls outside that specified. If it does, the shim between the follower and the valve must be replaced with one of a thickness that will restore the correct clearance.

9 Changing a shim requires removal of the relevant camshafts (see Chapter 2). Lift the follower and remove the shim from the top of the valve **(see illustrations)** – using a magnet makes removing the shim easy, but if you don't have one ease it out using a small screwdriver and pliers.

10 The shim size (thickness) should be marked on its face – but the shim should be measured to check that it has not worn **(see illustration)**. If the shim has worn, this

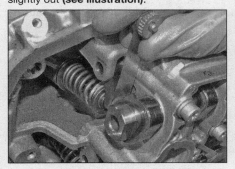

2.7 Check valve clearance with a feeler gauge

2.9a Lift the cam follower...

2.9b ...and remove the shim using a magnet

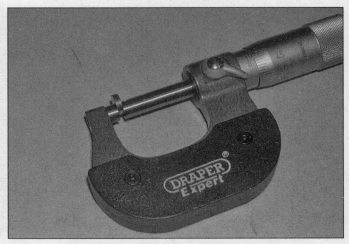

2.10 Measuring the shim with a micrometer

2.13 Fit the shim into its recess

3.1 Keep stand pivots clean and lubricated, and check the springs

must be taken into account when calculating the size of the new shim.

11 Compare the measured valve clearance with the specified clearance to determine the difference, which is the amount by which the shim size should be increased or decreased. If the measured clearance is too large, add the difference to the thickness of the existing shim to determine the size of the new shim. If the measured clearance is too small, subtract the difference from the thickness of the existing shim to determine the size of the new shim.

12 New shims are available in 0.02 mm increments from 1.72 to 2.40 mm and can be obtained from a BMW dealer. **Note:** *If the required replacement shim is greater than 2.40 mm (the largest available), the valve is probably not seating correctly due to a build-up of carbon deposits or valve damage. Remove the valve for checking (see Chapter 2).*

13 Lubricate the shim with engine oil and fit it into its recess in the top of the valve **(see illustration)**. Check that the shim is correctly seated, then pivot the follower onto it **(see illustration 2.9a)**. Install the camshafts (see Chapter 2).

14 Rotate the crankshaft several turns to seat the new shim(s), then check the clearances again.

15 Follow the same procedure to check and adjust the valve clearances on the other cylinder.

16 On completion, lubricate the valve assemblies, cam followers and camshafts with clean engine oil, then install the covers (see Chapter 2)

17 Install the remaining components in the reverse order of removal.

3 Stand pivots

1 Since the stands on a motorcycle are exposed to the elements, the pivots should be lubricated periodically to ensure safe and trouble-free operation **(see illustration)**.

2 In order for the lubricant to be applied where it will do the most good, the component should be disassembled (see Chapter 5). However, if chain or dry film lubricant is being used, it can be applied to the pivot joint gaps and will usually work its way into the areas where friction occurs. If engine oil or light grease is being used, apply it sparingly as it may attract dirt (which could cause the pivots to bind or wear at an accelerated rate).

3 Check the stand springs for damage and distortion. The springs must be capable

of retracting the stand fully and holding it retracted when the motorcycle is in use. If a spring has sagged or is broken, it must be replaced with a new one (see Chapter 5).

4 Spark plugs

Special tool: *An ignition coil extractor (Part No. 123621) is required for this job* **(see illustration 4.4a)**.

Note: *The spark plug caps are integral with the ignition coils. To avoid damaging the wiring, always disconnect the wiring connectors before removing the coils. Do not attempt to lever the coils off the spark plugs – use the special tool. Do not drop the coils.*

Note: *Make sure your spark plug socket is the correct size before attempting to remove the plugs.*

Removal

1 On GS and GS Adv models remove the engine protection bars, where fitted (see Chapter 7).

2 Undo the spark plug cover screw **(see illustration)**. Ease the cover off, noting how the tab locates **(see illustration)**.

3 Carefully push the ignition coil wiring connector away from the locking tab, then disconnect the connector **(see illustrations)** – do not bend the locking tab away from the connector as it will break.

4 Using the special tool pull the coil off the spark plug **(see illustrations)**.

5 Using either the BMW plug socket (tool No. 121220) or a 14 mm thin-walled, deep socket, unscrew the plug from the cylinder head **(see illustration)**.

6 Remove the plug from the other cylinder in the same way. Inspect the spark plugs and compare them with the colour spark plug reading chart at the end of this manual **(see illustration)**. The condition of the plugs can give an indication of the general condition

4.2a Undo the screw ...

4.2b ...and remove the cover as shown to release the tab (arrowed)

4.3a Push the connector towards the engine to release it from the tab...

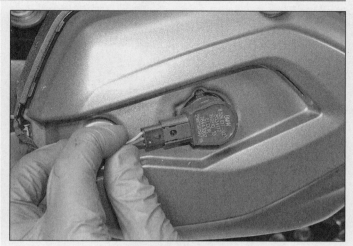

4.3b ...then draw it out

4.4a Fit the tool...

4.4b ...and pull the ignition coil out

4.5 Using a deep socket to unscrew the spark plug

4.6 Inspect the plug's firing end

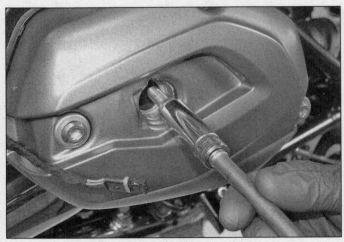

4.8 Take care not to cross-thread the plugs

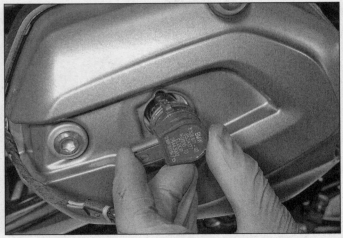

4.9 Align the tab with the cut-out in the valve cover and push the coil fully onto the plug

of the engine. Do not attempt to clean and re-use the old plugs, new ones must be fitted.

Installation

7 Before fitting the new plugs, refer to the Specifications and make sure they are the correct type and heat range. New plugs are pre-set to the correct gap.

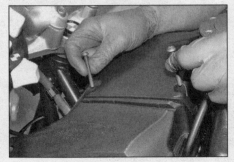

5.2a Undo the screws on each side...

8 Since the cylinder head is made of aluminium, which is soft and easily damaged, thread the plugs into the heads turning the plug socket by hand **(see illustration)**. Once the plugs are finger-tight, tighten them to the torque setting specified at the beginning of this Chapter – do not over-tighten them.

9 Fit the ignition coils, making sure they are correctly aligned and push them onto the plugs **(see illustration)**. Make sure that the terminals inside the wiring connectors are clean, then connect them, making sure the locking tab engages **(see illustration 4.3b)**.

10 Fit the spark plug covers **(see illustrations 4.2b and a)**. Fit the engine protection bars, as required.

> **HAYNES HINT** *Stripped plug threads in the cylinder head can be repaired with a thread insert – see 'Tools and Workshop Tips' in the Reference section.*

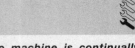

5 Air filter

Caution: If the machine is continually ridden in wet or dusty conditions, the filter should be changed more frequently.

1 Remove the fuel tank covers (see Chapter 7) – on GS models you can get away with just removing the top cover, and the air filter cover and filter can be removed with the tank side covers in place to save having to remove the side panels and covers as well.

2 Remove the air filter cover **(see illustrations)**.

3 Lift the filter unit out, then remove the element from the cage and discard it **(see illustration)**.

4 Fit the new filter element into the cage, then fit the filter unit into the housing.

5 Fit the filter cover and tighten the screws.

6 Install the fuel tank covers (see Chapter 7).

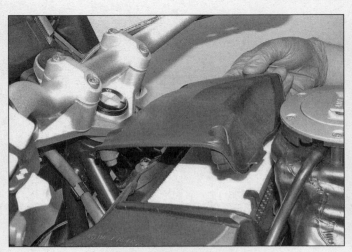

5.2b ...and remove the cover

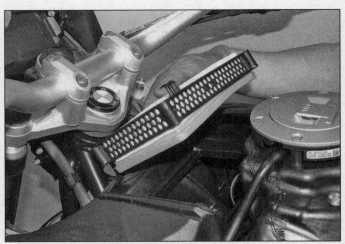

5.3 Remove the air filter element

6.2 Final drive oil filler plug

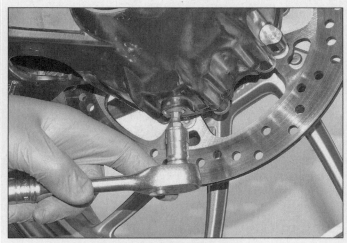

6.3a Unscrew the drain plug...

6 Final drive oil change

1 Before changing the oil, ride the machine for a few miles so that it reaches normal operating temperature and the oil will drain easily. Make sure the bike is on level ground. On GS and GS Adventure models remove the spray guard (see Chapter 7).
2 Unscrew the oil filler plug **(see illustration)**. Check the condition of the sealing washer and replace it with a new one if necessary.
3 Position a clean drain tray below the housing and cover the tyre and wheel with some rag. Unscrew the drain plug and allow the oil to drain – leave it several minutes to drain fully **(see illustrations)**. Remove the O-ring – a new one must be used.
4 Clean any muck off the magnetic tip in the drain plug, and replace the O-ring with a new one **(see illustration)**.

6.3b ...and drain the oil

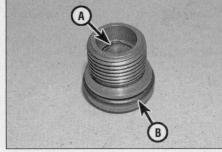

6.4 Drain plug magnet (A) and O-ring (B)

5 When the oil has completely drained, fit the drain plug using a new O-ring and tighten it to the torque setting specified at the beginning of the Chapter **(see illustration)**. Do not overtighten the plug as the threads in the casing could be damaged.
6 Refer to the Specifications at the beginning of the Chapter and pour the specified quantity of the specified oil into the housing via the filler hole **(see illustration)**. Use a suitably small funnel if pouring directly from the bottle, or use a clean syringe – do not use a syringe that has been in contact with any other fluids. BMW produces a service tool for this purpose (No. 342551).

6.5 Thread the drain plug into the final drive housing

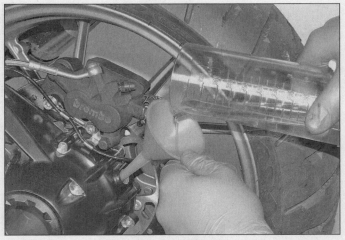

6.6 Make sure you measure the specified quantity – there is no level line to go by

6.7 Fit a new sealing washer if necessary

7.8 Undo the cover screws and lift off the cover and the diaphragm

7 On completion, refit the filler plug, using a new sealing washer if necessary, and tighten it to the specified torque setting **(see illustration)**. Do not over-tighten the plug as the threads in the housing could be damaged.

7 Clutch

General check

1 All models are fitted with an hydraulically operated clutch, for which there is no requirement for adjustment.
2 Inspect the clutch hose connections at the master cylinder on the handlebars and the release cylinder at the rear of the gearbox on the right-hand side for signs of fluid leakage, deterioration and wear.

3 If any leaks or damage are found they must be rectified immediately. Refer to Chapter 2 for details of the clutch release mechanism components.
4 Check the operation of the clutch. If there is evidence of air in the system (spongy feel to the lever, difficulty in engaging gear), bleed the system (see Chapter 2). If the lever feels stiff or sticky, check the operation of the master cylinder and the release cylinder (see Chapter 2).
5 The clutch lever has a span adjuster that alters the distance of the lever from the handlebar. The setting is altered by turning the adjuster **(see illustration 8.7)**. Push the lever forwards, then turn the adjuster as required to increase or decrease the span – position 1 gives the smallest span and position 4 the largest. Make sure the chosen setting aligns with the index mark on the lever.

Clutch fluid level

6 Position the handlebars so that the top of the master cylinder reservoir is as level as possible.
7 Make sure you have the correct clutch fluid – Vitamol V10, available from BMW dealers. Do not use conventional brake and clutch hydraulic fluid. Wrap a rag around the reservoir to ensure that any spillage does not come into contact with painted surfaces.
8 Remove the reservoir cover **(see illustration)**.
9 The fluid level should be up to the top of the vertical bar on the inside of the reservoir wall **(see illustration)**. Clutch wear causes the fluid level to rise, so make sure there is not too much fluid, and if there is remove some. If the level is low top up to the line with the specified fluid only **(see illustration)** – if you have to repeatedly top the level up there is a leak somewhere in the system that must be located and repaired.

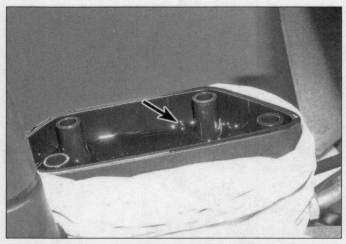

7.9a The fluid should be up to the top of the vertical bar (arrowed)

7.9b Top up with new Vitamol V10 clutch fluid almost to the top of the bar. Do not overfill.

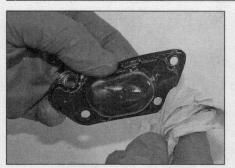

7.10a Wipe the diaphragm

7.10b Make sure that the diaphragm is correctly seated before fitting the cover

8.7 Lever span adjuster

10 Wipe any moisture off the diaphragm using a clean absorbent lint-free cloth, then fit the diaphragm and cover **(see illustrations)**.

8 Brake system

Brake system check

1 Make sure all brake fasteners are tight.
2 Make sure the fluid level in the front and rear brake reservoirs is correct (see *Pre-ride checks*).
3 Check the brake pads and discs for wear (see below).
4 Remove the fuel tank (see Chapter 4), then look for leaks at the hose and pipe connections and check for damage to the hoses (see below).
5 If the brake lever or pedal feels spongy, it is likely that there is air in the brake system and it will need bleeding – follow the procedure in Chapter 6.

Front brake lever

6 Check the brake lever for loose fitting, improper or rough action, excessive play, bends, and other damage. Replace any

damaged parts with new ones (see Chapter 6).
7 The front brake lever has a span adjuster that alters the distance of the lever from the handlebar. The setting is altered by turning the adjuster **(see illustration)**. Push the lever forwards, then turn the adjuster as required to increase or decrease the span – position 1 gives the smallest span and position 4 the largest. Make sure the chosen setting aligns with the index mark on the lever.

Rear brake pedal

8 Check the brake pedal for loose fitting, improper or rough action, excessive play, bends, and other damage. Replace any damaged parts with new ones (see Chapter 5).
9 On GS Adventure models, the adjustable pedal toe can be lowered for use when riding standing up, or raised for normal use – slide it rearwards and fold it down or up until it locks in position.

Brake light

10 Make sure the brake light operates when the front brake lever is pulled in and also when the rear brake pedal is depressed. The brake light switches are incorporated

in the ABS modulator assembly and are maintenance-free. If the brake light does not work refer to Chapter 8.

Brake pad wear check

Note: *Uneven pad wear in any one caliper indicates sticking piston(s) – refer to Chapter 6 to displace and clean the calipers.*
11 Pad wear can be determined without removing the pads from the caliper. On the front brakes, the friction material has wear indicator grooves that are visible on the bottom edge of each pad – the grooves are visible from the front of the machine **(see illustration)**. If the friction material has worn down to the bottom of the grooves, the pads must be renewed (see Chapter 6). On the rear brake the pads must be renewed when the friction material has worn to a thickness of 1 mm – the friction material is visible from the rear of the caliper **(see illustration)**.
12 If required, remove the pads for closer inspection (see Chapter 6). Measure the thickness of the friction material – the wear limit is 1 mm.
13 Always replace both pads in the caliper at the same time, and, in the case of the front brake, replace both sets of pads at the same time (see Chapter 6).

8.11a Front brake pad wear indicator grooves (arrowed)

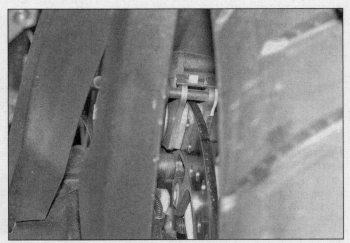

8.11b Check rear brake pad friction material thickness

8.15 Measure disc thickness with a micrometer

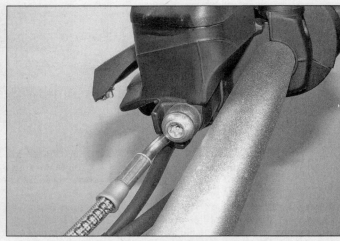

8.18 The exposed banjo unions are the most likely areas to be affected

Brake discs

14 Inspect the front and rear brake discs for wear and damage – light scratches are normal after use and won't affect brake operation, but deep grooves and heavy score marks will reduce braking efficiency and accelerate pad wear. If the disc is badly grooved fit a new disc (see Chapter 6).

15 Measure the thickness of each disc and compare the results with the specifications at the beginning of this Chapter **(see illustration)**. If any disc is worn down to the minimum thickness it must be replaced with a new one.

16 Follow the procedure in Chapter 6 to check disc runout.

Brake fluid change

17 The brake fluid should be changed at the prescribed service interval – follow the procedure in Chapter 6.

Brake hoses

18 Even though top quality brake hoses are fitted regular checks should be made for damage and leaks, particularly where the hose joins the banjo union **(see illustration)**. Damaged or leaking hoses must be replaced with new ones (see Chapter 6). Always use new sealing washers.

19 If a brake hose is disconnected, air will enter the brake system and the system will need bleeding – follow the procedure in Chapter 6.

Brake caliper and master cylinder seals

20 Hydraulic seals will deteriorate over a period of time, particularly if the bike has been in long-term storage, and lose their effectiveness, leading to sticking operation or fluid loss, or allowing the ingress of air and dirt.

21 If the brake caliper shows signs of sticking, remove the brake pads from the caliper (see Chapter 6). Carefully ease up the dust seals around the caliper pistons and check for fluid behind the seals. If brake fluid is leaking from the caliper, the piston seals have failed and the caliper must be overhauled – this procedure must be undertaken by a BMW dealer.

22 If brake fluid is leaking from the front or rear master cylinder a new master cylinder must be fitted – seal kits are not available. Follow the procedure in Chapter 6.

9 Nuts and bolts

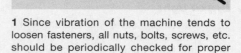

1 Since vibration of the machine tends to loosen fasteners, all nuts, bolts, screws, etc. should be periodically checked for proper tightness.

2 Pay particular attention to the following:
a) Spark plugs
b) Engine and final drive housing oil filler and drain plugs
c) Gearchange lever, front brake lever and rear brake pedal bolts
d) Footrest and stand bolts
e) Engine mounting bolts
f) Shock absorber mounting bolts and Telelever/swingarm pivot bolts
g) Handlebar clamp bolts
h) Front axle bolt and axle clamp bolts
i) Front fork yoke bolts
j) Rear wheel bolts
k) Brake caliper mounting bolts
l) Brake hose banjo bolts and caliper bleed valves
m) Brake disc bolts
n) Exhaust system bolts/nuts

3 If a torque wrench is available, use it together with the torque specifications at the beginning of this and other Chapters.

10 Wheels and wheel bearings

General

1 Make sure the valve stem cap is in place and tight **(see illustration)**. Check the valve stem for signs of damage and have a new one fitted if necessary. Note that on machines fitted with tyre pressure sensors, the sensor is integral with the valve assembly as indicated by the decal on the wheel rim.

2 Check that any wheel balance weights are fixed firmly to the wheel rim. If there are signs that a weight has fallen off, have the wheel rebalanced by a motorcycle tyre specialist.

3 From time to time, and especially if the bike has been dropped or hit any large potholes, check the wheel runout and front/rear wheel alignment as described in Chapter 6.

Cast wheels

4 Cast wheels are virtually maintenance free, but they should be kept clean and checked periodically for cracks and other damage. Never attempt to repair damaged cast wheels; they must be replaced with new ones.

10.1 A valve stem cap must be fitted

10.7 Checking for play in the front wheel bearings

10.10 Checking for play in the final drive bearings

Wire spoked wheels

5 Inspect the spokes for damage, breakage or corrosion. A single loose spoke can be tightened carefully (see Chapter 6), but if a number of spokes are loose, follow the procedure in Chapter 6 to check the radial and axial runout of the wheel and, if necessary, take it to a wheel building expert for correction. A broken or bent spoke must be renewed immediately because the load taken by it will be transferred to adjacent spokes which may in turn fail.

Front wheel bearings

6 The bearings in the front wheel will wear over a period of time and result in handling problems.

7 Support the motorcycle upright on its centre stand or an auxiliary stand, and take the weight off the front wheel. Check for any play in the bearings by pushing and pulling the wheel against the hub **(see illustration)**. Also spin the wheel and check that it rotates smoothly.

8 If any play is detected in the hub, or if the wheel does not rotate smoothly (and this is not due to brake drag), remove the wheel and inspect the bearings for wear or damage (see Chapter 6).

Final drive bearings

9 The rear wheel and brake disc are bolted to the final drive unit and pivot on the bearings contained within the drive unit – there are no bearings in the rear wheel. Before checking for play, first check that the rear wheel bolts are tight.

10 Support the motorcycle upright on its centre stand or an auxiliary stand, and take the weight off the rear wheel. Grasp the wheel and check for any play between the rear wheel and final drive unit **(see illustration)**. If play is evident the final drive bearings may need attention – have the machine checked by a BMW dealer. Note: Play felt at the rear wheel may be due to worn pivot bearings between the swingarm and the final drive unit (see Section 11).

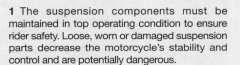

11 Suspension

1 The suspension components must be maintained in top operating condition to ensure rider safety. Loose, worn or damaged suspension parts decrease the motorcycle's stability and control and are potentially dangerous.

Front suspension

2 Hold the front brake on and check that the front suspension operates smoothly and without binding by pushing down on the handlebars **(see illustration)** – on models with ESA you need to have the ignition turned on to do this or the forks will feel solid.

3 Inspect the area above or below (according to model) the dust seal on each fork inner tube for signs of oil leakage, then carefully lever out the dust seal using a flat-bladed screwdriver and inspect the area around the fork seal **(see illustration)**. If leakage is evident, the seals

11.2 Checking the front suspension

11.3 Check the inner tube in this area for oil leakage

11.4a Inspect the shock for leakage and corrosion

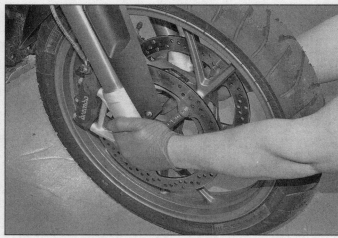

11.4b Checking the front suspension bushes and bearings

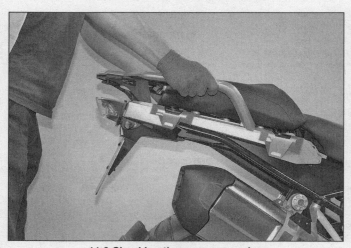

11.6 Checking the rear suspension

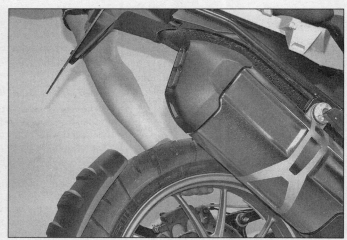

11.7 Checking for play in the shock absorber mountings

must be replaced with new ones (see Chapter 5). Also inspect the chrome finish on the inner tube for evidence of pitting and scratches that could cause seal falilure. If necessary replace the inner tubes with new ones.

4 On GS, GS Adv and RT models, inspect the

11.8 Checking for play in the swingarm pivots

shock absorber for pitting on the damper rod and fluid leakage **(see illustration)**. If leakage is found, the shock should be replaced with a new one (see Chapter 5). Make sure that the upper and lower mountings are tight. Have an assistant push down on the back of the bike to raise the front wheel off the ground, then grasp the bottom of each fork and gently push and pull them back and forward **(see illustration)** – if any freeplay is felt refer to Chapter 5 and check the Telelever pivot bolt is tight. If it is, check the Telelever bearings, the fork top bushes in the top yoke, and the Telelever ball joint.

Rear suspension

5 On RT models remove the shock absorber covers (see Chapter 7). On all models, inspect the shock absorber for pitting on the damper rod and fluid leakage. If leakage is found, the shock should be replaced with a new one (see Chapter 5). Make sure that the upper and lower mountings are tight.

6 With the aid of an assistant to support the bike, compress the rear suspension several times by pressing down on the passenger grab-rail **(see illustration)**. It should move up and down freely without binding. If any binding is felt, the worn or faulty component must be identified and replaced. The problem could be due to either the shock absorber or the swingarm components.

7 Support the bike on its centrestand or an auxiliary stand so the rear wheel is off the ground. Grasp the top of the rear wheel and pull it upwards – there should be no discernible freeplay before the shock absorber begins to compress **(see illustration)**. If freeplay is felt, check that the shock absorber mountings are tight, then check for wear in the mountings.

8 Grab the swingarm and rock it from side to side to check for freeplay **(see illustration)**. If freeplay is detected, this could be due to worn swingarm bearings or loose pivots.

9 First check that the pivots are tightened

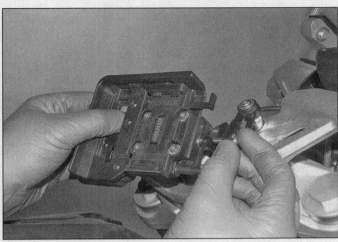

12.8a Undo the screw on each side and displace the holder, leaving the brackets in place

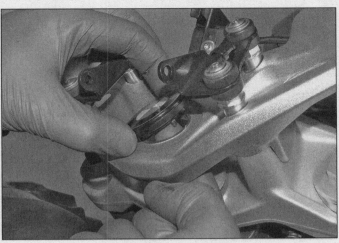

12.8b Push the badge out from the underside

correctly (see Chapter 5). Then remove the rear wheel (see Chapter 6) and shock absorber (see Chapter 5) to make an accurate assessment of the swingarm components.

10 The swingarm should move smoothly about its pivots, without any binding or rough spots. There should be no discernible freeplay felt front-to-back or side-to-side. Next, check for freeplay in the bearings between the swingarm and the final drive unit.

11 If bearing damage or freeplay is evident, the swingarm should be removed and the swingarm and final drive unit bearings and pivots inspected (see Chapter 5).

12 Steering head bearings

1 Steering head bearings can become dented, rough or loose during normal use of the machine. In extreme cases, worn or loose steering head bearings can cause steering wobble – a condition that is potentially dangerous.

GS, GS Adventure and RT models

2 Refer to Chapter 5 Section 8.

R and RS models

Check

3 Place the bike on its centrestand where fitted, or on an auxiliary stand (but not a front paddock stand), so the front wheel is off the ground. On models with a centrestand have an assistant push down on the back of the bike to raise the wheel. If using a stand under the engine, where fitted remove the engine spoilers (see Chapter 7). Always make sure that the bike is properly supported and secure.

4 Detach the steering damper from the bottom yoke (see Chapter 5).

5 Point the front wheel straight-ahead and slowly move the handlebars from lock to lock – the movement should feel smooth and free. Any dents or roughness in the bearing races will be felt and if the bearings are too tight the bars will not move smoothly and freely. Again point the wheel straight-ahead, and tap the front of the wheel to one side. The wheel should 'fall' under its own weight to the limit of its lock, indicating that the bearings are not too tight (take into account the restriction that the brake hose and wiring may have). Check for similar movement to the other side. If the bearings feel tight you can adjust them, but if they feel rough and/ or notchy remove the steering stem (see Chapter 5) and either replace them with new ones, or clean and re-grease them, as required.

6 Next, grasp the bottom of the forks and gently pull and push them forward and backward **(see illustration 11.4b)**. Any looseness or freeplay in the steering head bearings will be felt as front-to-rear movement of the forks. If play is felt, adjust the bearings as described below.

> **HAYNES HiNT** *Make sure you are not mistaking any movement between the bike and stand, or between the stand and the ground, for freeplay in the bearings. Do not pull and push the forks too hard – a gentle movement is all that is needed. Freeplay between the fork tubes due to worn bushes can also be misinterpreted as steering head bearing play – do not confuse the two.*

Adjustment

7 To prevent the possibility of damage should a tool slip cover the fuel tank, and on RS models the cockpit panels, with plenty of rag.

8 On RS models, where fitted displace the Satnav holder, then remove the badge from the handlebar centre **(see illustrations)**.

9 Slacken the fork clamp bolt in each side of the top yoke **(see illustration)**.

10 Unscrew the steering stem bolt **(see illustration)**.

11 Ease the top yoke assembly up the forks until there is enough space to lift the tabbed

12.9 Slacken the clamp bolt on each side

12.10 On RS models unscrew the bolt via the badge hole, then slide it to one side between the yoke and the handlebars

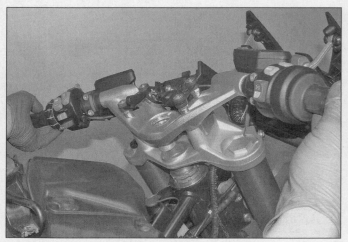

12.11 Ease the assembly up to the top of the forks

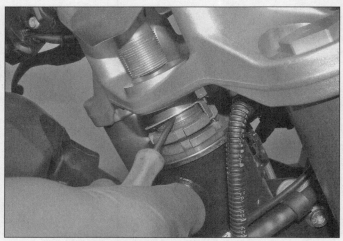

12.12a Lift the lockwasher...

12.12b ...then turn and position it as shown

12.12c Thread the locknut up off the adjuster nut

12.13 Turn the adjuster nut as described to set the bearings

12.14 Seat the lockwasher tabs in the notches

lockwasher clear of the nuts **(see illustration)**.

12 Lift the tabbed lock washer, noting how it locates, and when the tabs are clear of the locknut turn it to offset the tabs from the notches and rest it on top of the nut **(see illustrations)**. Slacken the locknut, using a C-spanner or drift if necessary, though it should only be finger-tight **(see illustration)**.

13 Using either a C-spanner or a drift located in one of the notches, slacken the adjuster nut until pressure is just released, then tighten it until all freeplay is removed, then tighten it a little more **(see illustration)**. Now slacken the nut, then tighten it again, setting it so that all freeplay is just removed, yet the steering is able to move freely from side to side. To do this tighten the nut only a little at a time, and after each tightening repeat the checks outlined above (Steps 5 and 6) until the bearings are correctly set. The object is to set the adjuster nut so that the bearings are under a very light loading, just enough to remove any freeplay. The torque setting at the beginning of this Chapter can be applied if you have access to the BMW tools, Nos. 313721 and 313723 – to apply the tools lift the top yoke assembly clear of the forks and lay it carefully aside on some rag, then remove the locknut and the rubber washer and locate the tool directly onto the adjuster nut.

Caution: Take great care not to apply excessive pressure because this will cause premature failure of the bearings.

14 With the bearings correctly adjusted, tighten the locknut until the rubber washer seats lightly, then tighten it a little further until its notches align with those in the adjuster nut – do not tighten it any further than the first alignment of the notches, it does not need to be tight. Fit the tabbed lock washer so that the tabs fit into the notches in both the locknut and adjuster nut **(see illustration)**.

15 Slide the top yoke down the forks. Tighten the steering stem bolt to the torque setting specified at the beginning of the Chapter. Now tighten the fork clamp bolts to the specified torque setting **(see illustration 12.9)**.

16 Re-check the bearing adjustment as described above and re-adjust if necessary.

17 Install all remaining components.

Lubrication

18 Over time the grease in the bearings will be dispersed or will harden allowing the ingress of dirt and water.

19 At the specified interval disassemble the steering head and clean and re-grease the bearings.

13 Cooling system

Check

⚠️ *Warning: The engine must be cool before beginning this procedure.*

1 Check the coolant level in the reservoir (see *Pre-ride checks*).

2 Check each hose connection and the hose unions on the engine for signs of leakage. If a hose connection is leaking it may need a new clamp and/or a new hose. If a union is leaking it may need a new O-ring. Refer to Chapter 3 for details on hose and union replacement.

3 Examine each rubber coolant hose along its entire length. Look for cracks, abrasions and other damage. Squeeze each hose at various points to see whether they are dried out or hard **(see illustration)**. They should feel firm, yet pliable, and return to their original shape when released. If necessary, replace them with new ones (see Chapter 3).

4 Check the radiator(s) for leaks and other damage. Leaks in the radiator leave tell-tale scale deposits or coolant stains on the outside of the core below the leak. If leaks are noted, remove the radiator (see Chapter 3) and have it repaired or replace it with a new one – do not use a liquid leak stopping compound to try to repair leaks.

5 Check the radiator fins for mud, dirt and insects, which may impede the flow of air through it. If the fins are dirty, remove the radiator (see Chapter 3) and clean it using water or low pressure compressed air directed through the fins from the back of the radiator. If the fins are bent or distorted, straighten them carefully with a screwdriver **(see illustration)**. If the air flow is restricted by bent or damaged fins over more than 20% of the radiator's surface area, replace the radiator with a new one.

⚠️ *Warning: Do not remove the pressure cap from the radiator when the engine is hot. It is good practice to cover the cap with a heavy cloth and turn the cap slowly anti-clockwise. If you hear a hissing sound (indicating that there is still pressure in the system), wait until it stops, then continue turning the cap until it can be removed.*

6 On GS models remove the right-hand side panel, on GS Adv models remove the coolant reservoir access panel from the right-hand side panel, on R models remove the right-hand radiator cowl, on RT and RS models remove the right-hand fairing side panel (see Chapter 7). On R and RS models clamp the reservoir hose at the filler neck **(see**

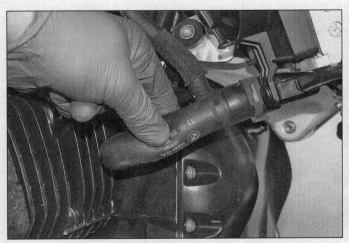

13.3 Check the hoses for cracks and hardening

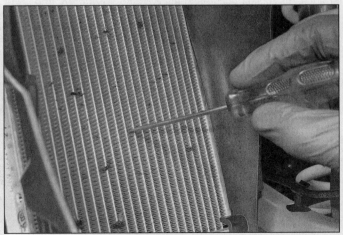

13.5 Straighten any bent fins using a small screwdriver

13.6a Clamp the hose (arrowed) to prevent the reservoir draining

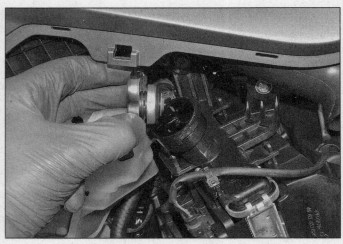

13.6b Remove the pressure cap as described

illustration). Remove the pressure cap from the radiator filler neck by turning it anti-clockwise until it reaches the stop. If you hear a hissing sound (indicating there is still pressure in the system), wait until it stops. Now press down on the cap and continue turning it until it can be removed **(see illustration)**.

7 Check the condition of the coolant in the system. If it is rust-coloured or if accumulations of scale are visible, drain, flush and refill the system with new coolant (see below). If available check the antifreeze content of the coolant with an antifreeze hydrometer. The system must have the correct coolant mixture, as specified at the beginning of the chapter – if the coolant is too weak (too little anti-freeze) there will not be adequate protection against freezing and corrosion, and if it is too strong the ability to cool the engine is reduced. If the hydrometer indicates an incorrect mixture, drain, flush and refill the system (see below).

8 Check the cap seal for cracks and other damage. If in doubt about the pressure cap's condition, or if problems such as overheating or a loss of coolant occur (and there are no signs of leakage), have it tested by a BMW dealer or fit a new one.

9 Fit the cap by turning it clockwise until it reaches the first stop then push down on it and continue turning until it can turn no further.

On R and RS models remove the clamp from the reservoir hose. Start the engine and let it reach normal operating temperature, then check for leaks again. As the coolant temperature increases, the electric fan mounted on the back of the radiator should come on automatically and the temperature should begin to drop. If it does not, check the fan and fan circuit (see Chapter 3, Section 2).

10 If the coolant level is consistently low, and no evidence of leaks can be found, have the entire system pressure checked by a BMW dealer.

Change the coolant

⚠️ *Warning: Allow the engine to cool completely before performing this maintenance operation. Also, don't allow anti-freeze to come into contact with your skin or the painted surfaces of the motorcycle. Rinse off spills immediately with plenty of water. Anti-freeze is highly toxic if ingested. Never leave anti-freeze lying around in an open container or in puddles on the floor; children and pets are attracted by its sweet smell and may drink it. Check with local authorities (councils) about disposing of anti-freeze. Many communities have collection centres which will see that anti-freeze is disposed of safely.*

Anti-freeze is also combustible, so don't store it near open flames.

Draining

11 On GS models remove the right-hand side panel, on GS Adv models remove the coolant reservoir access panel from the right-hand side panel, on RT and RS models remove the right-hand fairing side panel, and on R models remove the right-hand radiator cowl (see Chapter 7). On R and RS models clamp the reservoir hose at the filler neck **(see illustration 13.6a)**.

12 Remove the pressure cap from the top of the radiator by turning it anti-clockwise until it reaches a stop. If you hear a hissing sound (indicating there is still pressure in the system), wait until it stops. Now press down on the cap and continue turning the cap until it can be removed **(see illustration 13.6b)**.

13 Position a suitable container below the left-hand cylinder. Unscrew the drain plug and allow the coolant to completely drain **(see illustrations)**. Repeat for the right-hand cylinder **(see illustration)**. Remove the sealing washer from each plug – new ones must be fitted.

14 On GS, GS Adv and RT models place a container below the left-hand radiator. Release the hose clamp and slide it along the hose – you can release the clamps by

13.13a Unscrew the left-hand cylinder drain plug...

13.13b ...and allow the coolant to drain

13.13c Right-hand cylinder drain plug (arrowed)

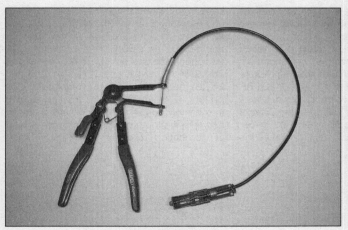

13.14a Hose clamp tool

13.14b Fit the tool onto the clamp...

13.14c ...then squeeze the handle to release the clamp

13.14d Pull the hose off and drain the coolant

squeezing the ends together using pliers, but it is much easier to use the proper tool designed for the type of clamp used, available from an automotive tool supplier **(see illustrations)**. Pull the hose off its union and allow the radiator to drain **(see illustration)**.

15 Suck the coolant out of the reservoir using a syphon pump or syringe **(see illustration)**.

Flushing

16 Flush the system with clean tap water by inserting a hose in the radiator filler neck. Allow the water to run through the system until it is clear and flows out cleanly. If the radiator(s) is/are corroded, remove it/them (see Chapter 3) and have it/them cleaned by a specialist. Also flush the reservoir.

Refilling

17 Fit each drain plug using a new sealing washer and tighten them to the torque settings specified at the beginning of the Chapter **(see illustration)** – note that the torque setting for each is different.

18 On GS, GS Adv and RT models connect the hose to the left-hand radiator, aligning the

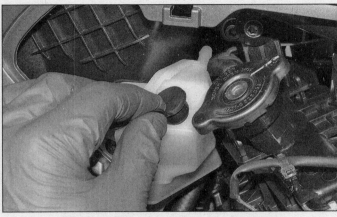

13.15 Open the cap and draw the coolant out

13.17 Fit a new sealing washer onto each plug

cut-out with the lug, and secure it with the clamp **(see illustration 13.14b)**.

19 On GS, GS Adv and RT models put the bike on its sidestand – this helps to distribute the coolant to the left-hand radiator.

20 Fill the system to the base of the radiator filler neck with the specified coolant mixture. Pour the coolant in slowly to minimise the amount of air entering the system, and when full carefully waggle the bike from side to side to dislodge any trapped air. Fill the reservoir to the MAX line. Fit the radiator cap and the reservoir cap. On R and RS models remove the clamp from the reservoir hose.

21 Start the engine and allow it to reach normal operating temperature, then shut it off. Let the engine cool then remove the pressure cap as described in Step 12 – on R and RS models clamp the reservoir hose again. Check that the coolant level is still up to the base of the wide section of the filler neck. If it's low, add the specified mixture until it reaches the base of the wide section. Refit the cap. On R and RS models remove the clamp.

22 Check the coolant level in the reservoir and top up if necessary.

23 Check the system for leaks. Install the body panels (see Chapter 7).

24 Do not dispose of the old coolant by pouring it down the drain. Instead pour it into a heavy plastic container, cap it tightly and take it into an authorised disposal site or service station – see *Warning*.

Chapter 2
Engine, clutch and transmission

Contents

Degrees of difficulty

| Easy, suitable for novice with little experience | 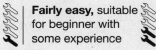 | Fairly easy, suitable for beginner with some experience | | Fairly difficult, suitable for competent DIY mechanic | | Difficult, suitable for experienced DIY mechanic | | Very difficult, suitable for expert DIY or professional | |

Specifications

General

Cylinder identification......................................	No. 1 cylinder – left, No. 2 cylinder – right
Capacity	1170 cc
Bore and stroke	101 x 73 mm
Compression ratio	12.5: 1
Cylinder compression	
Good	203 psi (14 Bars)
Normal	174 psi (12 Bars)
Poor	145 psi (10 Bars)
Engine oil pressure (at 80°C operating temperature)	
At idle speed...	10 to 22 psi (0.7 to 1.5 Bars)
At 5000 rpm	58 to 72.5 psi (4.0 to 5.0 Bars)

Camshafts and followers

Camshaft end-float	
Standard..	0.05 to 0.25 mm
Service limit	0.35 mm
Camshaft radial play	
Standard..	0.020 to 0.071 mm
Service limit	0.085 mm
Camshaft gear backlash..................................	0.003 to 0.020 mm
Cam follower end-float...................................	0.10 to 0.30 mm

Valves and valve guides

Valve clearances.	see Chapter 1
Valve spring free length	45.71 to 46.71 mm

Valve radial clearance
Intake
    Standard. . . . . 0.023 to 0.043 mm
    Service limit . . . . 0.055 mm
Exhaust
    Standard. . . . . 0.047 to 0.054 mm
    Service limit . . . . 0.07 mm
Valve guides
    Inside diameter. . . . . 5.5 to 5.507 mm

Cylinders

Bore diameter
    Standard. . . . . 100.995 to 101.005 mm
    Service limit . . . . 101.030 mm
Ovality (out-of-round) service limit
    20 mm from top . . . . 0.010 mm
    100 mm from top . . . . 0.015 mm

Pistons

Piston-to-bore clearance
    Standard. . . . . 0.008 to 0.052 mm
    Service limit . . . . 0.080 mm
Piston-to-piston pin clearance
    Standard. . . . . 0.005 to 0.015 mm
    Service limit . . . . 0.025 mm

Piston rings

	Standard	Service limit
Ring installation	'TOP' mark facing up	
Top ring		
Ring end gap (installed)	0.20 to 0.35 mm	0.40 mm
Ring float (ring-to-groove clearance)	0.03 to 0.07 mm	0.085 mm
Second ring		
Ring end gap (installed)	0.44 to 0.46 mm	0.60 mm
Ring float (ring-to-groove clearance)	0.01 to 0.07 mm	0.075 mm
Oil ring		
Ring end gap (installed)	0.20 to 0.40 mm	0.45 mm
Ring float (ring-to-groove clearance)	0.02 to 0.06 mm	0.075 mm

Connecting rods

Big-end bearing shell identification – colour mark on edge of shells. . . red, violet or blue
Big-end side clearance
    Standard. . . . . 0.130 to 0.312 mm
    Service limit . . . . 0.5 mm
Weight class identification
    2 white dots (class 1) . . . . 542.0 to 547.9 g
    2 blue dots (class 2) . . . . 548.0 to 553.9 g
    3 white dots (class 3) . . . . 554.0 to 559.9 g
    3 yellow dots (class 4) . . . . 560.0 to 565.9 g
    1 blue dot (class 5) . . . . 566.0 to 571.9 g

Crankshaft and bearings

Crankshaft end-float
    Standard. . . . . 0.075 to 0.258 mm
    Service limit . . . . 0.30 mm
Main bearing oil clearance
    Standard. . . . . 0.025 to 0.057 mm
    Service limit . . . . 0.080 mm
Thrust bearing radial play. . . . . 0.025 to 0.057 mm
Main and thrust bearing shell identification – colour mark on
    edge of shells. . . . . yellow, green or violet

Clutch

Clutch plate pack thickness (new)	38 to 39 mm
Friction plate pack thickness	24 mm
Maximum wear per friction plate	0.1 mm
Clutch fluid	Vitamol V10
Primary drive gear backlash	0.003 to 0.025 mm

Transmission

Gear ratios (no. of teeth)	
Primary ratio	1.000 to 1 (60/60)
Input ratio	1.650 to 1 (33/20)
1st gear	2.438 to 1 (39/16)
2nd gear	1.714 to 1 (36/21)
3rd gear	1.296 to 1 (35/27)
4th gear	1.059 to 1 (36/34)
5th gear	0.943 to 1 (33/35)
6th gear	0.848 to 1 (28/33)
Output ratio	1.061 to 1 (35/33)

Torque settings

Cam chain blade pivot bolts	19 Nm
Cam chain driven sprocket screws	10 Nm
Cam chain tensioner body	32 Nm
Camshaft driven gear bolts	65 Nm
Camshaft holder bolts	10 Nm
Clutch	
Clutch centre nut	150 Nm (see text)
Clutch housing nut	See text
Clutch spring bolts	10 Nm
Clutch release mechanism	
Clutch hose nuts	7 Nm
Master cylinder clamp screws	8 Nm
Release cylinder screws	8 Nm
Connecting rod bolts	
Initial stage	5 Nm
Second stage	20 Nm
Final stage	150°
Crankcase bolts	
10 mm bolts	
Initial stage	25 Nm
Final stage	90°
8 mm bolts	19 Nm
6 mm bolts	10 Nm
Crankshaft locking pin access plug	30 Nm
Cylinder head 10 mm bolts	
Initial stage	5 Nm
Second stage	20 Nm
Third stage	40 Nm
Final stage	120°
Cylinder head 6 mm bolts	12 Nm
Engine breather cover screws	12 Nm
Engine mounting bolts	
Upper (12 mm) mounting bolts	100 Nm
Lower (10 mm) mounting bolts	55 Nm
Front crankcase cover bolts	10 Nm
Gearbox housing bolts	10 Nm
Gearchange mechanism cover screws	10 Nm
Intermediate shaft axle retaining screw	8 Nm
Oil gallery plug	10 Nm
Oil pressure relief valve cap	42 Nm
Oil pump cover screws	12 Nm
Oil pump driven gear nut	10 Nm
Starter clutch screws	35 Nm
Starter driven gear retaining washer screw	10 Nm
Starter idle gear shaft	18 Nm
Starter idle gear shaft screw	8 Nm
Starter reduction gear shaft screw	8 Nm
Valve cover bolts	10 Nm

1 General information

1 The engine unit is an air/liquid-cooled, horizontally-opposed twin. There are four valves per cylinder, operated by twin overhead camshafts. The camshafts are gear driven off the intermediate shafts, which in turn are driven by chain, with the right-hand cylinder chain driven off the balancer shaft and the left-hand off the crankshaft. The intermediate shafts run at half crankshaft speed.

2 The crankcase divides vertically and incorporates a wet sump, pressure-fed lubrication system with a dual-rotor oil pump gear driven off the front of the balancer shaft. An oil filter is located externally on the left-hand side of the crankcase.

3 The engine is both air and liquid-cooled. The water pump is on the front of the engine, housed internally behind the front crankcase cover, and is driven directly by the crankshaft.

4 Power from the crankshaft is routed to the transmission input shaft in the gearbox via a wet multi-plate clutch. The input shaft has a sprung damper. The transmission is a six-speed constant-mesh unit, and drive to the rear wheel is by shaft via bevel gears in a final drive unit.

2 Component access

Operations possible with the engine in the frame

1 The components and assemblies listed below can be removed without having to remove the front or rear sub-frames and suspension systems.
a) *Valve covers*
b) *Cam chain tensioners*
c) *Camshaft driven gears, camshafts and followers*
d) *Intermediate shafts*
e) *Cylinder heads and valves*
f) *Clutch*
g) *Front crankcase cover*
h) *Water pump*
i) *Oil pump, pressure relief valve and oil level/temperature sensor*
j) *Starter motor*
k) *Clutch release cylinder*

Operations requiring removal of the engine from the frame

2 It is necessary to separate the engine and frame to gain access to the following components.
a) *Gearbox*
b) *Alternator*
c) *Starter clutch and gears*
d) *Balancer shaft*
e) *Cam chains, tensioner blades and guide blades*
f) *Pistons and piston rings*
g) *Connecting rods and bearings*
h) *Crankshaft and bearings*
i) *Oil strainers*

3 Engine wear assessment

⚠️ *Warning: Be careful when working on the hot engine – the exhaust pipes, the engine and engine components can cause severe burns.*

Cylinder compression test

1 Special tool: A compression gauge with threads that match the threads of the spark plug is required – a gauge should come with a selection of threaded adapters.

2 Among other things, poor starting and engine performance may be caused by leaking valves, a leaking head gasket or worn pistons, rings and/or cylinder walls. A cylinder compression check will help pinpoint these conditions.

3 Before carrying out the test, check that the valve clearances are correct (see Chapter 1).

4 Run the engine until it reaches normal operating temperature, then turn the ignition OFF. Put the bike on its centrestand, or an auxiliary stand, so that it is upright.

5 Remove the spark plugs (see Chapter 1).

6 Reconnect the ignition coil wiring connectors. Fit the spark plugs back into the coils. Securely earth the threaded section of each plug against the engine or a known good earth point on the frame, or better still to the battery negative (-) terminal – you can do this using jump leads.

7 Thread the adapter (if required) onto the gauge hose, then thread it into the spark plug hole on the cylinder being tested **(see illustrations)**.

8 Open the throttle fully and crank the engine over on the starter motor until the gauge reading stabilises **(see illustration)** – after one or two revolutions the pressure should build up to a maximum figure and then remain stable. Make a note of the pressure reading

3.7a Match the gauge hose adapter to the spark plug threads...

3.7b ...and thread it into the plug hole

3.8 Measuring cylinder compresion

and then repeat the procedure on the other cylinder. Turn the ignition OFF when the test has been completed.

9 Compare the results with the specifications at the beginning of this Chapter. If they are both within the specified range (normal to good) and relatively equal, the engine is in good condition. If there is a marked difference between the readings, or if the readings are lower than specified, inspection of one or both engine top-ends is required.

10 Install the spark plugs (see Chapter 1).

Note: *High compression pressure indicates excessive carbon build-up in the combustion chamber and on the top of the piston. If this is the case, remove the cylinder heads and clean the carbon deposits off. Note that excessive carbon build-up is less likely with the use of modern fuels.*

Engine oil pressure check

11 Special tool: An oil pressure gauge with threads that match the the threads of the oil gallery plug is required – a gauge should come with a selection of threaded adapters, or the tools are available from BMW (part Nos. 114601, 114602 and 114608).

Note: *Even if the engine appears to be in good condition, an oil pressure check can provide useful information about the internal condition of the engine.*

12 If the oil level indicator comes on whilst the engine is running, low oil level is indicated – stop the engine immediately and carry out an oil level check (see *Pre-ride checks*). Note that the indicator is for oil level, not oil pressure. If the oil level is correct check the level sensor (see Chapter 8).

13 To check the oil pressure, a suitable gauge and adapter piece (that screws into the crankcase) will be needed – see the example shown in *Tools and Workshop Tips* at the end of this manual.

14 Run the engine until it reaches normal operating temperature then turn the ignition OFF. Support the bike upright on its centre stand or an auxiliary stand.

15 Unscrew the oil gallery plug, located above the oil filter, then quickly screw the adapter in its place **(see illustration)**. Connect the pressure gauge to the adapter. Note that

a new sealing washer for the plug will be needed.

16 Start the engine and let it idle, noting the oil pressure reading on the gauge. Increase engine speed to 5000 rpm and note the pressure reading again, then stop the engine.

17 Remove the sealing washer from the gallery plug and fit a new one. Unscrew the gauge and adapter from the crankcase. Fit the plug and tighten to the torque setting specified at the beginning of the Chapter.

⚠️ **Warning: Wear gloves to prevent scalding from the hot engine oil.**

18 The oil pressure should be similar to that given in the Specifications at the beginning of this Chapter. If the pressure is significantly lower than that specified, either the pressure relief valve is stuck open, the oilstrainer(s) and/or filter is/are blocked, the oil pump is worn or there is other engine wear or damage.

19 Begin diagnosis by checking the pressure relief valve (see Section 19) and fitting a new oil filter (see Chapter 1). Next inspect the oil pump (see Section 19) and finally the strainers – this last procedure requires engine removal and crankcase separation (see Section 23). If everything is in good condition, it is likely that the crankshaft bearing oil clearances are excessive and the engine needs to be overhauled.

20 If the pressure is too high, either an oil passage is clogged, the relief valve is stuck closed or the wrong grade of oil is being used.

4 Engine removal and installation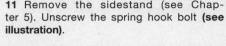

Note: *Models were available from new fitted with a range of optional electrical extras. When working on your machine, take care to ensure that all relevant electrical components are disconnected on disassembly and subsequently reconnected during the rebuild. Always take the precaution of disconnecting the battery negative (-) terminal before disconnecting an electrical wiring connector.*

Removal

1 Support the bike upright on its centre stand

or on an auxiliary stand – if using an auxiliary stand note that to remove the engine both wheels must be removed, and on GS, GS Adv and RT models the forks, front shock absorber and Telelever arm must be removed, so the stand must support the bike though the frame. Also the rear of the frame will have to be tied down to prevent it falling forwards when the engine is removed – if you are not working on a bike ramp with tie-down brackets you could place a sheet of thick plywood under the full length of the bike so the stand sits on the centre of it and the back extends under the rear wheel, then a ratchet strap can be placed under the ply at the back and attached to the rear sub-frame. Before removing the engine mounting bolts, the engine will have to be supported on a jack.

2 Remove the seats, side panels, side covers, battery cover, frame cover, fairing side panels, fuel tank covers, protection bars, sump guard and brackets, and engine spoilers and brackets, as appropriate to your model, to gain access to the engine and related components (see Chapter 7).

3 If the engine is dirty, particularly around its mountings, wash it thoroughly before starting any major dismantling work. This will make work much easier and rule out the possibility of dirt falling into some vital component.

4 Remove the battery (see Chapter 8).

5 Drain the engine oil, and if required remove the oil filter, and drain the coolant (see Chapter 1).

6 Remove the fuel tank, the air filter housing, the throttle bodies, the fuel injectors, and the fuel hose and pressure sensor assembly (see Chapter 4).

7 Remove the radiator(s) and the thermostat, along with all the coolant hoses (see Chapter 3).

8 Remove the exhaust system (see Chapter 4).

9 Remove the ignition coils (see Chapter 4). Detach the coil earth leads from the cylinder heads and free the wiring guide clips from the tops of the blocks **(see illustration)**.

10 Remove the starter motor (see Chapter 8).

11 Remove the sidestand (see Chapter 5). Unscrew the spring hook bolt **(see illustration)**.

3.15 Oil gallery plug (arrowed)

4.9 Displace the guide clip (arrowed) on each side

4.11 Unscrew the spring hook

4.12a Disconnect the ECT sensor connector (arrowed)...

4.12b ...the CKP sensor connector (arrowed)...

4.12c ...and the CMP sensor connector

4.12d Undo the screw and displace the guide

4.13 Disconnect the light grey connector with the three yellow wires

12 Disconnect the ECT, CKP and CMP sensor wiring connectors **(see illustrations)**. Release the wiring from any guides on the engine. Release the wiring guide from the bottom left-hand side of the gearbox **(see illustration)**.
13 Disconnect the alternator wiring connector from the regulator/rectifier **(see illustration)**.
14 Release and disconnect the oil level/ temperature sensor and gear position sensor wiring connectors, and release the wiring on the loom side of the connectors from the back of the gearbox **(see illustration)**. If required remove the sensors now, but it is easier after removing the engine.
15 Displace the clutch release cylinder from the gearbox (Section 21) – there is no need to slacken the hose nut or disconnect the hose.
16 Release and remove the clip securing the front end of the gearchange linkage rod, then pull the rod off the ball joint **(see illustrations)**.
17 Remove the rear wheel (see Chapter 6).
18 Remove the driveshaft (see Chapter 5). Reconnect the Paralever arm to the final drive housing and tighten the bolt finger-tight.
19 Place four blocks of 4x2 inch thick wood under the final drive housing **(see illustration)**. Tie the rear of the bike down using ratchet straps so the final drive housing rests on the wood.
20 Place a trolley jack under the engine. Remove the front wheel (see Chapter 6).
21 On GS, GS Adv and RT models remove the front forks and shock absorber (see Chapter 5). If required either remove, or displace and tie up, the Telelever arm – it

4.14 Release and disconnect the connectors (arrowed) and the wiring

4.16a Release the clip and swivel it round...

4.16b ...then withdraw it from the hole

4.16c Pull the head of the rod off the ball joint

4.19 Blocks under the final drive housing

4.21 Telelever arm displaced and tied up to the frame

4.22 Wiring guide (arrowed)

4.23 Unscrew the two nuts

is easier to tie the arm up as shown **(see illustration)** as the removal process involves removing the ABS modulator, and note that there is no need to displace the front of the arm from the ball joint (as the forks have been removed the bottom yoke can stay attached to the arm). If preferred the arm can be left on the engine and removed after the engine has been removed, as long as care is taken when removing the engine to keep the front frame tubes clear of the arm. If the arm is not removed place place some rag between it and the engine after removing the shock.

22 Check that all the wiring and hoses that will not be removed with the engine are free and clear of the engine – note that there is a wiring guide on the top of the engine that sits under the back of the telelever arm and the ABS modulator, and unless you have removed the modulator and arm you will have to displace this as you lower the engine on the jack **(see illustration)**. Check around the engine for any brackets, air deflectors or heat shields that need to be removed, as required according to model, and remove them, noting how they fit.

23 Unscrew the nuts from the left-hand ends of the upper mounting bolts **(see illustration)**.

4.24a Unscrew the lower mounting bolts on the left-hand side...

4.24b ...and on the right-hand side

24 Unscrew the two lower mounting bolts on each side, noting the washers **(see illustrations)**.

25 Double-check that you are now ready to remove the engine, and make sure the engine is properly supported on the jack. Summon the aid of an assistant or two. Withdraw the upper mounting bolts **(see illustration)**. Have an assistant hold the engine, then remove one of the blocks from under the final drive housing and pivot the frame up off the engine

by lowering the back of the bike, pivoting it on the centrestand or equivalent until the frame mounts are clear of the engine mounts **(see illustration)**. Now carefully lower the jack and draw it forwards, all the time making sure the engine and frame are clear of each other, until the engine can be manoeuvred out from under the bike.

⚠️ *Warning: The engine is very heavy. It is strongly recommended that you have at least one assistant*

4.25a Withdraw the upper mounting bolts...

4.25b ...then pivot the frame up off the engine

to help lift the engine if it is being moved. Personal injury or damage could occur if the engine falls or is dropped.

Installation

26 Installation is the reverse of removal, noting the following:

● Clean the threads of the mounting bolts. Apply some grease to the shanks of the upper bolts.

● Manoeuvre and raise the engine into position then lower the frame onto it so the mounting bolt holes align, then insert the upper mounting bolts from the right-hand side – the longer bolt goes into the front mount **(see illustration 4.25a)**. Apply some threadlock to the nuts and tighten them finger-tight **(see illustration 4.23)**. Fit the lower mounting bolts with their washers and tighten them finger-tight **(see illustrations 4.24a and b)**.

● Tighten the nuts on the upper (12mm) mounting bolts to the torque setting specified at the beginning of this Chapter, then tighten the lower (10mm) mounting bolts to their specified torque.

● Refer to the relevant Chapters where directed for installation of all components.

● Refill the engine and cooling system with the correct type and amount of oil and coolant respectively (see Chapter 1).

● Check the operation of the brakes and suspension and all electrical systems before taking the bike on the road.

5 Engine overhaul – general information

Disassembly

1 Before disassembling the engine, the external surfaces of the unit should be thoroughly cleaned and degreased. This will prevent contamination of the engine internals, and will also make working a lot easier and cleaner. A high flash-point solvent, such as paraffin (kerosene) can be used, or better still, a proprietary engine degreaser such as Gunk. Use old paintbrushes and toothbrushes to work the solvent into the various recesses of the engine casings. Take care to exclude solvent or water from the electrical components and from the intake and exhaust ports.

 Warning: The use of petrol (gasoline) as a cleaning agent should be avoided because of the risk of fire.

2 When the engine is clean and dry, clear a suitable clear area for working – a workbench is desirable for all operations once a component has been removed from the machine. Gather a selection of small containers and plastic bags so that parts can be grouped together in an easily identifiable manner. Some paper and a pen should be on hand so that notes can be made and labels attached where necessary. A supply of clean rag is also required. If the engine has

been removed from the bike (see Section 4), have an assistant help you lift it onto the workbench.

3 Before commencing work, read through the appropriate section so that some idea of the necessary procedure can be gained. When removing components it should be noted that great force is seldom required, unless specified. In many cases, a component's reluctance to be removed is indicative of an incorrect approach or removal method – if in any doubt, re-check with the text.

4 When disassembling the engine, keep 'mated' parts together (e.g. valve and camshaft assemblies, cylinders, pistons and connecting rods, that have been in contact with each other during engine operation). These 'mated' parts must be reused or renewed as assemblies.

5 A complete engine stripdown should be done in the following general order with reference to the appropriate Sections.

a) *Remove the valve covers*
b) *Remove the camchain tensioners*
c) *Remove the camshafts and intermediate shafts*
d) *Remove the cylinder heads*
e) *Remove the clutch*
f) *Remove the oil pump*
g) *Remove the water pump (see Chapter 3)*
h) *Remove the gearbox*
i) *Remove the alternator (see Chapter 8)*
j) *Remove the cam chains and blades*
k) *Remove the balancer shaft*
l) *Separate the crankcase halves*
m) *Remove the crankshaft, connecting rods and pistons*
n) *Remove the oil strainers and engine breather valve*

Reassembly

6 Reassembly is accomplished by reversing the general disassembly sequence.

6 Valve covers

Removal

1 Support the bike upright on its centre stand or an auxiliary stand.

2 Remove the injector cover **(see illustration)**. Remove the ignition coil (see Chapter 4). Undo the coil wiring earth lead screw.

3 Place a drain tray under the cylinder head to catch any residual oil as the cover is removed. Undo the valve cover bolts and pull the cover off the cylinder head **(see illustration)**. If it is stuck, tap it gently around the sides with a soft-faced mallet or block of wood to dislodge it – do not try to lever it off and risk damaging the sealing surface.

4 Remove the outer cover seals and the dowels if loose **(see illustration)**. Remove the inner cover seal **(see illustration)**. Clean and check the seals – they are re-usable, but

6.2 Undo the screw and remove the cover

6.3 Undo the bolts and remove the cover

6.4a Remove the outer seal, noting how it locates over the dowels (arrowed)...

6.4b ...and the inner seal

6.6 Remove the support block

6.9 Align the cut-out (arrowed) in the seal with the channel in the bore

if they are damaged or deteriorated, or if there are signs of oil leakage, replace them with a new set.

5 Check the condition of the cover bolt seals. If they are damaged or deteriorated, or if there are signs of oil leakage, fit new bolts – they come with the seals fitted, and the seals are not available separately.

6 Note how the support block fits and remove it if required **(see illustration)**.

Installation

7 Clean the sealing surfaces of the cylinder head and the valve cover with suitable solvent.
8 If removed fit the support block **(see illustration 6.6)**.
9 Fit the inner seal, aligning the cut-out in the seal with the channel in the bore **(see illustration)** – on the right-hand cylinder the channel is along the bottom of the bore, and on the left-hand cylinder it is along the top **(see illustration 6.4b)**. Fit the dowels if removed, then fit the outer seal onto them **(see illustration 6.4a)**.
10 Position the cover on the cylinder head, making sure the seals stay in place, then tighten the bolts finger-tight at first, and then to the torque setting specified at the beginning of the Chapter **(see illustration 6.3)**.
11 Connect the earth lead. Fit the ignition coil (see Chapter 4). Fit the injector cover **(see illustration 6.2)**.
12 Check the engine oil level and top-up as necessary (see *Pre-ride checks*).

7 Cam chain tensioners

Note: *The cam chain tensioners can be removed with the engine in the frame. To access the tensioner blades and guide blades the engine must be removed and the gearbox removed.*
Special tool: *A crankshaft locking tool to*

hold the engine at top dead centre (TDC) is required for this procedure (see Step 6), and is also required for many other procedures related to working on the engine (it not only acts as a tool to ensure the correct timing is maintained, but it also acts to lock the crankshaft when unscrewing various nuts related to the engine). BMW can provide a tool (No. 110822), which has an 8 mm sprung locking pin on its end marked A, that when fitted will automatically locate in an 8 mm hole in the alternator rotor to lock the crankshaft as it is turned. The tool also has a 6 mm pin on its other (B) end that can be used to lock the crankshaft at bottom dead centre (BDC) via the 6 mm hole in the rotor if removing the gearbox. Note that while this tool works well and is nicely made, it is not essential, and a home-made tool for locking the crankshaft at TDC is easy enough to make (and while it is necessary to position the engine at BDC to remove the gearbox, it is not necessary to lock it in this position). To make a tool order a spare access plug for the locking pin from a BMW dealer (see Step 5). Drill out the centre of the plug using a 7.5 mm drill, then tap it with an 8 mm tap. Get a high strength 8 mm bolt (it must be high strength to act as a sturdy lock when tackling the tight nuts) about 6 cm long with a

thread pitch to match that of the tap used, and thread a flanged nut onto it. Thread the bolt part-way into the tapped access plug, then use it as described below **(see illustration)**.

Removal

1 The tensioner for each cylinder is located on the underside of the cylinder.
2 Support the bike upright on its centre stand or an auxiliary stand so the rear wheel is off the ground. Remove the engine protection bars or spoilers as required according to model (see Chapter 7).
3 Remove the spark plugs (see Chapter 1).
4 Unscrew the access plug for the crankshaft locking pin from the left-hand side of the engine **(see illustration)** – a new sealing washer will be needed.
5 Remove the valve cover (see Section 6).
6 Before removing the tensioner, the piston for the cylinder being worked on must be at top dead centre (TDC) on the compression stroke. To turn the engine to this position, select a high gear and have an assistant turn the rear wheel slowly by hand in the normal direction of rotation (forwards), while you watch the positions of the camshafts and lobes and look for the 8 mm locking pin hole via the aperture in the crankcase (do not mistake the 6 mm

Home-made crankshaft locking tool

7.4 Unscrew the plug

7.6a Right-hand cylinder camshafts positioned at TDC on the compression stroke

7.6b 8 mm locking hole centered in the aperture

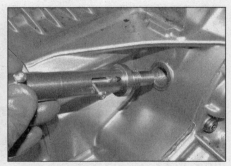

7.6c Thread the end marked A into the aperture…

7.6d …then unlock the handle to extend the pin…

7.6e …so it locates in the hole

7.6f Thread the access plug into the aperture…

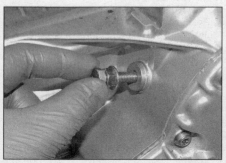

7.6g …then thread the bolt in so it locates in the locking hole…

7.6h …and thread the locknut against the plug to secure the bolt

7.7 Cable-tie the chain to the sprocket

7.8 Unscrew and remove the tensioner

hole at the BDC position for the 8 mm hole at the TDC position) – the piston is at TDC when the lobes are facing as shown and the flats on the ends of the camshafts are vertical and parallel, and the hole for the pin is centred in the aperture **(see illustrations)**. If you are using the BMW tool, fit the end marked A, with the sprung pin retracted, into the aperture, then extend the pin using the handle so it locates in the hole (turn the engine slightly to make sure) **(see illustrations)**. If you are using the home-made tool align the 8 mm hole centrally in the aperture, then thread the tapped access plug (with its washer) into it, then thread the bolt into the plug until its end locates in the hole and locks the crankshaft (try to turn the engine to make sure), then tighten the locknut down onto the access plug to hold the bolt **(see illustrations)**.

Caution: Be sure to turn the engine in its normal direction of rotation only. If the engine has been removed from the frame you can turn the crankshaft via the breather rotor bolt in the rear end of the crankshaft, after removing the breather cover – if doing this turn the crankshaft clockwise (see illustration 26.6a).

7 To make sure the chain does not jump a tooth on the sprocket while the tensioner is out, fit a cable-tie through one of the holes in the sprocket and around the chain **(see illustration)**.

8 Unscrew the tensioner and remove the spring and piston **(see illustration)**. Note that a new sealing washer is needed.

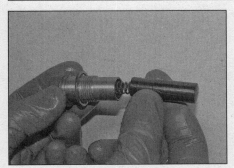

7.9 Remove the plunger and spring and check for wear and damage

Inspection

9 Examine the tensioner components for signs of wear, scoring or damage (see illustration).

10 Check that the plunger moves freely in and out of the tensioner body, and that the spring tension is good.

11 If any of the tensioner components are worn or damaged a new tensioner must be fitted.

Installation

12 Refer to Step 6 and make sure that the piston is at TDC on the compression stroke for the cylinder being worked on with the crankshaft locking pin engaged and the camshafts positioned as described and shown.

13 Fit a new sealing washer onto the tensioner body, then fit the spring into the body and the piston over the spring (see illustration 7.9). Insert the assembly and tighten the tensioner body to the torque setting specified at the beginning of this Chapter (see illustration 7.8).

14 Remove the cable-tie from the cam chain sprocket.

15 Remove the crankshaft locking tool. Turn the engine through two rotations by turning the rear wheel in a forwards direction. Fit a new sealing washer onto the access plug and tighten it to the specified torque.

16 Install the remaining components in the reverse order of removal. Check the engine oil level and top-up as necessary (see *Pre-ride checks*).

8 Camshaft driven gears, camshafts, and followers

Caution: The engine must be completely cool before beginning this procedure.

Note 1: *If there has been excessive gear whine (too little backlash) or clatter (too much backlash) from the top end, check the backlash between the camshaft drive and driven gears as described at the end of this section before removing the gears and/or camshafts. The amount of backlash can be adjusted by selecting different driven gear sizes for the camshafts. Backlash will become excessive through wear of the gear teeth, in which case you will have to replace both the drive and driven gears with new ones of the same size (the drive gear only comes in one size). The backlash should also be checked whenever new components are fitted. Note that for an exact measurement of the backlash according to the BMW specifications their own dial gauge and dial gauge holder must be used to ensure the correct angles between the gauge plunger and the teeth is obtained. If other tools are used and the relative angles are not correct a false reading may be obtained. The dial gauge part No. is 110861, and gauge holder is 110862. Due to the cost of these tools you may want to have the procedure carried out by a dealer.*

Note 2: *The gears, camshafts and followers can be removed with the engine in the frame. If the engine has been removed, ignore the steps that do not apply.*

Note 3: (Special tool): *The crankshaft locking tool (see Section 7) is required for this procedure. If the camshaft driven gears are being removed from the camshafts a camshaft holding/alignment tool (see Step 5) is also required – the BMW tool is recommended as it ensures accurate positioning of the camshafts relative to each other, and of the driven gears on the camshafts, though we relied on making our own accurate alignment marks between all related components as described in Step 2 and used a spanner to counter-hold the camshafts when unscrewing the driven gear bolts, and this worked perfectly well.*

Note 4: *The camshafts can be removed with the driven gears still on them, or the gears can be removed by themselves leaving the camshafts in place. It is best to remove the camshafts with the driven gears still on them. Only slacken the camshaft driven gear bolts and remove the gears from the camshafts if either the driven gears or the camshafts are being replaced with new ones. As there is no keyed alignment between the gears and the shafts the camshaft holding/alignment tool will be required if the bolts are slackened and the gears are removed to ensure accurate timing. For all other procedures requiring removal of the camshafts leave the gears bolted on them, and make sure you make your own alignment marks between the various components as described to ensure accurate timing without the need for special tools.*

Removal

1 Remove the valve cover (Section 6).

2 Make alignment marks using a bright marker paint between a tooth on each driven gear and the corresponding tooth on the drive gear, between the cam chain and the sprocket, and between the front of each camshaft and the camshaft holder (see illustrations). If you are removing the gears from the camshafts also mark between the inner face of each gear and its flange on the shaft, and mark each gear with an I or E according to whether it fits on the intake or exhaust camshaft. These marks will help to install the various components correctly, ensure accurate timing, and give peace of mind.

3 Remove the cam chain tensioner (Section 7) – make sure you fit the cable-tie around the cam chain sprocket.

4 If the camshaft driven gear is being removed from the left-hand cylinder head exhaust camshaft, slacken the bolt securing the camshaft position (CMP) sensor trigger and remove the trigger, noting how the index mark aligns with the tip of the sensor (see illustration).

8.2a Make alignment marks as described...

8.2b ...between the related components

8.4 Slacken the bolt (arrowed) and remove the trigger

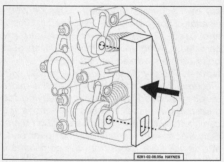

8.5a The BMW tool No. 110827 fits precisely over the shaped camshaft ends

8.5b Holding the camshaft with a spanner to unscrew the gear bolt

8.5c Unscrew the bolt and remove the gear...

8.5d ...noting the washer fitted in it

8.6a Camshaft holder bolts (arrowed)

8.6b Note the contact spring fitted under the head

8.6c Remove the holder...

8.6d ...and the camshafts

8.6e Remove the O-ring

5 If the camshaft driven gears are being removed you need to counter-hold the fronts of the camshafts while unscrewing the bolts – either fit the BMW holding/alignment tool (No. 110827) over the front ends of the camshafts **(see illustration)**, or counter-hold the relevant camshaft using a spanner on the flats **(see illustration)**. Unscrew the bolt, then remove the spacer and gear **(see illustration)**. Note the washer seated inside the inner side of the gear **(see illustration)**.

6 If you are removing the camshafts remove the holding/alignment tool, if used. Unscrew the camshaft holder bolts, initially slackening them evenly and a little at a time in a criss-cross sequence starting on the outer ends and working to the middle **(see illustration)**. Note the contact spring fitted under the head of the rear centre bolt **(see illustration)**. Lift the holder off the head, supporting the camshafts to prevent them dropping, then remove the camshafts **(see illustrations)**. Remove the spark plug bore O-ring **(see illustration)** – check its condition and replace it with a new one if necessary.

7 If required lift the follower off each valve and remove the valve shims **(see illustrations)** – store them in a container divided into four

8.7a Lift the followers...

8.7b ...and remove the shims using a magnet

compartments (there are four shims in each cylinder head, use a separate container for each head and mark them accordingly). Label each compartment with the location of its corresponding valve in the cylinder head. If containers are not available, use labelled plastic bags. **Note:** *It is essential that the cam followers and shims are stored according to their position in the head and fitted back on their original valves otherwise all the clearances will be wrong.*

8 If required withdraw the cam follower shaft retaining pin, withdraw the shaft and remove the followers for each camshaft – store each follower with its shim and each shaft and pin with its camshaft **(see illustrations)**.

Inspection

9 Inspect the bearing faces of the cam followers for wear, score marks, spalling (a pitted appearance) and cracks. Inspect the surface of the follower shafts for wear. The followers should be a sliding fit on their shafts with no discernible freeplay – if any components are worn or damaged, they must be replaced with new ones.

10 Inspect the camshaft bearing surfaces on the camshaft holder and cylinder head and the corresponding journals on the camshaft **(see illustrations)**.

11 Check the camshaft lobes for heat discoloration (blue appearance), score marks, chipped areas, flat spots and spalling. If there is evidence of damage or excessive wear, the camshaft must be replaced with a new one.

12 Check the camshaft driven gears for wear, chipped teeth and other damage. If they are worn, the drive gear on the intermediate shaft is probably worn as well and should be checked (Section 9). If new driven gears are being fitted make sure the correct size is selected according to the number marked on its inner face – there are four different numbers available, representing four different size teeth cuts, which is what affects backlash. If you are replacing the drive and driven gears with new ones replace the driven gears with the same size, according to the number on the back, then check the backlash as described below after fitting them to ensure the selection is the correct one. If you are only replacing the driven gears with new ones, it is probably

8.8a Pull out the pin...

8.8b ...withdraw the shaft and remove the followers

best to replace them with ones of the same size and then to check the backlash, but you may find that to allow for wear in the drive gear you may need to fit one size larger than that originally fitted to take up the excessive backlash, but you will only know whether this is the right thing to do after you have fitted the gears and checked the backlash. Before you commit yourself to buying what could end up being the wrong size ask the advice of a technician at a BMW dealer, and see whether they will allow you to exchange a wrong size bought in error for the correct size. Note that due to the extra costs of buying the special tools required to measure the backlash it may be wise to have the whole procedure performed by the dealer.

13 If available, blow through any oil passages with compressed air.

Installation

Note: *If both pairs of camshafts have been removed, position the appropriate cylinder at TDC compression (see Section 7).*

14 Select and lay out the correct parts for the cylinder being worked on, and the correct followers and shims for the camshaft being worked on, to ensure all parts are returned exactly where they came from, except in the case where new parts are being fitted.

15 Make sure the pistons are at TDC, and the cylinder head being worked on is on its compression stroke, and the crankshaft locking tool is fitted (Section 7). If components from both cylinder heads have been removed it does not matter which one you rebuild

first. If components from only one have been removed make sure the other cylinder is at TDC on its exhaust stroke – in this position the intake camshaft lobes will be pointing down into the head, and the exhaust camshaft lobes will be pointing vertically up. If it is on its compression stroke (with the intake camshaft lobes pointing up and away from the head and the exhaust camshaft lobes pointing vertically down as in illustration 7.6a), or if the first head has been rebuilt and so is at TDC on its compression stroke and you want to rebuild the second head, turn the crankshaft one full turn clockwise so the pistons are again at TDC, and so the installed camshafts have turned half a turn.

16 Lubricate the cam follower shafts with clean engine oil. Position each follower in turn over its valve and insert the shaft **(see illustration 8.8b)**. Make sure the groove in the shaft is centred in the retaining pin hole, then fit the pin **(see illustration 8.8a)**.

17 Lubricate the valve shims and fit them into the tops of the valves **(see illustration)** – make sure each shim is returned to its correct valve or the valve clearances will be wrong.

18 If the driven gears have been removed from their shafts, fit them after installing the shafts.

19 Fit the spark plug bore O-ring, using a new one of necessary **(see illustration 8.6e)**.

20 Lubricate the camshaft journals and hold the camshafts in position on the head. Make sure the camshaft lobes are positioned as shown and the flats on the ends of the shafts are vertical, and parallel to each other and

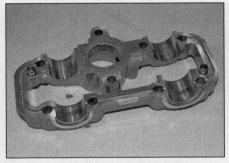

8.10a Inspect the camshaft holder and head...

8.10b ...and the camshaft journals and lobes

8.17 Fit each shim into its recess

8.20a Align and fit the intake camshaft...

8.20b ...and the exhaust camshaft

to the camshaft holder/cylinder head mating surface, with the alignment marks aligned, and if the driven gears are on the shafts aligning the marks made between the drive and driven gear teeth **(see illustrations)**.

21 Fit the camshaft holder and tighten its bolts finger-tight, not forgetting to fit the contact spring with the rear centre bolt **(see illustrations 8.6c, b and a)**. Tighten the bolts evenly and a little at a time in a criss-cross pattern, starting with the centre bolts and working outwards, to the torque setting specified at the beginning of the Chapter.

22 If the driven gears were removed, and if available, fit the camshaft holding and alignment tool over the front ends of the camshafts, turning them as required for alignment. If the tool is not available make sure the alignment marks made on removal are in exact alignment, and if not turn the camshaft so they are **(see illustration)**.

23 If the driven gears were removed from the shafts, make sure the washer is in the inner side of the gear **(see illustration 8.5c)**. Fit the gear onto the shaft, with the recessed side of the gear facing the shaft, making sure the gear marked I is fitted to the intake camshaft, and that marked E is fitted to the exhaust, and that the marks made between the teeth on the

drive and driven gears and between the gears and the shafts are in exact alignment **(see illustration)**. Fit and finger-tighten the bolt – when assembling the exhaust camshaft for the left-hand cylinder do not forget the spacer for the CMP sensor trigger and note that its bolt is longer than on the other shafts **(see illustration)**.

24 With the camshafts aligned and held, tighten the driven gear bolts to the torque setting specified at the beginning of the Chapter **(see illustration 8.5a)**. Remove the tool if used.

25 On the left-hand cylinder fit the camshaft position (CMP) sensor trigger all the way onto the camshaft, align the mark on the trigger with the groove in the sensor, and tighten the bolt **(see illustration 8.4)**.

26 Install the cam chain tensioner (Section 7). Remove the cable-tie.

27 Remove the crankshaft locking pin, and the camshaft holding/alignment tool if used.

28 Select a high gear and rotate the camshafts through one full revolution by turning the rear wheel in the normal direction of rotation until the marks made between the drive and driven gears align exactly as before. If the timing is correct you should be able to fit the crankshaft locking pin, and the camshaft

holding/alignment tool if available. If all is good remove the tool(s).

29 Check the valve clearances (see Chapter 1).

30 If new camshaft drive or driven gears have been installed check the backlash now (see below).

31 Install the remaining components in the reverse order of removal. Check the engine oil level and top up as necessary (0 Section 6).

Camshaft gear backlash check and adjustment

Note: *The engine must be cold.*

32 If there has been whine or clatter coming from the head area when the engine is running, or if new camshaft drive or driven gears have been fitted, the backlash between the gear teeth must be checked. To do this a dial gauge, BMW part No. 110861, and a holder for it, BMW part No. 110862, are required. Note that the use of any other dial gauge will result in a false reading as the specifications given are based upon the relative angles between the gauge plunger and the gear teeth determined by these tools. Due to the need for and cost of these tools you may want to have the procedure carried out by a BMW dealer.

33 Remove the valve cover (Section 6).

8.22 Align the marks made between the shaft and the holder

8.23a Align and fit the driven gear...

8.23b ...and secure with the bolt

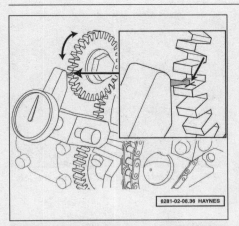

8.36 BMW dial gauge and holder for checking gear backlash

34 Set the cylinder being worked on at TDC on its compression stroke (Section 7).
35 Fit the dial gauge holder – when checking the backlash between the drive gear and the intake camshaft driven gear fit the holder between the drive gear and the exhaust camshaft driven gear, and when checking the backlash between the drive gear and the exhaust camshaft driven gear fit the holder between the drive gear and the intake camshaft driven gear. Locate the holder on the relative gear teeth and tighten the knurled nut to secure it.
36 Fit the dial gauge onto the holder so that the plunger is centred on and slightly compressed by a tooth on the driven gear being checked **(see illustration)**.
37 Turn the driven gear being checked lightly back and forth to record the backlash, i.e. the free movement, between it and the teeth on the drive gear – do not force the gear to turn against the drive gear, just take up the freeplay. Record the amount the dial moves around the gauge. If the amount of backlash recorded is outside the limits specified at the beginning of the Chapter a new driven gear must be selected to restore the correct amount of backlash.
38 To select a new gear remove the old one as described above, and take it along with the amount of backlash measured to a BMW dealer and ask them to replace it with one that will restore the backlash within the specified range. There is a number on the back of the gear that represents its size, and there are four sizes available – refer to the table below.

Number on gear	Part Number	Class, size
8 536 958 or 8 540 783	8 546 706	0.000
8 531 060 or 8 540 784	8 546 707	1, + 0.02 mm
8 531 061 or 8 540 785	8 546 708	3, + 0.04 mm
8 531 062 or 8 540 786	8 546 709	4, + 0.06 mm

39 Fit the new gear(s) onto the camshaft(s) as described above, then check the backlash again. If the backlash is now correct install all removed components as described above and in the preceding sections. If the backlash is still incorrect select a new gear and try again. Note that if the backlash is still excessive with the largest gear fitted, you must fit a new drive gear (Section 9).

9 Intermediate shaft and camshaft drive gear

Removal

1 Refer to the information in Note 4 of Section 8, and either remove the camshafts for the cylinder being worked on with the gears still bolted on them, or if required remove the driven gears from the camshafts and leave the camshafts in place – it is easier to remove the camshafts with the gears still on them than to do it the other way.
2 Make an alignment mark between a link on the cam chain and its position on the sprocket, and between the sprocket hub and its flange on the shaft **(see illustration 8.2a)**.
3 Undo the intermediate shaft axle retaining screw **(see illustration)**. Hold the shaft and withdraw the axle, then disengage the chain from the sprocket and remove the shaft **(see illustrations)**.

Inspection

4 Check the teeth on the drive gear and the cam chain driven sprocket for wear and damage. The sprocket can be removed and is available separately, the gear is part of the shaft. If the driven sprocket is worn it is likely the chain and drive sprocket are worn as well, so these should also be replaced with new ones.
5 Check the needle bearings in the shaft and the bearing surface on the axle **(see illustration)** – insert the axle and check it turns smoothly in the bearings, and make sure there is no side-to-side freeplay. If necessary replace the shaft and/or axle with a new one – the bearings are not available separately.
6 To remove the sprocket, clamp it in a soft-jawed vice and undo the screws. If you are fitting a new sprocket match its screw holes with those on the old one by laying the one on top of the other then make alignment marks on the new sprocket in the same places as made on the old one. If you are fitting a new shaft make an alignment mark on the flange in the same place as made on the old one. Fit the sprocket with the rounded side facing out, aligning the mark on the hub with that on the shaft flange, and tighten the screws to the torque setting specified at the beginning of the Chapter.

Installation

7 Lubricate the shaft axle with clean engine oil. Position the shaft in the head and lay the cam chain around it, aligning the marks made

9.3a Undo the screw...

9.3b ...withdraw the axle...

9.3c ...and remove the shaft

9.5 There are two needle bearings inside the shaft

9.7a Make sure the mark made on the chain aligns with that on the sprocket

9.7b The screw fits into the inner of the two holes in the axle on the right-hand head...

9.7c ...and into the outer hole on the left

on removal **(see illustration)**. Align the bores and insert the axle, shouldered end first and screw holes facing away from the head **(see illustration 9.3b)**. Align the screw holes and tighten the screw to the specified torque **(see illustrations)**.

8 Install the camshafts or camshaft driven gears as required (Section 8).

10 Cylinder head removal and installation

Caution: The engine must be completely cool before beginning this procedure or the cylinder head(s) may become warped.
Note: *The cylinder heads can be removed with the engine in the frame. If the engine has been removed, ignore the steps which do not apply.*
Special tool: *A degree disc is required for angle-tightening the cylinder head bolts.*

Removal

1 Disconnect the battery negative (-) terminal (see Chapter 8).

2 Drain the coolant (see Chapter 1).
3 Remove the exhaust system (see Chapter 4).
4 Remove the injector cover **(see illustration 6.2)**. Undo the fuel injector screw and displace the injector **(see illustration)**.
5 Remove the throttle body (see Chapter 4). Disconnect the by-pass air hose from the cylinder head.
6 Remove the camshafts with the driven gears on them, and the shims, and if required the followers (see Section 8).
7 Remove the intermediate shaft (Section 9).
8 On the left-hand cylinder head, release and disconnect the camshaft position (CMP) sensor wiring **(see illustration 4.12c)**.
9 Each cylinder head is secured by two 6 mm and four 10 mm bolts **(see illustration)**. First undo the two 6 mm bolts.
10 Slacken the 10 mm bolts evenly and a little at a time in a criss-cross pattern and remove them when loose.
11 Pull the cylinder head off **(see illustration)**. If it is stuck, tap around the joint face between the head and the cylinder with a soft-faced mallet to free it. Do not attempt to free the head by levering with a screwdriver between the head and cylinder – you'll

10.4 Displace the injector

damage the sealing surfaces. When removing the head note how the cam chain guide blade lug locates in the slot, and draw it out as you remove the head so it stays in the engine.
12 Remove the cylinder head gasket **(see illustration)** – a new one must be used. Remove the dowel and the locating pin if loose. Stuff some clean rag into the cam chain tunnel.
13 Check the old cylinder head gasket and the sealing surfaces on the cylinder head and

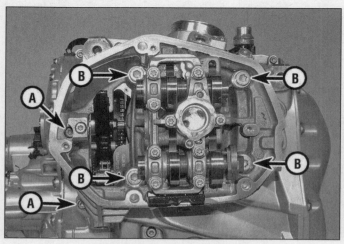

10.9 6mm bolts (A), 10mm bolts (B)

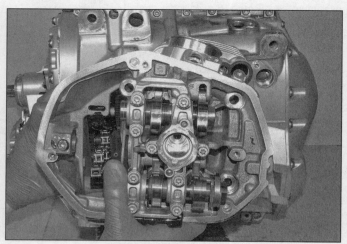

10.11 Remove the cylinder head

10.12 Remove the cylinder head gasket, noting how it locates on the dowel and pin (arrowed)

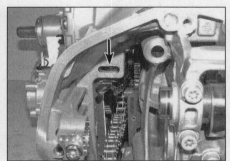

10.19 Lug on blade locates in slot (arrowed)

cylinder for signs of leakage, which could indicate a warped head. Discard the gasket once it has been inspected as a new one must be used.

14 Clean any traces of old gasket material from the cylinder head and cylinder. If a scraper is used, take care not to scratch or gouge the soft aluminium. Be careful not to let any of the gasket material fall into the crankcase or the oil and coolant passages.

15 If required, remove the camshaft position sensor from the left-hand head (see Chapter 4).

Installation

16 If removed, fit the CMP sensor into the left-hand head (see Chapter 4).

17 Check the cylinder head and cylinder mating surfaces are clean. Remove the rag from the cam chain tunnel.

18 Fit the dowel and locating pin if removed. Fit the new head gasket onto the dowel and pin, making sure all holes are correctly aligned (see illustration 10.12). Never re-use the old gasket.

19 Carefully fit the cylinder head onto the cylinder, feeding the cam chain through the tunnel and the guide and tensioner blades into it (see illustration 10.11) – make sure the lug on the cam chain guide blade seats in the cut-out in the head (see illustration).

20 Fit the cylinder head bolts and tighten them finger-tight (see illustrations).

21 Tighten the 10 mm cylinder head bolts first, tightening them evenly in a criss-cross sequence, first to the initial stage torque

setting specified at the beginning of this Chapter, then to the second stage torque, and then to the third stage torque. Next, using a degree disc (see Tools and Workshop Tips), angle-tighten each bolt in the same sequence and in one go through the final stage angle (see illustration).

22 Tighten the 6 mm bolts to the specified torque setting.

23 On the left-hand head connect and secure the CMP sensor wiring (see illustration 4.12c).

24 Follow the procedures in Section 9 to install the intermediate shaft and in Section 8 to install the followers, shims and camshafts.

25 Connect the by-pass air hose. Install the throttle body (see Chapter 4).

26 Check the condition of the injector O-ring and replace it with a new one if necessary. Fit the injector and tighten its screw (see illustration 10.4). Fit the injector cover (see illustration 6.2).

27 Install the remaining components in the reverse order of removal, noting the following:
● Refill the cooling system (see Chapter 1).
● Check the engine oil level and top-up if necessary (see Pre-ride checks).

11 Cylinder head and valve overhaul

1 Because of the complex nature of this job and the special tools and equipment required, most owners leave servicing of the

valves, valve seats and valve guides to a professional. However, you can make an initial assessment of whether the valves are seating correctly, and therefore sealing, by pouring a small amount of solvent into the valve ports. If the solvent leaks past the valve into the combustion chamber area the valve is not seating correctly and sealing.

2 With the correct tools (a valve spring compressor is essential – make sure it is suitable for motorcycle work), you can also remove the valves and associated components from the cylinder head, clean them and check them for wear to assess the extent of the work needed. Unless seat cutting or guide replacement is required, the head can then be reassembled.

3 A dealer service department or specialist engineer can fit new guides and re-cut the valve seats.

4 After the valve service has been performed, be sure to clean the head very thoroughly before installation on the engine to remove any metal particles or abrasive grit that may still be present from the valve service operations. Use compressed air, if available, to blow out all the holes and passages.

Disassembly

5 Before proceeding, arrange to label and store the valves along with their related components in such a way that they can be returned to their original locations without getting mixed up. A good way to do this is to obtain a container divided into eight compartments, and to label each compartment with the identity of the valve which will be stored in it (i.e. left or right-hand cylinder, intake front or rear and exhaust front or rear valve). Alternatively, labelled plastic bags will do just as well.

6 If not already done, when working on the left-hand head remove the CMP sensor (see Chapter 4).

7 Clean any traces of old gasket material from the cylinder head. If a scraper is used, take care not to scratch or gouge the soft aluminium.

8 Using a suitable valve spring compressor, compress the spring on the first valve, making sure the tool is correctly located onto both

10.20a Fit the 10 mm bolts...

10.20b ...and the 6 mm bolts

10.21 Angle-tighten the bolts using a degree disc

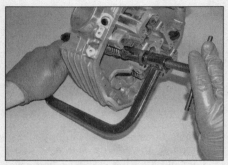

11.8a Fit the valve spring compressor...

11.8b ...making sure it seats correctly over the spring retainer...

11.8c ...and against the valve head...

11.8d ...then compress the spring and remove the collets

11.9 Remove the spring retainer and spring

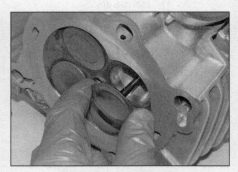

11.10a Remove the valve

ends of the valve assembly **(see illustrations)**. Do not compress the spring any more than is absolutely necessary, then remove the collets, using either needle-nose pliers, tweezers, a magnet, or a screwdriver with a dab of grease on it **(see illustration)**.

9 Carefully release the valve spring compressor and remove the spring retainer, noting which way up it fits, and the spring **(see illustration)**.

10 Push the valve down into the head and withdraw it from the underside **(see illustration)**. If the valve binds in the guide (won't pull through), push it back into the head and deburr the area above the collet groove with a very fine file or whetstone **(see illustration)**.

11 Pull the valve stem seal off the top of the valve guide using either a special removing tool or pliers **(see illustration)**. A new one must be fitted. Lift out the spring seat using a magnet, noting which way up it fits **(see illustration)**.

12 Repeat the procedure for the remaining valves. Remember to keep the components for each valve assembly together and in order so they can be reinstalled in the same location.

13 Carefully scrape all carbon deposits out of the combustion chamber area. A hand held wire brush or a piece of fine emery cloth can be used once the majority of deposits have been scraped away. Do not use a wire brush mounted in a drill motor as the head material is soft and may be eroded away. Next, wash the cylinder head with solvent and dry it thoroughly. Compressed air will speed the drying process and ensure that all holes,

recessed areas and oil passages are clean.

14 Carefully scrape off any deposits that may have formed on the valves. Make sure the valves do not get mixed up.

15 Clean the valve springs, collets, retainers and spring seats with solvent and dry them thoroughly. Clean the parts from one valve at a time so as not to mix them up.

Inspection

16 Inspect the head very carefully for cracks and other damage. If cracks are found, a new head will be required.

17 Examine the valve seats in the combustion chamber. If they are pitted, cracked or burned, the head will require work beyond the scope of the home mechanic. Check that the width of the valve seat-to-valve contact area is the same around the entire circumference of the

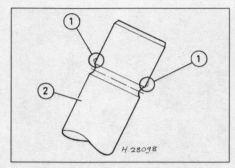

11.10b If necessary, deburr the valve stem (2) above the collet groove (1)

11.11a Pull the seal off the guide...

11.11b ...then remove the seat

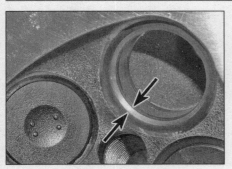

11.17 Inspect the valve seat

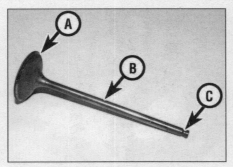

11.18 Valve face (A), stem (B) and collet groove (C)

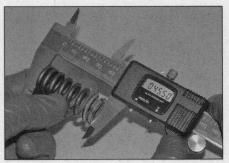

11.20 Measuring valve spring free length

seat **(see illustration)**. If the width varies, valve seat overhaul is required.

18 Carefully inspect each valve face for cracks, pits and burned spots, and check the valve stem and the collet groove area for scoring and cracks **(see illustration)**. Rotate the valve and check for any obvious indication that it is bent. Check the end of the stem for pitting and excessive wear. Any of the above conditions indicates the need for new valves.

19 If the necessary measuring equipment is available, fit the valves in their guides and check the radial play, then measure the internal diameter of the valve guides. Compare the results with the Specifications at the beginning of this Chapter. If the results indicate that the guides are worn, have the head inspected by a BMW dealer. Note: Carbon build-up inside the lower ends of the exhaust valve guides indicates worn valve stems and/or valve guides.

20 Check the end of each valve spring for wear and pitting. Measure the free length of each springs – if any have sagged below the specified range replace them all with a new set **(see illustration)**. It is good practice to fit new valve springs when an engine is being overhauled.

21 Check the spring retainers and collets for obvious wear and cracks. Any questionable parts should not be reused, as extensive damage will occur in the event of failure during engine operation.

22 If the inspection indicates that no overhaul

work is required, the valve components can be reinstalled in the head.

Reassembly

23 Unless a valve service has been performed, before fitting the valves they should be ground in (lapped) to ensure a positive seal between the valves and seats. This procedure requires fine valve grinding compound and a valve grinding tool. If a grinding tool is not available, a piece of rubber or plastic hose can be slipped over the valve stem (after the valve has been installed in the guide) and used to turn the valve.

24 Apply a small amount of fine grinding compound to the valve face **(see illustration)**. Lubricate the valve stem with engine oil and insert it into the guide. Note: Make sure each valve is installed in its correct guide and be careful not to get any grinding compound on the valve stem.

25 Attach the grinding tool (or hose) to the valve and rotate the tool between the palms of your hands **(see illustration)**. Use a back-and-forth motion (as though rubbing your hands together) rather than a circular motion (i.e. so that the valve rotates alternately clockwise and anti-clockwise rather than in one direction only). Lift the valve off the seat and turn it at regular intervals to distribute the grinding compound properly. Continue the grinding procedure until the valve face and seat contact area is of uniform width and unbroken around the entire circumference of the valve face and seat **(see illustration 11.17)**.

11.24 Apply grinding compound sparingly to the valve face only

26 Carefully remove the valve from the guide and wipe off all traces of grinding compound. Use solvent to clean the valve and wipe the seat area thoroughly with a solvent soaked cloth.

27 Repeat the procedure for the remaining valves.

28 Rebuild each valve assembly in turn. Fit the spring seat with its shouldered side facing up **(see illustration 11.11b)**.

29 Push the new valve stem seal squarely onto the top of the valve guide until it is felt to clip into place **(see illustration)**.

30 Lubricate the stem with engine oil and fit the valve into its guide **(see illustration 11.10a)**.

31 Fit the spring with the paint mark facing up **(see illustration)**.

11.25 Rotate the valve grinding tool back and forth between the palms of your hands

11.29 Press the seal into place

11.31 Fit the spring...

11.32 ...and the spring retainer

11.33 Seat the rib on each collet in the groove in the valve stem

11.34 Collets seated correctly in retainer and around top of valve stem

32 Fit the spring retainer, with its shouldered side facing down so that it fits into the top of the spring **(see illustration)**.

33 Apply a small amount of grease to the collets to hold them in place during installation, then compress the spring with the valve spring compressor and fit the collets **(see illustration)**. Do not compress the spring any more than is absolutely necessary to slip the collets into position. Make certain that the collets are securely located in the collet groove, then release the spring compressor.

34 Support the cylinder head on blocks so the valves can't contact the workbench top, then gently tap the valve stem to check the collets are securely seated in their grooves **(see illustration)**.

35 Repeat for the remaining valves.

12 Pistons

Note: *The pistons cannot be removed with the engine in the frame – the engine must be removed and the crankcases separated.*
Special tool: *A piston ring clamp is required for installing the pistons.*

Removal

1 Remove the engine from the frame (Section 4), then separate the crankcase halves (Section 23), and remove the crankshaft (Section 25) – you can leave the connecting rod for the left-hand piston on the crankshaft unless you need to remove it for other purposes.

2 Each piston is identical and has a triangular mark on the rim of the crown and a corresponding mark cast on the underside – the right-hand piston is fitted in the cylinder with the triangle at the top and pointing to the front, the left-hand piston is fitted in the cylinder with the triangle at the bottom and pointing to the front. The mark on the top may not be visible before the piston is cleaned, so unless you know that you will be fitting new pistons make your own mark at the top (RH piston) or bottom (LH piston) of the piston – marking the right-hand piston R and left-hand one L ensures they cannot get mixed up.

3 Push the left-hand piston out through the top of the cylinder **(see illustration 12.4a)**. If the piston is being re-used carefully prise out the circlip from the rear side of the piston **(see illustration 12.4b)** – new circlips must be used.

4 Push the right-hand piston/connecting rod assembly out through the top of the cylinder **(see illustration)**. Carefully prise out the circlip from one side of the piston using a small flat-bladed screwdriver in the notch, then push the piston pin out and detach the piston from the connecting rod **(see illustrations)**. If the piston is being re-used remove the circlip from the other side – new circlips must be used.

5 If new pistons are being fitted they come as a paired assembly along with new rings, circlips and piston pins. If the pistons are being re-used it is advisable to fit new rings, which are available separately, as are the circlips and the piston pins, but again in pairs – you cannot get components for one piston only, at least not from BMW.

6 Using your thumbs or a thin blade, carefully ease the rings off the piston **(see illustration)**. Do not nick or gouge the piston in the process. Note which way up each ring fits and in which groove as they must be installed in their original positions if being re-used.

7 Scrape all traces of carbon from the piston crown. A hand-held wire brush or a piece of fine emery cloth can be used once most of the deposits have been scraped away. Do not, under any circumstances, use a wire brush mounted in a drill motor to remove deposits from the piston – the piston material is soft and will be eroded away by the wire brush.

12.4a Remove the piston from the top of the bore

12.4b Prise the circlip out...

12.4c ...push the pin out and detach the rod

12.6 Remove the rings carefully, using your thumbs, or a thin blade such as a feeler gauge

12.12 Measuring piston diameter

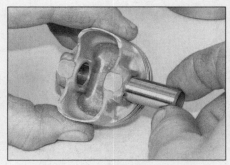

12.13 Check for freeplay between the piston and pin

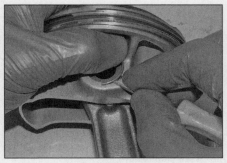

12.15 Carefully push the circlip into its groove

8 Use a piston ring groove cleaning tool to remove any carbon deposits from the ring grooves. If a tool is not available, a piece broken off an old ring will do the job. Be very careful to remove only the carbon deposits. Do not remove any metal and do not nick or gouge the sides of the ring grooves.

9 Once the deposits have been removed, wash the piston with solvent and dry it thoroughly. Make sure the oil return holes in the back of the oil ring groove are clear. If the identification mark made on removal is cleaned off, be sure to re-mark the piston in the same place with the correct identity (L or R) – you should now be able to see the triangle mark.

Inspection

10 Inspect the piston for cracks and damage around the skirt, at the pin bosses and at the ring lands. Normal wear appears as light, vertical marks on the thrust surfaces of the skirt. If the skirt is scored or scuffed, the piston and cylinder are probably worn beyond the service limit. Alternatively, the engine may have been suffering from overheating caused by lack of lubrication or abnormal combustion. If so check the operation of the oil pump (see Section 19) and, if necessary, have the engine management system checked by a BMW dealer.

11 A hole in the top of the piston (only likely in extreme circumstances) or burned areas around the edge of the piston crown, indicate that pre-ignition or knocking under

load have occurred. The engine management system should ensure correct ignition under all circumstances, but if a sensor fails, or if it is fitted incorrectly, the engine management system will not be able to set the correct ignition timing. If you find evidence of any problems, the causes must be corrected or the damage will occur again.

12 Measure the piston diameter 6 mm up from the bottom of the skirt and at 90° to the piston pin axis and record it **(see illustration)**. Refer to Section 14 to measure the cylinder bore and calculate the piston-to-bore clearance.

13 Apply clean engine oil to the piston pin, insert it part way into the piston and check for any freeplay between the two – there should be no discernible freeplay **(see illustration)**. If there is, it is more likely that the piston is worn than the pin, and this should be visually evident. The best course of action is fit new pistons, as they come with new pins, thus covering all bases.

Installation

14 Fit the piston rings, and make sure that the ring end gaps are correctly staggered (see Section 13).

15 Fit a new circlip into the groove in one side of the right-hand piston. Lubricate the piston pin with clean engine oil. Align the piston with the connecting rod so that the arrow mark on the underside of the piston is at the top and pointing to the left as you look at it, and the marking across the big-end and cap of

the connecting rod is facing down. Slide the piston pin in, then fit the other new circlip into the groove **(see illustration)**.

16 Fit a new circlip into the groove in the rear side of the left-hand piston.

17 Lubricate the piston, rings and the inside of the ring clamp with clean engine oil. Make sure the second ring ends are seated on either side of the pin, and not on it **(see illustration 13.7)**. Fit the clamp over the rings and tighten it enough to compress the rings into their grooves, but not so tight that it locks onto the piston **(see illustrations)** – as the piston is pressed into the cylinder bore, the clamp must be able to slide off. Once the clamp is in place, don't rotate it as the position of the ring end gaps will alter.

18 Sit the crankcase half being worked on onto its mating surface on some clean rag so the cylinder is vertical. Lubricate the cylinder wall with clean engine oil. Ease the lower end of the piston into the top of the bore, on the right-hand piston making sure the connecting rod does not contact the cylinder wall **(see illustration)** – if the pistons are being re-used check that the L marked piston is fitted in the left cylinder and the R marked piston in the right cylinder (see Step 2). Also make sure that the piston is the right way round with the triangle on the right-hand piston at the top of the cylinder and pointing to the front, and the triangle on the left-hand piston at the bottom of the cylinder and pointing to the front.

19 Tap down on the top of the piston using the handle-end of a hammer to slowly ease it

12.17a Fit the clamp over the piston…

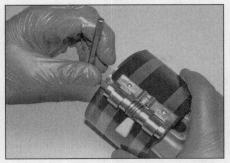

12.17b …and tighten it to compress the rings

12.18 Fit the piston into the top of the bore

into the bore **(see illustration)**. If the rings snag on the top lip of the bore, tighten the clamp slightly to compress the rings further into their grooves. Do not try to force a snagged ring in as it will break; if necessary start again.

Caution: Do not force the piston down – this will only result in broken rings.

20 The ring clamp will become free once the piston is safely inside the cylinder.

21 Position the left-hand piston in the cylinder so the piston pin bore is in direct alignment with the pin removal/installation hole **(see illustration)**.

22 Install the crankshaft (Section 25) then reassemble the crankcases (Section 23).

13 Piston rings

1 It is good practice to fit new piston rings when an engine is being overhauled. Before fitting the rings onto the pistons, the ring end gaps should be checked with the rings fitted in the cylinder.

2 First, check that the cylinder bore is not worn beyond the service limit (Section 14).

3 Lay out the pistons and ring sets so the rings will be matched with the same piston and cylinder during the measurement procedure and engine assembly. The upper surface of each ring is marked GOE TOP **(see illustrations)**.

4 To measure the installed ring end gap, insert each ring in turn into the top of the cylinder and square it up with the cylinder walls by pushing it in with the top of the piston. The ring should be about 20 mm below the top edge of the cylinder. To measure the end gap, slip a feeler gauge between the ends of the ring and compare the measurement to the specifications at the beginning of this Chapter for the ring being checked.

5 If the gap is larger or smaller than specified, and the bore is within limits, replace the rings with a new set.

6 Fit the oil control ring (lowest on the piston) first. It is composed of two separate components – the expander and the ring. Pull the ends of the expander apart enough to fit it over the top of the piston and slip it into its groove, then press the ends back together **(see illustration)**. Make sure that the straight wire is not pulled out of either end of the coiled wire. Now fit the oil control ring over the expander with the marked side facing the top of the piston, and positioning the end gap in the ring on the opposite side of the triangle on the right-hand piston and in line with the triangle on the left-hand piston, so when the piston is fitted the gap is at the bottom of the cylinder **(see illustration)**. Do not expand the ring any more than is necessary to slide it into place.

7 Fit the second ring next into the middle groove in the piston, with the GOE TOP mark facing the top of the piston, and locating its ends on each side of the pin in the ring groove **(see illustration)**.

8 Fit the top ring into the top groove in the piston, with the GOE TOP mark facing the

12.19 Tap the piston down the bore carefully

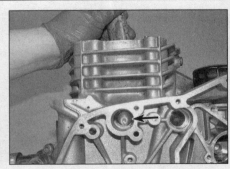

12.21 Align the pin bore centrally in the hole (arrowed)

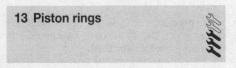

13.3a Upper surface mark (arrowed) – top ring

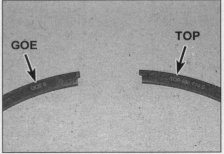

13.3b Upper surface marks (arrowed), and note the shaped ends – second ring

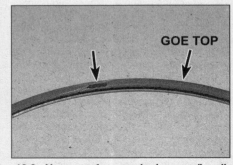

13.3c Upper surface marks (arrowed) – oil control ring

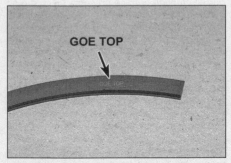

13.6a Fit the expander into the groove…

13.6b …then fit the control ring over it – this is the left-hand piston so the ends are aligned with the triangle on the top of the piston

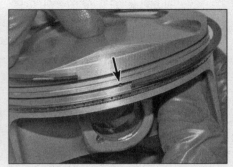

13.7 Fit the ends of the second ring on either side of the pin (arrowed)

13.8 Fitting the top ring – left hand piston shown, so the ends are on the opposite side to the triangle on the top of the piston

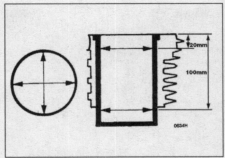

14.3 Take measurements in the directions shown

15.2 Measuring big-end side clearance

top of the piston, and so the end gap in the ring is next to the triangle on the right-hand piston and on the opposite side to the triangle on the left-hand piston, so when the piston is fitted the gap is at the top of the cylinder **(see illustration)**.

9 Double-check that all rings are correctly located in their grooves with the end gaps positioned as described above.

14 Cylinders

Note: *The cylinders are an integral part of the crankcases and cannot be separated from them*

1 The cylinder bores have a wear resistant coating that should last the life of the engine unless damage, caused by a broken piston ring or seizure, has occurred.

2 Working on one cylinder at a time, inspect the cylinder walls carefully for flaking, scratches and score marks. If damage is noted, yet the bore diameter is still within the service limit, seek the advice of a BMW dealer or engine specialist as to the suitability of the cylinder for continued use. The cylinders cannot be rebored.

3 Using telescoping gauges and a micrometer (see *Tools and Workshop Tips* in the Reference section), check the dimensions of each cylinder to assess the amount of wear

and ovality. Take measurements 20 mm and 100 mm from the top of the bore, both parallel with the piston pin and at 90° to it, taking a total of four measurements **(see illustration)**.

4 Compare the results with the specifications at the beginning of this Chapter, then calculate any difference between the measurements to determine ovality in the bore. Also calculate the piston-to-bore clearance, having measured the piston as described in Section 12.

5 If a cylinder is worn beyond the service limit, or bore ovality exceeds the service limits, check with a BMW dealer as to the best course of action. At the time of writing, replacement crankcase halves are not available, therefore a new engine would be required.

15 Connecting rods

Note 1: *The connecting rods cannot be removed with the engine in the frame – the engine must be removed and the crankcases separated.*
Note 2: *The big-end bolts are of the stretch type – new bolts must be fitted when the engine is finally reassembled.*
Special tool: *A degree disc is required for angle-tightening the connecting rod big-end bolts.*

Removal

1 Separate the crankcase halves (see Section 23).

2 Before removing the rods from the crankshaft, measure the big-end side clearance as follows: push the rod to one side on the crankpin and measure the clearance between the big-end and the crankshaft with a feeler gauge **(see illustration)**. If the clearance is greater than the service limit listed in the Specifications at the beginning of this Chapter, the rods must be replaced with a new pair – they are not available individually.

3 Using paint or a marker pen, mark the cylinder identity (L or R) on the front facing side of each connecting rod and cap to ensure they can be fitted the same way round on installation. The manufacturer's markings across the big-end and cap face the bottom of the engine.

4 Undo the big-end bolts, remove the caps and detach the rods from the crankpins **(see illustrations)** – remove the left-hand cylinder connecting rod, and push the right-hand connecting rod/piston up into the bore a little so it is clear of the crankpin. Keep the rod, cap and the bearing shells together to ensure correct installation **(see illustration)**.

5 Remove the crankshaft (Section 25). Remove the right-hand piston/connecting rod assembly from the cylinder, then detach the piston from the rod (Section 12).

15.4a Undo the big-end bolts…

15.4b …remove the cap…

15.4c …and push the rod off the crankpin

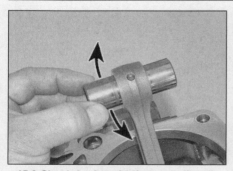

15.9 Check for freeplay between the pin and the rod

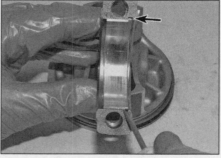

15.11a Ease the shells out carefully – note the locating tab (arrowed)

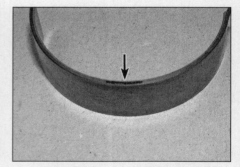

15.11b Shell colour code (arrowed)

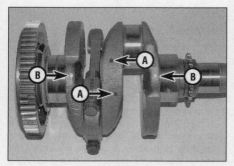

15.11c Big-end bearing colour codes (A), main bearing colour codes (B)

15.13 Fit the shells, locating the tabs in the notches

15.18 Angle-tighten the big-end bolts using a degree disc

Inspection

6 The connecting rods are fitted as paired sets dependent upon their weight. Weight class identification is represented by coloured dots (white, blue or yellow) painted on the sides of the rods (see Specifications at the beginning of this Chapter for details).

7 The joint between the connecting rod and the cap is a fractured joint that can only be assembled one way round. Take care not to damage the joint surfaces – if the surfaces are not a perfect match, the two halves of the big-end will not mate properly and a new pair of connecting rods will have to be fitted.

8 Check the connecting rods for cracks and other obvious damage.

9 Apply clean engine oil to the piston pin, insert it into the connecting rod and check for any freeplay between the two – there should be no discernible freeplay **(see illustration)**. If there is, it is more likely that the rod is worn than the pin, and this should be visually evident.

10 Examine the big-end bearing shells. If they are scored, badly scuffed or appear to have seized, check the crankpins. If the pins are worn or damaged, a new crankshaft will have to be fitted. If there is any doubt about the condition of the crankshaft, have it checked by a BMW dealer.

11 If the bearing shells show signs of normal wear they should be replaced with new ones – always replace the shells in both big-ends as a set. Ease the shells out using a small screwdriver in the notch **(see illustration)**. The shells are colour-coded red, violet or blue – the colour mark is on the edge of the shell, and

must match the colour code mark on the crank web adjacent to the crankpin **(see illustrations)**.

12 If you are in doubt about their straightness, have the rods checked for twist and bend by a BMW dealer, and replace them with new ones if any is found.

Installation

13 Press the bearing shells into the rods and caps, locating the tabs in the notches and making sure they are flush with the edges **(see illustration)**.

14 Fit the right-hand piston onto its rod, then fit the right-hand piston/connecting rod assembly into the cylinder (Section 12).

15 Fit the crankshaft (Section 25).

16 Lubricate the threads and under the heads of a set of new big-end bolts with clean engine oil.

17 Seat the connecting rod on the crankpin and fit the cap, making sure they are the right way round (see Step 3) **(see illustrations 15.4c and b)**. Double-check that the two halves of the fractured joint are a perfect fit, then fit the new bolts and tighten them finger-tight **(see illustration 15.4a)**.

18 Referring to the torque settings given at the beginning of the Chapter, tighten the bolts evenly to the initial stage torque setting, then to the second stage torque, then use a degree disc (see *Tools and Workshop Tips* in the Reference section) to tighten them through the final stage angle in one continuous movement **(see illustration)**. Now slacken the bolts until loose, then tighten them again through the two stages and the angle in the same way.

19 Check that the connecting rod is free to

rotate smoothly and freely on the crankpin. If the rod feels tight, tap on the bottom of the cap with a soft-faced mallet to free it. If there are still signs of roughness or tightness, detach the rod and recheck the assembly. Note: New big-end bolts must be used.

20 Assemble the crankcases (Section 23).

16 Front crankcase cover

Note: *The front crankcase cover can be removed with the engine in the frame.*

Removal

1 Drain the engine oil (see Chapter 1).

2 On R and RS models remove the radiator (see Chapter 3).

3 Unscrew the crankcase cover bolts and remove the cover **(see illustration)**. The

16.3 Crankcase cover bolts

16.7a Apply an even bead of sealant ...

16.7b ...to the perimeter and around the hole (A). Dowel locations (B)

16.8a The shouldered end of the black tube goes into the hole below the oil pump gear

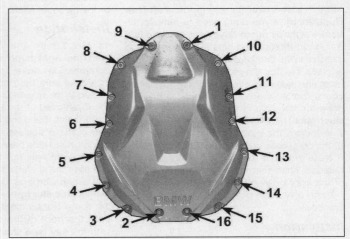

16.8b Cover bolt tightening sequence

sealant used between the cover and the crankcase can form a strong bond – if the cover is stuck, tap around the joint with a soft-faced mallet to free it from the crankcase. Do not attempt to free the cover by levering with a screwdriver between the cover and the crankcase – you'll damage the sealing surfaces.

4 Note the location of the dowels in either the cover or the crankcase and remove them if they are loose **(see illustration 16.7b)**.

5 Clean all traces of sealant from the cover and crankcase mating surfaces. If a scraper is used, take care not to scratch or gouge the soft aluminium. Be careful not to let any of the old sealant fall into the crankcase.

Installation

6 If removed, fit the dowels into the crankcase or cover **(see illustration 16.7b)**.

7 Apply an even bead of suitable sealant

to the perimeter mating surface on the crankcase, going round the inside of the bolt holes and outside the dowels, and completely around the hole in the left-hand side **(see illustrations)** – BMW recommend using Dow Corning sealant (part No. 07580397777).

8 Fit the cover, making sure the dowels locate correctly, then fit the bolts and tighten them finger-tight at first **(see illustration)**. Now tighten the bolts as follows to the torque setting specified at the beginning of this Chapter – as you look at the cover **(see illustration)**. Tighten the top right bolt first, then tighten the bottom left to top left bolts in a clockwise sequence, then tighten the second top right bolt to bottom right bolts in a clockwise sequence.

9 On R and RS models install the radiator and refill the cooling system (see Chapter 3).

10 Refill the engine with oil to the correct level (see Chapter 1).

17 Balancer shaft

Note: *The balancer shaft cannot be removed with the engine in the frame – the engine must be removed, and the gearbox removed from the engine.*

Removal

1 Remove the engine (Section 4).

2 Remove the clutch assembly (Section 20).

3 Remove the gearbox (Section 26).

4 Remove the right-hand cylinder intermediate shaft (Section 9).

5 Make an alignment mark between the cam chain and its drive gear on the balancer shaft. Unscrew the right-hand cylinder cam chain tensioner blade pivot bolt and remove the

17.6a Note the alignment of the holes (A) and how the weight locates over the key (B)

17.6b Slide the weight off the shaft if required

17.7 Slide the shaft out of the crankcase

blade (see illustration 18.7). Slip the cam chain off its sprocket on the balancer shaft (see illustration 18.8).

6 With the right-hand piston at TDC note how the hole in the front balancer weight aligns with the hole in the crankcase, and how the weight locates over the key in the shaft (see illustration). If you don't need to remove the front weight/oil pump drive gear you can fit a 6 mm pin through the hole in the weight and into that in the crankcase, and the gear will stay in place, held by the pin and the pump driven gear and keeping everything aligned, when you withdraw the balancer shaft. Otherwise draw the weight off the end of the shaft (see illustration). Remove the key if loose.

7 Withdraw the balancer shaft from the rear of the crankcase (see illustration).

8 Note there is a thrust washer for the balancer shaft that is fitted on the inner side of the front bearing housing in the crankcase – it can only be removed after separating the crankcases.

Inspection

9 Check the teeth of the oil pump drive gear on the front weight and of the right-hand cylinder cam chain drive sprocket on the rear of the shaft for wear and damage and replace with new ones if necessary. Check for corresponding wear and damage on the pump driven gear, and the sprocket on the intermediate shaft.

10 Check for wear on the balancer shaft

journals and their bearings in the crankcase. Check for wear on the surface of the transmission input shaft – it runs on two needle bearings fitted inside the balancer shaft. None of the bearings are listed as being available separately from either the crankcase or the balancer shaft.

Installation

11 Make sure the crankshaft is locked with the right-hand piston at TDC on its compression stroke.

12 Make sure the thrust washer is correctly seated in the housing.

13 If removed fit the key for the front weight into its slot. Slide the balancer shaft into the rear of the crankcase with the rear weight on the left-hand side (see illustration 17.7). If the front weight was not removed support it as you slide the shaft through, and make sure the key aligns with and locates in the slot in the weight (see illustration 17.6a).

14 If the front weight was removed slide it onto the front of the shaft, aligning the slot with the key (see illustrations 17.6b and a). Make sure the holes in the gear and crankcase align and fit the locking pin.

15 Engage the right-hand cylinder cam chain around the sprocket, aligning the marks (see illustration 18.8). Lubricate the right-hand cylinder tensioner blade pivot with oil, fit the blade and tighten the bolt to the torque setting specified at the beginning of the Chapter (see illustration 18.7). Install the intermediate

shaft (Section 9). Check that all components are in correct alignment for timing purposes, then remove the locking pin from the balancer weight.

16 Install the gearbox and the clutch.

18 Cam chains and blades

Note: *The cam chains and blades cannot be removed with the engine in the frame – the engine must be removed, and the gearbox removed from the engine.*

Removal

1 Remove the engine (Section 4).
2 Remove the cylinder heads (Section 10).
3 Remove the right-hand cylinder cam chain guide blade, noting how it locates (see illustration).
4 Remove the gearbox (Section 26).
5 Remove the alternator stator and rotor (see Chapter 8).
6 Remove the starter idle and reduction gears, and the starter driven gear (Section 22).
7 Make an alignment mark between the right-hand cylinder cam chain and its drive sprocket on the balancer shaft. Unscrew the right-hand cylinder tensioner blade bolt and remove the blade (see illustration).
8 Remove the right-hand cylinder cam chain (see illustration).

18.3 Note how the blade locates over the idle gear shaft

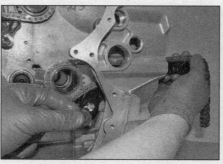

18.7 Undo the pivot bolt and remove the blade

18.8 Remove the chain

18.9a Remove the left-hand guide blade...

18.9b ...tensioner blade...

18.10 ...and cam chain

9 Make an alignment mark between the left-hand cylinder cam chain and its drive sprocket on the crankshaft. Unscrew the left-hand cylinder guide and tensioner blade bolts and remove the blades **(see illustrations)**.

10 Remove the left-hand cylinder cam chain **(see illustration)**.

Inspection

11 Except in cases of oil starvation, the cam chains wear very little. If the chains have stretched, indicated by play between the links, they must be replaced with new ones. If the chains have worn, it is likely that the sprockets on the crankshaft, balancer shaft and intermediate shafts are worn also.

12 Check the tensioner and guide blades and their pivots for signs of wear and damage and replace them with new ones if necessary – they come as a set of four blades and three pivot bolts.

Installation

13 Installation is the reverse of removal – lubricate the blade pivot bolts with clean engine oil and tighten the bolts to the torque setting specified at the beginning of the Chapter. Check the tensioner blades pivot freely on the bolts.

19 Oil pump, pressure relief valve, and level/temperature sensor

Note: *The oil pump can be removed with the engine in the frame.*

Oil pump

Removal

1 Remove the clutch assembly (Section 20).

2 With the pistons at TDC note how the hole in the front balancer weight aligns with the hole in the crankcase **(see illustration 17.6a)**. Fit a 6 mm pin through the hole in the weight and into that in the crankcase.

3 Unscrew the oil pump driven gear nut, remove the square washer and draw the gear off the shaft **(see illustrations)** – if the

front balancer weight has been removed counter-hold the gear using a spanner on the square washer. A new nut must be fitted.

4 Unscrew the oil pump cover screws and remove the cover **(see illustration)**. Remove the locating pins if loose.

5 Grasp the end of the shaft and draw it out along with the rotors **(see illustration)**.

6 Remove the front outer and inner rotors, then withdraw the drive pin **(see illustrations 19.11d, c and b)**. Slide the spacer off the shaft **(see illustration 19.11a)**. Remove the rear outer rotor from the pump housing if it did not come away with the shaft **(see illustration 19.10)**. The rear inner rotor is integral with the shaft.

Inspection

7 Clean all the components in a suitable solvent.

8 Inspect the pump cover, housing and rotors for scoring and wear. If any damage or wear is evident, fit a new pump – individual components are not available. Note that at the time of writing, replacement crankcase halves are not available, therefore a new engine would be required.

Installation

9 Lubricate the pump rotors with clean engine oil. The marks made on the pump rotors must face out, i.e. towards the front of the engine

19.3a Unscrew the nut...

19.3b ...and remove the washer and the gear

19.4 Remove the cover

19.5 Draw the shaft and rotors out as an assembly

19.10 Fit the rear outer rotor

19.11a Fit the spacer...

19.11b ...the drive pin...

19.11c ...the front inner rotor...

19.11d ...and outer rotor

10 Fit the rear outer rotor (the narrower of the two outer rotors) into the pump housing with the punch mark facing out **(see illustration)**.
11 Slide the spacer onto the front of the shaft with its recessed side facing the rear inner rotor **(see illustration)**. Fit the drive pin into its hole, then seat the cut-outs in the inner face of the front inner rotor over the drive pin ends **(see illustrations)**. Slide the front outer rotor over the inner rotor, with its punch mark facing out **(see illustration)**.
12 Slide the shaft into the housing, making sure the rear inner rotor fits into the outer rotor, and aligning the recess in the inner face of the spacer with the pin in the housing, so the pin fits into the recess **(see illustration)**. Make sure the outer faces of the front rotors are flush with the housing surface, and turn the shaft to check the pump turns smoothly and freely.

13 Fit the cover locating pins if removed. Fit the cover, making sure it locates over the pins **(see illustration 19.4)**. Tighten the screws to the torque setting specified at the beginning of the Chapter.
14 Fit the driven gear onto the shaft with its recessed side facing out, engaging it with the drive gear on the balancer shaft (unless it has been removed) **(see illustration 19.3b)**. Fit the square washer onto the flats on the shaft and in the recess in the face of the gear. Fit a new nut and tighten to the specified torque setting **(see illustration 19.3a)**. Remove the locking pin from the balancer shaft weight if in place.
15 Install the clutch (Section 20).

Oil pressure relief valve

16 Remove the exhaust system (see Chapter 4).

17 The pressure relief valve cap is in the bottom of the crankcase **(see illustration 19.18)**. If the engine oil has not been drained, position a drain tray below the engine to catch any residual oil when the valve is removed.
18 Unscrew and remove the cap and sealing washer, then withdraw the spring and valve **(see illustration)**.
19 Wash the components in a suitable solvent and examine them for signs of wear, scoring or damage.
20 No specifications are available for checking the valve. If any of the valve components are worn or damaged, or if an oil pressure test (see Section 3) suggests the valve is not operating correctly, fit a new valve – it comes as an assembly.
21 Installation is the reverse of removal. Fit a new sealing washer to the cap and tighten it to the torque setting specified at the beginning of this Chapter.
22 Check the engine oil level and top-up as necessary (see *Pre-ride checks*)

Oil level/temperature sensor

23 The oil level and temperature sensor is on the back of the engine on the right-hand side. Remove the starter motor (see Chapter 8) – on RT models remove both engine covers when doing so.
24 Trace the wiring from the sensor and disconnect it at the connector **(see illustration)**. Feed the wiring down to the sensor, releasing it from the tie and guide and noting its routing.

19.12 Align and seat the recess (A) over the pin (B)

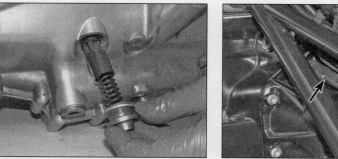

19.18 Remove the cap and withdraw the spring and relief valve

19.24 Oil level/temperature sensor wiring connector (arrowed)

19.25a Undo the screws...

19.25b ...and withdraw the sensor

19.26 Sensor O-ring (arrowed)

25 Place some rag under the sensor. Undo the screws, displace the sensor and withdraw the tube, catching the residual oil **(see illustrations)**.

26 Check the condition of the O-ring and replace it with a new one if necessary **(see illustration)**.

27 Installation is the reverse of removal. Clean the threads of the screws and apply some fresh threadlock.

20 Clutch

Note 1: *The clutch can be removed with the engine in the frame. If you are just replacing the clutch plates with new ones there is no need to remove the clutch housing.*

Note 2: *If there has been excessive gear whine (too little backlash) or clatter (too much backlash) coming from the primary drive and driven gears on the front of the engine, check the backlash between the gears as described in this section. The amount of backlash can be adjusted by selecting different primary driven gear sizes for the clutch housing. Backlash will become excessive through wear of the gear teeth, in which case you may need to replace both the drive and driven gears with new ones (the drive gear, an integral part of the crankshaft, only comes in one size). The backlash should also be checked whenever new components are fitted. Note that for an exact measurement of the backlash according to the BMW specifications their own dial gauge and dial gauge holder must be used to ensure the correct angles between the gauge plunger and the teeth is obtained. If other tools are used and the relative angles are not correct a false reading will be obtained. The dial gauge part No. is 110861, and gauge holder is 110863. Due to the cost of these tools you may want to have the procedure carried out by a dealer.*

Note 3: *Poor clutch disengagement and clunky gear changes in GS models up to engine No. 122EN36130280 may be caused by a clutch component that has since been upgraded – refer to your BMW dealer for*

details. Similar symptoms on all models may be caused by too much oil, the incorrect oil, or oil additives.
Special tool: *Some form of clutch holding method or tool will be required (see Step 6).*

Removal

1 Remove the front crankcase cover (see Section 16).

2 If you are removing the complete clutch assembly, rather than just removing the clutch plates, and if required the clutch centre, set the engine so the right-hand cylinder is at TDC on its compression stroke and lock the crankshaft in this position, as described in Section 7. If available also fit the camshaft alignment/holding tool onto the

right-hand cylinder camshafts as described in Section 8.

3 If the crankshaft and camshafts aren't locked you need to prevent the clutch from turning as you unscrew the spring bolts – the bolts shouldn't be very tight so cover the clutch with a rag and hold it, or better still have an assistant hold it. Working in a criss-cross sequence, gradually and evenly unscrew the bolts until spring pressure is released, then remove the bolts, the spring plate, the springs, the pressure plate (which may come away with the outermost clutch plates on it), turning it slightly anti-clockwise as you do, and the short pushrod **(see illustrations)**.

4 Remove the clutch friction and plain plates, noting how they fit and keeping them in order

20.3a Unscrew the bolts and remove the spring plate...

20.3b ...the springs...

20.3c ...the pressure plate...

20.3d ...and the short pushrod

20.4 Draw the plates out as a pack and keep them in order – the outermost plate(s) may have come away with the pressure plate

20.5 Hook the spring and its seat off using a piece of wire or draw them off with a magnet

20.6 Using a commercially available holding tool and an air ratchet to hold the clutch and unscrew the nut

(see illustration). Note how the outer three plates (two friction plates and one dimpled plain plate), and the inner friction plate, have a larger internal diameter – the inner one seats around the anti-judder spring and spring seat. The inner plain plate has a smooth surface, while all other plain plates have a dimpled surface.

5 Remove the anti-judder spring and spring seat, noting which way round they fit **(see illustration)**.

6 To unscrew the clutch centre nut, the input shaft must be locked or the clutch centre must be held – if the engine is in the frame, engage 6th gear and have an assistant hold the rear brake on hard with the rear tyre in firm contact with the ground; alternatively, and if the engine has been removed, the BMW tool (No. 110828) must be used to stop the clutch centre from turning. Note that the

clutch nut is very tight. We found that using an air ratchet together with a commercially available clutch holding tool was successful, but there is a danger of the holding tool slipping and damaging the clutch centre grooves, particularly if using a socket and hand pressure on the nut. You will, however, still need the BMW tool when tightening the nut on installation. With the clutch centre held, unscrew the nut **(see illustration)**. Note that a new nut must be fitted.

7 Slide the clutch centre off the shaft, followed by the thrust washer **(see illustrations)**. A new nut and thrust washer must be used.

8 To remove the clutch housing, the crankshaft and camshafts must be locked with the right-hand piston at TDC on its compression stroke – this is to ensure that the relative positions of the crankshaft and balancer shaft are not disturbed with the clutch housing

removed. With the engine at TDC a punch mark on the primary drive gear tooth (which you won't be able to see until the housing has been removed – see illustration 20.14) aligns with the rib on the clutch housing and the rib on the crankcase **(see illustration)**. The clutch housing nut is encapsulated with a thread locking compound that must be heated to 150°C using a hot air gun to release it. Heat the nut, then unscrew it and remove the washer, using a magnet or wearing heat resistant gloves **(see illustration)** – if the engine has been removed you can counter-hold it using a metal bar in one of the engine mounting bolt holes as shown while slackening the nut. Slide the clutch housing off the shaft (it may be hot), noting how the slot in its centre locates over the key in the shaft. A new nut and washer must be used, but keep the old nut if you need to check the backlash between the primary drive and driven gears.

Inspection

9 After an extended period of service the clutch friction plates will wear and promote clutch slip. Clean the oil off the plates, then measure the thickness of the friction plates as a pack. BMW specify the pack thickness to be 24 mm and give a wear maximum of 0.1 mm in each plate. Therefore the pack thickness should not be less than 23.2 mm and no friction plate must be less than 2.9 mm **(see illustration)**. If the plate pack or any plate has worn, or if any of the plates smell burnt or is glazed, the plates must be replaced with

20.7a Remove the clutch centre...

20.7b ...and thrust washer

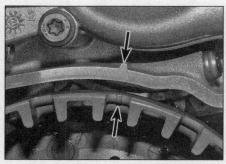

20.8a Clutch housing alignment ribs (arrowed)

20.8b Slackening the clutch but with the engine removed

20.9 Measuring the thickness of an individual friction plate

20.10 Check the plain plates for warpage

20.12a Check the friction plate tabs and housing slots...

20.12b ...and the plain plate teeth and centre slots as described

a new set – they come as a complete pack with new plain plates as well as friction plates (there is also a clutch package available, that also includes the clutch centre, pressure plate, springs and spring plate, if further investigation as described below reveals the need). If you are unsure about the measurements, the bottom line is that if the clutch has been slipping, and you have not used any oil additives, then the best thing to do is fit a new clutch plate pack, and a new set of springs as well.

10 The plain plates should not show any signs of excess heating (bluing). Check for warpage using a flat surface and feeler gauges **(see illustration)**. If any plate is warped, or shows signs of bluing, fit a new clutch plate pack.

11 No specifications are given for the free length of the clutch springs, but as stated above if the clutch has been slipping it is best to fit a new set. Place the springs upright on a flat surface and check they are all the same height, and check them for bend by placing a ruler against them, or alternatively lay them against a set square. If any spring has sagged or is bent, replace the springs – they come as a set along with the bolts and spring plate.

12 Inspect the friction plate tabs and the clutch housing slots for burrs and indentations on the edges **(see illustration)**. Similarly check for wear between the inner teeth of the plain plates and the slots in the clutch centre **(see illustration)**. Wear of this nature will cause clutch drag and slow disengagement during gear changes as the plates will snag when the pressure plate is lifted. With care a small amount of wear can be corrected by dressing with a fine file, but if this is excessive the worn components should be replaced with new ones.

13 Check the mating ramps on the pressure plate and clutch centre, the pressure plate bearing, and the short pushrod for signs of wear or damage **(see illustration)**. There are also two long pushrods inside the transmission shaft – to remove them remove the clutch release cylinder (Section 21).

14 Check the teeth of the primary driven gear on the back of the clutch housing and the corresponding teeth of the primary drive gear on the crankshaft **(see illustration)**. Replace the clutch housing and/or crankshaft with a new one if worn or chipped teeth are discovered. Refer below for driven gear selection and backlash measurement.

Primary driven gear backlash check and adjustment

Note: *The engine must be cold.*

15 If there has been whine or clatter coming from the front when the engine is running, or if a new clutch housing or crankshaft have been fitted, the backlash between the gear teeth must be checked. To do this a dial gauge, BMW part No. 110861, and a holder for it, BMW part No. 110863, are required. Note that the use of any other dial gauge will result in a false reading as the specifications given are based upon the relative angles between the gauge plunger and the gear teeth determined by these tools. Due to the need for and cost of these tools you may want to have the procedure carried out by a BMW dealer.

16 Remove the clutch assembly as described above, if not already done.

17 Remove all traces of old sealant from the bottom of the crankcase, on its mating surface with the front cover.

18 Fit the clutch housing back onto the shaft aligning the slot with the key and making sure the gear teeth engage. Fit a new washer and the old clutch housing nut and tighten the nut finger-tight.

19 Remove the right-hand cylinder cam chain tensioner (Section 7).

20 Fit the dial gauge holder and secure it with the screws and washers.

21 Fit the dial gauge onto the holder so that the plunger is centred on and slightly compressed by a tooth on the driven gear.

22 Turn the driven gear lightly back and forth to record the backlash, i.e. the free movement, between it and the teeth on the primary drive gear – do not force the gear to turn against the drive gear, just take up the freeplay. Record the amount the dial moves around the gauge. Remove the gauge and holder. If the amount of backlash recorded is outside the limits specified at the beginning of the Chapter a new driven gear must be selected to restore the correct amount of backlash.

23 To select a new gear remove the clutch housing as described above, and take it along with the amount of backlash measured to a BMW dealer and ask them to replace it with one that will restore the backlash within the specified range. Each tooth on the gear has either one, two or three grooves cut into its edge that represents the size of the whole gear (all teeth will have the same number of grooves) – one groove in each tooth denotes the smallest size, giving the greatest amount of backlash, two grooves denotes the middle size, and three the largest, giving the least backlash.

24 Fit the new clutch housing as described

20.13 Check the pressure plate/clutch centre mating surfaces (that form the ramps for the back-torque limiter), and the bearing in the centre

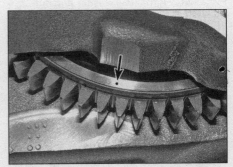

20.14 Check the primary drive (shown) and driven gear teeth for wear and damage – note the alignment punch mark (arrowed)

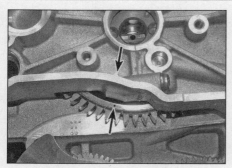

20.26 At TDC the punch mark on the drive gear and the rib on the crankcase align

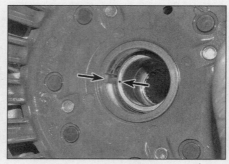

20.27a The slot and the punch mark (arrowed) must align...

20.27b ...and the ribs (arrowed) must align

above, then check the backlash again. If the backlash is still incorrect select a new gear and try again. Note that if the backlash is still excessive with the largest gear fitted, you must replace the crankshaft with a new one (Section 25). When the backlash is correct remove the gauge and holder and the old nut securing the clutch housing, then continue rebuilding the clutch using a new nut as described below.

25 Install the cam chain tensioner (Section 7).

Installation

26 Before installing the clutch housing, and if the crankshaft and/or balancer shaft have been removed, make sure each is positioned correctly, and with the crankshaft locked at TDC, as described in the relevant sections, before fitting the clutch housing **(see illustration and 17.6a)**.

20.28a Fit the new washer and nut...

20.28b ...and tighten the nut as described

27 Slide the clutch housing onto the balancer shaft, aligning the slot in its centre with the punch mark on the end of the shaft and the key and the ribs on the housing with that on the crankcase (if something does not align recheck the positions of the crankshaft and balancer shaft), making sure that the teeth of the primary driven gear on the back of the housing engage with those of the primary drive gear **(see illustrations)**.

28 Make sure the threaded end of the balancer shaft is free of any oil and grease – use a solvent to clean the threads. Prepare a high range torque wrench (two settings of 170 and 250 Nm are needed), and a socket to fit – once the new clutch housing nut has been threaded onto the shaft the threadlock with which it is encapsulated begins to cure, and will set in about a minute, so the tightening process must be completed within a minute.

Slide the new washer and thread the new nut onto the shaft and tighten it to 170 Nm, then slacken the nut by a quarter turn (90°), then tighten the nut to 250 Nm **(see illustrations)**.

29 If are fitting a new set of clutch plates onto the original clutch centre BMW specify to check the assembled height of the complete clutch pack – to do this assemble all the plates onto the clutch centre and pressure plate as described below (before fitting the centre onto the shaft), then fit the pressure plate, springs, spring plate and bolts and tighten the bolts to the specified torque, again as described below. Now measure the height of the assembled pack, from the top of the uppermost friction plate tabs to the bottom of the lowermost tabs, in three different places around the assembly, and check the height is within the range specified at the beginning of the Chapter – if it is not within the range swap for a new set of plates and measure again, until the height is correct. Disassemble the pack and continue to build the clutch as described below.

30 If you are fitting a new clutch package, that includes the clutch centre, pressure plate etc, you can assume that the assembled height of the pack is correct, but it will come assembled and so you need to disassemble it all, then rebuild it on the bike as described below – when disassembling it make sure you keep all the plates in order and refit them as such.

31 Slide a new thrust washer onto the shaft, then fit the clutch centre **(see illustrations 20.7b and a)**.

32 Lubricate the threads and seating surface of the new clutch centre nut with clean oil. Thread the nut on **(see illustration)**. Using the method employed on removal to lock the input shaft or hold the clutch centre (see Step 6), tighten the nut to the torque setting specified at the beginning of the Chapter, then fully slacken the nut, then tighten it again to the same torque setting.

33 Fit the anti-judder spring seat into the clutch centre, then fit the spring so that its outer edge is raised off the seat and facing outwards **(see illustration and 20.5)**.

34 Coat each plate with engine oil prior to installation, then build up the plates as follows.

20.32 Thread the new nut on and tighten as described

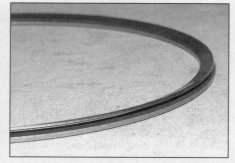

20.33 Fit the spring seat and the spring with its outer edge raised off the seat

20.34a Fit a friction plate with the larger internal diameter first...

20.34b ...then the smooth plain plate

20.34c Follow this with the standard friction plates...

20.34d ...and dimpled plain plates alternately...

20.34e ...finishing with a large ID friction plate

20.34f Fit a large ID friction plate onto the pressure plate...

First fit a friction plate with the larger internal diameter, seating it around the anti-judder spring and spring seat (see illustration), then fit the plain plate with the smooth surface (see illustration), then fit the five standard diameter friction plates, alternating them with the five standard diameter dimpled plain plates, until all are installed, then fit a friction plate with the larger internal diameter (see illustrations). Fit the final friction plate with the larger internal diameter onto the pressure plate, followed by the plain plate with the larger ID (see illustrations).

35 Fit the short pushrod into the shaft with its shouldered end facing out (see illustration 20.3d).

36 Fit the pressure plate, engaging the back-torque limiter mechanism ramps then turning the plate slightly clockwise, and seating the tabs of the outer friction plate in the shallow slots in the housing (see illustration).

37 Lubricate the threads of the spring bolts with oil. Fit the clutch springs, spring plate and bolts and tighten the bolts evenly and a little at a time in a criss-cross sequence to the specified torque (see illustration 20.3b and a).

38 If removed install the long pushrods and the clutch release cylinder (Section 21). Pull the clutch lever in and check that action of the release mechanism.

39 Install the front crankcase cover (see Section 16) and all other removed parts as required according to model.

20.34g ...then fit the large ID plain plate onto it

40 Refill with oil and coolant as required (see Chapter 1).

41 Run the engine and check the operation of the clutch.

21 Clutch release mechanism

1 All the models covered in this manual are fitted with an hydraulic clutch. The clutch system comprises the master cylinder on the handlebars, the hose and the release cylinder on the back of the gearbox. The system requires no maintenance other than inspection and a check of the fluid level at the specified service interval (see Chapter 1).

20.36 Fit the pressure plate, engaging the ramps and locating the plate tabs in the shallow offset slots

2 If there is evidence of air in the system (spongy feel to the lever, difficulty in engaging gear), bleed the system (see below).

3 If clutch fluid is leaking from the hose joint with the master or release cylinder first check that the nut is tight. If necessary, disconnect the hose and replace the O-ring on the nut with a new one, then bleed the system (see below). If either the master cylinder or the release cylinder is leaking, a new one will have to be fitted – no rebuild kits are available.

Clutch lever

4 If the clutch lever feels stiff, check the lever and bracket for damage. If there is no damage remove the lever and lubricate it as follows.

5 On GS models where fitted, and on GS Adv models, remove the hand protector (see

21.5a Undo the locknut...

21.5b ...withdraw the pivot bolt and remove the lever

21.5c Withdraw the sleeve to release the pushrod piece

Chapter 7). Hold the lever pivot bolt and unscrew the locknut on the underside **(see illustration)**. Withdraw the pivot bolt and draw the lever out, noting how the pushrod locates in the rubber boot **(see illustration)**. If required remove the pivot sleeve and pull the pushrod piece out of the lever, noting that there is a spring that fits between them in the front **(see illustration)**. The pushrod piece is part of the master cylinder. Note that BMW specify to use a new locknut.

6 Check the condition of the rubber boot in the master cylinder and replace it with a new one if necessary – it is available separately.

7 Clean the contact surfaces of the lever, pushrod piece, bracket, sleeve and pivot bolt, and check for wear and damage.

8 Lubricate all components with a Teflon spray prior to reassembly. Make sure the spring is in place then fit the pushrod piece into the lever and insert the sleeve **(see illustration 21.5c)**. Fit a new rubber boot into the master cylinder if necessary, using a blunt tool to carefully push the inner lip into place. Fit the lever into the bracket, making sure the pushrod enters the boot and seats against the master cylinder piston, and the outer lip of the boot seats correctly around the base of the rod, and insert the pivot bolt **(see illustration 21.5b)**. Fit and tighten the new locknut **(see illustration 21.5a)**.

9 If, after cleaning, lubricating and refitting the lever, the clutch action is still stiff, the problem probably is in the master or release cylinder (see below).

Master cylinder

Removal

10 Before starting, make sure you have some new Vitamol V10 clutch fluid, some clean rags and a suitable container for the old clutch fluid.

11 On GS, GS Adv and R models remove the mirror (see Chapter 7).

12 Remove the clutch lever (see above).

13 Remove the clutch switch (see Chapter 8).

14 Undo the reservoir cover screws and remove the cover and diaphragm **(see illustrations)**. Remove all the fluid from the reservoir using a syringe, then wipe it out using absorbent cloth or tissue.

15 Undo the clutch hose nut and detach the hose from the master cylinder **(see illustration)**. Be prepared to catch any residual fluid in the end of the hose and master cylinder. Wrap a clean plastic bag over the end of the hose to prevent dirt entering the system and secure the hose in an upright position to minimise fluid loss. Plug the end of the master cylinder.

16 Note the alignment of the line on the master cylinder clamp with that on the handlebar, then undo the clamp screws and lift the master cylinder off **(see illustration)**.

17 If there has been a problem with clutch operation and the lever has been checked, to check the action of the master cylinder piston, temporarily install the reservoir cover or cap. Wrap some clean rag over the open end of the master cylinder hose union and push the piston in against the spring using a suitable tool. If the action is rough or stiff, there is a fault with the master cylinder piston. No rebuild kit is available – if it is not working correctly, a new one will have to be fitted. If the piston moves in smoothly and returns quickly under spring pressure, it is likely that the release cylinder is faulty (see below).

Caution: Do not, under any circumstances, use a petroleum-based solvent to clean the master cylinder.

Installation

18 Installation is the reverse of removal, noting the following:

21.14a Undo the screws...

21.14b ...and remove the cover and diaphragm

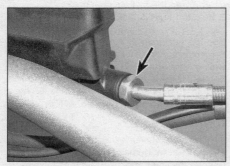

21.15 Clutch hose banjo nut (arrowed)

21.16 Master cylinder alignment marks (arrowed)

21.24a Slacken the hose nut (arrowed), then undo the screws...

21.24b ...and displace the release cylinder

21.25 Disconnect the hose. Note the O-ring (arrowed)

- Align the line on the master cylinder clamp with that on the handlebar **(see illustration 21.16)**. Tighten the clamp screws to the torque setting specified at the beginning of the Chapter, tightening the upper screw first, then the lower, so that gap in the clamp is at the bottom.
- Check the condition of the O-ring on the clutch hose nut and replace it with a new one if necessary, though it is best to use a new one as a matter of course.
- Tighten the hose nut to the torque setting specified at the beginning of this Chapter, using a torque wrench if you have the correct tools, or by feel if not – do not overtighten it.
- Top up and bleed the system with new Vitamol V10 clutch fluid (see below) – note that it is worth trying to bleed the upper end of the system by pumping the clutch lever before going through the process described below, which involves displacing the starter motor.
- Check the operation of the clutch before riding the motorcycle.

Release cylinder

19 The release cylinder is on the back of the gearbox.

20 If the clutch action is stiff, and the lever and master cylinder are good, it is likely that the release cylinder is faulty. No rebuild kit is available – if it is not working correctly, a new one will have to be fitted.

Removal

21 Before starting, make sure you have some new Vitamol V10 clutch fluid, some clean rags and a suitable container for the old clutch fluid.

22 On RT models remove the right-hand engine and shock absorber covers (see Chapter 7).

23 Remove the battery and starter motor (see Chapter 8), and the exhaust system (see Chapter 4).

24 Slacken the clutch hose nut, then lightly re-tighten it **(see illustration)**. Undo the release cylinder screws evenly and a little at a time and detach it from the gearbox, using pliers to prevent the pushrod

coming out with it if necessary **(see illustration)**.

25 Undo the hose nut and disconnect the hose – be prepared to catch some fluid **(see illustration)**. Place the end of the hose in a container supported on the gearbox.

Caution: Do not operate the clutch lever while the hose is disconnected.

Installation

26 Installation is the reverse of removal, noting the following:

- Check the condition of the release cylinder O-ring and replace it with a new one if necessary **(see illustration 21.25)**.
- Check the condition of the O-ring on the clutch hose nut and replace it with a new one if necessary, though it is best to use a new one as a matter of course. Connect the hose to the cylinder and tighten the nut.
- Pull the pushrod out slightly and locate it in the hole in the piston, then seat the release cylinder and tighten the screws evenly and a little at a time to the torque setting specified at the beginning of this Chapter **(see illustrations 21.24b and a)**.
- Tighten the hose nut to the torque setting specified at the beginning of this Chapter, using a torque wrench if you have the correct tools, or by feel if not – do not overtighten it.
- Top up and bleed the system with new Vitamol V10 clutch fluid (see below).
- Check the operation of the clutch before riding the motorcycle.

Bleeding the clutch release mechanism

27 Bleeding the clutch is simply the process of removing air from the master cylinder, hose and the release cylinder. Bleeding is necessary whenever an hydraulic connection is loosened, or when a component or hose is renewed. Leaks in the system may also allow air to enter, but leaking clutch fluid will reveal their presence and warn you of the need for repair.

28 To bleed the clutch fully you will need some new Vitamol V10 clutch fluid, some rags, a spanner to fit the bleed valve, a length of clear vinyl or plastic tubing, and if required (though it is not essential) a syringe with a capacity of 100 cc (BMW produces service tool Part No. 342551). Note: It is essential that the hose and syringe are not contaminated with any other fluids.

29 If not already done remove the starter motor (see Chapter 8).

30 Remove the master cylinder cover and remove all old clutch fluid from it (see Step 14 above).

31 Turn the handlebars so that the top of the master cylinder reservoir is as level as possible.

32 Completely remove the cap from the bleed valve, then connect one end of the clear tubing to the valve **(see illustrations)**.

33 Fill the master cylinder reservoir to the upper level with Vitamol V10, then cover the

21.32a Remove the cap...

21.32b ...and fit the tube onto the valve

reservoir **(see illustration)**. Make sure you keep it topped up during the bleeding process.
34 Carefully squeeze the clutch lever to ensure no air is trapped in the upper end of the system, then release the lever slowly.
35 Open the bleed valve on the release cylinder and pull the clutch lever slowly in to the handlebar, then close the bleed valve and release the lever, and repeat this process until all the air is expelled from the hose and master cylinder via the bleed valve and tube and only new clutch fluid is coming out **(see illustration)**. Tighten the bleed valve, remove the tube and refit the cap.
36 Install the starter motor.
37 Check the fluid level in the reservoir and top up to the top of the vertical bar. Fit the diaphragm and cover.
38 Check the operation of the clutch before riding the motorcycle.

 HAYNES HiNT *If it's not possible to produce the correct feel to the lever the clutch fluid may be aerated. Let the fluid in the system stabilise for a few hours and then check for air trapped in the upper end of the system again.*

22 Starter clutch and gears

Note: *The starter clutch cannot be removed with the engine in the frame – the engine must be removed, and the gearbox removed from the engine.*

21.33 Fill reservoir to the top of the vertical bar (arrowed)

Check

1 The operation of the starter clutch can be checked while it is in situ. Remove the starter motor (see Chapter 8). Check that the starter idle/reduction gear is able to rotate freely anti-clockwise as you look at it via the starter motor aperture, but locks when rotated clockwise. If not, the starter clutch is faulty and should be removed for inspection.

Removal

2 Remove the engine (Section 4).
3 If you need to remove the idle and reduction gears remove the right-hand cylinder head (Section 10).
4 Remove the gearbox (Section 26).
5 Remove the alternator stator and rotor (see Chapter 8) – the starter clutch is on the back of the rotor. Before removing the rotor, if you know that you need to remove the starter clutch from it, slacken the starter clutch

21.35 Bleed the release mechanism as described until all air is expelled and only fluid is coming out

screws after fitting the crankshaft locking pin to save having to hold the rotor on the bench.
6 To remove the starter driven gear undo the retaining washer screw and remove the washer and spacer **(see illustration)**. Slide the gear off the crankshaft **(see illustration)**.
7 To remove the idle and reduction gears remove the right-hand cam chain guide blade, noting how it locates **(see illustration 18.3)**.
8 Undo the idle gear shaft screw, noting the washer, then unscrew the shaft, turning it clockwise as it has left-hand threads, and remove the gear **(see illustrations)**.
9 Undo the reduction gear shaft screw, noting the washer **(see illustration)**. Thread an M10 x 1 bolt into the shaft to use as a handle, then pull the shaft out and remove the gear **(see illustration)**.

Inspection, disassembly and reassembly

10 With the alternator rotor face down on

22.6a Unscrew the retainer...

22.6b ...then slide the gear off

22.8a Undo the screw...

22.8b ...then unscrew the shaft and remove the gear

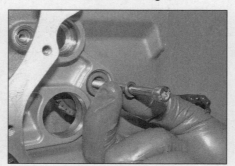

22.9a Undo the screw...

22.9b ...then withdraw the shaft, using a bolt as shown, and remove the gear

22.10 Fit the driven gear and check the operation of the clutch as described

22.11 Check the sprags and the hub for wear and damage

22.12 Hold the rotor and undo the screws

a workbench, fit the starter driven gear into the clutch, turning it clockwise as you do, and check that it rotates freely clockwise and locks against the rotor anti-clockwise **(see illustration)**. Remove the driven gear, rotating it clockwise as you do.

11 Check the condition of the sprags and the corresponding surface on the driven gear hub **(see illustration)**. If the sprags or hub are damaged, marked or flattened at any point, remove the starter clutch from the rotor (see below) and replace the sprag assembly with a new one.

12 To remove the starter clutch from the back of the alternator rotor, if the screws weren't slackened before removing the rotor hold the rotor using a strap, undo the six screws **(see illustration)**. Remove the sprag housing then remove the sprag assembly, noting which way round they fit.

13 Fit the new sprag assembly with the wide rim facing the rotor, then fit the housing with its flat side facing the rotor, and depending on the type fitted, either with the weighted section on the opposite side to the slot for the key in the rotor hub, or with the cut-way section aligned with the slot. Align the screw holes, fit the screws and tighten them to the torque setting specified at the beginning of the Chapter, either holding the rotor using a strap, or finger-tight now and tightening them to the specified torque after installing the rotor and while the crankshaft is locked, as preferred.

14 Check the bush in the starter driven gear hub for wear **(see illustration)**. Replace the driven gear with a new one if necessary.

If there are any signs of scoring or other abnormal damage also check the bearing surface on the crankshaft.

15 Check the teeth of the idle and reduction gears and the corresponding teeth of the starter driven gear and starter motor drive shaft. Replace the gears and/or starter motor if worn or chipped teeth are discovered on related gears. Also check the gear shafts for damage, and check that the gears are not a loose fit on them. Check the shaft ends and the bores they run in for wear.

Installation

16 Check the condition of the idle and reduction gear shaft O-rings and screw washers and replace them with new ones if necessary. Clean the threads of the screws.

17 Lubricate the reduction gear shaft and its O-ring with oil, position the gear and insert the shaft, pushing it all the way in **(see illustrations)**. Apply some threadlock to the screw threads, fit the screw with its washer and tighten to the torque setting specified at the beginning of the Chapter **(see illustration 22.9a)**.

18 Lubricate the idle gear shaft and its O-ring with oil, position the gear and insert the shaft, and tighten it anti-clockwise to the specified torque setting **(see illustration 22.8b)**. Apply some threadlock to the screw threads, fit the screw with its washer and tighten it to the specified torque **(see illustration 22.8a)**.

19 Lubricate the driven gear hub bush with oil and slide the gear onto the crankshaft **(see illustrations 22.14 and 22.6b)**. Clean the threads of the retaining washer screw and apply some threadlock, then fit the spacer

and the washer and tighten the screw to the specified torque **(see illustration 22.6a)**.

20 Install the starter clutch and alternator rotor (see Chapter 8). If not already done, before removing the crankshaft locking tool and fitting the stator tighten the starter clutch screws to the specified torque.

21 Install all remaining components.

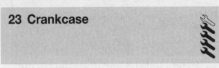

23 Crankcase

Note: *To separate the crankcase halves, the engine must be removed from the frame (see Section 4).*
Special tool: *A degree disc is required for angle-tightening the 10 mm crankcase bolts.*

Separation

1 To access the crankshaft and its bearings, the connecting rods and pistons, and the oil strainers, the crankcase must be split into two parts. When the crankcases are split the left-hand half is lifted off the right-hand half with the piston in the left-hand cylinder, and the crankshaft stays seated in the right-hand half.

2 Before the crankcase halves can be separated, the following components must be removed:

● Front crankcase cover (Section 16)
● Water pump (see Chapter 3)
● Clutch (Section 20)
● Oil level/temperature sensor (Section 19)
● Cylinder heads (Section 10)
● Gearbox (Section 26)

22.14 Check the bush for wear

22.17a Fit the gear with its smaller pinion to the front

22.17b Push the shaft in until it is flush

23.6a Removing the circlip requires care and patience

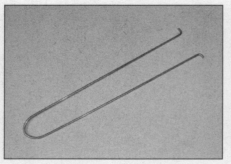

23.6b Make this simple tool as described and shown...

23.6c ...squeeze the ends together and insert in the the hole and through the pin...

23.6d ...relax it and draw the pin out

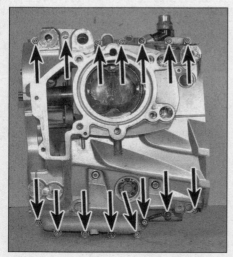

23.7a Unscrew the 6 mm bolts (arrowed) around the top and bottom...

- Alternator stator (see Chapter 8)
- Cam chains and blades as required (Section 18)

3 The following components should also be removed for a complete engine strip and for maximum convenience when separating the crankcases, though they can be left in place if required to save time if for example you just need to access the pistons or the crankshaft and connecting rod (main and big-end) bearings.

- Oil pump (Section 19)
- Alternator rotor (see Chapter 8)
- Cam chains and blades (Section 18)
- Balancer shaft (Section 17)

4 If not already done remove the crankshaft locking tool.

5 Before separating the crankcase halves, measure the amount of crankshaft end-float using a dial gauge (see *Tools and Workshop Tips* in the Reference section). Press the front end of the crankshaft into the crankcase, then mount the dial gauge with its pointer sitting against the front of the crankshaft. Zero the gauge, then pull the crankshaft out of the casing and record the end-float. Compare the result to the specifications at the beginning of this Chapter. If the end-float exceeds the service limit, replace the thrust bearings with new ones.

6 Turn the crankshaft so the left-hand cylinder piston pin is centred in the hole in the front of the crankcase **(see illustration 12.21)**. Remove the piston pin circlip, using a small headed but long-shafted flat-bladed screwdriver in the notch to lever it out of the groove, and using long-nosed pliers or equivalent (such as fish-hook pliers) to grip it and bend it as

required to remove it **(see illustration)** – do not worry about bending the circlip out of shape as you will fit a new one, but take care not to mark or gouge the rim of the groove the circlip sits in as any rough surface could interfere with the withdrawal of the piston pin. Get a piece of thick wire or welding rod about 560 mm long and bend it back on itself in the middle, then bend each end outwards at right-angles to make a tool to withdraw the piston pin as shown **(see illustration)**. Squeeze the ends of the tool together and insert them into the hole and through the piston pin, and when the ends protrude from the opposite end of the pin relax the tool so the bent ends expand and locate against the end of the pin, then pull on the tool to withdraw the pin **(see illustrations)**. If you cannot remove the circlip and pin in this way, you need the BMW tools 110826 and 110843 to remove the circlip, and 110829 to remove the pin, using them as follows: first, if necessary, turn the circlip in its groove using a suitable tool so the open ends are centred in the notch. Fit the adapter (tool 110843) into the circlip puller (110826), then insert the puller and turn it until the adapter engages with the gap in the circlip ends. Now turn the puller a quarter to half a turn anti-clockwise, then withdraw the puller and remove the adapter from it. Insert the puller again and turn it anti-clockwise until the lever engages in the cut-out with an audible click. Withdraw the puller – it will (or should) bring the circlip with it. Now insert the pin puller (tool 110829) and withdraw the pin.

7 Unscrew the seventeen 6 mm bolts, followed by the two 8 mm bolts, then the two 10 mm bolts **(see illustrations)**.

23.7b ...and the two in the front...

23.7c ...then unscrew the 8 mm bolts...

23.7d ...and the 10 mm bolts

23.9 Unscrew the 10 mm bolts

23.10a Initially break the seal by levering the halves apart in the two places provided...

23.10b ...then lift the left-hand crankcase half off the right-hand half

8 Turn the engine so that it rests on the top of its right-hand cylinder, making sure it is properly supported using blocks of wood.

9 Unscrew the two 10 mm bolts in the left-hand side **(see illustrations)**.

10 Use a screwdriver in the leverage points to break the seal, then carefully lift the left-hand crankcase off **(see illustrations)**. If the halves do not separate easily, make sure all the bolts have been removed, and tap around the joint with a soft-faced mallet.

11 Note the crankshaft main bearing and thrust bearing shells in the left-hand crankcase half and take care not to dislodge them.

12 Remove the balancer shaft thrust washer **(see illustration)**.

13 Remove the two dowels if loose, and the O-ring, from the right-hand crankcase **(see illustration)** – a new O-ring must be used.

14 Remove the crankshaft and bearings, connecting rods and pistons as required, referring to the relevant sections.

Inspection

15 Undo the screws securing the oil strainers and ease the strainers out of their sockets **(see illustration)**. Remove the O-rings – new ones should be used.

16 Undo the crankcase vent valve screws and remove the valve, noting which way round it is fitted **(see illustration)**.

17 Clean the crankcases thoroughly

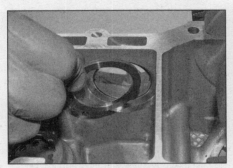

23.12 Remove the thrust washer

with suitable solvent and dry them with compressed air. Blow out all oil passages with compressed air.

18 Remove all traces of old sealant from the mating surfaces. If a scraper must be used, be very careful not to nick or gouge the soft aluminium or oil leaks will result.

19 Check the cases for any damage. Small cracks or holes in aluminium castings can be repaired with an epoxy resin adhesive as a temporary measure or a more secure repair can be made with one of the low temperature home welding kits, such as Lumiweld. Argon-arc welding is another solution, but only a specialist in this process is in a position to advise on the economy or practical aspect of such a repair. If any damage is found that

23.13 Crankcase dowels and O-ring (arrowed)

can't be repaired, renew the crankcase halves as a set.

20 Damaged threads can be economically reclaimed by using a diamond section wire insert. These are easily fitted after drilling and re-tapping the affected thread.

21 Sheared screws can usually be removed with stud extractors – if you are in any doubt, consult a BMW dealer or a specialist motorcycle engineer.

HAYNES HINT *Refer to Tools and Workshop Tips in the Reference section for details of installing a thread insert and using stud extractors.*

23.15 Oil strainer screws (arrowed)

23.16 Crankcase vent valve screws (arrowed)

23.24a Make sure each reed is not stuck and is clean...

23.24b ...and forms a good seal

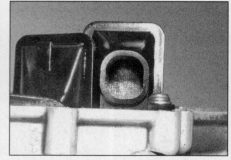

23.25 Check and clean the gauze in the strainer

Reassembly

22 Clean the threads of all the crankcase bolts.

23 If not already done remove all traces of old sealant from the mating surfaces. If a scraper must be used, be very careful not to nick or gouge the soft aluminium or oil leaks will result.

24 Carefully lift the crankcase vent valve reeds to make sure they are not stuck and to check for trapped dirt **(see illustration)**. If necessary, wash the valve with suitable solvent and dry it with compressed air. Do not attempt to scrape dirt off the surface of the valve reeds – they are fragile and easily damaged. At rest the reeds should lay flat against the body of the valve **(see illustration)** – hold the valve up to the light to check for a good seal. If necessary fit a new valve. Check that the screws securing the reed stopper plates are secure, then fit the vent valve in the left-hand crankcase **(see illustration 23.16)**.

25 Make sure that the oil strainers are thoroughly clean **(see illustration)**. Do not attempt to prise the gauze filters off the strainers – they must remain a tight fit. If necessary, wash the strainers with suitable solvent and dry them with compressed air. Fit a new O-ring onto each strainer, then fit the strainers carefully, taking care not to displace the O-rings, and secure them with the screws **(see illustration 23.15)**.

26 Install the connecting rods and pistons, and the crankshaft and bearings, referring to the relevant sections. Make sure the crankshaft bearings are in the left-hand crankcase Section 25.

27 Make sure the right-hand crankcase is properly supported using blocks of wood. Use a rag soaked in high flash-point solvent to wipe over the mating surfaces of both crankcase halves to remove all traces of oil.

28 Fit the balancer shaft thrust washer, using oil or dabs of grease to hold it in place **(see illustration 23.12)**.

29 Fit a new O-ring into the groove in the top of the right-hand crankcase, and fit the dowels if removed **(see illustration 23.13)**.

30 Apply a thin, even bead of suitable sealant to the mating surface of the right-hand crankcase half **(see illustrations)**.

Caution: Don't apply an excessive amount of sealant as it will ooze out when the case halves are assembled and may obstruct oil passages. Do not apply the sealant on or too close to any of the bearing shells or surfaces.

31 Carefully lower the left-hand crankcase half down onto the right-hand half **(see illustration 23.10b)** – it is worthwhile having an assistant to support the left-hand connecting rod as the left-hand crankcase half is fitted.

Make sure the crankshaft bearings remain in position in the left-hand crankcase. Check that the crankcase halves are correctly seated all the way round before fitting any bolts.

Caution: The crankcase halves should fit together without being forced. If they're not correctly seated, separate them and investigate the problem. DO NOT attempt to pull them together by tightening the crankcase bolts.

32 Fit the two 10 mm bolts and two 6 mm bolts into the left-hand crankcase and tighten them finger-tight, tight enough so the crankcases cannot move as you turn the engine over **(see illustrations 23.9 and 23.7b)**.

33 Sit the engine upright, making sure it is properly supported using blocks of wood.

34 Fit the two 10 mm bolts, the two 8 mm bolts, then the fifteen 6 mm bolts, tightening them all finger-tight **(see illustrations 23.7d, c and a)**.

35 Tighten the 10 mm bolts evenly and a little at a time to the initial torque setting specified at the beginning of this Chapter, then use a degree disc (see *Tools and Workshop Tips* in the Reference section) to tighten each bolt through the final angle setting in one continuous movement **(see illustration)**.

36 Tighten the two 8 mm bolts evenly and a little at a time to the specified torque setting, then tighten the seventeen 6 mm bolts to the specified torque setting.

37 Sit the engine on its left-hand cylinder with a block under the crankcase as shown, so the left-hand cylinder connecting rod hangs vertically down, making it easier to align with

23.35 Using a degree disc to angle-tighten the 10 mm bolts

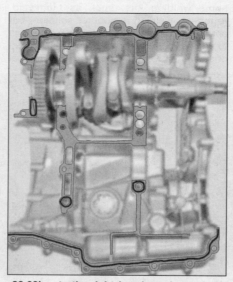

23.30b ...to the right-hand crankcase half

23.30a Apply an even bead of sealant...

23.37a Sit the crankcase as shown

23.37b Make sure the rod and piston are aligned with each other and in the hole

the bore in the piston **(see illustration)**. Align the left-hand connecting rod and the piston pin bore centrally with each other and in the hole using a screwdriver **(see illustration)**.

38 If you used the BMW tools to remove the circlip and piston use them as follows to fit them, but before doing so note that we tried them, and while the tool inserted the piston pin well enough it did not succeed in locating the circlip in its groove and left it precariously dangling in the gap between the piston and the cylinder, twice. Instead we made a very simple tool out of scrap metal tubing that worked very well first time, as described in Step 39. To use the BMW tools, fit the new front circlip into the arrowed end of the sleeve that comes with tool 110829, then slide the sleeve onto the tool with the circlip facing out and push it over the sprung ball on the wide section **(see illustrations)**. Slide the piston pin up against the sleeve so the sprung ball in the end of the narrow section protrudes from the outer end **(see illustrations)**. Insert the tool all the way in, making sure the gap in the circlip is not in line with the cut-out, then push the knob on the outer end of the tool in, which hopefully pushes the circlip into its groove and release the pin, and remove the tool **(see illustration)**. Check the piston pin is all the way in and the circlip is correctly located in its groove.

39 To do it the cheaper, more rewarding and more successful way, first insert the piston pin and push it in until it comes up against the

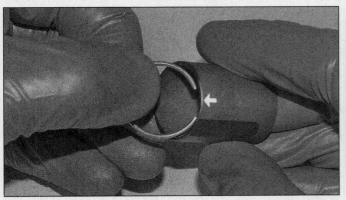

23.38a Seat the circlip in the end of the sleeve marked with the arrow

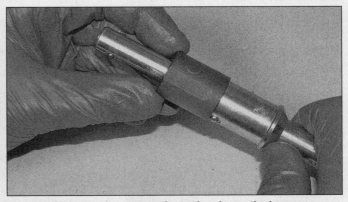

23.38b Slide the sleeve onto the tool and over the inner sprung ball

23.38c Slide the piston pin on...

23.38d ...so it sits against the inner side of the outer sprung ball

23.38e Fully insert the tool, then push the end knob in to seat the circlip and release the piston pin, then withdraw the tool

23.39a A piece of fuel hose can be used to insert the piston pin, then use a screwdriver to push it through once it has entered the piston

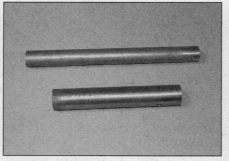

23.39b The two pieces of scrap tube we used to make our tool

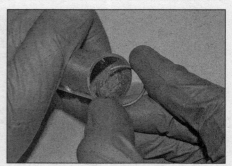

23.39c Fit the circlip into one end of the outer tube...

rear fitted circlip (see illustration). Now you need two pieces of tubing, and they can be steel, aluminium, copper or plastic, as long as the dimensions are as follows: the outer tube needs to be 140 to 150 mm long, and must have an external diameter of 25 mm and an internal diameter of 21.5 mm, giving a wall thickness of 1.75 mm – depending on the finish of the tube you may need to sand the outside to ensure it slides smoothly in the hole in the crankcase; the inner tube needs to be 210 to 215 mm long, and must have an external diameter of 20 or 21 mm (the internal diameter is not important), and again sand it if necessary so it slides smoothly in the outer tube (see illustration). Note that for the inner tube you could use a socket on an extension bar instead of actual tube – the requirement

of the inner section of the tool is that it is a close enough fit inside the outer tube so it locates up against the cirlip and will not not pass through it. Fit the new circlip a few mm into one end of the outer tube, then slide the inner tube in and set the circlip square in the tube by pushing it down against the inner tube using a screwdriver (see illustrations). Insert the circlip end of the tube assembly into the hole and up against the piston, then push the outer end of the inner tube in so it pushes the circlip out of the inner end of the outer tube and into the groove in the piston (see illustrations). Remove the tool and check the circlip is correctly located in its groove.

40 Check that the crankshaft is free to rotate. If there are any signs of undue stiffness or rough spots (taking into account the

resistance of the pistons in the cylinders), or of any other problem, the fault must be rectified before proceeding further.

41 Set the crankshaft so the pistons are at TDC and fit the locking tool.

42 Install the remaining components in the reverse order of removal.

24 Crankshaft bearings and connecting rod big-end bearings – general information

1 Even though the crankshaft and connecting rod bearings are generally replaced with new ones during an engine overhaul, the old bearings should be examined before as they may reveal valuable information about the condition of the engine.

2 Bearing failure occurs mainly because of lack of lubrication, the presence of dirt or other foreign particles, overloading the engine and/or corrosion. Regardless of the cause of bearing failure, it must be corrected before the engine is reassembled to prevent it from happening again.

3 When examining the bearings, match them with their corresponding journal on the crankshaft to help identify the cause of any problem. Note that the bearing shells are pressed into their locations in the crankcase halves and connecting rods and caps, and should only be disturbed when required for examination. It is essential to keep the bearing shells in the right order – lay them on a clean sheet of card and mark the locations on the card.

4 Dirt and other foreign particles get into the engine in a variety of ways. They may be left in the engine during assembly or they may pass through filters or breathers, then get into the oil and from there into the bearings. Metal chips from machining operations and normal engine wear are often present. Abrasives are sometimes left in engine components after reconditioning operations, especially when parts are not thoroughly cleaned using the proper cleaning methods. Whatever the source, foreign objects often end up imbedded in the soft bearing material and are easily

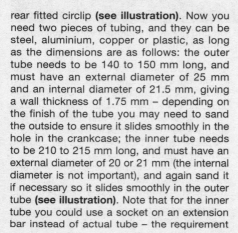

23.39d ...then insert the inner tube...

23.39e ...and square up the circlip

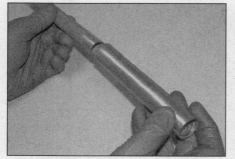

23.39f Slide the outer tube into the hole and up against the piston...

recognised. Large particles will not imbed in the bearing and will score or gouge the bearing and journal. The best prevention for this type of bearing failure is to clean all parts thoroughly and keep everything spotlessly clean during engine reassembly. Regular oil and filter changes are also essential.

5 Lack of lubrication or lubrication breakdown has a number of interrelated causes. Excessive heat (which thins the oil), overloading (which squeezes the oil from the bearing face) and oil leakage or throw off (from excessive bearing clearances, worn oil pump or high engine speeds) all contribute to a breakdown of the protective lubricating film. Blocked oil passages will starve a bearing of lubrication and destroy it. When lack of lubrication is the cause of bearing failure, the bearing material is wiped or extruded from the steel backing of the bearing. Temperatures may increase to the point where the steel backing and the journal turn blue from overheating.

Refer to Tools and Workshop Tips in the Reference section for bearing fault finding.

6 Riding habits can have a definite effect on bearing life. Full throttle, low speed operation, or labouring the engine, puts very high loads on bearings, which tend to squeeze out the oil film. These loads cause the bearings to flex, which produces fine cracks in the bearing face (fatigue failure). Eventually the bearing material will loosen in pieces and tear away from the steel backing. Short trip riding leads to corrosion of bearings, as insufficient engine heat is produced to drive off the condensed water and corrosive gases produced. These products collect in the engine oil, forming acid and sludge. As the oil is carried to the engine bearings, the acid attacks and corrodes the bearing material.

7 Incorrect bearing installation during engine assembly will lead to bearing failure as well.

25.3 Carefully remove the crankshaft – it is quite heavy

Tight fitting bearings which leave insufficient bearing oil clearances result in oil starvation. Dirt or foreign particles trapped behind a bearing shell result in high spots on the bearing which lead to failure.

8 To avoid bearing problems, clean all parts thoroughly before reassembly, double check all bearing clearance measurements and lubricate the new bearings with clean engine oil during installation.

25 Crankshaft

Note: *To remove the crankshaft the engine must be removed from the frame (see Section 4).*

Removal

1 Follow the procedure in Section 23 and separate the crankcase halves.

2 Detach the connecting rod(s) from the crankshaft (Section 15) – the left-hand cylinder rod can stay on the crankshaft if you have no reason to remove it.

3 Lift the crankshaft out of the right-hand crankcase half, taking care not to dislodge the bearing shells **(see illustrations)**.

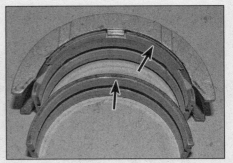

25.5 Main and thrust bearing colour codes (arrowed)

Inspection

4 Clean the crankshaft with suitable solvent and blow dry it with compressed air – also blow through the oil passages to ensure they are clear.

5 Examine the main and thrust bearing shells in both halves of the crankcase. If there are any signs of wear on the bearing surfaces they should be replaced with new ones – always replace the main bearing shells as a complete set. The shells are colour-coded violet, green or yellow according to their original tolerance fit – the colour mark is on the edge of the shell **(see illustration)**. The crankshaft should be identically colour-coded with a mark on each web adjacent to the main journals **(see illustration 15.11c)**. Always fit new shells that match the colour code on the crankshaft.

6 Refer to the general information in Section 24. If the bearing shells are scored, badly scuffed or appear to have seized, check the corresponding crankshaft journal. Damage to the surface of the journal cannot be corrected – a new crankshaft will have to be fitted. If there is any doubt about the condition of the crankshaft, have it checked by a BMW dealer.

7 Remove the main bearing shells from each crankcase half, using a small flat-bladed screwdriver in the notch to dislodge them **(see illustrations)**. If there are no obvious signs of

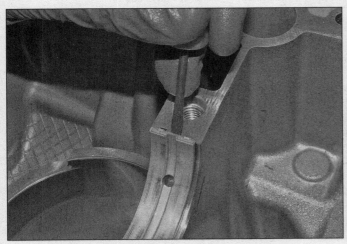

25.7a Dislodge each shell using a screwdriver...

25.7b ...then lift them out

25.10 Measure the diameter of the crankshaft journals (arrowed)

25.11 Make sure the tab (arrowed) engages with the notch in the case

damage, keep the shells in order so that they can be returned to their original locations for accurate oil clearance measurement prior to reassembly.

8 The rear end of the crankshaft runs in a bearing housed in the alternator stator carrier – refer to Chapter 8 Section 24 for details.

Oil clearance check

9 Whether new bearing shells are being fitted or the original ones are being re-used, the crankshaft bearing oil clearance should be checked before the engine is reassembled. Bearing oil clearance can be measured by using a micrometer and telescoping gauge.

10 First measure the diameter of both crankshaft journals in two different planes with the micrometer and note the results **(see illustration)**.

11 Next, clean the backs of the bearing shells and the bearing housings in both crankcase halves with a suitable solvent. Press the shells into their locations **(see illustration 25.7b)**, locating the tab on each shell in the notch in its crankcase **(see illustration)**. Make sure the shells are fitted in their correct locations and take care not to touch any shell's bearing surface with your fingers.

12 Carefully lower the left-hand crankcase half down onto the right-hand half. Make sure the crankshaft bearings remain in position in the left-hand half and the crankcase seats correctly all the way round.

13 Check that the threads of all the crankcase bolts are clean, then follow the procedure in Section 23 to tighten the crankcase bolts.

14 Measure the diameter of the crankshaft journal housings with a telescoping gauge and micrometer and note the results.

15 Subtract each crankshaft journal diameter from its journal housing diameter to obtain the oil clearance, and compare the results with the service limits specified at the beginning of this Chapter.

16 If the original bearing shells have been used for the check and the clearances are well

within the service limit, they can be re-used (if they are within, but only just, you may as well fit a new set). If the clearances are beyond the service limit select and fit new bearing shells according to the colour codes (see Step 5), then check the oil clearances once again. If the clearances are still beyond the service limit the journals are worn and a new crankshaft must be fitted. If a new crankshaft is fitted new main and thrust bearing shells must be selected according to the colour codes on the new crankshaft – do not use the new shells that were selected for the old crankshaft, unless the colour codes are identical.

Installation

17 Clean the backs of the bearing shells and the bearing housings in both crankcase halves. If new shells are being fitted, clean off any traces of protective grease using suitable solvent.

18 Press the shells into their locations, locating the tab on each shell in the notch in the crankcase **(see illustrations 25.7b and 25.11)**. Make sure the shells are fitted in their correct locations and take care not to touch any shell's bearing surface with your fingers.

19 Lubricate the crankshaft bearing journals and shells with clean engine oil, then lay the

crankshaft in the right-hand crankcase **(see illustration 25.3)**.

20 Fit the connecting rod(s) onto the crankshaft (Section 15).

21 Reassemble the crankcase halves (Section 23).

---

26 Gearbox removal and installation

Removal

1 Remove the engine (Section 4).

2 Remove the oil level/temperature sensor (Section 19).

3 Undo the engine breather cover screws and remove the cover **(see illustration)**.

4 Remove the spark plugs (see Chapter 1).

5 Unscrew the access plug for the crankshaft locking tool from the left-hand side of the engine **(see illustration)** – a new sealing washer will be needed.

6 Before removing the gearbox, the crankshaft must be positioned so the pistons are at bottom dead centre (BDC). Turn the crankshaft clockwise to this position using a hex bit on the breather rotor bolt via the

26.3 Remove the breather cover

26.5 Remove the plug

26.6a Turn the crankshaft clockwise...

26.6b ...so the 6 mm hole is centred in the aperture

26.9a Withdraw the rear pushrod...

26.9b ...then draw the front one out

7 Remove the clutch plates and clutch centre, leaving the housing in place (Section 20).

8 If required remove the gearchange mechanism cover and shaft (Section 28) – note that this is not necessary if you are just removing the gearbox to work on the engine.

9 Withdraw the rear long clutch release pushrod from inside the transmission input shaft, then draw the front one out using a magnet **(see illustrations)**.

10 Unscrew the gearbox housing bolts **(see illustration)**. The sealant used between the gearbox and engine can form a strong bond – break the seal using a suitable pry bar or large flat-bladed screwdriver in the leverage slots provided (do not lever between the sealing surfaces themselves), then draw the gearbox off until the input shaft is clear of the balancer shaft **(see illustrations)**. Remove the two dowels if loose **(see illustration 26.16)**.

hole in the gearbox cover, where the breather cover fits **(see illustration)**, and as you turn the crankshaft look for the 6 mm locking pin hole via the aperture in the crankcase **(see**

illustration) – the pistons are at BDC when the 6 mm hole for the pin is centred in the aperture (there is also an 8 mm hole, which is the top dead centre (TDC) position).

26.10a Unscrew the bolts (arrowed)

26.10b Break the seal using the leverage points...

26.10c ...and remove the gearbox

26.11a Check all the gears and shafts...

26.11b ...and the bearings (arrowed) they run in

26.11c The selector drum and forks are in the bottom of the gearbox

Inspection

11 Check all components for wear and damage, in particular looking for broken gear teeth, evidence of metal chips or dust in the bottom of the housing, and noisy and rough bearings **(see illustrations)**. Check the selector drum and forks for wear and damage, particularly looking for bent forks or shafts and worn or damaged fork ends **(see illustration)**.

12 The gearbox and all its components come as a complete assembly – with the exception of the output shaft oil seal (see Section 27) there are no individual components available. If there are any problems within the gearbox a complete new one must be fitted. Note that the gearchange mechanism cover, shaft and its oil seals are not part of the gearbox, and must be removed from the old one (if not already done) and transferred to the new one (Section 28). The selector arm will come

away with the gearchange mechanism cover, remove it – a new arm will be supplied with the gearbox, and must be fitted into the cover before installing the cover. Also remove the wiring clips from the old housing and fit to the new.

Installation

13 Make sure the engine is securely supported using blocks of wood.

14 Remove all traces of old sealant from the gearbox and crankcase mating surfaces. If a scraper must be used, be very careful not to nick or gouge the soft aluminium or oil leaks will result.

15 Lubricate the ends of the shafts and their bearings in the crankcase, the gears and the selector drum and forks with clean engine oil of the specified grade **(see illustrations 26.11a, b and c)**.

16 Use a rag soaked in high flash-point solvent to wipe over the mating surfaces of both crankcase halves to remove all traces of oil. Fit the two dowels if removed **(see illustration)**.

26.16 Gearbox locating dowels (arrowed)

26.17 Apply the sealant round the inside of the bolts holes and all around the dowels

26.18 Slide the input shaft into the balancer shaft

17 Apply a thin, even bead of suitable sealant to the mating surface on the crankcase **(see illustration)**.

18 Carefully manoeuvre the gearbox into place, keeping it square to the engine so the input shaft slides all the way though the balancer shaft, and making sure the ends of the other shafts all engage in their housings/bearings **(see illustration)**. Check that the gearbox is fully seated against the crankcases all the way round before fitting any of the bolts, then fit the bolt above the output shaft (bolt No. 1) and the bottom right-hand bolt (bolt No. 2) and tighten them finger-tight to secure the gearbox, then fit the rest, tightening them all finger-tight at first **(see illustration 26.10a)**.

19 Now tighten bolts 1 and 2 to the torque setting specified at the beginning of the Chapter. Next tighten the bolts from No. 2 to No. 1 in a clockwise direction, i.e. along the bottom then up the left-hand side, to the specified torque. Finally tighten the bolts from No. 2 to No. 1 in an anti-clockwise direction, i.e. up the right-hand side then around the top, to the specified torque.

20 Lubricate the clutch release pushrods and insert them in the input shaft – fit the longer rod first with its shouldered end first, then fit the shorter one with its shouldered end facing out, so the knurled and rounded ends of the shafts push against each other **(see illustrations 26.9b and a)**.

21 If removed fit the gearchange mechanism components (Section 28).

22 Install the clutch (Section 20).

23 Remove the crankshaft locking tool. Fit a new sealing washer onto the access plug and tighten it to the specified torque.

24 Check the condition of the engine breather cover oil seal and O-ring and replace them with new ones if necessary **(see illustration)**. Lubricate the seal and O-ring with the oil then fit the cover and tighten the screws to the specified torque.

25 Install all remaining components in the reverse order of removal.

27 Gearbox output shaft oil seal

1 The output shaft oil seal must be replaced with a new one if there are signs of oil leakage – this can be done with the gearbox in place.

2 Remove the swingarm/final drive unit assembly (see Chapter 5).

3 Remove the circlip from its groove in the seal housing **(see illustration)**.

4 Carefully drill two holes on opposite sides of the old seal using a 2 or 3 mm drill bit – take care to only just drill through the outer surface of the seal rather than let the drill go deeper. Thread a self-tapping screw part-way into each hole, leaving enough exposed to get a good grip on the head. Either grip the screw head using a pair of standard pliers and pull the seal out, alternating sides to pull it out evenly, or use a pair of curved nose pliers to lever it out, along with some card to protect the housing rim, again swopping sides to lever it out evenly.

5 Wrap a single layer of insulating tape over the shaft splines to protect the inner lip of the new seal. Lubricate the tape and the inner lip with a smear of clean oil – do not lubricate the outer rim. Slip the seal onto the shaft with its marked side facing out and press it into the housing, then drive it in until the circlip groove is just fully exposed using a deep socket or suitable piece of tubing that bears on the outer rim of the seal, or a drift.

6 Remove the tape. Fit a new circlip into the groove.

7 Install the swingarm/final drive unit.

28 Gearchange mechanism

Note: *The gearchange mechanism can be removed with the engine in the frame.*

Removal

1 Drain the engine oil (see Chapter 1).

2 On models with a standard gearchange lever, note the alignment of the gearchange linkage arm on the shaft, then slacken

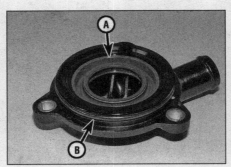

26.24 Check the oil seal (A) and O-ring (B)

27.3 Remove the circlip (arrowed)

28.2 Slacken the bolt and slide the arm off

28.7 Cut the cable-tie (arrowed)

28.8a Undo the screws...

28.8b ...and remove the cover

the pinch bolt and draw the arm off **(see illustration)**.

3 On models with gearshift assist, release and remove the retaining clip from the gearchange linkage rod, then pull the rod off **(see illustrations 4.16a, b and c)**. Unscrew the bolt securing the gearshift assist unit and remove the washer. Pull the unit off and disconnect the wiring, then remove the sleeve from the shaft if it doesn't come with the unit. If you can't pull the unit off thread the BMW tool 230831 or a bolt to fit the outer threads in the unit (not the inner threads in the shaft) into the hole and keep turning it to draw the

unit off the shaft, and when clear disconnect the wiring connector. Remove the sleeve from the shaft. Note that BMW specify to fit a new sleeve when installing the unit.

4 Displace the gear position sensor (see Chapter 8) – there is no need to disconnect the wiring at the connector, but you need to cut the cable-tie near the sensor.

5 Remove the exhaust system (see Chapter 4).

6 Release and displace the wiring/hose guide, and release the hoses from it **(see illustration 4.12d)**.

7 Cut the cable-tie securing the rubber gaiter around the output shaft housing then pull the gaiter back **(see illustration)**.

8 Undo the gearchange mechanism cover screws and remove the cover **(see illustrations)** – there is a lug on the bottom left corner that can be used to lever the cover off to break the seal if required. Do not use anything to lever between the cover mating surfaces as they are easily scored. Remove the dowels if loose.

9 If required remove the selector arm from the cover, noting how it locates **(see illustration)**. Note the fitting of the centralising spring and how its ends locate on either side of the post on the arm.

10 To remove the gearchange shaft or to

inspect its bearing, first remove the oil seal (see below).

11 The gearchange shaft and caged ball bearing are retained by a circlip – remove the circlip and draw the shaft out. The inner end of the shaft is supported by a needle roller bearing. The bearings are not available separately.

Inspection

12 Inspect the pawls on the selector arm and the pins on the selector drum camplate **(see illustration)**. Note the small spring on the pawl mechanism – the mechanism should move smoothly, but not be loose.

13 Inspect the stopper arm return spring, the stopper arm and the roller and the corresponding lobes on the gearchange cam **(see illustration 28.12)**.

14 If any of the selector arm, selector drum or stopper arm components are found to be worn or damaged a new gearbox must be fitted – individual components are not available.

15 Inspect the gearchange shaft splines for wear and damage **(see illustration 28.18)**. Check the peg on the shaft and the corresponding hole in the selector arm for wear **(see illustration 28.9)**. Check the condition of the shaft bearing(s). The caged ball bearing is part of the shaft. Fit a new shaft if necessary.

28.9 Remove the selector arm, noting how it engages the centralising spring

28.12 Selector drum camplate and pins (A), stopper arm (B)

28.18 Gearchange shaft splines and seal

28.22 Pushing the selector drum seal out

28.23 Fit the new seal as shown

Gearchange shaft seal

16 If the gearchange shaft oil seal is leaking, or to inspect the shaft bearings, remove the old seal as follows.

17 If not already done, remove the linkage arm or gearshift assist unit from the shaft as described above.

18 Carefully drill two holes on opposite sides of the old seal using a 2 or 3 mm drill bit – take care to only just drill through the outer surface of the seal rather than let the drill go deeper **(see illustration)**. Thread a self-tapping screw part-way into each hole, leaving enough exposed to get a good grip on the head. Either grip the screw head using a pair of standard pliers and pull the seal out, alternating sides to pull it out evenly, or use a pair of curved nose pliers along with some card to protect the housing rim, to lever the seal out, again swopping sides to lever it out evenly

19 Wrap a single layer of insulating tape over the shaft splines to protect the inner lip of the new seal. Lubricate the tape and the inner lip with a smear of clean oil – do not lubricate the outer rim. Slip the seal onto the shaft with its marked side facing out and press it into the housing, then drive it in until seated using a deep socket or suitable piece of tubing that bears on the outer rim of the seal.

20 Fit the gearchange linkage arm or gearshift assist unit (see below).

Selector drum seal

21 The seal is located behind the gear position sensor at the rear of the gearbox. If not already done, remove the gearchange mechanism cover (see above).

22 Carefully push the seal out from the outside using a screwdriver, or lever it out from the inside using a small, flat-bladed screwdriver, taking care not to damage the surface of the housing **(see illustration)**. Note which way round the seal is fitted.

23 Lubricate the lip of the new seal with a smear of clean oil. Press the seal in with your fingers, or drive it in using a socket that bears on the outer rim **(see illustration)**.

24 Fit the cover.

Installation

25 Clean all traces of old sealant from the cover and gearbox housing mating surfaces.

26 Lubricate the gearchange shaft and bearing(s), then slide the shaft in and secure it with the circlip. Fit a new gearchange shaft oil seal (see above).

27 Fit the centralising spring if removed, and the selector arm **(see illustration 28.9)**.

28 Fit the cover dowels if removed. Wipe the mating surfaces with solvent, then apply a smear of sealant to the mating surface on the cover. Fit the cover, locating it on the dowels, and tighten the screws in a criss-cross sequence to the torque setting specified at the beginning of the Chapter **(see illustrations 28.8b and a)**.

29 Fit the rubber gaiter over the housing and secure it using a new cable-tie **(see illustration 28.7)**.

30 Fit the wiring/hose guide and secure the hoses in it **(see illustration 4.12d)**.

31 Install the exhaust system (see Chapter 4).

32 Fit the gear position sensor (see Chapter 8).

33 On models with a standard gearchange lever align the slit in the linkage arm clamp with the lines on the shaft, slide the lever on and tighten the pinch bolt **(see illustration 28.2)**.

34 On models with gearshift assist slide a new sleeve into the unit so it is flush, aligning the wide splines (it can only fit one way). Clean the threads of the bolt, and inside the shaft using the correct tap. Apply some fresh threadlock to the bolt. Reconnect the wiring, then align the unit on the shaft, fit the bolt with its washer and tighten the bolt to push the unit on. Fit the linkage rod and secure

it with the clip **(see illustrations 4.16c, b and a)**.

35 Refill the engine with oil (see Chapter 1).

29 Running-in procedure

1 Make sure the engine oil level and coolant level are correct (see *Pre-ride checks* and Chapter 1).

2 Check that the kill switch is in the RUN position and the gearbox is in neutral, then turn the ignition switch ON.

3 Start the engine and allow it to run until it reaches operating temperature.

4 If a lubrication failure is suspected, stop the engine immediately and try to find the cause. If an engine is run without the oil circulating, even for a short period of time, severe damage will occur.

5 Check carefully for oil leaks and make sure the transmission and controls, especially the brakes, function properly before road testing the machine.

6 Treat the machine gently for the first few miles to make sure oil has circulated throughout the engine and any new parts installed have started to seat.

7 Extra care is necessary if new pistons, rings or bearing shells have been fitted. If this is the case, the bike will have to be run in as when new. This means greater use of the transmission and a restraining hand on the throttle until at least 600 miles (1000 km) have been covered.

8 Upon completion of the road test, and after the engine has cooled down completely, recheck the valve clearances (see Chapter 1) and check the engine oil level and coolant level (see *Pre-ride checks* and Chapter 1).

9 BMW advise that the engine should not exceed 5000 rpm for the first 600 miles (1000 km). The throttle position should be varied, but not fully open. Avoid running the engine at a constant rpm.

Chapter 3
Cooling system

Contents

Degrees of difficulty

Easy, suitable for novice with little experience		Fairly easy, suitable for beginner with some experience		Fairly difficult, suitable for competent DIY mechanic		Difficult, suitable for experienced DIY mechanic		Very difficult, suitable for expert DIY or professional	

Specifications

General

Coolant mixture type and capacity .... see Chapter 1
Cooling system test pressure .... 22 psi (1.5 Bars), maintained for 5 mins.
Cooling fan cut-in temp. .... 105°C
Temperature warning cut-in temp. .... 118°C

Torque settings

Coolant outlet union screws .... 12 Nm
ECT sensor .... 15 Nm
Water pump mounting bolts .... 12 Nm

1 General information

1 The cooling system uses a water/anti-freeze coolant to carry away excess heat from the engine and maintain as constant a temperature as possible. Each cylinder is surrounded by a water jacket from which the heated coolant is circulated by thermo-syphonic action in conjunction with a water pump, which is on the front of the engine and driven directly off the crankshaft. The hot coolant passes through the thermostat and to the radiator(s). The coolant then flows across the core of the radiator(s) and back to the water pump and the engine.

2 A thermostat is fitted to prevent the coolant flowing when the engine is cold, therefore accelerating the speed at which the engine reaches normal operating temperature. The ECT (engine coolant temperature) sensor mounted in the coolant outlet union on the engine transmits information to the ECU (electronic control unit). If the engine gets too hot the ECU actuates the cooling fan on the back of the radiator (right-hand one on GS and RT models) to draw extra air through, and if necessary turns on the temperature warning light in the instrument cluster.

3 The complete cooling system is partially sealed and pressurised, the pressure being controlled by a valve contained in the spring-loaded radiator cap. By pressurising the coolant the boiling point is raised, preventing premature boiling in adverse conditions. The overflow pipe from the system is connected to a reservoir into which excess coolant is expelled under pressure. The discharged coolant automatically returns to the radiator by the vacuum created when the engine cools.

⚠ *Warning: Do not remove the pressure cap from the radiator when the engine is hot. Scalding hot coolant and steam may be blown out under pressure, which could cause serious injury. When the engine has cooled, place a thick rag, like a towel, over the pressure cap; slowly rotate the cap anti-clockwise to the first stop. This procedure allows any residual pressure to escape. When the steam has stopped escaping, press down on the cap while turning it anti-clockwise and remove it.*

Caution: Do not allow anti-freeze to come in contact with your skin or painted surfaces of the motorcycle. Rinse off any spills immediately with plenty of water. Anti-freeze is highly toxic if ingested. Never leave anti-freeze lying around in an open container or in puddles on the floor; children and pets are attracted by its sweet smell and may drink it. Check with the local authorities about disposing of used anti-freeze. Many communities will have collection centres which will see that anti-freeze is disposed of safely.

Caution: If preparing a mix of anti-freeze and distilled water, take care to mix it in the correct proportion. The anti-freeze contains corrosion inhibitors which are essential to avoid damage to the cooling system. A lack of these inhibitors could lead to a build-up of corrosion which would block the coolant passages, resulting in overheating and severe engine damage. Distilled water must be used as opposed to tap water to avoid a build-up of scale which would also block the passages.

2 Cooling fan

Check

1 The cooling fan is on the back of the radiator, the right-hand one on GS, GS Adv and RT models. Refer to the removal procedure below for your model and disconnect the wiring connector **(see illustration 5.4b)**.

2 Using a 12 volt battery and two jumper wires with very small probes, connect the battery positive (+) lead to the blue wire terminal on the fan, and the battery negative (–) lead to the black wire terminal on the connector – take care as the connector and its terminals are very small and it will be easy to touch the probes together and short the battery. Once connected the fan should operate. If it does not, replace the fan assembly with a new one.

Removal and installation

 Warning: The engine must be completely cool before carrying out this procedure.

GS, GS Adv and RT models

3 On GS models remove the right-hand side panel (see Chapter 7). On GS Adv models remove the right-hand fuel tank cover (see Chapter 7). On RT models remove the right-hand knee support panel (see Chapter 7).

4 Disconnect the fan wiring connector **(see illustration 5.4b)**.

5 Release the trim clip at the bottom, then draw the fan down to free the tabs at the upper end **(see illustrations)**.

6 Installation is the reverse of removal.

R and RS models

7 Remove the radiator (see Section 5).

8 Undo the screws on the front, then lift the fan off the peg at the top.

9 Installation is the reverse of removal.

3 Temperature display and ECT sensor

Temperature display

Caution: If the high temperature warning display comes on during normal use, stop the engine then wait for it to cool down and check the coolant level in the reservoir (see Pre-ride checks).

1 On GS and GS Adv models the display consists of the general warning symbol and a high temperature warning symbol – if the engine temperature is too high the general warning symbol shows red and the temperature warning symbol comes on. On RT models the display consists of a segmented temperature gauge, with the segments coming on as the coolant

2.5a Release the trim clip…

temperature rises, and the general warning symbol – if the coolant temperature is too high the general warning symbol shows red and the temperature gauge turns red. On R and RS models the display consists of the general warning symbol and a high temperature warning symbol – if the engine temperature is too high the general warning symbol flashes red and the temperature warning symbol comes on.

ECT sensor

Function

2 The ECT (engine coolant temperature) sensor is threaded into the coolant outlet union, which is on the top of the engine on the right-hand side at the front **(see illustration)**. The resistance of the sensor changes as engine coolant temperature changes. The information is sent to the ECU, which uses it to determine fuel and ignition requirements, and to run the temperature display in the instrument cluster according to model (see above).

Removal and installation

 Warning: The engine must be completely cool before carrying out this procedure.
Caution: The ECT sensor is fragile and could be damaged if dropped or struck.

3 Drain the cooling system (see Chapter 1).

4 On GS and GS Adv models remove the left-hand side panel, on RT models remove the left-hand fairing side panel (see Chapter 7).

3.2 ECT sensor (arrowed)

2.5b …and remove the fan

On R and RS models remove the radiator (Section 5). On all models remove any air deflector and heat shield panels as required for best access to the sensor.

5 Cut the cable-tie and disconnect the sensor wiring connector **(see illustration 3.2)**. Unscrew and remove the sensor, and discard the sealing washer.

6 Fit a new sealing washer onto the sensor. Fit the sensor and tighten it to the torque setting specified at the beginning of the Chapter. Connect the wiring and secure it with a new cable-tie.

7 Refill the cooling system (see Chapter 1).

4 Thermostat

1 The thermostat is fitted in the top of the coolant outlet union, which is on the top of the engine on the left-hand side at the front. It is closed when the engine coolant is cold, restricting the flow of coolant around the system and allowing the engine to warm up quickly, and opens as the coolant warms up, allowing the coolant to flow and be cooled by passing through the radiator(s). It is automatic in operation and should give many years service without requiring attention. In the event of a failure, the valve will either jam open, in which case the engine will take much longer than normal to warm up, or shut, in which case the coolant will be unable to circulate and the engine will overheat. Neither condition is acceptable, and the fault must be investigated promptly.

Removal

 Warning: The engine must be completely cool before carrying out this procedure.

2 Drain the cooling system (see Chapter 1).

3 On GS and GS Adv models remove the left-hand side panel, on RT models remove the left-hand fairing side panel (see Chapter 1). On R and RS models remove the radiator (Section 5). On all models remove any air deflector and heat shield panels as required for best access to the thermostat.

4 Trace the hoses from the thermostat to their unions on the radiators, release the clamps and disconnect the hoses – refer to the illustrations in Section 5.

5 Pull the thermostat retaining clip out, lift the thermostat off the union and remove it along with the hoses **(see illustrations)**.

6 To remove the coolant outlet union disconnect the ECT sensor wiring connector **(see illustration 3.2)**, then undo the screws and remove the union **(see illustration)** – a new O-ring must be fitted **(see illustration)**.

Installation

7 Installation is the reverse of removal. If the coolant outlet union was removed fit a new O-ring and tighten the screws to the torque setting specified at the beginning of the Chapter **(see illustrations 4.6b and a)**. Seat the cut-out in the end of each coolant hose around the rib on its union, and secure the hoses using new clamps where necessary **(see illustration 7.7)**. Make sure the thermostat retaining clip is pushed fully in **(see illustration 4.5a)**.

8 Refill the cooling system (see Chapter 1). Install the body panels (see Chapter 7).

5 Radiator(s)

Note: *If the radiator(s) is/are being removed as part of the engine removal procedure, detach the hoses from their unions on the engine rather than on the radiator and remove the radiator complete with its hoses. Note the routing of the hoses.*

Removal

 Warning: The engine must be completely cool before carrying out this procedure.

1 Drain the cooling system (see Chapter 1).

GS, GS Adv and RT models

Right-hand radiator

2 On GS models remove the right-hand side panel, on GS Adv models remove the fuel tank right-hand side cover, and on RT models remove the right-hand knee support panel (see Chapter 7).

3 Displace and support the reservoir, then release the clamp securing its hose to the radiator filler neck, detach the hose and remove the reservoir, draining it if required and not already done (if you don't drain it keep the hose above the level of the coolant to prevent it draining itself) **(see illustrations)**.

4 Release and disconnect the cooling fan wiring connector and wiring **(see illustrations)**.

5 Place a container under the radiator to catch any residual coolant. Release the

4.5a Pull the clip out…

4.5b …then lift the thermostat off the coolant outlet union

4.6a Coolant outlet union screws (arrowed)

4.6b Replace the O-ring (arrowed) with a new one

5.3a Displace the reservoir…

5.3b …and disconnect the hose

5.4a Release the connector from its clip…

5.4b …then disconnect it and release the wiring clip

5.5a Release the clamps...

5.5b ...and detach the hoses

5.6 Undo the screw to release the cowl

5.7 Undo the three radiator screws

5.8a On RT models lift the radiator off the lugs

clamps securing the hoses to the bottom of the radiator and disconnect them **(see illustrations)**.

6 On RT models undo the screw securing the radiator cowl **(see illustration)**.

7 Undo the radiator mounting screws and remove the washers **(see illustration)**. On GS Adv models remove the mounting bracket.

8 Displace the radiator, then release the clamp and disconnect the hose from the top of the radiator and remove the radiator **(see illustrations)**.Note the arrangement of the collars and grommets in the radiator mounts **(see illustration 5.13)**. Replace the grommets with new ones if they are damaged, deformed or deteriorated.

Left-hand radiator

9 On GS models remove the left-hand side panel, on GS Adv models remove the fuel tank left-hand side cover, and on RT models remove the left-hand knee support panel (see Chapter 7). On RT models undo the screw securing the radiator cowl **(see illustration)**.

10 Place a container under the radiator to catch any residual coolant. Release the clamp securing the small-bore hose to the top of the radiator and disconnect it **(see illustration)**.

11 Undo the radiator mounting screws and remove the washers **(see illustration)**.

12 Displace the radiator, then if required

5.8b Release the clamp...

5.8c ...and detach the hose

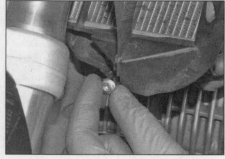

5.9 Undo the screw to release the cowl

5.10 Detach the small-bore hose

5.11 Undo the three radiator screws

5.12 Remove the radiator, detaching the top inner hose if required, or removing it with the radiator if not

5.13 Check the grommets for cracks and hardening

(if the right-hand radiator has not been removed), release the clamp and disconnect the inner hose from the top, and remove the radiator **(see illustration)**.

13 Note the arrangement of the collars and grommets in the radiator mounts **(see illustration)**. Replace the grommets with new ones if they are damaged, deformed or deteriorated.

R and RS models

14 On R models remove the radiator cowls (see Chapter 7). Release the trim clips from the top of the radiator **(see illustration 5.15)**.

15 On RS models remove the fuel tank side covers and fairing inner panels (see Chapter 7). Release the trim clip securing the air deflector to the top of the radiator on each side **(see illustration)**.

16 Release the hose from the clip, then release the clamp and disconnect the hose from the radiator filler neck **(see illustration)** – if you haven't drained the reservoir you need to clamp the hose, or place the end in a container to catch the coolant from the reservoir.

17 Release the hose clamps and disconnect the hoses, being ready with a container to catch any residual coolant **(see illustrations)**.

18 Undo the two screws and remove the washers. Displace the radiator to the right, being ready with a container to catch any residual coolant. Disconnect the cooling fan connector and release the wiring ties(s) and guide, and remove the radiator. Note the arrangement of the collars in the right-hand mounts, and the grommets in all the mounts. Replace the grommets with new ones if they are damaged, deformed or deteriorated.

All models

19 Check the radiator for signs of damage and clear any dirt or debris that might obstruct air flow and inhibit cooling. If the radiator fins are badly damaged or broken the radiator must be replaced with a new one. To enable full examination and cleaning, remove the cooling fan from the radiator (see Section 2).

Installation

20 Installation is the reverse of removal, noting the following.

● Make sure the coolant hoses are in good condition. Seat the cut-out in each hose around the rib on each union **(see illustration 7.7)**. Fit the hose clamps, using new ones where necessary.

● Make sure the rubber grommets and collars are correctly fitted.

● Make sure that the fan wiring is securely connected.

● On completion refill the cooling system as described in Chapter 1.

Pressure cap check

21 If problems such as overheating or unexplained loss of coolant occur, check the entire system. The radiator cap opening pressure should be checked by a BMW dealer with the special tester required to do the job. If the cap is defective, replace it with a new one.

5.15 There is a clip (arrowed) on each side – lever the head of the clip up then draw the body out

5.16 Release the hose clip (arrowed), then detach the hose from the filler neck

5.17a Detach the hose from the left-hand side...

5.17b ...and the hoses from the right-hand side. Radiator mounting screws (arrowed)

6.4 Unscrew the mounting bolts – do not undo the darker pump assembly screws

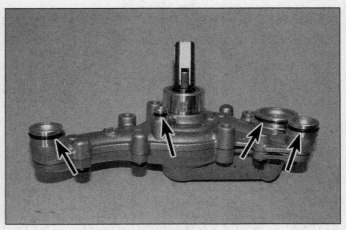

6.5 Water pump O-rings (arrowed)

6 Water pump

Removal

1 The water pump is mounted on the front of the engine behind the front crankcase cover. Drain the engine oil and coolant (see Chapter 1).
2 On R and RS models remove the radiator (Section 5).
3 Remove the front crankcase cover (see Chapter 2).
4 Unscrew the six mounting bolts and remove the pump assembly **(see illustration)**.
5 Remove the O-rings – new ones must be used **(see illustration)**.

Inspection

6 Check the impeller by turning the shaft. If it is noisy or rough when turned, the pump must be replaced with a new one.
7 If there is evidence that coolant has been leaking from around the shaft replace the pump with a new one.

Installation

8 Clean the pump and crankcase mating surfaces.

9 Fit new O-rings onto the pump **(see illustration 6.5)**.
10 Fit the pump, aligning the slot in the end of the impeller shaft with the drive tab, and making sure the O-rings stay in place **(see illustration)**. Tighten the pump bolts to the torque setting specified at the beginning of the Chapter.
11 Install the crankcase cover (see Chapter 2), and on R and RS models refit the radiator. Refill with engine oil and coolant (see Chapter 1).

7 Coolant hoses

Removal

1 Before removing a hose, drain the coolant (see Chapter 1).
2 Where single-use clamps are fitted (such as on the thermostat), they can be released using a screwdriver. The clamps must obviously be replaced with new ones, and special pliers, obtainable from BMW (part No. 13 1 500) or any good automotive tool supplier, are needed to secure them. Note that if preferred

the single-use clamps can be replaced with multi-use ones, as long as they are the correct size and can be correctly fitted and tightened.
3 Where spring clamps are fitted (such as on the radiator), they can be released by squeezing the ends together using pliers, but it is much easier to use the proper tool designed for the type of clamp used, available from an automotive tool supplier **(see illustrations 13.14a and b in Chapter 1)**.
4 Slide the released clamp along the hose away from the union.
5 Before detaching a hose have a container ready to catch any residual coolant – even though the system has been drained there is always some left.
Caution: The radiator unions are fragile. Do not use excessive force when attempting to remove the hoses.
6 Carefully pull the hose off, using a twisting motion to help break the seal. If a hose proves too difficult to pull off its union, carefully cut the hose with a sharp knife – this means replacing the hose with a new one.

Installation

7 Slide the clamps onto the hose and then work the hose on to its union, seating the cut-out in the end around the rib on the union **(see illustration)**.

> **HAYNES HiNT** *If the hose is difficult to push on its union, soften it by soaking it in very hot water, or alternatively a little soapy water on the union can be used as a lubricant.*

8 Slide the clamp onto the union, and where necessary crimp it tight using the special pliers. If a single-use clamp has been replaced with a screw type one, tighten the clamp using a screwdriver.
9 Refill the cooling system with fresh coolant (see Chapter 1).

6.10 Locate the drive tab (A) in the slot (B)

7.7 Seat the cut-out (A) in the end of the hose around the rib (B)

Chapter 4
Engine management systems

Contents

Degrees of difficulty

Easy, suitable for novice with little experience	Fairly easy, suitable for beginner with some experience	Fairly difficult, suitable for competent DIY mechanic	Difficult, suitable for experienced DIY mechanic	Very difficult, suitable for expert DIY or professional

Specifications

Fuel
Grade
  All models . . . .   Unleaded, minimum 95 RON (Research Octane Number)
  R1200 GS and GS Adventure (optional – requires dealer reset) . . . .   Unleaded, minimum 91 RON (Research Octane Number)
Tank capacity
  R1200 GS . . . .   20 litres
  R1200 GS Adventure . . . .   30 litres
  R1200 RT . . . .   25 litres
  R1200 R and RS . . . .   18 litres
Quantity remaining when level warning light comes on . . . .   4 litres

Throttle bodies
Internal diameter . . . .   52 mm
Fuel pump output pressure . . . .   5 Bars

Torque settings
Exhaust system
  Silencer mounting bolt . . . .   19 Nm
  Silencer clamp nut . . . .   22 Nm
  Servo/downpipe assembly bracket screws . . . .   19 Nm
  Downpipe nuts . . . .   28 Nm
  Oxygen sensors . . . .   45 Nm
Fuel pump retaining ring (not GS Adventure models) . . . .   35 Nm
Sensors
  Camshaft position sensor screw . . . .   8 Nm
  Crankshaft position sensor screw . . . .   8 Nm

1 General information and precautions

General information

1 BMW's digital engine management system monitors, controls and co-ordinates both the fuel and ignition system functions.

2 The system is operated by the ECU (BMW's DME (Digital Motor Electronics) unit). A second unit, the ground module (BMW's GM), is responsible for monitoring and control of all other electrical systems such as lighting, switches and accessories. The two units are linked for such functions as starting and engine immobilisation.

3 The ECU uses engine speed and throttle valve position as the basis for determining optimum engine operation. Additional data, supplied by temperature sensors, oil pressure, and gear position sensors, and exhaust gas analysers, when combined with control maps and correction values embedded within the ECU, fine tune injection volume and ignition timing to meet the engine's requirements in any given circumstance.

4 The engine management system has in-built diagnostic functions which record and store all data should a fault occur. If this happens, the engine warning light in the instrument cluster illuminates and, unless the fault is serious, the engine runs in emergency 'limp home' mode. Otherwise, the engine will stop. BMW advise that in 'limp home' mode, full engine power may not be available and the machine should be ridden with this in mind. Refer to Section 14 for details of fault finding.

5 Because of their nature, individual system components cannot be repaired. Once the faulty component has been isolated, the only cure is to replace the part with a new one. Keep in mind that most electrical parts, once purchased, cannot be returned. To avoid unnecessary expense, make very sure the faulty component has been positively identified before buying a new part.

Fuel system

6 The fuel system consists of the fuel tank, fuel pump and strainer, fuel hoses and pressure regulator, throttle bodies, fuel injectors, and the air intake system.

7 The fuel pump, with integral filter, is housed inside the tank. The fuel strainer is mounted on the bottom of the pump.

8 There is an injector for each cylinder, housed in the cylinder head. Cold starting, warm-up and engine idle speed are controlled by the ECU acting on information sent by the engine and intake air temperature sensors – there is no manual method (i.e. a choke) for assisting cold starting.

9 Information on fuel level is provided by a level sensor in the tank, which is linked to the fuel gauge and/or low fuel level warning in the instrument cluster, according to model. The tripmeter will calculate the range available on the remaining fuel and present this information on the multi-function panel in the instrument cluster.

10 The exhaust system is a two-into-one design, incorporating a catalytic converter, oxygen sensors and exhaust control valve.

 Warning: Petrol (gasoline) is extremely flammable, so take extra precautions when you work on any part of the fuel system. Don't smoke or allow open flames or bare light bulbs near the work area, and don't work in a garage where a natural gas-type appliance is present. If you spill any fuel on your skin, rinse it off immediately with soap and water. When you perform any kind of work on the fuel system, wear safety glasses and have a fire extinguisher suitable for a class B type fire (flammable liquids) on hand.

Ignition system

11 The ignition system, due to its lack of mechanical parts, is totally maintenance-free.

12 On all models, the ignition coil for each spark plug is incorporated in the spark plug cap. The system incorporates ignition advance controlled by the ECU, which reacts to the information sent to it from the various sensors to provide the sparks at the optimum time.

13 The system incorporates a safety interlock circuit that prevents the engine from being started with the sidestand down unless the gearbox is in neutral. The interlock circuit will also cut the ignition if the sidestand is put down whilst the engine is running and in gear, or if a gear is selected whilst the engine is running and the sidestand is down.

 Warning: The very high output of the engine management system means that it can be very dangerous or even fatal to touch live components or terminals of any part of the system while in operation. Take care not to touch any part of the system when the engine is running, or even with it stopped and the ignition ON. Before working on an electrical component, make sure that the ignition switch is OFF, then disconnect the battery negative lead (-ve) and insulate it away from the battery terminal.

Precautions

14 Always perform fuel-related procedures in a well-ventilated area to prevent a build-up of fumes.

15 Never work in a building containing a gas appliance with a pilot light, or any other form of naked flame. Ensure that there are no naked light bulbs or any sources of flame or sparks nearby.

16 Do not smoke (or allow anyone else to smoke) while in the vicinity of petrol (gasoline) or of components containing it. Remember the possible presence of vapour from these sources and move well clear before smoking.

17 Check all electrical equipment belonging to the house, garage or workshop where work is being undertaken (see the *Safety first!* section of this manual). Remember that certain electrical appliances such as drills, cutters etc. create sparks in the normal course of operation and must not be used near petrol (gasoline) or any component containing it. Again, remember the possible presence of fumes before using electrical equipment.

18 Always mop up any spilt fuel and safely dispose of the rag used.

19 Any stored fuel that is drained off during servicing work must be kept in sealed containers that are suitable for holding petrol (gasoline), and clearly marked as such; the containers themselves should be kept in a safe place. Note that this last point applies equally to the fuel tank if it is removed from the machine; also remember to keep its filler cap closed at all times.

20 Read the *Safety first!* section of this manual carefully before starting work.

21 Owners of machines used in the US, particularly California, should note that their machines must comply at all times with Federal or State legislation governing the permissible levels of noise and of pollutants such as unburnt hydrocarbons, carbon monoxide etc. that can be emitted by those machines. All vehicles offered for sale must comply with legislation in force at the date of manufacture and must not subsequently be altered in any way which will affect their emission of noise or of pollutants.

22 In practice, this means that adjustments may not be made to any part of the fuel, ignition or exhaust systems by anyone who is not authorised or mechanically qualified to do so, or who does not have the tools, equipment and data necessary to properly carry out the task. Also if any part of these systems is to be replaced it must be replaced with only genuine BMW components or by components which are approved under the relevant legislation. The machine must never be used with any part of these systems removed, modified or damaged.

2 Fuel tank

 Warning: Refer to the precautions given in Section 1 before starting work.

Removal

1 Remove the fuel tank covers (see Chapter 7).

2 On GS, GS Adv and RT models displace

2.2a Use a pointed tool in the hole to release the fuse holder

2.2b Undo the screws and bolts…

2.2c …withdraw the sleeves…

the fuse holder **(see illustration)**. Undo the seat bracket screws and the tank mounting bolts, then withdraw the sleeves from the tank mounts and remove the bracket **(see illustrations)**.

3 On R and RS models undo the seat bracket bolts and the tank mounting bolts and withdraw the collars, then ease the sides of the seat bracket out and remove the bracket **(see illustration)**.

4 Disconnect the breather and overflow hoses from the filler neck **(see illustration)**.

5 On models with keyless ride disconnect the filler cap wiring connector and free the wiring from its ties and guides, and note its routing **(see illustration)** – on RS models undo the left-hand air intake duct and remove the duct for best access.

6 Lift the rear of the tank and ease it back off its front mounts **(see illustration)**.

2.2d …and remove the bracket

7 Disconnect the fuel pump and fuel level sensor wiring connectors **(see illustration)**. Check the connectors and sockets for corrosion (which could affect their function) and clean if necessary.

2.3 Unscrew the bolts (arrowed) and remove the bracket

8 Push the fuel hose retainer across and disconnect the hose **(see illustrations)**. Note the O-ring(s) on the hose connector – GS and GS Adv models have two, all other models one. BMW specify to check the O-ring(s) and

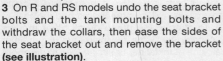

2.4 Detach the hoses

2.5 Release and disconnect the wiring connector (arrowed) and wiring – RT shown

2.6 Ease the tank back, noting how it locates

2.7 Disconnect the wiring connectors

2.8a Push the metal retainer across…

2.8b …and pull the hose off

replace if necessary, but do not list them as being available separately from the connector itself.

9 Make sure the fuel filler cap is secure, then carefully lift the tank off. Support the tank on some rag or a cushioned surface.

Installation

10 Installation is the reverse of removal, noting the following:

- Check the condition of the front mounting rubbers and the rear mounting grommets and replace them with new ones if they are damaged or have deteriorated (see illustration 2.6 and 2.2c).
- Make sure the fuel hose is correctly routed. Check the O-ring(s) on the hose connector (see Step 8). Lubricate the O-ring(s) with a smear of Molykote 111 or silicone grease.
- To connect the fuel hose, push the retaining clip across, then gently push the hose connector in straight until it clicks into place, then release the clip.
- Make sure the fuel pump and level sensor wiring connectors are secure.
- Make sure the tank locates correctly on its front mounts (see illustration 2.6).
- On models with keyless ride make sure the wiring is correctly routed and secured (see illustration 2.5).
- Check for leakage around the fuel pump and hose connector before fitting the bodywork.

4.5a Unscrewing the retaining ring using a metal bar works perfectly well

3 Evaporative emission control system – US models

1 When the engine is stopped, fuel vapour from the tank vents through a hose into a cylindrical charcoal filter, rather than venting directly into the atmosphere as on other market models. When the engine is running, a control valve, operated by the ECU, directs the vapour stored in the filter canister back into the fuel system via the left-hand throttle body.

2 Apart from periodic checks of the hoses, the system is essentially maintenance-free. If the hoses become cracked or split replace them with new ones, removing the body panels, fuel tank, radiator(s), coolant reservoir and any other components as required according to model to access them. Trace the hose from the tank to the canister, and from the canister to the control valve and so on, releasing the hoses from any ties and guides and noting their routing.

4 Fuel pump, strainer, and level sensor

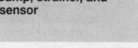

> **Warning: Refer to the precautions given in Section 1 before starting work.**

4.5b Take care when drawing the pump assembly out – the seal will probably come away with it

Note: *Cleaning the fuel strainer is not a service item. However, if fuel delivery problems are suspected, the strainer should be inspected.*

1 The fuel pump is located inside the fuel tank on the left-hand side. A filter is incorporated in the body of the pump and a strainer is located on the bottom of the pump. Only the strainer is available separately. The pump has an electronic controller fitted externally that can be replaced with a new one if faulty.

2 Before removing the pump from the tank, any fuel should be emptied from the tank using a commercially available pump.

Fuel pump

Removal

3 Remove the fuel tank (Section 2).

4 To remove the pump on GS Adv models undo the retaining plate screws and remove the plate. Carefully pull the pump assembly out of the tank, taking care not to snag the level sensor float arm – do not try to lever the pump free as you will damage the rim and the seal.

5 To remove the pump on all other models unscrew the pump retaining ring, using either a piece of metal bar or similar (see illustration) located against the castellations, or if preferred BMW produces a service tool to do this (No. 161021) (see illustration). Carefully ease the pump assembly out of the tank, taking care not to snag the float arm (see illustration) – do not try to lever the pump free as you will damage the rim and the seal.

6 Remove the seal and check it for damage – replace it with a new one if necessary, though it is best to fit a new one whatever the apparent condition.

7 Check the strainer (see below).

Check

8 Pump efficiency will be severely restricted if the strainer is blocked (see below). If the strainer is good, test the pump as follows:

9 Using a fully charged 12 volt battery and two insulated jumper wires, connect the positive (+) battery terminal to the positive terminal on the pump controller, and the negative (-) battery terminal to the negative terminal (see illustration). The pump should operate.

10 If the pump does not work disconnect

4.9 Fuel pump terminals (A) and pump controller screws (B)

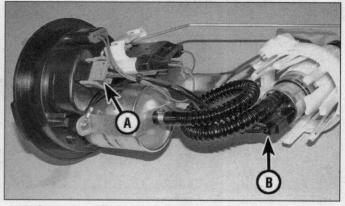

4.10 Controller wiring connector (A), pump motor connector (B)

4.14a Fit the seal...

4.14b ...then carefully manoeuvre the pump in...

4.14c ...seating the tab in the cut-out

the wiring connector from the controller and connect the jumper wires as before to the terminals in the connector **(see illustration)**. If the pump operates the controller is faulty and a new one must be fitted – it comes with a new seal, which must be lubricated with silicone grease. If it still doesn't work connect the jumper wires directly to the pump motor terminals. If it still doesn't work it is faulty and must be replaced with a new one.

11 If the pump operates when tested, check that the terminals in the pump wiring connector are clean, then connect the connector and turn the ignition ON. The pump should operate. If not, inspect the wiring and terminals for physical damage or loose or corroded connections. Turn the ignition OFF when the test is complete.

12 If the pump operates but is thought to be delivering an insufficient amount of fuel, check that the fuel tank breather hose is not obstructed, pinched or trapped.

13 If all appears to be good, have the fuel pump's output pressure checked by a BMW dealer.

Installation

14 Installation is the reverse of removal, noting the following:
- Fit the sealing ring into the tank, making sure it is correctly seated all round **(see illustration)**. Lubricate the ring with a silicone spray to ease fitting.
- Ease the pump into the tank with the tab on the rim at the top, making sure the seal

does not dislodge and that the seal and the pump rim seat correctly all round **(see illustrations)**.
- On GS Adv models align the retaining ring screw holes with those in the tank, then make sure the pump is correctly aligned for the tab on the rim to seat in the recess in the retaining ring. Tighten the screws evenly in a criss-cross sequence.
- On all other models tighten the retaining ring securely **(see illustration 4.5a)** – if the BMW service tool is available, tighten the ring to the torque setting specified at the beginning of this Chapter.

Fuel strainer

15 Remove the fuel pump (see above).

16 The strainer is on the lower end of the pump assembly **(see illustration)**. Allow the strainer element to dry, then use a soft brush to remove any dirt or sediment. If the strainer is heavily soiled, clean accumulated dirt out of the tank.

17 Inspect the strainer for splits and holes – if any damage is found, a new one should be fitted. **Note:** *If it is damaged, and if there is evidence of sediment inside the tank and on the undamaged portions of the strainer, it is possible sediment will have entered the pump body and the internal filter may have become blocked. Under these circumstances, a new pump will have to be fitted, and it comes with a strainer.*

18 To remove the strainer pull it off the bottom of the filter.

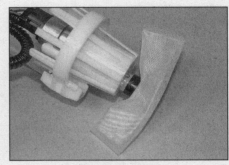

4.16 Fuel strainer

19 Installation is the reverse of removal

Fuel level sensor

20 Remove the fuel pump (see above).

21 To check the sensor connect a multimeter set to read resistance to the terminals in the sensor, then manually move the float arm up and down – the resistance should vary as the arm is moved **(see illustrations)**. No specifications are available, but we measured around 100 ohms with the float lowered (empty tank) and around 30 ohms with the float raised (full tank), and there should be a constant variation in resistance as you move the arm. If there is no reading, or if the reading is constant, the sensor is faulty.

22 To remove the sensor disconnect the wiring connector and cut the cable-tie **(see illustration)**. Undo the two bracket screws

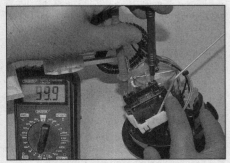

4.21a Testing sensor resistance with the float lowered...

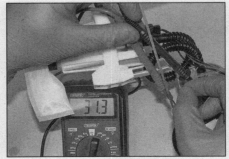

4.21b ...and raised

4.22a Sensor wiring connector (arrowed)...

4.22b ...and bracket screws (arrowed)

5.4 Release the hoses from the clips (arrowed)

5.5 Release the union and disconnect the wiring

and displace the bracket from pump **(see illustration)**. Release the catch to free the sensor from the bracket.

23 Installation is the reverse of removal.

5 Fuel hoses and pressure sensor

⚠️ **Warning: Refer to the precautions given in Section 1 before starting work.**

Removal

1 The fuel hoses, between the tank union and the fuel injectors, are part of a one-piece distribution assembly that incorporates the fuel pressure sensor **(see illustration 5.5)**.

2 To remove the fuel distribution assembly, remove the fuel tank (Section 2) and the fuel injectors (Section 7).

3 Cut the cable-tie securing the injector wiring to the fuel hose.

4 Release the fuel tank drain and breather hoses from the clip and the fuel hoses from the clips, and note the routing of the hoses **(see illustration)**.

5 Draw the three-way union out of its holder, disconnect the pressure sensor wiring connector and remove the hose assembly **(see illustration)**.

6 The fuel hose connector (that goes onto the fuel pump), and the hose clamps, are the only parts available. The connector can be pulled out of the hose after releasing the clamp. Fit a new clamp when fitting the new connector. If any of the hose sections are kinked, cracked or split renew the complete hose assembly – it will come with a new connector.

Installation

7 Installation is the reverse of removal, noting the following:

● Make sure the hoses are correctly routed and secured **(see illustration 5.4)**.
● Refer to Section 7 to fit the injectors.
● Check that there are no leaks by turning the ignition switch on to pressurise the system before installing the bodywork.

6 Throttle bodies

⚠️ **Warning: Refer to the precautions given in Section 1 before starting work.**

Removal

1 Remove the fuel tank (Section 2).

2 Undo the screws securing the back of the air filter housing **(see illustration)**.

3 Release and remove the throttle body clamps, using the special pliers (BMW tool No. 131512) if available or water pump pliers if not **(see illustration)** – take care not to damage or distort the clamps.

4 Disconnect the wiring connector and cut the cable-tie securing the wiring to the throttle body **(see illustration)**.

5 Lift the air filter housing and draw the throttle body out of the ducts **(see illustration)**.

6 Stuff some clean rag into the intake duct on the cylinder head.

Inspection

7 Inspect the throttle bodies and air ducts for cracks or any other damage which may result in air leakage and replace any damaged components with new ones.

8 Make sure that the inside of the body is completely clean.

9 Check the condition of the clamps – if they were damaged during removal, replace them with new ones.

Installation

10 Installation is the reverse of removal, noting the following:

● Remove the rag from the intake duct.
● Fit the right-hand throttle body with the servo motor at the front, and the left-hand

6.2 Undo the two air filter housing screws

6.3 Using water pump pliers to release the clamps – locate the ends as shown and squeeze the clamp gently to release its catch

6.4 Disconnect and release the wiring

6.5 Lift the upper duct off then lift the throttle body out of the lower duct and remove it

6.10a Orientation of right-hand throttle body

6.10b Orientation of left-hand throttle body

6.10c Fit the clamp…

throttle body with the servo motor at the rear, in each case aligning the recessed section on the intake duct with the raised section on the throttle body **(see illustrations 6.10a and b)**.

● Use new clamps if necessary. Fit the clamp around the duct and place it on the first catch to hold it in place, then use the pliers or tool to squeeze the clamp onto its main catch **(see illustrations 6.10c, d and e)**.

6.10d …place it on the first catch…

6.10e …then squeeze it onto the main catch

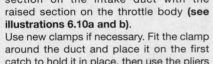

7 Fuel injectors

⚠ *Warning: Refer to the precautions given in Section 1 before starting work.*

Removal

1 Undo the fuel injector cover screw and remove the cover **(see illustration)**.
2 Release the clip securing the fuel injector wiring connector and disconnect the connector **(see illustration)**.
3 Undo the fuel hose connector screw, then carefully withdraw the injector **(see illustrations)**.
4 Release the clip securing the fuel hose to the fuel injector and disconnect the hose, being prepared to catch any residual fuel **(see illustrations)**.

7.1 Remove the injector cover

7.2 Disconnect the injector wiring connector

7.3 Undo the screw and lift the injector off

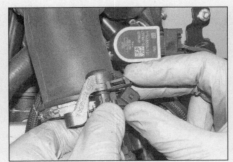

7.4a Release the clip…

7.4b …and disconnect the hose

7.5 Injector O-rings (arrowed)

8.3 Pull the hose unions out of the air ducts

8.4a Displace the reservoir...

8.4b ...it can be cable-tied to the handlebar

8.5a Air intake duct screw (arrowed)

8.5b Release the tabs (arrowed) and displace the ducts

5 Remove the O-rings from the injector, noting which fits where as they are slightly different sizes (and to help should be different colours, top black and bottom brown) **(see illustration)** – new ones must be used.
6 Modern fuels contain detergents which should keep the injectors clean and free of gum or varnish. If either injector is suspected of being blocked, flush it through with injector cleaner.

Installation

7 Installation is the reverse of removal, noting the following:
● Fit new O-rings onto each fuel injector – the top O-ring is black and the bottom one is brown **(see illustration 7.5)**.
● Make sure the injector is secure in the hose and the clip is slid fully across. Make sure the injector wiring connector is secure.

● Check that there are no leaks by turning the ignition on to pressurise the system.

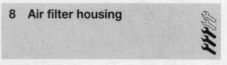

8 Air filter housing

Removal

1 Remove the fuel tank (see Section 2).
2 Release and remove the clamp securing the air duct to the top of the throttle body **(see illustration 6.10c)**, using the special pliers (BMW tool No. 131512) if available or water pump pliers if not **(see illustration 6.3)** – take care not to damage or distort the clamps.
3 Disconnect the air by-pass hose from each duct **(see illustration)**.

4 On GS, GS Adv and RT models undo the coolant reservoir screw and secure the reservoir upright clear of the air filter housing **(see illustrations)**.
5 On GS Adv and RT models undo the screw securing the air intake duct on each side **(see illustration)**. On RT models release the air intake duct tabs top and bottom and draw the ducts out of the air filter housing **(see illustration)**.
6 On GS Adv models undo the radiator bracket screws and remove the bracket for each radiator **(see illustration)**.
7 On R models disconnect the ambient air temperature sensor wiring connector **(see illustration)**.
8 Release the hoses from the back of the housing, noting their routing **(see illustration)**.
9 Release the clip securing the intake air

8.6 Radiator bracket screws (arrowed)

8.7 Ambient air temperature sensor connector (arrowed)

8.8 Release the hoses

8.9 Disconnect the IAT sensor wiring connector

8.10 Detach the breather hose

9.1 Remove the silencer cover

temperature sensor wiring connector and disconnect the connector **(see illustration)**.

10 Release the clamp securing the crankcase breather hose to the back of the air filter housing and detach the hose **(see illustration)**.

11 Undo the air filter housing screws and remove the washers, then lift the housing off **(see illustration 6.2)**.

Installation

12 Installation is the reverse of removal, noting the following:

● Make sure all hoses and wiring are correctly routed and secured.

● Secure the throttle body clamps with the clamp pliers to avoid damage.

9 Exhaust system

⚠ **Warning: If the engine has been running the exhaust system will be very hot. Allow the system to cool before carrying out any work.**

Silencer

Removal

1 Undo the silencer cover screws, noting the washer with the front screw on RT models, and remove the cover, on R and RS models noting how the front locates in the holder **(see illustration)**.

2 Loosen the nut on the clamp securing the silencer to the downpipe assembly and slide the clamp back **(see illustration)**.

3 Undo the silencer mounting bolt and remove it along with its shaped washer **(see illustration)** – on some GS and GS Adv models there is a second washer fitted on the inner side of the clamp mount, between it and the sub-frame.

4 Draw the silencer off **(see illustration)**.

5 Note the rubber bush and the collar inside the silencer clamp on GS and GS Adv models, and in the mount on the sub-frame on RT, R and RS models **(see illustration)**.

Installation

6 Check the condition of the rubber mounting grommet and replace it with a new one if necessary. Make sure the collar is fitted in the back of the grommet **(see illustration 9.5)**.

7 Clean the exhaust clamp and lubricate the inside surface with high-temperature assembly grease such as Copaslip. Fit the clamp over the end of the silencer front pipe.

8 Push the silencer over the end of the downpipe assembly and secure it to the rear sub-frame with the bolt and washer, not forgetting the inner washer between the clamp and the frame where removed on GS and GS Adv models **(see illustration 9.3)**. Tighten the bolt to the torque setting specified at the beginning of this Chapter.

9 Align the recess in the clamp with the tab on the downpipe and tighten the clamp nut to the specified torque setting **(see illustration)**.

Downpipe assembly

Removal

10 On GS and GS Adv models remove the sump guard, on RT models remove the engine

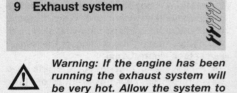

9.2 Loosen the silencer clamp nut

9.3 Undo the silencer bolt – note the inner washer fitted on some models

9.4 Draw the silencer off

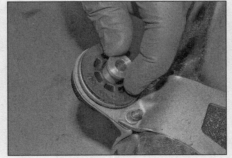

9.5 Note collar in the rubber bush

9.9 Make sure the clamp is correctly aligned

9.12a Remove the cover…

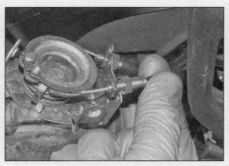

9.12b …then release the outer cables…

9.12c …and the cable ends

9.13a Release the connector…

9.13b …then disconnect it

covers, and on R and RS models remove the engine spoilers if fitted (see Chapter 7).

11 Remove the silencer (see above).

12 Undo the exhaust flow control valve cover screws and remove the cover **(see illustration)**. Note the location of each cable according to its nipple size in the pulley. Slacken the cable locknuts, release the outer cables from the brackets and the inner cable ends from the pulley **(see illustrations)**.

13 Release and disconnect the right-hand oxygen sensor wiring connector **(see illustrations)**. Disconnect the exhaust flow control valve servo wiring connector and release the wiring guide from the servo **(see illustration)**. Undo the servo mounting screw and remove the washer, then draw the servo out of the grommets and remove it along with the cables, noting the routing of the sensor wiring **(see illustrations)**.

14 Release and disconnect the left-hand oxygen sensor wiring connector **(see illustration)**. Feed the connector back to the sensor, noting the routing and releasing it from the cable-tie.

15 Place a support under the back of the downpipe assembly. Undo the servo/downpipe bracket screws **(see illustration)**.

16 Undo the nuts securing the downpipes to the cylinder heads, then remove the support,

9.13c Disconnect the servo wiring…

9.13d …then undo the screw…

9.13e …and remove the servo

9.14 Left-hand oxygen sensor wiring connector (arrowed)

9.15 Undo the two screws

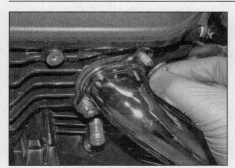

9.16a Undo the nuts...

9.16b ...and draw the pipes off the studs

9.17 Discard the old exhaust port gaskets

carefully draw the assembly down off the studs and remove it from under the bike (see illustrations).

17 Remove the old gaskets from the exhaust ports and discard them as new ones must be fitted (see illustration). Clean any corrosion off the cylinder head studs with a wire brush.

18 If required, remove the oxygen sensors (see Section 10).

Installation

19 Check the condition of the grommets in the servo/downpipe bracket and replace them with new ones if necessary (see illustration). Smear oil into the grommets. Fit the bracket onto the downpipe.

20 If removed, install the oxygen sensors (see Section 10).

21 Fit a new gasket into each exhaust port with the raised section facing up (see illustration). If required, apply a smear of grease to the gaskets to keep them in place whilst fitting the downpipe assembly. Lubricate the cylinder head studs with a smear of copper-based grease.

22 Manoeuvre the assembly into position, align the head of each downpipe with its exhaust port and slide them onto the studs (see illustration 9.16b). Tighten the nuts finger-tight (see illustration 9.16a).

23 Position the bracket and tighten the screws finger-tight (see illustration 9.15).

24 Tighten the nuts on the cylinder head studs evenly to the torque setting specified at the beginning of this Chapter.

25 Tighten the servo/downpipe bracket screws to the specified torque setting.

26 Fit the exhaust flow control valve servo and connect the wiring connectors for it and both oxygen sensors, and route and secure the connectors and wiring in a reverse of the removal procedure in Step 13.

27 Connect the control valve cables to the valve pulley – the lower cable from the servo is the opening cable and goes into the inner run and socket in the valve pulley (see illustration 9.12c). Fit the outer cables into the bracket and tighten the locknuts (see illustration 9.12b) – check that there is a small amount of free deflection in each cable,

9.19 Make sure the grommets are in good condition

so they are not holding the pulley off its stops. Clean the threads of the cover screws and apply some copper grease, then fit the cover (see illustration 9.12a).

28 Install the silencer.

29 Run the engine and check that there are no air leaks from the joints.

30 Install the remaining components in the reverse order of removal.

Exhaust flow control valve

Check

31 Remove the silencer (see above).

32 Note the position of the valve in the end

9.21 Fit the gasket with the raised section facing up

of the downpipe assembly, then turn the ignition ON to actuate the servo – it should move through its range then return to its start position. Turn the ignition OFF.

Removal

33 Follow the procedure in Steps 12 and 13 above to disconnect the cables from the valve pulley in the downpipe assembly and to remove the servo. Note that the valve pulley and valve are integral parts of the downpipe assembly.

34 To remove the cables from the servo undo the servo housing screws and remove the cover (see illustrations). Release the inner cable ends from their sockets and the cable

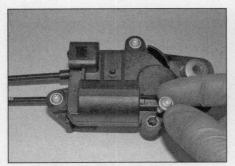

9.34a Undo the screws...

9.34b ...and remove the cover

9.34c Release the cable ends...

9.34d ...and the holders

holders from the housing and remove the cables **(see illustrations)**.

Installation

35 The cables have different size and colour nipples on each end – the silver nipples go onto the servo pulley, and the gold ones go onto the valve pulley. Match each cable to its location in the servo according to the size of its nipple and the nipple socket on the pulley. Fit the cable holders onto the servo housing and the cable ends into the pulley **(see illustrations 9.34d and c)**. Fit the cover, making sure it seats correctly over the cable holders, and tighten the screws.

36 Fit the servo and connect the cables to the valve pulley as described in the downpipe assembly installation procedure above. Check the operation of the valve as described above before fitting the silencer.

10 Catalytic converter and oxygen sensors

Warning: If the engine has been running the exhaust system will be very hot. Allow the system to cool before carrying out any work.

Catalytic converter

1 All models have a catalytic converter in the exhaust system to minimise the amount of pollutants that escape into the atmosphere. Hot exhaust gasses pass through the flow channels in the converter that are coated with a precious metal catalyst. The catalyst reduces nitrous oxides into nitrogen and oxygen, and oxidises unburned harmful hydrocarbons and carbon monoxide into water and carbon dioxide. The efficiency of the catalyst is reduced if the flow channels become clogged or if the precious metal coating becomes covered with carbon, lead or oil.

2 The catalytic converter is simple in operation and requires no maintenance, although the following precautions should be noted.

● Always use unleaded fuel – the use of leaded fuel will destroy the converter.
● Do not use any fuel or oil additives.
● Keep the fuel and ignition systems in good order.
● Handle the downpipe assembly with care when it is off the machine – the catalyst is fragile.

Oxygen sensors

3 The oxygen sensors measure exhaust gas oxygen content and relay this information to the ECU. The ECU compares exhaust gas oxygen content with the oxygen content in the ambient air and, depending on whether the engine is running rich or lean, adjusts the fuel/air mixture accordingly.

4 The sensors are threaded into the left and right-hand exhaust downpipes **(see illustration)**.

5 To remove a sensor, release and disconnect the sensor wiring **(see illustrations 9.13a or 9.14)**. Feed the wiring back to the sensor, noting its routing

6 Unscrew the sensor carefully to avoid damage to its tip. If the sensor threads are corroded, soak them with penetrating oil.

7 Deposits on the sensor tip are an indication of poor engine running – light rust coloured deposits indicate lead contamination through the use of the wrong fuel, black or dark brown deposits are a sign that oil is getting into the combustion chamber through worn valve stem seals or piston rings.

10.4 Right-hand oxygen sensor

8 A contaminated sensor will send an inaccurate signal to the ECU, which should, in turn, illuminate the engine warning light in the instrument cluster. Do not attempt to clean the sensor – if it is contaminated, a new one will have to be fitted.

9 Use a diagnostic tester (see Section 14) for further testing of the sensors.

10 Before installing the oxygen sensor, clean the threads and lubricate them with a smear of high temperature assembly grease. If the correct tool is available (it is a deep slotted socket that accommodates the wiring while allowing a torque wrench to be used), tighten the sensor to the torque setting specified at the beginning of this Chapter.

11 Make sure that the terminals in the wiring connector are clean and the connection is secure.

11 Ignition system checks

Warning: Refer to the Warning given in Section 1 before starting work.

1 As no means of adjustment is available, any failure of the system can be traced to failure of a system component or a simple wiring fault. Of the two possibilities, the latter is by far the most likely. In the event of failure, check the system in a logical fashion, as described below. Note: Before making any tests, check that the battery is in good condition and fully charged.

2 Ignition faults can be divided into two categories, namely those where the ignition system has failed completely, and those which are due to a partial failure. The likely faults are listed below, starting with the most probable source of failure. Work through the list systematically, referring to the subsequent sections for full details of the necessary checks and tests, where information is available.

● Loose, corroded or damaged wiring connections, broken or shorted wiring between any of the component parts of the ignition system (see Chapter 8).
● Faulty spark plug, dirty, worn or corroded plug electrodes, or incorrect gap between electrodes (see Chapter 1).
● Faulty ignition coil (Section 12).
● Faulty ignition switch or engine kill switch (see Chapter 8).
● Faulty starter interlock circuit (Section 13).
● Faulty engine control unit (ECU) (Section 14).
● Faulty crankshaft position sensor or camshaft position sensor (Section 16).

3 If the above checks don't reveal the cause of the problem, refer to Section 14

12 Ignition coils

 Warning: Refer to the Warning given in Section 1 before starting work.

1 Follow the relevant steps in the spark plug procedure in Chapter 1, to access the coil and pull it off the spark plug.

2 Check that the terminals inside the wiring connector are clean, then reconnect the wiring connector. Connect the coil to a new spark plug of the correct type and lay the plug on the cylinder head with the threads contacting it. If necessary, hold the plug in position with an insulated tool.

 Warning: Do not remove either of the spark plugs from the engine to perform this check – atomised fuel being pumped out of the open spark plug hole could ignite, causing severe injury!

3 Check that the kill switch is in the RUN position and the transmission is in neutral, then turn the ignition switch ON and turn the engine over on the starter motor. If the system is in good condition a regular, fat blue spark should be evident at the plug electrodes. If the spark appears thin or yellowish, or is non-existent, further investigation is necessary. Turn the ignition OFF. Repeat the check for the other coil.

4 The ignition system must be able to produce a spark that is capable of jumping a particular size gap. BMW provide no specification, but a healthy system should produce a spark capable of jumping at least 6 mm. A commercially available ignition spark gap tester tool will be required for this check **(see illustration)**.

5 Connect the coil to the protruding electrode on the test tool, and connect the tool to a good earth (ground) on the engine. Check that the kill switch is in the RUN position, turn the ignition switch ON and turn the engine over on the starter motor. If the system is in good condition a regular, fat blue spark should be seen to jump across the gap on the tool. Repeat the test for the other coils. If the test results are good the entire ignition system can be considered good.

6 If the spark at one plug appears thin or yellowish, or is non-existent, substitute the appropriate ignition coil from the other cylinder and test again. If the result is good it is likely the original coil is defective. If there is no improvement the fault lies with the ignition system.

7 Use a diagnostic tester (see Section 14) to determine conclusively that an ignition coil, or some other part of the ignition system, is defective.

8 Follow the procedure in Chapter 1, to install the ignition coil.

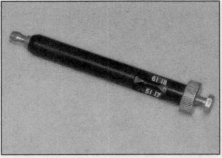

12.4 A commercially available spark gap test tool

13 Starter interlock circuit

1 Check the operation of the starter interlock system as follows:
- Position the bike on its centrestand. Make sure the transmission is in neutral, and the sidestand retracted (up), then start the engine. Pull in the clutch lever and select a gear. Extend the sidestand – the engine should stop as the sidestand is extended.
- Check that when the sidestand is extended (down), the engine can only be started if the transmission is in neutral.
- Make sure the engine is in neutral and the sidestand is extended (down). Start the engine, pull in the clutch lever and select a gear – the engine should cut out.
- Check that when the sidestand is retracted (up) and the transmission is in gear, the engine can only be started if the clutch lever is pulled in.

2 If the circuit does not operate as described, refer to Chapter 8 and check the operation of the sidestand switch, gear position sensor and clutch switch, and check the wiring between the switches and the engine control unit (ECU).

14 Engine management system and ECU – fault finding

1 For a general description of the system, see Section 1.

Diagnostic tester and fault identification

2 Fault diagnosis requires the use of BMW's dealer-only diagnostic equipment or an aftermarket tester such as the GS-911 tool with appropriate wifi interface.

3 The engine management system has in-built diagnostic functions which record and store all data should a fault occur. Recorded faults can then be checked using the diagnostic tester, which connects to the diagnostic plug

14.3 Diagnostic tester plug (arrowed) is next to the battery

next to the battery and analyses the data and identifies the exact fault **(see illustration)**.

4 Should a fault occur, the engine warning light in the instrument cluster illuminates. If this happens, the management system switches itself into 'limp home' mode, so that in theory you should not be left stranded. Depending on the problem, it is possible that you will notice no difference in the running of the motorcycle. However, BMW advise that in 'limp home' mode, full engine power may not be available and the machine should be ridden with this in mind.

5 In order to diagnose the problem and to turn the warning light off, the diagnostic tester is essential.

6 It is possible to perform certain tests and checks to identify a particular fault, but the difficulty is knowing in which part of the system the fault has occurred, and therefore where to start checking. Further details on the location and function of the individual sensors are given in the following Sections.

Fault finding

7 If a fault is indicated, first check the wiring and connectors to and from the ECU and the various sensors and all their related components. It may be that a connector is dirty or corroded or has come loose – a dirty or corroded terminal or connector will affect the resistance in that circuit, which will distort the information transmitted to the ECU, and therefore affect its control of the system. To deter corrosion, spray the wiring loom connector pins lightly with electrical contact cleaner.

8 A wire could be pinched and is shorting out – a continuity test of all wires from connector to connector will locate this. Albeit a fiddly and laborious task, the only way to determine any wiring faults is to systematically work through the wiring diagrams at the end of Chapter 8 and test each individual wire and connector for continuity – all wires are colour-coded. The wiring diagrams show the terminal number for each wire on the ECU – match these to the terminals on the ECU connectors when making the tests. Refer also to Chapter 8, Section 26.

15.3a Lift and remove the centre part of the clip...

15.3b ...then lift the front and remove the rubber holder...

15.3c ...and draw the ECU out of the rear holder

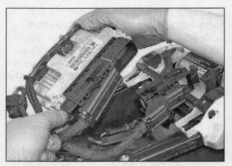

15.3d Pull the release catches out and disconnect the connectors

15.3e Release the clips...

15.3f...and lift the holder off

15 Control units

⚠️ *Warning: Refer to the Warning given in Section 1 before starting work.*

Caution: If a control unit is faulty, do not replace it with a second-hand one as this will cause problems with the other control units. Always have a new control unit replaced by a BMW dealer so the correct installation procedure can be carried out.

Removal

Main ECU

Note: *The ECU is also known as the DME (Digital Motor Electronics) unit.*

1 Remove the rider's seat (see Chapter 7).
2 Disconnect the battery negative (-) lead (see Chapter 8).
3 Release and remove the trim clip at the front, then displace the ECU, noting how it locates in the rubber holder at the back, and disconnect the wiring connectors **(see illustrations)**. Release the fuse holder clips from the underside of the ECU and displace the holder **(see illustrations)**.

Ground module

4 Remove the battery and the starter relay (see Chapter 8). Remove the fuel tank (Section 2).
5 Release the battery housing cover tabs and remove the cover **(see illustrations)**. Release the diagnostic connector from its clip, then

undo the screw and remove the clip **(see illustration)**. Remove the jump-start terminal cover, then undo the terminal and detach the lead **(see illustration)**. Release and displace the main relay **(see illustration)**. Cut the various cable ties securing the wiring loom around the battery tray, and release the trim clip securing

the wiring guide **(see illustrations)** – we only cut the three ties shown, but there are others that you may want to cut for extra freedom of movement. Cut the cable-tie securing the brake hose, then release the hose from the clip on the inside and move it to the rear **(see illustration)**. Release the rubber straps holding the battery

15.5a Release the tabs on the front side...

15.5b ...on the rear side...

15.5c ...and on the left-hand end...

15.5d ...and draw the cover out

15.5e Release the plug then undo the screw (arrowed) and remove the clip

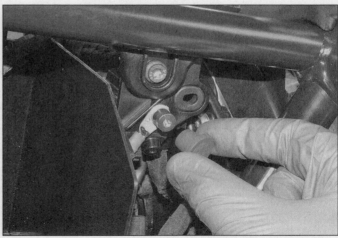

15.5f Remove the cover from the terminal, then unscrew the terminal

15.5g Release the main relay holder

15.5h Cut the cable-ties (arrowed)...

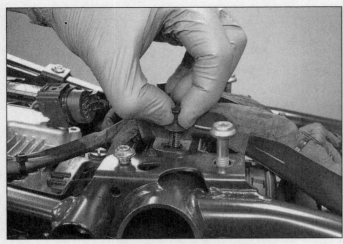

15.5i ...and release the trim clip

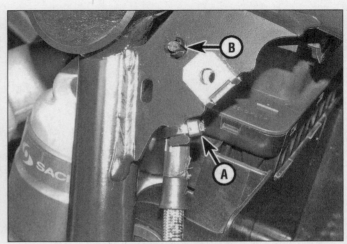

15.5j Cut the cable-tie (A) and release the brake hose clip (B)

15.5k Release the rubber straps

15.5l Undo the screw on each side

housing (see illustration). Undo the screw on each side (see illustration). Lift the housing to release the pegs from the grommets, then free the hoses from the clips and draw the housing out far enough for access to the ground module's wiring connector (see illustration).

6 Disconnect the wiring connector from the ground module then lift it out of the holder (see illustrations).

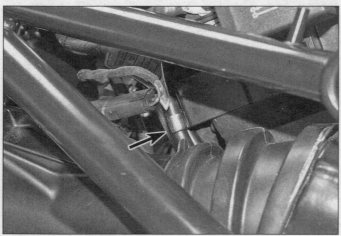

15.5m Release the hoses from the clip (arrowed)

15.6a The ground module is in the rear holder. Pull the catch and disconnect the wiring…

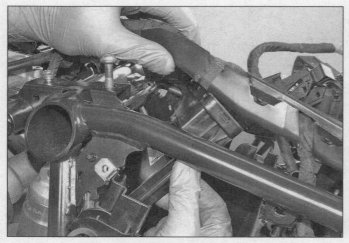

15.6b …then lift the ground module out

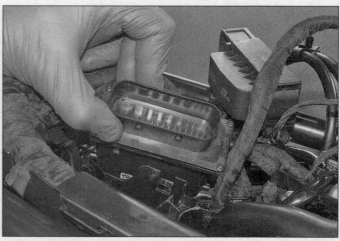

15.6c There may be another module in the left-hand end, according to OE equipment fitted

7 If required draw the housing out **(see illustration)**.

Installation

8 Installation is the reverse of removal, noting the following:

- Make sure that the terminals in the multi-pin connectors are clean and undamaged.
- Spray the connector pins lightly with electrical contact cleaner.
- Make sure the connectors are secure.

16 Sensors

⚠️ *Warning: Refer to the Warning given in Section 1 before starting work.*
Caution: Before disconnecting the wiring connector from any sensor, make sure the ignition is switched OFF, then disconnect the battery (see Chapter 8).

15.7 Remove the housing if required

1 No data is available for testing the sensors which supply data to the ECU. If a sensor is faulty, the engine warning light in the instrument cluster will illuminate. Use of a diagnostic tester (see Section 14) is required to identify the faulty component. Once the faulty component had been renewed, the fault code can be erased from the engine management system.

Crankshaft position sensor
Function

2 The sensor reads the position of the crankshaft and how fast it is turning; this information is used by the ECU to determine which cylinder is on its ignition stroke and when it should fire. The ECU combines engine speed with information from other sensors to determine fuelling and ignition requirements.

Removal and installation

3 The crankshaft position sensor is located on the top of the front crankcase cover **(see illustrations)**.

4 On GS and GS Adv models remove the right-hand side panel (see Chapter 7). Undo the radiator surround screw, then release the tabs along the top and remove the surround **(see illustration)**.

5 On RT models remove the right-hand fairing side panel (see Chapter 7). Displace the electrical unit, and where fitted the aerial connector, from the radiator cowl, then release the two trim clips and undo the four screws and remove the cowl **(see illustration)**.

16.3a Crankshaft position sensor and its screw (arrowed)...

16.3b... and wiring connector (arrowed)

16.4 Undo the screw (arrowed) and remove the surround

16.5 Displace the control unit and aerial connector (where fitted) from the cowl, then release the clips and undo the screws

16.11 Camshaft position sensor wiring connector and screw (arrowed)

16.21 Release the clip and draw the IAT sensor out, noting the O-ring (arrowed)

6 On R and RS models remove the radiator (see Chapter 3). Remove the air guides and heat shield as required for access to the sensor.
7 Release the wiring from its guide, then release and disconnect the connector **(see illustration 16.3b)**.
8 Undo the screw securing the sensor and pull it out **(see illustration 16.3a)**. Check the condition of the O-ring and replace it with a new one if necessary.
9 Installation is the reverse of removal, noting the following:
● Fit a new O-ring if necessary. Lubricate the O-ring with a smear of clean engine oil.
● Tighten the sensor screw to the torque setting specified at the beginning of this Chapter.
● Check the terminals in the wiring connector are clean.
● Make sure the wiring is securely connected and correctly routed.

Camshaft position sensor

Function

10 The sensor reads the position of the camshaft and how fast it is turning. This information is used by the ECU to determine which cylinder is on its ignition stroke and when it should fire.

Removal and installation

11 The camshaft position sensor is located in the underside of the left-hand cylinder head **(see illustration)**.
12 On RT models remove the left-hand engine cover (see Chapter 7).
13 Disconnect the sensor wiring connector – cut the cable-tie to release the wiring if required.
14 Undo the screw securing the sensor and pull it out. Check the condition of the O-ring

and replace it with a new one if necessary.
15 Installation is the reverse of removal, noting the points in Step 9.

Intake air temperature sensor

Function

16 The sensor reads the temperature of the air in the airbox. As changes in temperature affect air density, the ECU uses the information to determine fuelling requirements.

Removal and installation

17 The intake air temperature sensor is located in the right-hand side of the airbox just behind the air duct.
18 On GS, GS Adv, and RT models remove the fuel tank (Section 2).
19 On R models remove the right-hand side cover, and on RS models remove the right-hand fuel tank cover (see Chapter 7).
20 Release the clip securing the sensor wiring connector and disconnect the connector **(see illustration 8.9)**.
21 Release the clip securing the sensor in the airbox, then draw the sensor out, noting the O-ring **(see illustration)**.
22 Check the condition of the O-ring and replace it with a new one if necessary.
23 Installation is the reverse of removal, noting the relevant points in Step 9.

Engine oil level/temperature sensor

Function

24 The sensor warns if the oil level is low, and reads the temperature of the oil.

Removal and installation

25 The oil level/temperature sensor is covered in Chapter 2 Section 19.

Oxygen sensors

Function

26 The oxygen sensors measure exhaust gas oxygen content and the ECU uses the information to determine fuelling requirements.

Removal and installation

27 Refer to the procedure in Section 10 to remove and install the oxygen sensors.

Engine coolant temperature (ECT) sensor

Function

28 The ECT (engine coolant temperature) sensor is threaded into the coolant outlet union, which is on the top of the engine on the right-hand side at the front. The resistance of the sensor changes as engine coolant temperature changes. The information is sent to the ECU, which uses it to determine fuel and ignition requirements, and to run the temperature display in the instrument cluster according to model.

Removal and installation

29 The ECT sensor is covered in Chapter 3, Section 3.

Gear position sensor

Function

30 The sensor monitors the position of the selector drum, and therefore which gear is selected, and the ECU uses the information, combined with engine speed, to determine fuelling and ignition requirements.

Removal and installation

31 The gear position sensor is covered in Chapter 8, Section 14.

Chapter 5
Frame, suspension and final drive

Contents

Degrees of difficulty

Easy, suitable for novice with little experience	**Fairly easy,** suitable for beginner with some experience	**Fairly difficult,** suitable for competent DIY mechanic	**Difficult,** suitable for experienced DIY mechanic	**Very difficult,** suitable for expert DIY or professional

Specifications

Front suspension

Type
   R1200 GS, GS Adventure and RT . . . . BMW Telelever
   R1200 R and RS. . . . . Telescopic fork
Fork oil type (all models). . . . . BMW telescopic fork oil (10W)
Fork oil capacity
   R1200 GS and GS Adventure. . . . . 485 ml
   R1200 RT . . . . 545 ml
   R1200 R without ESA. . . . . 590 ml
   R1200 R with ESA
      Right-hand fork. . . . . 682 ml
      Left-hand fork . . . . 290 ml
   R1200 RS without ESA. . . . . 590 ml
   R1200 RS with ESA
      Right-hand fork. . . . . 682 ml
      Left-hand fork. . . . . 304 ml
Fork oil level (see text)
   R1200 GS and GS Adventure. . . . . 133 to 137 mm
   R1200 RT . . . . 88 to 92 mm
   R1200 R without ESA. . . . . 110 mm
   R1200 R with ESA
      Right-hand fork. . . . . 80 mm
      Left-hand fork. . . . . 75 mm
   R1200 RS without ESA. . . . . 110 mm
   R1200 RS with ESA
      Right-hand fork. . . . . 82 mm
      Left-hand fork. . . . . 65 mm
Fork tube runout limit . . . . 0.1 mm

Rear suspension

Type . . . . BMW Paralever

Final drive

Final drive oil type . . . . Castrol SAF-XO
Final drive oil capacity
   Initial filling . . . . 200 ml
   Oil change. . . . . 180 ml

Torque settings

Brake pedal pivot bolt	19 Nm
Final drive unit pivot bolt	100 Nm
Footrest bracket bolt for gearchange lever – R1200 RT	38 Nm
Front suspension and steering – R1200 GS, GS Adv and RT	
Steering head bearing stud bolt	130 Nm
Fork top stud nuts	40 Nm
Fork air bleed screw	2.5 Nm
Fork clamp bolts (bottom yoke)	19 Nm
Ball joint stud nut on bottom yoke	130 Nm
Shock absorber mounting bolts	56 Nm
Telelever pivot shaft bolt	120 Nm
Steering damper-to-bottom yoke nut	19 Nm
Steering damper-to-Telelever arm bolt	24 Nm
Front suspension and steering – R1200 R and RS	
Damper cartridge bolt – standard forks	25 Nm
Damper cartridge bolt – forks with ESA	30 Nm
Fork clamp bolts, top and bottom yokes	19 Nm
Fork top bolts	20 Nm
Steering stem bolt	130 Nm
Steering damper bolts	19 Nm
Steering head bearing adjuster nut using BMW service tools	15 Nm
Gearchange lever pivot bolt – R1200 GS, GS Adv, R and RS	19 Nm
Handlebar bolts	
R1200 GS, GS Adventure and R	
Handlebar clamp bolts	19 Nm
Handlebar end-weight bolts	38 Nm
R1200 RT	
Steering head bearing stud bolt	130 Nm
Fork top stud nuts	40 Nm
Handlebar end-weight bolts	19 Nm
R1200 RS	
Handlebar mounting bolts	19 Nm
Handlebar end-weight bolts	19 Nm
Rear brake master cylinder mounting bolts – R1200 RT	6 Nm
Rear suspension	
Paralever arm mounting bolts	56 Nm
Rear shock absorber mounting bolts	100 Nm
Swingarm right-hand bearing pin	
Initial setting	15 Nm
Final setting	7 Nm
Swingarm right-hand bearing pin locknut	145 Nm
Swingarm left-hand bearing pin	100 Nm
Sidestand pivot pin	40 Nm

1 General information

1 All models have a tubular steel frame that uses the engine as a stressed member.
2 On GS, GS Adventure, and RT models, front suspension and steering are managed separately by BMW's Telelever system. Telelever uses an arrangement of telescopic fork legs to support the front wheel and provide steering, together with a swingarm and shock absorber to provide suspension control – unlike conventional front forks, the Telelever forks contain neither damping mechanism nor springs, only oil to lubricate the friction surfaces.
3 At the top of the Telelever system, the fork inner tubes are held in a yoke, which is mounted to the frame via the steering head bearing.

Midway down the assembly, the fork outer tubes are bridged by the lower yoke which is attached to the front of the Telelever swingarm via a ball joint. The swingarm pivots around a shaft that passes through the front of the engine crankcases, with the shock absorber located between the swingarm and the frame.
4 On R and RS front suspension and steering are managed together by a conventional pair of telescopic forks mounted in two yokes that pivot in the steering head on the frame.
5 Rear suspension on all models is provided by a single-sided swingarm and centrally mounted shock absorber. The drive shaft to the rear wheel is housed inside the swingarm. The joint between the swingarm and the final drive unit is pivoted, with a link arm, BMW's Paralever system, controlling movement between the two. The Paralever system counteracts the adverse effect of the shaft drive on suspension movement.

2 Frame

1 The frame should not require attention unless accident damage has occurred. In most cases, fitting a new frame is the only satisfactory remedy for such damage. A few frame specialists have the jigs and other equipment necessary for straightening a frame to the required standard of accuracy, but even then there is no simple way of assessing to what extent the welded joints in the frame may have been over-stressed.
2 A frame that is out of alignment (bent) will cause handling problems. If misalignment is suspected, first check the wheel alignment (see Chapter 6).
3 Loose bolts can cause ovaling or fracturing of the frame mountings. On a high mileage

bike, the frame should be examined closely for signs of cracking or splitting at the welded joints. Minor damage can often be repaired by welding, depending on the extent and nature of the damage, but this is a task for an expert. Always remove the battery, the main ECU and the basic control module, any other electronic control units according to fitment, and the instrument cluster before using electric welding equipment. Frames on which the coating has come off to expose bare metal that is rusting can be blasted and re-coated.

3 Footrests, brake pedal and gearchange lever

Footrests

R1200 GS and GS Adventure

1 The front footrest rubber can be removed for greater grip on the footrest when riding off-road, and both front and rear footrest rubbers can be replaced with new ones if worn, without having to remove the footrest. The front rubber has pegs on its underside that locate in holes – pull the rubber up off the footrest **(see illustration)**. The rear rubber has a single locating peg – pull the outer end of the rubber up, release the peg then draw the rubber off the footrest, noting how the inner plate fits **(see Illustration 3.3)**.

2 To remove the rider's footrests, remove the E-clip from the bottom of the footrest pivot pin, then withdraw the pivot pin and remove the return spring and sleeve, and the footrest **(see illustration)** – note how the spring ends locate on the footrest and in the mounting bracket **(see illustration)**.

3 To remove the passenger footrests, remove the E-clip from the bottom of the footrest pivot pin, then withdraw the pivot pin and remove the footrest **(see illustration)**.

R1200 RT

4 Front and rear footrest rubbers can be replaced with new ones if worn, without having to remove the footrest. The rubbers are shaped to seat over the shaped end of the footrest – pull the outer end of the rubber up to release it then draw the rubber off the footrest, noting how the inner plate fits.

5 To remove the rider's footrests, remove the E-clip from the bottom of the footrest pivot pin, then remove the collar and return spring, noting how its ends locate **(see illustration 3.1)**. Withdraw the pivot pin and remove the footrest.

6 To remove the passenger footrests, remove the E-clip from the bottom of the footrest pivot pin, then withdraw the pivot pin and remove the footrest **(see illustration 3.3)**.

R1200 R and RS

7 Front and rear footrest rubbers can be replaced with new ones if worn, without having to remove the footrest – undo the two screws on the underside and remove the rubber **(see illustration)**. There is a threaded retainer plate inside the rubber – the new rubber comes with it. Either use new screws, or clean the threads of the original ones and apply some fresh threadlock. If the rubbers are riveted on (as factory fitted on some models) you need to drill the rivets out to remove the rubber, then buy the screws along with the new rubber, and then you may have to drill the holes in the footrest out to accommodate the screws, depending on their size relative to the size of the rivet.

8 To remove the rider's footrests, remove the E-clip from the bottom of the footrest pivot pin, then withdraw the pivot pin and remove the footrest and return spring, noting how its ends locate **(see illustration)**.

9 To remove the passenger footrests, remove the E-clip from the bottom of the footrest pivot pin, then withdraw the pivot pin **(see illustration 3.7)**. Ease the footrest out of the holder, noting that there is a detent ball and spring fitted in the footrest that will spring out unless you take care to cover the inner end with your fingers as you remove it. Remove the detent plate from the footrest holder if required.

Installation

10 Installation is the reverse of removal. Lubricate the pivot pin and sliding surfaces. Make sure the return spring ends are correctly located where applicable. Use new E-clips if necessary.

3.1 Pull the rubber up to release the locating pegs

3.2a Remove the E-clip (arrowed) to release the pivot pin

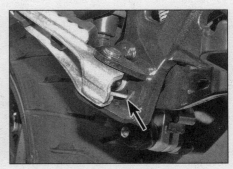

3.2b Note how the spring end locates in the hole (arrowed)

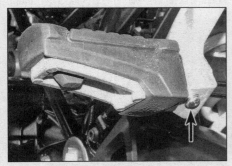

3.3 Remove the E-clip (arrowed) to release the pivot pin

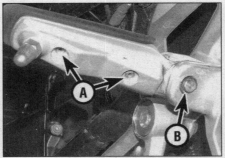

3.7 Screws or rivets (A) secure the footrest rubbers. Passenger footrest pivot pin E-clip (B)

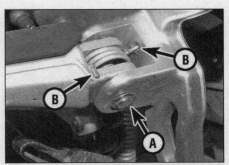

3.8 Remove the E-clip (A) to release the pivot pin – note how the spring ends (B) locate

3.12 Remove the split pin and washer (A) then withdraw the clevis pin (B)

3.13 Remove the spring (arrowed)

3.14 The pivot bolt threads into the pivot bush (arrowed), that fits into the inner side of the pedal

3.20 Unhook the spring (arrowed)

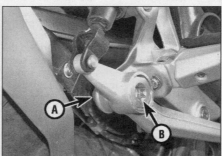

3.21 Hold the bolt (A) and unscrew the pivot bush (B)

Installation

22 Installation is the reverse of removal, noting the following:

- Lubricate the pedal pivot with a smear of grease.
- Make sure the spring ends are correctly positioned.
- Tighten the pivot bolt to the torque setting specified at the beginning of this Chapter.
- Secure the clevis pin using a new split pin and bend its ends round to lock it.
- On GS and GS Adventure models make sure there is a 1 mm gap between the top of the pedal shank and the bottom of the bracket so there is no pressure in the brake master cylinder with the pedal at rest **(see illustration)** – the gap is preset at the factory so unless the position of the clevis on the pushrod has been altered for some reason the gap should be there. If there is no gap, slacken the locknut above the clevis, then turn the pushrod clockwise using the hex at its upper end to reduce the effective length of the pushrod and so draw the pedal down away from the bracket **(see illustration)**. Tighten the locknut.

Brake pedal

R1200 GS and GS Adventure

11 Remove the footrest (see above).
12 Straighten the ends of the split pin and remove it and the washer **(see illustration)**. Withdraw the clevis pin and separate the pushrod from the brake pedal.
13 Unhook and remove the pedal return spring **(see illustration)**.
14 Counter-hold the pivot bush on the inner side and undo the bolt, noting its washer, then remove the pedal, collecting the washer between it and the footrest holder **(see illustration)**.

R1200 RT

15 Separate the pushrod from the brake pedal (see Step 12).
16 Unhook and remove the pedal return spring.

17 Undo the pivot bolt and remove the pedal, collecting the washer that fits between it and the bracket. Remove the pivot bush from the pedal.

R1200 R and RS

18 Refer to Chapter 4 Section 9 and remove the silencer cover and the exhaust flow control valve cover.
19 Separate the pushrod from the brake pedal (see Step 12).
20 Unhook and remove the pedal return spring **(see illustration)**.
21 Counter-hold the bolt on the inner side and undo the pivot bush, then remove the pedal, collecting the washer between it and the bracket **(see illustration)**. Note the washer fitted with the pivot bolt. There is an inner bush in the pedal that can be removed and replaced with a new one if worn.

Gearchange lever

Removal

23 On GS, GS Adv, R and RS models, counter-hold the bolt on the inner side and undo the pivot bush, then displace the lever, collecting the washer between it and the bracket, and noting the washer with the bolt **(see illustration)**.

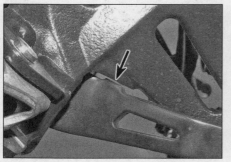

3.22a Make sure there is a gap (arrowed) between pedal and bracket

3.22b Loosen the locknut (arrowed) and adjust the pushrod

3.23 Hold the bolt and unscrew the pivot bush

3.25a Release the clip from around the rod...

3.25b ...then draw it out of the head...

3.25c ...and pull the head off the ball joint. Note the protective bush fitted behind the balljoint head

Release and remove the linkage rod retaining clip and detach the lever from the rod **(see illustrations 3.25a, b and c)**. There is an inner bush in the lever that can be removed and replaced with a new one if worn.

24 On RT models release and remove the linkage rod retaining clip and detach the rod from the lever **(see illustrations 3.25a, b and c)**. Unscrew the footrest bracket bolt and remove the footrest/lever/bracket assembly, collecting the washer that fits between the lever and the frame. Remove the lever from its pivot, and remove the washer that fits between the lever and the footrest bracket.

25 If required detach the linkage rod from the linkage arm or gearshift assist unit (as fitted) in the same way as detaching it from the lever **(see illustrations)**.

26 On models with a standard gearchange lever, note the alignment of the gearchange linkage arm on the shaft, then slacken the pinch bolt and draw the arm off.

27 On models with gearshift assist unscrew the bolt securing the gearshift assist unit and remove the washer. Pull the unit off and disconnect the wiring, then remove the sleeve from the shaft if it doesn't come with the unit. If you can't pull the unit off thread the BMW tool 230831 or a bolt to fit the outer threads in the unit (not the inner threads in the shaft) into the hole and keep turning it to draw the unit off the shaft, and when clear disconnect the wiring connector. Remove the sleeve from the shaft. Note that BMW specify to fit a new sleeve when installing the unit later.

Installation

28 Installation is the reverse of removal, noting the following:
- Clean any corrosion off the gearchange shaft splines and smear them with grease.
- On models with a standard gearchange lever align the wide splines and the slit in the linkage arm clamp with the lines on the shaft, slide the lever on and tighten the pinch bolt.
- On models with gearshift assist slide a new sleeve into the unit so it is flush, aligning the wide splines (it can only fit one way). Clean the threads of the bolt, and inside the shaft using the correct tap. Apply some

3.26 Marks on shaft align with slot in linkage arm, and there is a wide spline so the arm can only be fitted in one position

fresh threadlock to the bolt. Reconnect the wiring, then align the unit on the shaft, fit the bolt with its washer and tighten the bolt to push the unit on.
- Clean all old grease off the lever pivot, off the ball joint heads on the lever and linkage arm or gearshift assist unit, and from inside the sockets in the linkage rod.
- Make sure the ball joint heads are tight.
- Make sure the protective bushes are fitted behind the heads of the ball joints in the lever and linkage arm or gearshift assist unit **(see illustration 3.25c)**.
- Lubricate the ball joint heads and sockets and the pedal pivot with a smear of grease.
- Use new retaining clips to secure the linkage rod if necessary.
- On GS, GS Adv, R and RS models tighten the pivot bolt to the torque setting specified at the beginning of this Chapter.
- On RT models clean the threads of the footrest bracket bolt and apply some fresh threadlock, and tighten the bolt to the torque setting specified at the beginning of the Chapter.

Lever adjustment

29 On models with an adjustable toe-piece, slacken the screw on the top of the lever end and rotate the toe-piece until it is in the desired position, then tighten the screw.
30 On all models, the height of the lever can be adjusted slightly by holding the hex in the middle of the linkage rod and slackening the locknut on each end, then turning the rod

3.30 Slacken the nuts (arrowed) and turn the rod as required within the limits

using the hex **(see illustration)** – the rod is reverse-threaded on one end so turning it one way increases its length and so lowers the lever, and turning it the other shortens it and so raises the lever. To ensure there are always enough threads left to hold the linkage rod securely BMW specify a maximum length of the linkage rod measured between the centres of the ball joint sockets – on GS models it is 107 mm, on RT models it is 124 mm, and on R and RS models it is 145 mm. Tighten the locknuts after making any adjustment.

4 Stands

1 Lubricating the stand pivots is part of routine maintenance (see Chapter 1).
2 Make sure the stand springs (there are 2 on each stand) are in good condition and capable of holding the stand fully retracted when not in use. A broken or weak spring is an obvious safety hazard – always renew a spring that is damaged or has sagged.
3 Before removing a stand, make sure the machine is securely supported, either on its other stand or using an auxiliary stand, and tie the front brake lever to the handlebar so the front wheel is locked.

Centre stand

4 With the centre stand retracted, unhook the

4.4 The springs hook onto the plates that hook over the lugs on the frame and stand

4.5 Centrestand pivot bushes are secured by circlips (arrowed)

4.11 Note how the springs hook up on each end

stand springs and remove them along with the spring plates – a spring hook located in one of the holes in the spring plate is a useful tool to do this (see illustration). If you don't have a spring hook or similar, lower the centre stand to the point at which the springs are most stretched, then fit washers between the coils so when the stand is retracted again the springs are unable to close up so much, making them easier to remove.

5 Remove the circlip on the outer end of each pivot bush (see illustration). Support the stand and push each bush out from the outside.

6 Inspect the stand, pivot holes and bushes for signs of wear and replace any components with new ones as necessary. Replace the circlips with new ones if they distorted on removal.

7 Clean the bushes and the bush holes in the frame, and lubricate the bushes with grease.

8 Position the stand and insert the bushes

from the inner side of each pivot. Secure each bush with its circlip, using new ones if necessary and making sure they are secure in the groove all round (see illustration 4.5).

9 Hook up the stand springs, making sure the ends are securely located with the spring plates under the heads of the posts (see illustration 4.4).

10 Check the operation of the stand before riding the motorcycle.

Sidestand

11 With the sidestand retracted, unhook the stand springs and remove them along with the spring plate (see illustration) – a spring hook is a useful tool to do this. If you don't have a spring hook or similar, lower the sidestand to the point at which the springs are most stretched, then fit washers between the coils so when the stand is retracted again the springs are unable to close up so much, making them easier to remove. Alternatively,

and with care, you can leave the springs hooked up while displacing the stand and unhook them once the stand is free and there is no tension in the springs.

12 Displace the sidestand switch, on early GS models by releasing the two circlips and removing the washer, and on all other models by undoing the screw, then lift the switch off the pivot pin, noting how the slot in the body locates over the tab or pin on the bracket, and how the pin on the back locates in the offset hole in the stand (see illustration). Note that new circlips should be used on early GS models.

13 Unscrew the pivot pin and remove the stand, then unhook the springs if not already done (see illustrations).

14 Clean off all old grease and check all components for wear damage – in particular look for wear in the pivot pin and the bushes in the bracket, and replace them with new ones if necessary.

15 On installation, clean the threads of the pivot pin and apply a suitable non-permanent thread locking compound. Lubricate the pivot bushes and pin with grease. Position the stand, hooking the springs up now if required, fit the pivot pin and tighten it to the torque setting specified at the beginning of this Chapter.

16 If not already done hook up the stand springs, making sure the ends are securely located with the spring plate under the head of the post (see illustration 4.11).

17 Fit the sidestand switch, locating the pin on its back in the hole in the stand (see illustration), and the slot in the body over

4.12 Undo the screw and displace the switch

4.13a Unscrew the pivot pin...

4.13b...slide the stand off the bracket...

4.13c ...and unhook the springs

4.17 Locate the pin in the hole

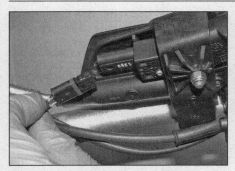

5.5a Release the connector from the catch on the underside

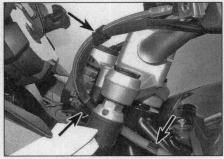

5.5b Release the wiring from the clips (arrowed)

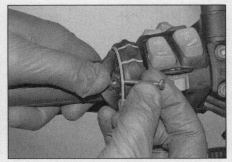

5.5c Undo the screw...

the pin **(see illustration 4.12)**. On early GS models secure the switch with the washer and two new circlips, making sure each locates correctly. On all other models clean the threads of the switch screw and apply some fresh threadlock, and secure the switch with the screw.

18 Check the operation of the starter interlock system (see Chapter 4 Section 13).

19 Check the operation of the stand before riding the motorcycle.

5 Handlebars and levers

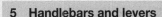

5.5d ...release the catches and remove the cover...

5.5e ...and slide the assembly off

Handlebars

Note 1: *The handlebars can be displaced without having to remove the lever or switch assemblies – take care to avoid straining the handlebar wiring and support or tie the handlebar assembly using rags to cushion it and anything it sits against. Wrap the master cylinders with rag in case of leakage. It is advisable to remove any painted panels as required according to model to prevent possible damage if components are being displaced rather than removed, and in case a tool should slip (see Chapter 7).*

Note 2: *The machines covered in this manual were available from new fitted with a range of optional electrical extras. When working on your machine, take care to ensure that all relevant electrical components are disconnected on disassembly and subsequently reconnected during the rebuild. Always take the precaution of disconnecting the battery negative (-) terminal before disconnecting an electrical wiring connector.*

R1200 GS, GS Adventure and R

1 Disconnect the battery negative lead (see Chapter 8). Remove the mirrors, and where fitted the hand protectors (see Chapter 7).

2 On models without hand protectors unscrew the end-weight bolts and remove the weights **(see illustration 5.21)**.

3 Where fitted displace the SatNav holder and rest it to one side on some rag **(see illustration 5.20a)** – cut the cable-tie securing

the wiring if required. Undo the SatNav holder bracket screws and displace/remove the brackets **(see illustration 5.20b)**.

4 Follow the procedure in Chapter 2 Section 21 and displace the clutch master cylinder – there is no need to disconnect the clutch hose. Secure the reservoir upright and make sure no strain in placed on the hose.

5 Disconnect the clutch switch wiring connector **(see illustration)**. Release the handlebar switch wiring from the clips **(see illustration)**. Pull the inner end of the grip back to reveal the screw and undo it **(see illustration)**. Release the connector cover from the housing **(see illustration)**. Slide the handlebar grip/switch housing assembly off the handlebar **(see illustration)**. If required

refer to Chapter 8 to separate the switch housing from the grip.

6 Follow the procedure in Chapter 6 and displace the front brake master cylinder – there is no need to disconnect the brake hose. Secure the reservoir upright and make sure no strain in placed on the hose.

7 Follow the procedure in Chapter 8 and remove the right-hand switch housing. Undo the throttle twistgrip screw and slide the twistgrip off the handlebar **(see illustration)**.

8 On GS and GS Adv models note the alignment of the marks on the front of the handlebar with the mating surfaces of the right-hand holder and clamp **(see illustration)**. On R models note the alignment of the marks on the back of the handlebar

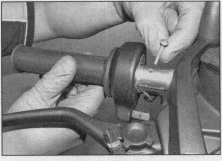

5.7 Twistgrip is secured by a screw

5.8a Handlebar alignment marks – GS models

5.8b Handlebar alignment marks – R models

5.8c Handlebar clamp bolts (arrowed) – GS models

with the gap between the each handlebar holder and clamp (see illustration). Loosen the handlebar clamp bolts (see illustration). Support the handlebars and remove the clamps, then lift the handlebars off.

9 Installation is the reverse of removal, noting the following:

● On GS and GS Adv models, make sure the handlebars are central in the holders using the vertical lines on the front of the handlebar, and set the reach using the horizontal lines, with both being set in relation to the mating surfaces of the holder and clamp, either as noted on removal or as required (see illustration 5.8a) – the upper horizontal line is set as a standard for riding off-road in the standing position, and the lower line is set as a standard for normal seated riding, but really these positions will depend on arm length and rider preference and riding style as well as intended use.

● On R models, make sure the handlebars are central in the holders using the vertical lines on the back of the handlebar, and set the horizontal lines in the gaps between the holders and clamps (see illustration 5.8b).

● Tighten the front clamp bolts first, then the rear, so the gap is at the back of the clamp, and tighten them to the torque setting specified at the beginning of the Chapter.

● Refer to the relevant Chapters as directed for installation and alignment of the various handlebar assemblies. Make sure all wiring connectors are securely reconnected.

● On models without hand protectors tighten the end-weight bolts to the specified torque setting.

R1200 RT

10 Place the bike on its centre stand. Disconnect the battery negative lead (see Chapter 8). Unscrew the end-weight bolts and remove weights (see illustration 5.21).

11 Refer to Steps 4 to 7 above to displace or remove the handlebar mounted assemblies.

12 The handlebars are an integral part of the top yoke. Carefully lever the badge from the centre of the yoke.

13 Take the weight off the front wheel either using a jack and block of wood under the engine, or by tying the rear of the bike down.

14 Disconnect the wiring connector(s) from the ignition switch or keyless ride unit, as fitted. Release the wire from its guide.

15 Carefully prise out the fork top caps (see illustration 6.6). Counter-hold the fork top bolt underneath the yoke and unscrew the nut from the top of the stud (see illustration 6.7). Pull each fork inner tube down out of its bearing in the yoke (see illustration 6.8b).

16 Unscrew the bearing stud bolt and lift the handlebar/yoke assembly off.

17 If required refer to Chapter 8 and remove the ignition switch or keyless ride unit, and to Section 8 and remove the steering head bearing and fork top bushes.

18 Installation is the reverse of removal, noting the following:

● Clean the threads of the steering head bearing stud bolt and apply some fresh

threadlock. Tighten the bolt to the torque setting specified at the beginning of the Chapter.

● Clean the threads of the fork top studs and apply some fresh threadlock. Tighten the stud nuts to the torque setting specified at the beginning of the Chapter.

● Refer to the relevant Chapters as directed above for installation and alignment of the various handlebar assemblies. Make sure all wiring connectors are securely reconnected.

● Tighten the end-weight bolts to the specified torque setting.

R1200 RS

19 Disconnect the battery negative lead (see Chapter 8).

20 Where fitted displace the SatNav holder and rest it to one side on some rag (see illustration) – cut the cable-tie securing the wiring if required. Undo the SatNav holder bracket screws and displace/remove the brackets (see illustration).

21 Unscrew the end-weight bolts and remove the weights (see illustration).

22 Refer to Steps 4 to 7 above to remove or displace the handlebar mounted assemblies.

23 Unscrew the bolts securing the handlebars and lift the handlebars off.

24 Installation is the reverse of removal, noting the following:

● Tighten the handlebar mounting bolts to the torque setting specified at the beginning of the Chapter.

● Refer to the relevant Chapters as directed above for installation and alignment of the various handlebar assemblies. Make sure all wiring connectors are securely reconnected.

● Tighten the end-weight bolts to the specified torque setting.

Levers

25 Follow the procedure in Chapter 2, Section 21, to remove and install the clutch lever.

26 Follow the procedure in Chapter 6 Section 5 to remove and install the front brake lever.

27 To adjust the lever span, refer to Chapter 1 Section 7 or 8.

5.20a Undo the screw on each side and displace the SatNav holder from the brackets…

5.20b …then undo the bracket screws (arrowed)

5.21 Handlebar end-weight bolt (arrowed)

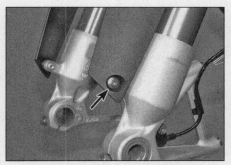

6.4 Undo the screw (arrowed) on the relevant side

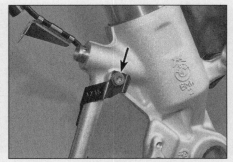

6.5 ABS sensor wire guide screw (arrowed)

6.6 Prise off the fork top cap

6 Front suspension – GS, GS Adventure and RT models

Fork leg

Removal

Note: *Unlike a conventional telescopic fork leg, the fork inner tube is not secured in the outer tube by the fork bushes or damper rod. When removing the fork leg, take care not to pull the inner tube out accidentally. If the inner tube and outer tube are separated, new oil seals must be fitted.*

1 Position the bike on its centre stand or support it securely on an auxiliary stand. Work can be made easier by raising the machine to a suitable working height on an hydraulic ramp or a suitable platform. Make sure the machine is secure and will not topple over.

2 On RT models, for best access remove the fairing side panels (see Chapter 7).

3 Remove the front wheel (see Chapter 6).

4 Undo the screw securing the bottom of the front mudguard to the fork leg **(see illustration)**.

5 Undo the screw securing the ABS sensor wire guide to the left-hand fork **(see illustration)**. Secure the sensor clear of the fork, noting the routing of the wire.

6 Carefully prise out the fork top cap **(see illustration)**.

7 Counter-hold the fork top bolt and unscrew the nut from the top of the stud **(see illustration)** – depending on the tools available you may need to displace the handlebars from the yoke on GS models (Section 5). Slide the fork inner tube down until the stud is clear of the bush **(see illustration 6.26a)**.

8 Loosen the clamp bolts in the bottom yoke **(see illustration)**. Note the routing of all cables and wiring around the forks, then slide the fork leg down and out through the yoke **(see illustration)**.

Overhaul

Note: *The fork seal kit comes with both seals for both forks along with new washers and retaining clips. The fork bushes in the top yoke are covered in Section 8.*

9 Undo the air bleed screw **(see illustration)** – check the condition of its O-ring and replace it with a new one if necessary.

10 Support the fork leg upright and withdraw the inner tube from the outer tube **(see illustration)**. Drain the oil in the outer tube into a suitable container **(see illustration)**. **Note:** *Do not loosen the bolt in the bottom of the outer tube – it is not a drain plug.*

6.7 Counter-hold the fork top bolt and undo the nut

6.8a Loosen the clamp bolts in the bottom yoke...

6.8b ...then slide the fork leg down and out

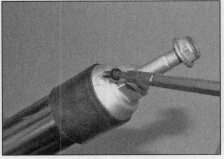

6.9 Undo the air bleed screw

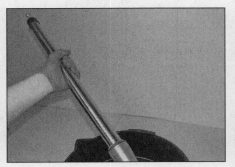

6.10a Slide the inner tube out...

6.10b ...then tip the oil from the outer tube

6.11 Use a flat-bladed screwdriver to prise out the dust seal

6.12 Remove the retaining clip

6.13a Seat the adapter under the seal...

6.13b ...then fit the slide-hammer...

6.13c ...and jar the seal out

6.13d Remove the oil seal washer

11 Carefully prise out the dust seal **(see illustration)**.

12 Carefully prise the oil seal retaining clip out of its groove **(see illustration)**.

13 To remove the oil seal you need an internal expanding puller with slide-hammer attachment – select the correct adapter and locate it behind the seal, then tighten the nut to expand it so it is tight, but make sure it does not expand so much that it contacts the inner wall of the tube **(see illustration)**. Fit the slide-hammer attachment then jar the seal out

(see illustrations) – note which way up it is fitted. Remove the washer **(see illustration)**.

14 If the fork inner tube is thought to be bent, check it for runout using V-blocks and a dial gauge **(see illustration)**. If the amount of runout exceeds the service limit specified, the tube must be replaced with a new one.

 Warning: If either fork tube is bent, it should not be straightened; replace both fork tubes with new ones.

15 If, when the fork oil was drained, it contained metallic particles, wear has been

taking place on the bushes. Slide the inner tube into the outer tube and check for play between the two. If there is any play, the bushes are worn. The bushes are located inside the outer tube. You should be able to draw the top bush out using your fingers **(see illustration)**. If it is tight remove it using an internal expanding knife-edge puller with slide-hammer in the same way as the oil seal. Remove the three top spacers, the bottom bush and the two bottom spacers – you can draw the first spacer out with your fingers, and

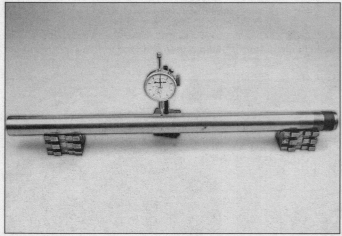

6.14 Check the inner tube runout using V-blocks and a dial gauge

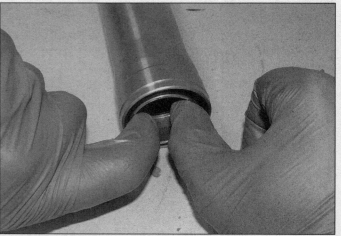

6.15a Remove the top bush and spacer with your fingers...

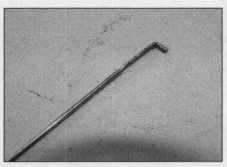

6.15b ...then shape a hook onto the end of a piece of wire...

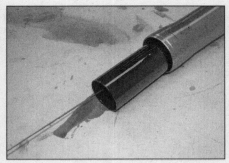

6.15c ...and use it draw out the spacers...

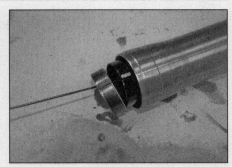

6.15d ...and the bottom bush and spacers

for the rest use a piece of wire bent over at the end to hook them out **(see illustrations)**.

16 Clean all the oil of the bushes and spacers and check them for wear and damage **(see illustration)** – if the grey (Teflon) coating has worn off the inner surfaces of the bushes replace them with new ones.

17 Fit the two bottom spacers, the new bottom bush, and the three top spacers into the outer tube, pushing the fitted parts down the tube with the next part being fitted until all are in and all the way down **(see illustrations)**. Fit the top bush into the top of the tube and push it in, all the way onto its seat if possible, then seat the washer on it **(see illustrations)** – if you can't seat the bush with finger pressure drive it onto its seat using a suitable driver or socket that bears fully on the washer but does not contact the wall of the tube – BMW make

tools for this if required, Nos. 234660 and 005500. Remove the washer and check the bush is fully seated.

6.16 Check the working surface of each bush

18 Fit the new oil seal and push or tap it into place using a 33 mm socket or driver **(see illustrations)**.

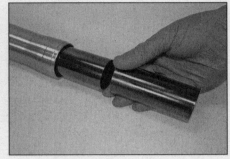

6.17a Slide in the two bottom spacers...

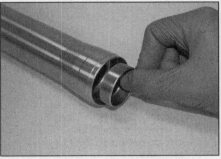

6.17b ...the bottom bush...

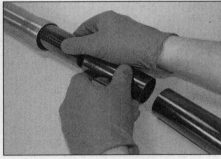

6.17c ...and the three top spacers...

6.17d...then fit the top bush...

6.17e ...and the washer

6.18a Make sure the seal is the correct way up

6.18b Using a socket to push the seal in

6.19 Fit the retaining clip into the groove

6.20 Slide the seal onto the bottom of the tube, making sure it is the correct way up

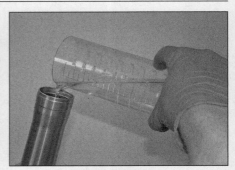

6.21a Add the oil...

6.21b ...and check the level

6.22 Make sure the inner tube is parallel to the outer tube to avoid distorting the seal lips

6.23 Press the seal into the top of the outer tube

19 When the seal is correctly seated, the groove for the retaining clip will be visible above the seal. Fit the new clip, making sure it is correctly located in its groove **(see illustration)**.
20 Slide the dust seal onto and up the inner tube **(see illustration)**.
21 Refill the outer tube with the type and amount of oil specified at the beginning of the Chapter for your model, then measure the oil level from the top of the tube and add or remove oil as required until the level is as specified **(see illustrations)**.
22 Insert the inner tube fully into the outer tube **(see illustration)**.
23 Slide the dust seal down the fork tube and press it into position **(see illustration)**.

24 Fit the O-ring onto the air bleed screw if removed, using a new one if necessary, then thread the screw loosely in so air can bleed **(see illustration 6.9)**.

Installation

25 Clean any dirt and corrosion off the fork outer tubes and the inside of the bottom yoke. Clean the threads of the top stud. If the air bleed screw in the top of the fork has not already been loosened, do so now. Check the condition of its O-ring and replace it with a new one if it is damaged or has deteriorated.
26 Slide the fork up through the bottom yoke as far as it will go (there is a ridge that butts up against the underside of the yoke), making

sure all cables, hoses and wiring are correctly routed, then lightly tighten the clamp bolts in the bottom yoke **(see illustrations 6.8b and a)**. Slide the inner tube up so the stud on its top goes into the bush in the top yoke, twisting it as required so the air bleed screw faces out **(see illustration)**. Apply some fresh threadlock to the stud, then fit the stud nut **(see illustration)**. Counter-hold the top bolt, and tighten the nut to the torque setting specified at the beginning of the Chapter **(see illustration 6.7)**. Fit the other fork if removed. Fit the handlebars if displaced on GS models. Fit the fork top caps **(see illustration)**.
27 Loosen the clamp bolts in the bottom yoke and slide the axle through the bottom

6.26a Slide the stud up into the bush...

6.26b ...and fit the nut

6.26c Push the caps into the yoke

of both forks so they are correctly aligned **(see illustration)**. Now tighten the clamp bolts in the bottom yoke to the torque setting specified at the beginning of this Chapter, tightening each of them alternately several times to counter the effect of the offset.
28 Tighten the air bleed screws.
29 Fit the mudguard screw(s) and ABS sensor wire guide **(see illustrations 6.4 and 6.5)**. Install the front wheel (see Chapter 6), and on RT models the fairing side panels if removed (see Chapter 7).

Shock absorber
Removal
Note: *On machines equipped with electronic suspension adjustment (ESA), the operation of the ESA should be checked with front and rear shocks in place on the bike (Section 12).*
30 Position the bike on its centre stand.
31 Raise the front wheel off the ground using a jack under the engine, then place a block of wood under the front wheel to so that no loading is placed on the shock absorber.
32 Remove the fuel tank and the air filter housing (see Chapter 4).
33 On machines equipped with electronic suspension adjustment (ESA), release the bottom of the ride height sensor linkage rod from the ball joint **(see illustration)**. Trace the wiring from the shock absorber to the connector then release and disconnect it, and free the wiring from the tie and guides **(see illustrations)**.
34 Unscrew and remove the shock absorber lower mounting bolt, then remove the support from under the front wheel and lower the Telever arm **(see illustration)**. Unscrew the upper mounting bolt, and remove the shock absorber **(see illustrations)**. Note that a high strength threadlock is used on the bolts.

Inspection
35 Inspect the shock absorber for obvious physical damage. Check the spring for looseness, cracks or signs of fatigue.
36 Inspect the damper rod for signs of pitting and oil leakage.
37 Inspect the pivot hardware at the top and bottom of the shock for wear or damage.
38 Apart from the shock mounting bolts and the splash guard on the front, individual component parts for the front shock absorber are not available. The entire unit must be

replaced with a new one if it is worn or damaged, although it may be worth first seeking advice from a suspension specialist.

Shock installation
39 Installation is the reverse of removal, noting the following:
● Clean the threads of the bolts and apply a suitable high strength thread-locking compound such as Loctite 270.
● Manoeuvre the shock into place and fit the upper mounting bolt (with the domed head) loosely, then lower the front of the bike to align the lower mounting holes and fit the lower bolt.
● Tighten the bolts to the torque setting specified at the beginning of the Chapter.
● On machines equipped with ESA, reconnect the wiring connector(s) and secure the wiring

in its guides and using a new cable-tie while the front of the bike is still supported, to avoid strain on the wiring when the machine is in use. Do not forget to clip the ride height sensor linkage rod back onto the ball head. When all work is completed the bike should be taken to a BMW dealer to recalibrate the ride-height sensor.
● Secure the throttle body clamps with the clamp pliers to avoid damage.

Telelever arm
Removal
Caution: The Telelever arm is a close fit in the frame and needs some care to be manoeuvred out – before removing it mask off the front frame tubes and the underside of the arm, and place some rag over the

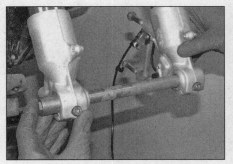
6.27 Slide the axle in to align the forks

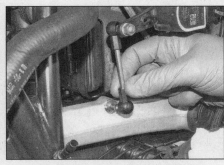
6.33a Pull the rod off the ball joint

6.33b Release the connector from its holder…

6.33c …then disconnect it

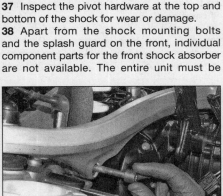
6.34a Unscrew the lower bolt…

6.34b …then the upper bolt…

6.34c …and remove the shock absorber

6.42 Release the guide from the tank bracket and disconnect the wiring

6.43 Undo the screws and remove the tank mounting bracket from each side

6.46a Prise off the covers on both ends of the Telelever pivot shaft…

6.46b …and undo the bolt from the right-hand end

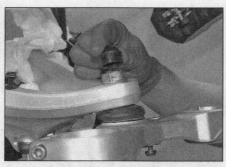

6.47a Remove the cap…

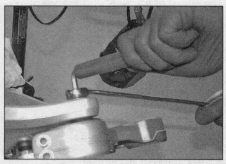

6.47b …then hold the stud and unscrew the nut

fins on the cylinder heads, as protection against scratches and knocks.

40 Remove the fuel tank and the fuel hose and pressure sensor assembly, the air filter housing and the throttle bodies (see Chapter 4).

41 Drain the cooling system and remove the radiators, and the thermostat and coolant outlet union (see Chapter 3). On RT models remove the left-hand inner fairing panel.

42 On machines equipped with electronic suspension adjustment (ESA), release the bottom of the ride height sensor linkage rod from the ball joint (see illustration 6.33a). Release the ride height sensor wiring guide and disconnect the connector (see illustration).

43 Remove the front fuel tank mounting brackets (see illustration).

44 Remove the ABS pressure modulator (see Chapter 6).

45 Remove the shock absorber as described above, supporting the bike as described, and ignoring anything applicable to components that have already been removed.

46 Prise off the Telelever pivot shaft covers (see illustration). Counter-hold the head of the pivot shaft and undo the bolt on the right-hand side (see illustration).

47 Remove the cap from the top of the ball joint on the front of the Telelever arm (see illustration). Counter-hold the stud on the top of the ball joint using a hex bit or an Allen key and extension holder, and undo the nut using a ring spanner (see illustration). If it is very difficult to undo, cover the front of the arm in heavy rag and heat the nut using a hot air gun, then try again – wear some heat resistant gloves when removing the nut. Lift the Telelever arm off the ball joint.

HAYNES HiNT *Heating the nut softens the threadlock and will make it easier to undo. This will work on the particular threadlock that BMW use on assembly, however if the nut has since been tightened using a different type of threadlock, heat may actually make it more difficult to remove. If this is the case, allow the parts to cool and try again.*

48 Lift the Telelever arm and unscrew the steering damper bolt, displace the damper and remove the washer and spacer (see illustration 10.8).

49 Support the Telelever arm and withdraw the pivot shaft (see illustration). Push the arm forwards and remove the spacer from the inner side of each pivot (see illustrations).

6.49a Withdraw the shaft…

6.49b …push the arm forwards…

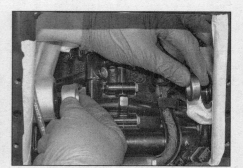

6.49c …and remove the spacers

6.49d Fit the shaft and bolt...

6.49e ...and tighten the bolt lightly

6.49f Manoeuvre the arm into the position shown

6.49g Slacken the bolt and tap on it to dislodge the shaft...

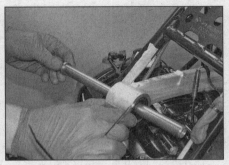

6.49h ...then unscrew the bolt and withdraw the shaft

6.49i Manoeuvre the arm into the position shown...

Refit the pivot shaft and tighten its bolt until it bottoms, but do not tighten it any further **(see illustrations)** – this squeezes the ends of the arm together slightly to get the clearance to remove the arm, otherwise it does not fit between the frame tubes. Manoeuvre the arm so the left-hand pivot is above the left-hand frame tube and the right-hand pivot is below the right-hand tube as shown **(see illustration)**. Partially unscrew the pivot shaft bolt, then lightly tap on its head to dislodge the shaft (as it will have probably been pinched in the bearings as the ends of the arm squeeze together slightly), then remove the bolt and withdraw the shaft **(see illustrations)**. Manoeuvre the arm so the pivots are out to the right with the right-hand frame tube up to the front of the arm, pull the

front of the arm rearwards past the inner side of the left-hand tube and remove the arm **(see illustrations)**.

Inspection

50 Thoroughly clean the arm, removing all traces of dirt, corrosion and grease. Inspect the arm and pivot components, looking for obvious signs of wear such as heavy scoring and cracks or distortion due to accident damage. Any damaged or worn component must be replaced with a new one.

51 Slide the pivot shaft through the bearings and check that there is no resistance due to distortion of the arm. If there is, first check that the pivot shaft is straight by rolling it on a true surface such as a sheet of glass.

If the shaft is straight, then the arm itself could be bent – have it checked by a BMW dealer.

52 There are two bearings fitted in each pivot with a spacer between them, and a seal on the inner side of each pivot **(see illustration)**. Refer to *Tools and Workshop Tips* in the Reference section and inspect the bearings and sleeves for wear or damage. If the bearings do not turn smoothly or if there is excessive freeplay, they must be replaced with new ones as follows: lever the grease seal out of the inner side of the pivot **(see illustration)**. To remove the outer bearing you need an internal expanding knife-edge puller with slide-hammer attachment. Select the correct adapter for the size of the bearing and attach it to the puller, then locate the knife edge

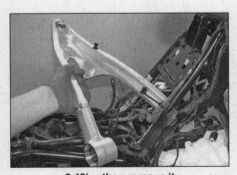

6.49j ...then remove it

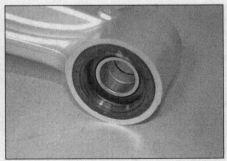

6.52a Seal and bearing arrangement in arm pivot

6.52b Lever the seal out

6.52c Locate the puller behind the bearing...

6.52d ...and jar it out with the slide-hammer

6.52e A socket can be used to drive the bearings in

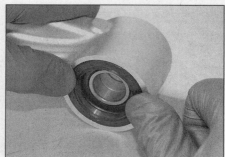

6.52f Press the new seal in with your fingers

behind the inner race of the outer bearing and expand it (see illustration). Heat the bearing housing with a hot air gun, then have an assistant to firmly hold the arm and use the slide-hammer attachment to jar the bearing out (see illustration). Remove the central spacer. Drive the inner bearing out using a bearing driver or socket on the inner race – place the arm on its side and support directly under the pivot. The new bearings are best drawn in using a drawbolt arrangement, which can be easily made as described in *Tools and Workshop Tips*. Cool the new bearings in a freezer for a while before fitting them, and heat the bearing housing immediately before. Make sure each bearing is drawn squarely onto its seat with the drawing washer sitting on the outer race not the inner, and do not forget to fit the central spacer after fitting the first bearing. Alternatively drive each bearing

in using a socket that bears on the outer race, and support the arm directly under the pivot (see illustration). Press a new seal into the inner side of the pivot, with its flat side facing out, using your fingers, or the drawbolt if necessary (see illustration) – note that the seal for the right-hand pivot is bigger than that for the left. Smear the seal lips with grease.

53 Inspect the ball joint on the bottom yoke for signs of wear or damage (see illustration 6.58b). It should move freely with no signs of roughness or notchiness. There should be no noticeable play in the joint. If the joint is worn, remove the forks and replace the bottom yoke with a new one – the ball joint is not available separately.

Installation

54 Clean the threads of the ball joint stud on the bottom yoke.
55 Manoeuvre the arm into position in an exact

reverse of the way it was removed – see Step 49. Fit the narrow spacer into the inner side of the right-hand pivot and the wide spacer into the left (see illustration 6.49c). Lubricate the pivot shaft with a smear of grease and slide it in from the left and all the way through. Fit the bolt and tighten it finger-tight.
56 Clean the threads of the steering damper bolt and apply some fresh threadlock. Fit the steering damper with its spacer and washer and tighten the bolt to the torque setting specified at the beginning of the Chapter (see illustration 10.8). Fit the arm down onto the ball joint.
57 Counter-hold the pivot shaft and tighten the bolt to the torque setting specified at the beginning of this Chapter.
58 Apply a high strength thread locking compound (such as Loctite 270) to the ball joint stud threads and fit the nut. Counter-hold the stud using an Allen key and tighten the nut securely (see illustration 6.47b) – the top of the ball joint has four spikes on it that bite into the seat in the underside of the Telelever arm when the nut is tightened, which means the nut can now be fully tightened to the specified torque setting without having to counter-hold the ball joint (see illustrations). Press the cap onto the top of the ball joint (see illustration 6.47a).
59 Fit the pivot shaft covers (see illustration 6.46a).
60 Install the shock absorber (see above).
61 Remove any protective tape previously fitted to the frame tubes and arm. Install all remaining components in a reverse of the removal procedure, referring to the relevant Chapters and Sections as directed.

7 Front suspension – R and RS models

Fork removal and installation
Removal

1 Work on one fork at a time. Note the routing of the cables, hose and wiring around the forks. Note the setting of the top of the fork in respect to the upper surface of the top yoke.
2 On models with ESA undo the screw securing the top cap to the left-hand fork and remove the cap (see illustration).

6.58a An initial tightening of the nut gets the spikes (arrowed)...

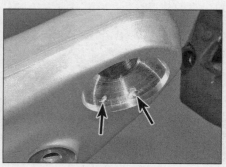

6.58b ...to bite into the seat...

6.58c ...preventing the joint from turning it as you tighten it to the full torque

7.2a Remove the cap…

7.2b …and release and disconnect the wiring

7.5 Undo the screw (arrowed)

Release the wire from its guides and disconnect the connector **(see illustration)**.
3 Remove the front wheel (see Chapter 6).
4 Remove the front mudguard (see Chapter 7).
5 When removing the left-hand fork undo the screw securing the ABS sensor wire guide **(see illustration)**. Secure the sensor clear of the fork.
6 Slacken the fork clamp bolt in the top yoke **(see illustration)**.
7 If the fork is to be disassembled, or if the fork oil is being changed, slacken the fork top bolt **(see illustration)** – it is advisable to stick a single layer of masking tape around the hex to protect the finish.
8 Slacken the fork clamp bolts in the bottom yoke **(see illustration)**. Remove the fork by twisting it and pulling it down **(see illustration)**.

> **HAYNES HiNT**
> *If the fork legs are seized in the yokes, spray the area with penetrating oil and allow time for it to soak in before trying again.*

Installation

9 Remove all traces of corrosion from the fork tubes and the yokes. Make sure you fit the fork with the ABS sensor mount on the left-hand side.

10 Slide the fork up through the bottom yoke and into the top yoke, making sure the cables, hose and wiring are routed on the correct side of the fork, and on the left-hand fork on models with ESA you draw the wiring up through the yoke **(see illustration 7.8b)**. Set the groove near the top of the outer tube flush with the upper surface of the top yoke **(see illustration)**. Tighten the clamp bolts in the bottom yoke to the torque setting specified at the beginning of the Chapter, tightening them alternately several times to counter the effect of the offset **(see illustration 7.8a)**.
11 If the fork has been dismantled or if the fork oil was changed, tighten the fork top bolt to the specified torque **(see illustration 7.7)**.

7.6 Slacken the clamp bolt

7.7 Slacken the top bolt if required

7.8a Slacken the fork clamp bolts in the bottom yoke…

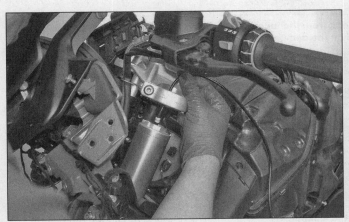

7.8b …then draw the fork down and out of the yokes, guiding the wiring through on the left fork on models with ESA

7.10 Set the groove in the tube level with the top surface of the yoke

12 Tighten the fork clamp bolt in the top yoke to its specified torque **(see illustration 7.6)**.

13 Install all remaining components – make sure the ABS sensor wire, and where applicable the ESA wire, is/are correctly routed and secured.

14 Check the operation of the front forks and brake before taking the machine out on the road.

Fork oil change

Standard forks (without ESA)

15 Cut a 14 mm wide slot to the centre of a 50 mm wide washer and prepare a holding tool using some threaded rod and nuts and a piece of shaped steel as shown **(see illustration 7.25)**.

16 Support the fork leg in an upright position and unscrew the top bolt from the top of the outer tube **(see illustration 7.26)**. If the bolt O-ring is damaged or deteriorated replace it with a new one.

17 Slide the outer tube down onto the base of the fork, then clean any oil off the spacer. Fit the holding tool onto the spacer, locating the rod ends in the holes **(see illustration 7.27a)**. Push the spacer down against the spring and fit the washer between the top of the spacer and the underside of the locknut, so the slot fits around the threaded rod, then relax the spring so the spacer seats against the washer **(see illustration 7.27b)**. Hold the top bolt and slacken the locknut, then thread the top bolt off **(see illustration 7.27c)**.

18 Remove the upper spacer. Hook the spring out, noting which way up it fits **(see illustration 7.28c)**. Wipe any excess oil off the spring and spacer.

19 Invert the fork leg over a suitable container to drain the oil and tip out the lower spacer, then pump the fork tubes and the damper rod to expel as much oil as possible. Support the fork upside down in the container and allow it to drain for a few minutes. If the oil contains metal particles disassemble the fork and inspect the bushes for wear (see below).

20 Slowly pour in the quantity and grade of fork oil specified at the beginning of the chapter, then pump the damper rod slowly ten times to distribute it evenly **(see illustrations 7.39a and 7.30a)**. Stand the fork upright for ten minutes to allow any air bubbles to rise. Slide the outer tube down until it is flush with the top of the inner tube, then measure the oil level from the top of the tube **(see illustration 7.30b)**. Add or subtract oil until it is at the level specified at the beginning of the Chapter.

21 Fit the lower spacer over the rod and into the fork, then fit the spring **(see illustration 7.28c)**. Draw the damper rod out, then fit a piece of hose onto the top of the rod to use as a handle to keep the rod extended **(see illustration 7.31a)**. Fit the spacer narrow end first over the wire and rod and seat the narrower bottom section in the top of the spring **(see illustration 7.31b)**. Hold the rod and push down on the spacer to compress the spring, then fit the slotted washer between the spacer and locknut **(see illustration 7.31d)**. Remove the hose.

22 Smear some fork oil onto the top bolt O-ring, using a new one if necessary. Thread the top bolt onto the damper rod until it seats, then hold it and tighten the locknut up against it **(see illustrations 7.27d and c)**. Push down on the spacer, remove the slotted washer, then allow the spacer to seat up against the top bolt.

23 Fully extend the outer tube and thread the top bolt into it **(see illustration 7.26)**. Lightly tighten the top bolt at this stage – tighten it further when the fork leg is being installed and is securely held in the bottom yoke.

24 Install the fork (see above).

Forks with ESA
Right-hand fork

25 Cut a 14 mm wide slot to the centre of a 50 mm wide washer and prepare a holding tool using some threaded rod and nuts and a piece of shaped steel as shown **(see illustration)**.

26 Support the fork leg in an upright position and unscrew the top bolt from the top of the outer tube **(see illustration)**. If the bolt O-ring is damaged or deteriorated replace it with a new one.

27 Slide the outer tube down onto the base of the fork, then clean any oil off the plastic spacer. Fit the holding tool onto the spacer, locating the rod ends in the holes **(see illustration)**. Push the spacer down against the spring using the holding tool and fit the washer between the top of the metal spacer and the underside of the locknut, so the slot fits around the threaded rod, then relax the spring so the spacer seats against the washer **(see illustration)**. Hold the top bolt and slacken the locknut, then thread the top bolt off **(see illustrations)**.

7.25 Prepare the tools as shown

7.26 Unscrew the top bolt from the tube – it will remain threaded on the damper rod

7.27a Fit the holding tool...

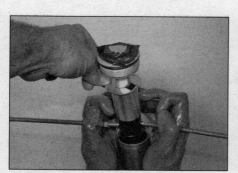
7.27b ...then compress the spring and slide the washer between the locknut and the spacer

7.27c Release the locknut...

7.27d ...and thread the top bolt off

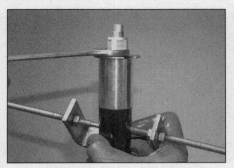

7.28a Thread the nut up the rod a bit...

7.28b ...and remove the slotted washer, spacers, spacer seat and washer...

7.28c ...and the spring

28 Thread the locknut part-way up the rod, leaving the top few threads exposed, to relax the spring a bit, then compress the spring and remove the washer from under the locknut **(see illustration)** – if the rod turns with the nut hold it on the plain unthreaded top section using pliers. Remove the metal spacer and the plastic spacer, then remove the spacer seat and washer, and the spring **(see illustrations)**. Remove the holding tool from the plastic spacer and wipe any excess oil off the spring and spacers.

29 Invert the fork leg over a suitable container to drain the oil and tip out the lower washer and the plate, then pump the damper rod to expel as much oil as possible. Support the fork upside down in the container and allow it to drain for a few minutes. If the oil contains metal particles disassemble the fork and inspect the bushes for wear (see below).

30 Slowly pour in the quantity and grade of fork oil specified at the beginning of the chapter **(see illustration 7.39a)**. Pump the damper rod slowly ten times to distribute the oil **(see illustration)**. Stand the fork upright for ten minutes to allow any air bubbles to rise. Slide the outer tube all the way down, then measure the oil level from the top of the tube **(see illustration)**. Add or subtract oil until it is at the level specified at the beginning of the Chapter.

31 Fit the plate and the washer over the rod and into the fork, then fit the spring with its closer-wound coils at the bottom **(see illustration 7.28c)**. Fit the upper washer and spacer seat over the rod and onto the spring **(see illustration 7.28b)**. Draw the damper rod out, and fit a piece of garden hose over the exposed threads to use as a handle to keep the rod extended **(see illustration)**. Fit

the plastic spacer narrow end first over the hose and rod and seat the narrower bottom section in the spacer seat and the top of the spring, then fit the narrow end of the metal spacer into the top of the second spacer **(see illustrations)**. Fit the holding tool onto the spacer **(see illustration 7.27a)**. Hold the rod and push down on the spacer to compress the spring, and fit the slotted washer between the spacer and locknut **(see illustration)**. Remove the hose. Thread the locknut down the rod until it seats lightly **(see illustration 7.28a)**.

32 Smear some fork oil onto the top bolt O-ring, using a new one if necessary. Thread the top bolt onto the damper rod until it seats, then hold it and tighten the locknut up against it **(see illustrations 7.27d and c)**. Push down on the spacer, remove the slotted washer, then allow the spacer to seat up against the top bolt **(see illustration 7.27b)**.

7.30a Pump the rod to distribute the oil...

7.30b ...then measure the level

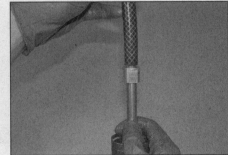

7.31a Fit a piece of hose onto the rod

7.31b Fit the plastic spacer...

7.31c ...and the metal spacer...

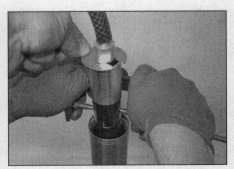

7.31d ...then compress the spring and fit the slotted washer

7.35 Unscrew the top bolt from the tube – it will remain threaded on the damper rod

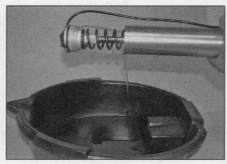

7.36 Tip the oil out into a container

7.37a Hold the disc and slacken the top bolt...

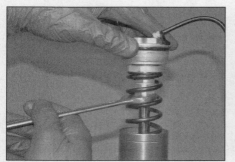

7.37b ...then hold the locknut and thread the top bolt off

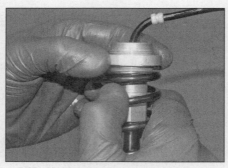

7.37c Hold the spring and unscrew the disc...

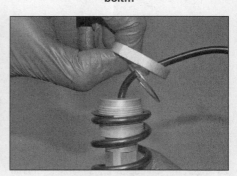

7.37d ...and remove it along with the washer

33 Fully extend the outer tube and thread the top bolt into it (see illustration 7.26). Lightly tighten the top bolt at this stage – tighten it further when the fork leg is being installed and is securely held in the bottom yoke.

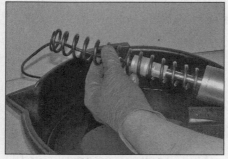

7.38 Remove the spring

34 Install the fork (see above).

Left-hand fork

35 Support the fork leg in an upright position and unscrew the top bolt from the top of the inner tube (see illustration). If the bolt O-ring is damaged or deteriorated replace it with a new one.

36 Tip the fork leg over a suitable container and drain as much oil as possible (see illustration). Support the fork upside down in the container and allow it to drain for a few minutes. If the oil contains metal particles disassemble the fork and inspect the bushes for wear (see below).

37 Slide the outer tube down onto the base of the fork, then clean any oil off the spring. Push the spring down and fit a spanner onto the flats of the disc that sits under the top bolt, then counter-hold the disc and slacken

the top bolt (see illustration). Now fit a spanner between the spring coils and onto the locknut threads, counter-hold the locknut and thread the top bolt off (see illustration). Hold the spring then thread the disc off and remove the upper washer (see illustrations).

38 Remove the spring (see illustration). Wipe any excess oil off the spring.

39 Slowly pour in the quantity and grade of fork oil specified at the beginning of the chapter (see illustration). Stand the fork upright for ten minutes to allow any air bubbles to rise. Slide the outer tube all the way down, then measure the oil level from the top of the tube (see illustration). Add or subtract oil until it is at the level specified at the beginning of the Chapter.

40 Fit the spring with its closer wound coils at the bottom (see illustration). Fit the washer onto the spring, then thread the disc on as far

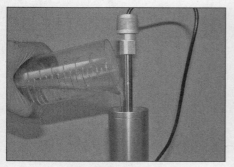

7.39a Add the oil...

7.39b ...to the correct level

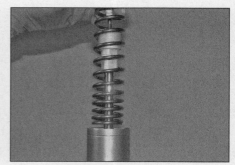

7.40a Make sure the spring is the correct way round

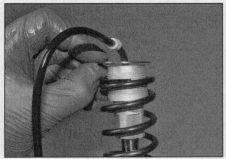

7.40b Fit the washer...

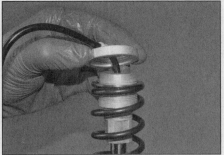

7.40c ...then thread the disc on

7.41a Fit the connector through the bolt from the underside...

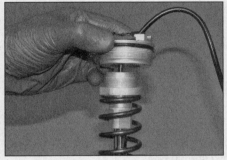

7.41b ...then thread the bolt on

7.45 Remove the axle clamp bolt(s)

7.46 Slacken the damper cartridge bolt as described

as it will go **(see illustrations)** – pull the spring down clear as you thread the disc down **(see illustration 7.37c)**.

41 Smear some fork oil onto the top bolt O-ring, using a new one if necessary. Pass the wiring connector through the top bolt, then thread the bolt onto the damper rod as far as it will go **(see illustrations)** – hold the locknut using a spanner between the coils of the spring as before if the rod turns with the bolt **(see illustration 7.37b)**. Now counter-hold the top bolt and tighten the disc up against it **(see illustration 7.37a)**.

42 Fully extend the outer tube and thread the top bolt into it **(see illustration 7.35)**. Lightly tighten the top bolt at this stage – tighten it further when the fork leg is being installed and is securely held in the bottom yoke.

43 Install the fork (see).

Fork overhaul

Disassembly

44 Remove the fork — make sure that the top bolt is loosened while the leg is still clamped in the bottom yoke (see above). Always dismantle the fork legs separately to avoid interchanging parts. Store all components in separate, clearly marked containers.

45 Remove the axle clamp bolt that is in line with the damper rod bolt hole from the bottom of the fork **(see illustration)** – the other clamp bolt can stay in place, or remove it as well if required.

46 If you need to remove the damper cartridge (fork seals and bushes can both be

replaced without removing it) slacken its bolt in the base of the inner tube **(see illustration)** – do not unscrew it at this stage or the fork oil will come out. On models with standard forks (without ESA), if the damper cartridge turns with the bolt, turn the leg upside down and compress the fork so the pressure of the spring holds the damper while the bolt is loosened. Alternatively use an air impact wrench, if available. If the bolt cannot be loosened at this stage, BMW produce tools (Nos. 313643 and 313724) which can be fitted together and inserted down inside the inner tube once the spring has been removed – tool 313724 is a peg spanner that engages slots in the top end of the damper cartridge to hold it while the bolt is loosened.

47 Refer to the relevant Steps above and drain the oil from the fork.

48 Withdraw the inner tube from the outer tube **(see illustration)**.

49 Carefully prise out the dust seal from the bottom of the outer tube **(see illustration 6.11)**. A new seal must be used on installation.

50 Carefully release the retaining clip, taking care not to scratch the surface of the tube **(see illustration 6.12)**.

51 Carefully lever the oil seal out using a screwdriver or seal hook, protecting the rim of the tube with BMW tool 36640, or a piece of rubber or wood. If the seal is difficult to remove use an expanding knife-edge puller with slide-hammer attachment **(see illustrations 6.13a, b and c)**. Remove the washer **(see illustration 6.13d)**.

52 Withdraw the spacer(s) from the top of the outer tube, using a piece of wire bent at the end to hook them out **(see illustration)**.

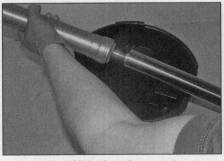

7.48 Slide the tubes apart

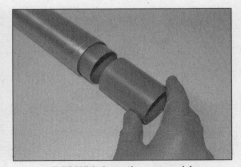

7.52 Withdraw the spacer(s)

7.53a Withdraw the cartridge from the inner tube

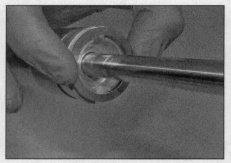

7.53b Remove the washer from the top of the left-hand fork cartridge on ESA models

7.56 Check the working surface of each bush (arrowed) for wear

53 If required, remove the damper cartridge bolt and its copper sealing washer from the bottom of the fork, on models with standard forks using a holding tool as described earlier if necessary. A new sealing washer must be used on reassembly. Withdraw the damper cartridge from the fork **(see illustration)**. On models with ESA remove the washer from the top of the cartridge for the left-hand fork **(see illustration)**.

Inspection

54 Clean all parts in solvent and blow them dry with compressed air, if available. Check the inner tube for score marks, scratches, rust spots and flaking of the chrome finish. Any such damage will result in premature seal failure. Fork inner tubes can be re-chromed using hard chrome, or replace them with new ones. Check the fork seal seat for nicks, gouges and scratches. If damage is evident, leaks will occur.

55 Check the inner tube for runout using V-blocks and a dial gauge. If the amount of runout exceeds the service limit specified at the beginning of the chapter, the tube must be replaced with a new one **(see illustration 6.14)**.

 Warning: If the tube is bent or exceeds the runout limit, it should not be straightened; replace it with a new one.

56 Check the working surface of each bush for wear **(see illustration)** – the surface should be Teflon grey all over. If the Teflon has worn to expose the material below remove

the bushes and replace them with new ones – to remove them use a long drift (such as a socket on an extension bar) inserted from the opposite end to the bush being removed and against the underside, or a knife-edged puller and slide-hammer (as for the oil seal) inserted from the end the bush is in and against the underside, and take care to drive or draw the bush out square and not damage the inner surface of the tube **(see illustrations 6.13a and b)**. Push the new bushes in initially with your fingers, then push or drive them onto their seats using a piece of plastic tubing.

57 Check the spring and all other components for cracks and other damage.

58 Check the damper cartridge for wear and damage. Check the oil passage holes are clear. Pump the rod in and out of the cartridge – it should move smoothly and freeely.

Reassembly

59 On models with ESA, when doing the left-hand fork fit the washer onto its seat on the top of the damper cartridge **(see illustration 7.53b)**. Slide the damper cartridge into the inner tube **(see illustration 7.53a)** – on forks with ESA when the cartridge seats agains the bottom turn in to get the flats on the bottom of the cartridge to locate in the flats in the seat, you will feel it drop into place and when seated the cartridge cannot turn. Fit a new sealing washer onto the damper cartridge bolt and apply a few drops of a suitable non-permanent thread locking compound **(see illustration)**. Fit the bolt into the bottom of the inner tube, thread it into the

cartridge and tighten it to the torque setting specified at the beginning of the Chapter for your type of fork. If the cartridge rotates inside the tube as you tighten the bolt, on models with standard forks use the same holding method as on disassembly, and on models with ESA forks the cartridge has not seated in the flats, so must be lifted and repositioned so it does.

60 Lubricate the plastic spacer(s) with new fork oil and slide it/them into the top of the outer tube and up against the top bush **(see illustration 7.53)**.

61 Stand the outer tube upside down and fit the washer **(see illustration 6.17e)**. Fit the new seal into the tube with its marked side (the side with the shallower recess) facing out, and push or drive it onto its seat using a driver or socket that bears on the outer rim **(see illustrations 6.18a and b)** – the seal is seated when the retaining clip groove is fully exposed.

62 Fit the retaining clip into the groove **(see illustration 6.19)**.

63 Lubricate the lip of the new dust seal with clean fork oil and slide it onto the inner tube, making sure it is the correct way round **(see illustration 6.20)**. Lubricate the oil seal lip and the inner tube with fork oil, then carefully slide the inner tube into the outer tube, turning the inner tube lightly as you do and making sure you keep them both parallel, and making sure the oil seal lip does not turn inside out. Slide the inner tube all the way in, then out and in again a few times to check the oil seal lip is correctly seated.

64 Press the dust seal into position **(see illustration)**.

65 Fit the axle clamp bolt(s) loosely into the bottom of the fork **(see illustration 7.45)**.

66 Refer above and fill the fork with oil and finish reassembly.

67 Install the fork (see above).

7.64 Press the dust seal into the outer tube

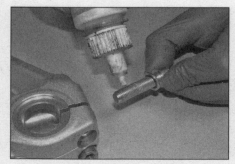

7.59 Fit a new sealing washer and apply threadlock

8 Steering bearings – GS, GS Adventure and RT models

1 The steering turns on a bearing in the top yoke and a ball joint that links the front of the Telelever arm to the fork bridge. These

8.6 Checking the bottom yoke ball joint

8.11a Unscrew the stud bolt…

8.11b …displace the yoke…

8.11c …release the wiring…

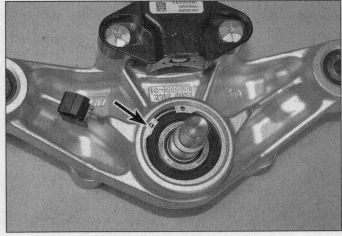

8.11d …and disconnect the connector(s)

could wear during normal use, and may cause steering wobble – a condition that is potentially dangerous.

Check

2 Position the bike on its centre stand. Raise the front wheel off the ground either by having an assistant push down on the rear, or by placing a support under the engine.
3 Detach the steering damper from the Telelever arm (Section 10).
4 Point the front wheel straight ahead, then slowly turn the handlebars from side to side. Any roughness in the bearings will be felt and the bars will not move smoothly and freely. If it is thought that the bearings are worn or damaged it will be necessary to partially disassemble the steering and suspension components for further investigation.
5 Remove the fork legs (Section 6).
6 The bottom yoke should move freely without any sign of roughness or play in the joint **(see illustration)**. Check that the boot shows no signs of deterioration and is free from cracks and splits. The ball joint is an integral part of the bottom yoke and is not available separately – to remove the bottom yoke follow the procedure in Section 6, Step 47.
7 The top yoke should turn freely on its bearing without any sign of roughness or play. To fit a new bearing proceed as follows.

Removal and installation

8 Carefully lever the badge from the top yoke.
9 On GS and GS Adv models displace the handlebars from the top yoke (Section 5) – there is no need to remove any of the assemblies from the handlebars. Lay the bars on a cushion or plenty of rag as protection.
10 Carefully prise out the fork top caps **(see illustration 6.6)**. Counter-hold the fork top bolt underneath the yoke and unscrew the nut from the top of the stud **(see illustration 6.7)**. Pull each fork inner tube down out of its bearing in the yoke **(see illustration 6.26a)**.
11 Unscrew the bearing stud bolt and lift the handlebar/yoke assembly off, then release the

ignition switch/keyless ride unit wiring from the clip and disconnect the connector(s) **(see illustrations)**.
12 Prise out the circlip securing the bottom edge of the bearing in the yoke **(see illustration)**.
13 The bearing must be driven out of the top yoke from the top. Support the yoke on blocks of wood with sufficient clearance to allow the bearing to come out. Cover the ignition switch or keyless ride unit in some rag. Use a hot air gun to heat the bearing housing, then drive the bearing and stud out with a suitably sized socket **(see illustration)**. Note which way round the bearing is fitted.

8.12 Remove the circlip (arrowed)

8.13 Heat the housing then drive the bearing out

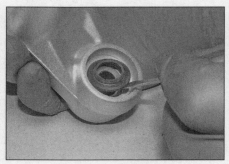

8.15a Remove the seal...

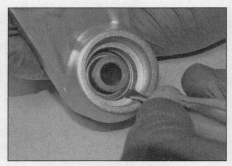

8.15b ...and the circlip...

8.15c ...then drive the bush out

8.15d Driving the new bush in using a socket

8.17 Driving the new bearing in using a socket

14 Press the stud out of the bearing, taking care not to damage the stud threads.
15 The fork top studs locate in bushes in the top yoke. If a new bearing is being fitted, it is good practice to fit new bushes also. Remove the seal and circlip from the top of each bush, then turn the yoke over, rest it under the bush being removed on a 21 mm socket and press or drive the bushes out from the underside of the yoke using a thin-walled 17 mm socket (**see illustrations**) – heat the bush housing using a hot air gun if necessary. Remove the seals from the top and bottom of each new bush, then lightly lubricate the bushes and fit them in

from the top, with the larger bevelled end facing down, using either a press, suitable driver (17 mm socket), or a drawbolt set-up, and some heat if required (see *Tools and Workshop Tips* in the Reference section) (**see illustration**). Secure the bushes with new circlips, then fit the seals, pushing them in using a 17 mm socket.
16 Press the stud into the new steering head bearing.
17 The new bearing must be pressed or driven into the top yoke from the underside. Support the top yoke on blocks of wood. Use a hot air gun to heat the top yoke bearing housing, then press or drive the bearing in

using a 33 mm socket or driver that bears only on the bearing's outer race (**see illustration**).
18 Secure the bearing with a new circlip, making sure it seats properly in its groove (**see illustration 8.12**).
19 Installation is the reverse of removal, noting the following:
● Clean the threads of the steering head bearing stud bolt and apply some fresh threadlock. Tighten the bolt to the torque setting specified at the beginning of the Chapter.
● Clean the threads of the fork top studs and apply some fresh threadlock. Tighten the stud nuts to the torque setting specified at the beginning of the Chapter (**see illustration 6.7**).

9 Steering stem and head bearings – R and RS models

Removal

1 On R models remove the headlight and instrument cluster (see Chapter 8). Release and disconnect the wiring and connectors from the front carrier brackets and the top yoke, noting the routing of the wiring (**see illustrations**). Undo the front carrier bracket

9.1a Release and disconnect all the wiring at the front...

9.1b ...and from the clip(s) (arrowed) on the underside of the yoke

9.1c Undo the bolts (arrowed) on each side

9.2 Remove the badge so you can access the stem bolt

9.4 Undo the screw (arrowed) and displace the hose joint

bolts and remove the bracket/turn signal assembly **(see illustration)**. If required displace the handlebars from the top yoke and rest them on a cushion or plenty of rag across the fuel tank, making sure they are secure – if you displace them the top yoke can be removed completely, if they stay on the yoke the whole assembly can be laid across the tank.

2 On RS models remove the fairing side and upper panels (see Chapter 8). Release the wiring from the guide(s) on the underside of the top yoke **(see illustration 9.1b)**. If you are going to remove the top yoke completely disconnect the ignition switch or keyless ride unit wiring connector(s). Release the hose

and wiring from the guide. If required displace the handlebars from the top yoke and secure them across the front – if you displace them the top yoke can be removed completely, if they stay on the yoke the whole assembly can be secured across the front **(see illustration 9.5c)**. If you don't displace them push the badge out from the underside **(see illustration)**.

3 Remove the front forks (Section 7).

4 Displace the brake hose joint from the bottom yoke **(see illustration)**. Displace the steering damper from the bottom yoke (Section 10).

5 Unscrew the steering stem bolt **(see illustration)** – on RS models, if the handlebars

are in place you cannot remove the bolt, but lift it out and slide across to the side **(see illustration)**. Lift the top yoke or top yoke/handlebar assembly up off the steering stem and either remove it, or if the handlebars weren't displaced rest it on a cushion or some rag on the fuel tank on R models, or tie it across the front on RS models **(see illustrations)**.

6 Remove the tabbed lock washer, noting how it fits **(see illustration)**. Unscrew and remove the locknut and its rubber washer, using either a C-spanner or a peg spanner if required, though it should only be finger-tight **(see illustration)**.

7 Support the bottom yoke and unscrew the

9.5a Unscrew the bolt – on RS models with the handlebars in place, via the badge hole...

9.5b ...then lift it and slide it across

9.5c Lift the yoke/handlebar assembly up off the stem...

9.5d ...securing it as shown on RS models

9.6a Lift the tabbed washer off...

9.6b ...then unscrew the locknut – the rubber washer will be stuck to the underside of it

9.7a Unscrew the adjuster nut...

9.7b ...and remove the bearing cover...

9.7c ...then draw the bottom yoke/steering stem out of the steering head

9.8a Remove the inner race and upper bearing from the top of the head...

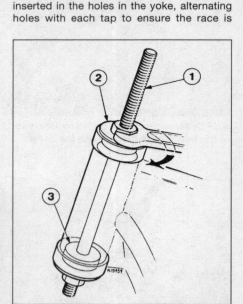

9.8b ...and the lower bearing from the stem

be solidly supported as all the force needs to be transmitted to the race). BMW can supply a drawbolt tool. Make sure that the drawbolt washer or drift (as applicable) bears only on the outer edge of the race and does not contact the working surface.

> **HAYNES HiNT** *Installation of new bearing outer races is made much easier if the races are left overnight in the freezer. This causes them to contract slightly making them a looser fit. Alternatively, use a freeze spray on the races just before you install them.*

bearing adjuster nut using a C-spanner **(see illustration)**. Remove the bearing cover, then gently lower the bottom yoke and steering stem out of the frame **(see illustrations)**.

8 Remove the upper bearing and its inner race from the top of the steering head **(see illustration)**. Remove the lower bearing from the steering stem **(see illustration)**. Refer below to remove the lower bearing inner race and the outer races in the steering head, but only remove them if they are to be replaced with new ones – once removed they cannot be re-used.

Inspection

9 Clean all traces of old grease from the bearings and races using paraffin or solvent, and check them for wear or damage.

10 Inspect the bearing balls, cages and races

for signs of wear, damage or discoloration – the races should be polished and free from indentations. If there are any signs of wear and damage on any of the above components both upper and lower bearing assemblies must be replaced with a new set (see below).

Replacement

11 The outer races are an interference fit in the steering head – you should be able to tap them out using a suitable drift located in the cut-outs, alternating cut-outs with each tap to ensure the races are driven out squarely **(see illustrations)**. Curve the end of the drift slightly to improve access if necessary.

12 Press the new outer races into the head using a drawbolt arrangement **(see illustration)**, or tap them in using a large diameter tubular drift (to do this the bike must

13 To remove the lower bearing inner race from the steering stem, position the yoke upside down on some blocks of wood, and tap on the underside of the race using a drift inserted in the holes in the yoke, alternating holes with each tap to ensure the race is

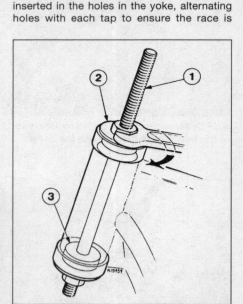

9.12 Drawbolt arrangement for fitting steering stem bearing races

1 Long bolt or threaded bar
2 Thick washer
3 Guide for lower race

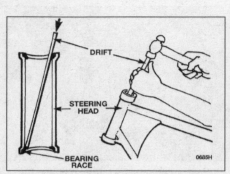

9.11a Locate the drift as shown...

9.11b ...in the cut-outs provided (arrow)

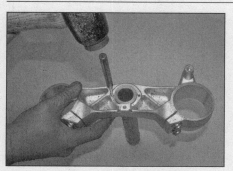

9.13 Remove the lower bearing race as described using a drift that is a snug fit in the holes

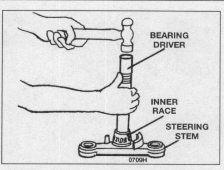

9.14 Drive the new race on using a suitable bearing driver or a length of pipe that bears only against the top of the race and not against the bearing surface

driven off squarely **(see illustration)**. If the race is very tight heat it using a hot air gun with a narrow nozzle so you can direct the heat onto the race and not the stem. The seal that sits under the race will come off as well – replace it with a new one.

14 Fit a new seal onto the steering stem. Heat the new bearing race then tap it into position using a length of tubing with an internal diameter slightly larger than the steering stem so that it locates on the top of the race, and not on its bearing surface **(see illustration)**.

9.17a Fit the adjuster nut...

Installation

15 If not already done clean all old grease from the bearings and races using solvent or paraffin.

16 Make sure the seal and the lower bearing inner race are correctly in place. Smear a liberal quantity of lithium-based multi-purpose grease onto the races and bearings, and a smear onto the seal on the underside of the upper bearing cover. Fit the lower bearing onto the stem **(see illustration 9.8b)**. Fit the upper bearing and its inner race into the head **(see illustration 9.8a)**.

17 Carefully lift the steering stem/bottom yoke up through the steering head and support it **(see illustration 9.7c)**. Fit the bearing cover onto the top of the steering head **(see illustration 9.7b)**. Thread the adjuster nut onto the steering stem and tighten it lightly **(see illustrations)**.

18 To adjust the bearings as specified by BMW, tool Nos. 313721 and 313723 and a torque wrench are required. Tighten the adjuster nut to the torque setting specified at the beginning of the Chapter. Make sure that the steering stem is able to move freely from lock-to-lock, but that all freeplay is eliminated.

19 If the tools are not available, using a C-spanner tighten the adjuster nut until all freeplay is removed, then tighten it a little more **(see illustration 9.17b)**. Now slacken the nut, then tighten it again, setting it so that all freeplay is just removed, yet the steering is able to move freely from side to side. *Caution: Take great care not to apply excessive pressure because this will cause premature failure of the bearings.*

20 Fit the rubber washer and the locknut and thread it down until the rubber washer seats lightly **(see illustration 9.6b)**. Tighten the locknut further until its notches align with those in the adjuster nut, then fit the tabbed lock washer so that the tabs fit into the notches in both the locknut and adjuster nut **(see illustration 9.6a)** – the lockwasher need not be tightened further than the first alignment of the notches.

21 Fit the top yoke/handlebar assembly onto the steering stem **(see illustration 9.5c)**. Fit the steering stem bolt and tighten it finger-tight **(see illustration 9.5b)**. Temporarily install one of the forks to align the top and bottom yokes, and secure it by tightening the bottom yoke clamp bolts only **(see illustration)**. Now tighten the steering stem bolt to the torque setting specified at the beginning of the Chapter **(see illustration 9.5a)**.

22 Install all remaining components in a reverse of the removal procedure, referring to the relevant Sections or Chapters where required, and to the torque settings specified at the beginning of the Chapter. Make sure the wiring, cables and hose are correctly routed.

23 Refer to the freeplay check procedure in Chapter 1 to make a final assessment of the bearings with the leverage and inertia of all components taken into account, and if necessary re-adjust – this should not be necessary if the torque settings were applied, but may be if they weren't.

9.17b ...and tighten lightly

9.21 Align the yokes with one of the forks before tightening the stem bolt

10.7 Hold the hex while undoing the nut

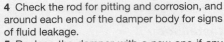

10.8 Note the arrangement of the mounting components

10.10 Steering damper bolts (arrowed)

10 Steering damper

Check

1 Turn the steering from lock-to-lock and check that there is no freeplay between the damper unit and its mountings.
2 If any freeplay is evident, check that the mountings are tight **(see illustrations 10.7 and 10.8 or 10.10)**. If the mountings are tight, then either the mounts or the damper itself are worn, or there is freeplay between the damper rod and the damping mechanism itself.
3 Check that the damper rod moves smoothly in and out of the damper body with no signs of roughness or binding.

4 Check the rod for pitting and corrosion, and around each end of the damper body for signs of fluid leakage.
5 Replace the damper with a new one if any of the above are evident.

Removal and installation

GS, GS Adventure and RT models

6 Remove the front wheel (see Chapter 6), then remove the front mudguard (see Chapter 7).
7 Counter-hold the hex below the rose joint and undo the nut on the underside of the bottom yoke **(see illustration)**. Lift the damper rod off the yoke.
8 Undo the damper mounting bolt on the underside of the Telelever arm and remove the damper, collecting the washer and spacer **(see illustration)**.
9 Installation is the reverse of removal. Clean the threads of the bolt and apply a suitable

non-permanent thread-locking compound, and either fit a new nut or apply threadlock to the stud threads. Tighten the nut and bolt to the torque settings specified at the beginning of the Chapter.

R and RS models

10 Undo the damper mounting bolts and remove the damper, collecting the spacers and collars **(see illustration)**.
11 Installation is the reverse of removal. Clean the threads of the bolts and apply a suitable non-permanent thread-locking compound, and tighten them to the torque setting specified at the beginning of the Chapter.

11 Rear shock absorber

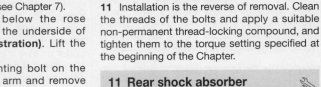
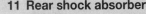

Removal

GS and GS Adventure

1 Place the bike on the centrestand.
2 Remove the ECU (see Chapter 4).
3 On models with ESA remove the battery cover (see Chapter 8). Remove the ride height sensor cover **(see illustration)**. Disconnect the ESA wiring connectors **(see illustration)**. Undo the screw securing the ECU tray to the rear sub-frame on the right-hand side **(see illustration)**. Release and displace the fuse holder **(see illustration)**. Release the ESA wiring from its guides and feed the connectors down between the tray and the sub-frame, noting its routing **(see illustration)** – it is easier to release

11.3a Pull the peg from the grommet then release the tab

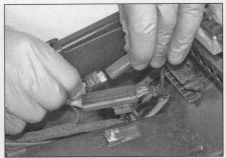

11.3b Disconnect the connectors

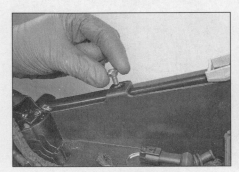

11.3c Undo the screw

11.3d Release the catch using a pointed tool and pull the holder off

11.3e Feed the connectors down

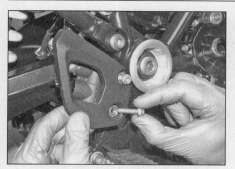

11.4 Remove both heel plates

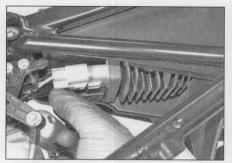

11.6 Disconnect the connectors

11.7a Unscrew the lower bolts…

11.7b …slacken the upper ones…

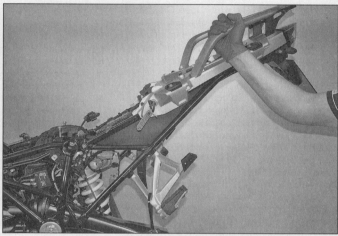

11.7c …and raise the sub-frame

the wiring that is just above the shock reservoir once the sub-frame has been raised (Step 7).

4 Remove the heel plate from each side of the frame **(see illustration)**.

5 Remove the silencer (see Chapter 4).

6 Disconnect the regulator/rectifier wiring connectors **(see illustration)**.

7 Unscrew the rear sub-frame lower bolt on each side, then slacken the upper bolts and raise the sub-frame so it is vertical, and secure it by re-tightening the upper bolts **(see illustrations)**. Release the wiring from the guide above the shock reservoir if not already done **(see illustration)**.

8 Place a block of wood under the rear wheel so the wheel is supported, but not lifted.

9 Unscrew the bolt securing the bottom of the shock absorber to the swingarm **(see illustration)**. Support the shock and unscrew the bolt securing the top, then lift the shock out **(see illustrations)**.

RT models

10 Remove the left-hand seat cowling (see Chapter 7) – when doing so remove the right-hand shock absorber cover as well as the left.

11 Remove the silencer (see Chapter 4).

11.7d On models with ESA now release the wiring

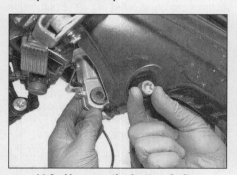

11.9a Unscrew the bottom bolt…

11.9b …the top bolt…

11.9c …and lift the shock absorber out

11.14 Pull the rod off the ball joint

12 Remove the rear wheel (see Chapter 6). Position a support (a block of wood or an axle stand is ideal) underneath the final drive unit so it is supported, but not lifted. Do not place the support under the rear brake disc.

13 Remove the mudflap.

14 On models with ESA remove the ECU (see Chapter 4). Release the ride height sensor linkage rod from the ball head joint on the swingarm **(see illustration)**. Disconnect the ESA wiring connectors **(see illustration 11.3b)**. Release and displace the fuse holder **(see illustration 11.3d)**. Release the ESA wiring from its guides and feed the connectors down.

15 Unscrew and remove the bolt securing the top of the shock absorber, raising or lowering the swingarm slightly if required to relieve any pressure **(see illustration 11.9b)**. Remove the support and lower the swingarm, then unscrew the bolt securing the bottom of the shock, withdraw the bolt and manoeuvre the shock out **(see illustration 11.9a)**.

R and RS models

16 Place the bike on the centrestand if fitted. If no centrestand is fitted you need to support the rear of the bike using axle stands or similar that hold the weight through the frame, not any part of the rear suspension, and so the rear wheel is off the ground.

17 On models with ESA remove the ECU (see Chapter 4). Release the ride height sensor linkage rod from the ball head joint on the swingarm **(see illustration 11.14)**. Disconnect the ESA wiring connectors **(see illustration 11.3b)**. Cut the cable-tie on the fuse holder, then release and displace the holder **(see illustration 11.3d)**. Release the ESA wiring from its guides and feed the connectors down.

18 Position a support (a block of wood or an axle stand is ideal) underneath the rear wheel or final drive unit so it is supported, but not lifted. Do not place the support under the rear brake disc.

19 Unscrew and remove the bolt securing the top of the shock absorber, raising or lowering the swingarm slightly if required to relieve any pressure **(see illustration 11.9b)**. Remove the support and lower the swingarm, then unscrew the bolt securing the bottom of the

shock, withdraw the bolt and manoeuvre the shock out **(see illustration 11.9a)**.

Inspection

20 Inspect the shock absorber for obvious physical damage. Check the spring for looseness, cracks or signs of fatigue. Where applicable, check the operation of the spring pre-load adjuster.

21 Inspect the damper rod for signs of bending, pitting and oil leakage.

22 Inspect the pivot bushes at the top and bottom of the shock for wear or damage.

23 Individual components for the rear shock absorber are not available. The entire unit must be replaced with a new one if it is worn or damaged.

Installation

24 Installation is the reverse of removal, noting the following.

● Lubricate the shoulders of the mounting bolts with a smear of grease.

● Clean the threads of the bolts and apply a high strength thread-locking compound (such as Loctite 270).

● Tighten the bolts to the torque setting specified at the beginning of the Chapter.

● On machines equipped with ESA, reconnect the wiring connectors and secure the wiring in its guides. Do not forget to clip the ride height sensor linkage rod back onto the ball head. When all work is completed the bike should be taken to a BMW dealer to recalibrate the ride-height sensor.

12 Suspension adjustment and ESA

Manually adjusted shock absorbers

1 Before adjusting the suspension, position the bike on its centre stand or support it securely upright on an auxiliary stand.

2 The front shock absorber is not adjustable.

3 The rear shock absorber is adjustable for spring pre-load and rebound damping. Suspension damping must be set-up to suit spring pre-load. An increase in pre-load requires firmer damping, a reduction in pre-load requires softer damping.

4 On RT models remove the pre-load adjuster cover by pulling the bottom out first, then releasing the tabs on the top. If required an extension handle is provided in the toolkit as an aid for turning the adjuster knob – locate the two prongs in the holes in the knob.

5 Spring pre-load adjustment is made by turning the adjuster knob on the shock. Turn the knob anti-clockwise (LOW) to reduce spring pre-load, and clockwise (HIGH) to increase it. For rider-only use on all models, turn the knob fully anti-clockwise (LOW arrow). Turn the knob clockwise to increase pre-load related to any

extra load carried, and rider preference. No recommendations are made for extra loads on GS models. On GS Adventure models BMW recommends (as a guide) 15 turns clockwise from fully LOW for rider plus luggage, and 30 turns clockwise for rider plus passenger and luggage. On RT models BMW recommends 10 turns clockwise from fully LOW for rider plus luggage, and as far as it will go clockwise for rider plus passenger and luggage. On R and RS models BMW recommend 15 turns clockwise from fully LOW for rider plus luggage, and as far as it will go clockwise for rider plus passenger and luggage.

6 The preferred setting for particular loads can be recorded by counting the number of grooves visible on the spindle of the adjuster knob.

7 Damping adjustment is made by turning the adjuster knob on the bottom of the shock at the front. Turn the knob clockwise to increase damping and anti-clockwise to reduce it. For rider use only, turn the knob fully clockwise until it seats, then turn it anti-clockwise 8 clicks on GS and GS Adv models, and 6 clicks on RT, R and RS models. Turn the knob clockwise to increase damping according to any extra load carried and the pre-load setting, and as required according to road conditions and rider preference. No recommendations are made for extra loads on GS models. On GS Adventure models BMW recommends 4 clicks anti-clockwise from full clockwise, or 4 clicks clockwise from the rider only recommended setting, for any extra loads, luggage and/or passenger. On RT models BMW recommends 4 clicks anti-clockwise from full clockwise, or 4 clicks clockwise from the the rider only recommended setting, for rider plus luggage, and 2 clicks anti-clockwise from full clockwise, or 6 clicks clockwise from the rider only recommended setting, for rider plus passenger and luggage. On R and RS models BMW recommends 4 clicks anti-clockwise from full clockwise, or 4 clicks clockwise from the rider only recommended setting, for rider plus luggage, and fully clockwise for rider plus passenger and luggage.

Electronic suspension adjustment (ESA)

8 A range of spring pre-load and damping options can be selected using the buttons on the handlebar switch assemblies as described in the owners handbook for your model.

9 If no changes in spring pre-load and damping are noticed when changes are dialled in using the switches, first check the wiring and connectors (see Section 6, Section 7, Section 11). If the wiring and connectors are good take the bike to a BMW dealer for testing using the diagnostic tools.

Ride height sensors

Front

10 Remove the fuel tank (see Chapter 4).

11 Detach the sensor arm from the Telelever **(see illustration 6.33a)**. Release the fuel

12.11a Release the hose from its clip

12.11b Disconnect and release the wirng

12.11c Tank bracket screws (arrowed)

hose from the left-hand fuel tank bracket **(see illustration)**. Disconnect the wiring connector from the sensor and release the wire guide from the tank bracket **(see illustration)**. Undo the tank bracket screws and remove the bracket with the sensor attached **(see illustration)**. Undo the screws and remove the sensor from the bracket.

12 Installation is the reverse of removal.

Rear

13 On RT models remove the left-hand shock absorber cover (see Chapter 7). On all other models remove the ride height sensor cover **(see illustration 11.3a)**.

14 Detach the sensor arm from the swingarm **(see illustration 11.14)**. Disconnect the wiring connector from the sensor **(see illustration)**. Undo the screws and remove the sensor **(see illustration)**.

15 Installation is the reverse of removal.

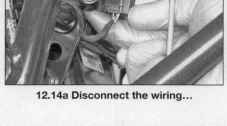

12.14a Disconnect the wiring…

12.14b …then undo the screws

13 Swingarm and driveshaft

Removal

1 The swingarm, driveshaft and final drive unit can be removed as an assembly, but note that as such it is heavy and awkward, and so it is advisable to remove the final drive unit completely. If required the driveshaft can be removed from the swingarm, leaving the swingarm/final drive unit in place, after pivoting the final drive unit down (see below).

2 Position the bike on its centre stand or support it securely on an auxiliary stand that takes the weight through the frame and not any part of the rear suspension. Tie the front brake lever on.

3 Remove the rear wheel (see Chapter 6).

4 Displace the rear wheel speed sensor **(see illustration)**.

5 Displace the rear brake caliper (see Chapter 6), then secure the caliper and rear wheel speed sensor to the rear sub-frame – it is not necessary to disconnect the brake hose from the caliper.

6 If required remove the final drive unit (Section 14).

7 If the final drive unit has not been removed place a support under it. Unscrew the bolt securing the Paralever arm to the final drive unit, noting the wiring guide, then pivot the arm up and secure it to the sub-frame **(see illustration)**. If you want to remove the arm completely undo the hose/wiring cover

13.4 Undo the screw and draw the sensor off

13.7a Detach the arm from the final drive unit

13.7b Undo the rear screw…

13.7c …and the front screw…

13.7d …release the hose and wire and remove the cover…

13.7e …then unscrew the bolt and remove the arm

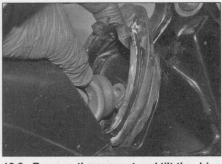

13.8a Remove the support and tilt the drive unit back…

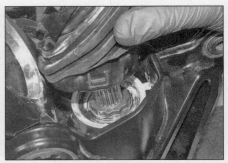

13.8b …and remove the boot

13.9 Pull the boot off the swingarm

screws and remove the cover, then unscrew the bolt securing the arm to the frame and remove the arm **(see illustrations)**.

8 If the final drive unit has not been removed, and if you want to withdraw the driveshaft from the swingarm, remove the support underneath it and place it under the swingarm, then carefully tilt the unit back, displacing the rubber boot from the swingarm – the final drive housing shaft will come out of the driveshaft coupling **(see illustration)**. Remove the rubber boot, noting the plastic insert **(see illustration)**.

9 Displace the front rubber boot forwards off the swingarm **(see illustration)**.

10 A retaining ring inside the front driveshaft coupling secures the coupling on the gearbox output shaft by seating in a groove. Insert a suitable bar or strong screwdriver between the two halves of the front driveshaft coupling so that it bears on the end of the gearbox output shaft, then lever the coupling off the gearbox shaft **(see illustration)**. If required withdraw the driveshaft from the swingarm, noting which way round it fits **(see illustration)**.

11 Remove the rear shock absorber (Section 11). Place a support (a block of wood or an axle stand is ideal) underneath the swingarm, or under the final drive unit (if not removed).

13.10a Lever the front driveshaft coupling off the gearbox output shaft…

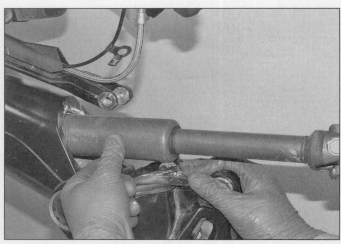

13.10b …and withdraw the driveshaft from the swingarm

13.12a Unscrew the nut, and remove the plug where fitted

13.12b Unscrew the pin

13.13a Heat the bearing pin...

12 Unscrew the right-hand bearing pin locknut and remove the anti-chafing plug where fitted, then unscrew the pin **(see illustrations)**.
13 Support the swingarm assembly. Heat the left-hand bearing pin using a hot air gun, then unscrew the pin, and remove the anti-chafing plug or washer, according to model **(see illustrations)**.
14 Carefully draw the swingarm out **(see illustration)**.
15 If required release and remove the front rubber boot, noting the plastic insert.

Inspection

16 Check the condition of the rubber boots and replace them with new ones it cracked or split.
17 Clean all the components thoroughly, removing all traces of dirt, corrosion and grease.
18 Inspect the components closely for signs of wear or accident damage. Any damaged or worn components must be renewed.
19 Check the driveshaft coupling universal joints for wear. The joints should move smoothly and freely with no sign of roughness and there should be no play between the halves of the coupling **(see illustration)**. If wear is evident, a new driveshaft must be fitted – individual components are not available.
20 Inspect the internal splines in each end of the driveshaft couplings and the corresponding external splines on the gearbox output shaft and the final drive unit input shaft for wear and damage. Check the fit of each

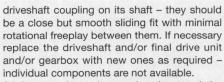

13.13b ...then unscrew it

13.14 Remove the swingarm

driveshaft coupling on its shaft – they should be a close but smooth sliding fit with minimal rotational freeplay between them. If necessary replace the driveshaft and/or final drive unit and/or gearbox with new ones as required – individual components are not available.
21 Inspect the swingarm bearings and the surface of the bearing pins **(see illustration)**. Refer to *Tools and Workshop Tips* in the Reference section for details of bearing inspection and renewal. Note that BMW specify to use a new left-hand bearing pin.
22 Inspect the bushes in the front end of the Paralever arm and the top of the final drive unit **(see illustration)**. If the bushes are worn or have deteriorated they should be replaced with new ones. Use a drawbolt arrangement to draw the old bushes out and the new bushes in (see *Tools and Workshop Tips* in the Reference section).

Installation

23 Lubricate the gearbox output shaft splines with molybdenum disulphide grease. If removed fit the rubber boot onto the back of the gearbox and secure it with a cable-tie. Make sure the plastic insert is correctly in place in the rear of the boot.
24 Lubricate the plain shoulder and the inner narrower section of threads on the right-hand swingarm bearing pin, and the plain shoulder on the left-hand pin. Apply a high strength thread locking compound (such as Loctite 270) to half of the threaded section on the left-hand pin, from the centre up to the head.
25 Carefully manoeuvre the swingarm into place and thread the bearing pins in finger-tight, fitting the anti-chafing plug or washer with the left-hand pin according to model **(see illustrations 13.14, 13.13b and 13.12b)**. Tighten the left-hand pin first, to

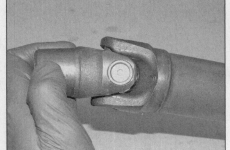

13.19 Check the universal joints for wear

13.21 Check the condition of the swingarm bearings

13.22 Check the bushes

13.26a Guide the driveshaft over the output shaft...

13.26b ...then lever it on to engage the retaining ring

13.31 Locate the tabs under the rim

the torque setting specified at the beginning of the Chapter. Next tighten the right-hand pin to its initial torque setting, then loosen it and tighten it to the final torque setting. Make a reference mark between the right-hand pin and part of the frame that won't be covered by the anti-chafing plug (when and where fitted), then fit the plug (where fitted) and the locknut and tighten the nut to the specified torque **(see illustration 13.12a)**. Check the reference marks after tightening to make sure the pin has not tightened with the nut. If it has loosen the nut and the pin, then use the BMW tool Nos. 33641 and 33642, that allow the pin to be counter-held while tightening the nut. Check the swingarm pivots up and down smoothly and freely, then place a support under it.

26 Lubricate the driveshaft splines with molybdenum grease. Slide the driveshaft into the swingarm with the wider section of shaft at the front **(see illustration 13.10b)**, and guide it onto the output shaft, turning it as required to align the splines **(see illustration)**. Lever the shaft fully on so the retaining ring engages in the groove, then try to pull it back to make sure it is secure on the shaft **(see illustration)**.

27 Lubricate the rear rim of the front rubber boot with silicone grease and fit over the front of the swingarm, making sure the plastic insert is correctly aligned and locates correctly **(see illustration 13.9)**.

28 Install the rear shock absorber (see Section 11).

29 If the Paralever arm was completely removed clean the threads of the front mounting bolt and apply a high strength

locking compound, fit the arm onto the frame and fit the bolt, and tighten it to the specified torque **(see illustration 13.7e)**. Fit the hose and wire into the cover, then fit the cover onto the arm **(see illustrations 13.7d, c and b)**.

30 If removed install the final drive unit (Section 14).

31 If the final drive unit was not completely removed lubricate the shaft splines with molybdenum grease, and the rear rubber boot flanges with silicone grease, and fit the boot onto the final drive unit, making sure it locates correctly **(see illustration 13.8b)**. Clean the threads of the Paralever rear bolt and apply a high strength locking compound. Pivot the final drive unit up and align and engage the splined shaft inside the driveshaft coupling **(see illustration 13.8a)**. Fit the Paralever arm, position the wiring guide, insert the bolt and tighten it to the specified torque **(see illustration 13.7a)**. Seat the boot in the end of the swingarm **(see illustration)**.

32 Install the remaining components in the reverse order of removal.

14 Final drive unit

Note: *This procedure covers removal and installation of the final drive unit. Further dismantling and set-up of the final drive unit requires special tools and is beyond the scope of this manual. If the final drive unit is thought to be faulty have it checked by a BMW dealer.*

Removal

1 Position the bike on its centre stand or support it securely on an auxiliary stand that does not interfere with removal of the rear wheel or final drive unit.

2 Remove the rear wheel (see Chapter 6).

3 Displace the rear wheel speed sensor **(see illustration 13.4)**.

4 Displace the rear brake caliper (see Chapter 6), then secure the caliper and rear wheel speed sensor to the rear sub-frame – it is not necessary to disconnect the brake hose from the caliper.

5 Place a support under the final drive unit. Unscrew the bolt securing the Paralever arm to the final drive unit, noting the wiring guide, then pivot the arm up and secure it to the sub-frame **(see illustration 13.7a)**.

6 Remove the support from under the drive unit and carefully tilt the unit back, displacing the rubber boot from the swingarm – the final drive housing shaft will come out of the driveshaft coupling **(see illustration 13.8a)**. Support the drive unit on a block of wood. Remove the rubber boot, noting the plastic insert **(see illustration 13.8b)**.

7 Prise the cover off the left-hand pivot sleeve on the drive unit **(see illustration)**. Counter-hold the pivot sleeve and unscrew and remove the pivot bolt on the inner side **(see illustrations)**.

8 Support the drive unit and use a suitable drift to drive the left-hand pivot sleeve out, then drive out the right-hand pivot stud **(see illustrations)**. Lift the drive unit off – it should be supported upright, but not on the disc,

14.7a Prise off the cover...

14.7b ...then counter-hold the pivot sleeve and undo the pivot bolt...

14.7c ...and withdraw it

14.8a Remove the sleeve...

14.8b ...and the stud

14.8c Remove the spacer and check its O-ring...

14.8d ...and the seal on the stud

14.9a Check for oil leakage around the brake disc flange...

14.9b ...and the shaft

and not allowed to rest on its side. Remove the spacer from the inside of the left-hand bearing housing (see illustration). Check the condition of the pivot stud seal and the spacer O-ring and replace them with new ones if necessary (see illustration).

Inspection

9 Clean the drive unit thoroughly, removing all traces of dirt and corrosion. Check for any evidence of oil leakage, particularly behind the brake disc flange and around the bevel gear shaft (see illustrations). Replacement of the drive unit seals must be undertaken by a BMW dealer.

10 Inspect the bearing surfaces of the pivot sleeve and the pivot stud (see illustrations 14.8a and b). If they are worn, pitted or scored, replace them with new ones. Inspect the corresponding bearings in the drive unit – a needle roller bearing is fitted in the right-hand side and a sealed ball bearing is in the left-hand side (see illustration). Note that the ball bearing is secured by a circlip on the outside (see illustration). Refer to Tools and Workshop Tips in the Reference section for details of bearing inspection and renewal.

11 Inspect the bush for the Paralever arm in the top of the unit housing (see illustration 13.22). If the bush has deteriorated it should be replaced with a new one, and the arm should be removed to check the front bush (Section 13). Use a drawbolt arrangement to draw the old bush out and the new bush in (see Tools and Workshop Tips in the Reference section).

12 Pull the breather out of the top of the

drive housing and clean it. If it is damaged or deteriorated, fit a new one.

Installation

13 If necessary fit a new O-ring onto the bearing spacer. Press the spacer into the inside of the left-hand bearing housing with the O-ring facing the bearing (see illustration 14.8c).

14 Lubricate the splined end of the shaft with molybdenum disulphide grease.

15 If necessary fit a new seal onto the pivot stud (see illustration 14.8d). Clean the threads of the pivot bolt.

16 Support the drive unit in position and press the pivot sleeve in from the left-hand side and the pivot stud in from the right-hand side (see illustrations 14.8a and b).

17 Apply some high strength threadlock (such as Loctite 270) to the threads of the pivot bolt, then fit the bolt in from the inner side (see illustration 14.7c). Counter-hold the

14.10a Check the bearings

pivot sleeve and tighten the pivot bolt to the torque setting specified at the beginning of this Chapter (see illustration 14.7b).

18 Lubricate the rear rubber boot flanges with silicone grease, and fit the boot onto the final drive unit, making sure it locates correctly (see illustration 13.8b). Clean the threads of the Paralever rear bolt and apply a high strength locking compound. Pivot the final drive unit up and align and engage the splined shaft inside the driveshaft coupling (see illustration 13.8a). Fit the Paralever arm, position the wiring guide, insert the bolt and tighten it to the specified torque (see illustration 13.7a). Seat the boot in the end of the swingarm (see illustration 13.31).

19 Fit the cover on the left-hand pivot sleeve (see illustration 14.7a).

20 Install the remaining components in the reverse order of removal.

14.10b Sealed ball bearing is secured by a circlip (arrowed)

Chapter 6
Brakes, wheels and tyres

Contents

Degrees of difficulty

Easy, suitable for novice with little experience	**Fairly easy,** suitable for beginner with some experience	**Fairly difficult,** suitable for competent DIY mechanic	**Difficult,** suitable for experienced DIY mechanic	**Very difficult,** suitable for expert DIY or professional

Specifications

Front brake

Brake fluid type	DOT 4
Brake pad friction material wear limit (min. thickness).	1.0 mm
Disc thickness	
Standard.	4.5 mm
Service limit	4.0 mm
Disc diameter	
R1200 GS and GS Adventure.	305 mm
R1200 RT, R and RS.	320 mm
Runout (service limit)	0.15 mm

Rear brake

Brake fluid type	DOT 4
Brake pad friction material wear limit (min. thickness).	1.0 mm
Disc thickness	
Standard.	5.0 mm
Service limit	4.5 mm
Disc diameter (all models)	276 mm
Runout (service limit)	0.35 mm

Wheels

Maximum wheel runout (axial and radial)	
Cast wheels (front and rear)	1.5 mm
Spoke wheels (front and rear).	1.7 mm

Tyres

	Front	Rear
Tyre pressures	see *Pre-ride checks*	
Tyre sizes*	**Front**	**Rear**
R1200 GS and GS Adventure.	120/70 R 19V	170/60 R 17V
R1200 RT and R1200 R	120/70 ZR 17W	180/55 ZR 17W

Also refer to your owners handbook or the tyre information label under the bike's seat.

ABS

Wheel speed sensor air gap	
Front	0.1 to 1.4 mm
Rear	0.1 to 1.6 mm

Torque settings

Brake hose banjo bolts.	24 Nm
Front axle bolt	
GS, GS Adv and RT models	30 Nm
R and RS models	50 Nm
Front axle clamp bolts	19 Nm
Front brake caliper bleed valve	10 Nm
Front brake caliper mounting bolts	38 Nm
Front brake disc bolts	19 Nm
Front brake lever pivot bolt nut	7 Nm
Front brake master cylinder clamp bolts	8 Nm
Rear brake caliper bleed valve	14 Nm
Rear brake caliper mounting bolts	24 Nm
Rear brake disc bolts	
Initial setting	12 Nm
Final setting	30 Nm
Rear brake master cylinder mounting screws	8 Nm
Rear wheel bolts.	60 Nm
Wheel spokes – R1200 GS Adventure	
Nipple initial setting	1 Nm
Nipple final setting	4 Nm
Grub screw	2 Nm
Wheel speed sensor screw	8 Nm

1 General information

1 All models covered in this manual are fitted with front and rear hydraulically operated disc brakes. The front brake calipers have four opposed pistons each, and the rear brake has two pistons in a sliding caliper. An ABS (anti-lock braking system) that prevents the wheels from locking-up under hard braking is fitted as standard equipment to all models.

2 The cast alloy wheels on GS, RT, R and RS models are designed for tubeless tyres only. GS Adventure models have wire spoked wheels, but these are of a cross-spoke design – the spokes are attached to the rim outside of the tyre's sealing area, thus permitting the use of tubeless tyres. These wheels are available as optional equipment (OE) on GS models.

Caution: Disc brake components rarely require disassembly. Do not disassemble components unless absolutely necessary.

The dust created by the brake system is harmful to your health – never blow it out with compressed air and don't inhale any of it. An approved filtering mask should be worn when working on the brakes. Do not use solvents for cleaning brake system components. Solvents will cause the seals to swell and distort. Use only clean brake fluid or dedicated brake system cleaner. Use care when working with brake fluid as it can injure your eyes and will damage painted surfaces and plastic parts.

2 Brake pads

⚠️ **Warning: The dust created by the brake system could be harmful to your health. Never blow it out with compressed air and don't inhale any of it. An approved filtering mask should be worn when working on the brakes.**

Front brake pads

1 Pull out the spring clip then unscrew the pad pin **(see illustrations)**. Remove the pad spring, noting how it fits, and withdraw the pads from the caliper **(see illustration)**.

Caution: Do not operate the front brake lever whilst the pads are out of the caliper.

2 Inspect the surface of each pad for contamination and check that the friction material has not worn down to the wear limits (see Chapter 1) or the minimum thickness (see Specifications).

3 If any pad is worn, fouled with oil or grease, or heavily scored or damaged, all the front pads must be replaced with a new set. Note that it is not possible to degrease the friction material – if the pads are contaminated in any way they must be replaced with new ones.

4 If the pads are in good condition clean them carefully, using a fine wire brush which is completely free of oil and grease to remove all traces of road dirt and corrosion. Use a pointed instrument to dig out any embedded

2.1a Pull out the spring clip...

2.1b ...then unscrew the pad pin and remove the spring...

2.1c ...and pull the pads out

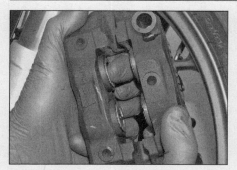

2.8 Finger pressure should be enough, but use a tool if necessary

2.10 Make sure the friction material on the pads faces the disc

2.11 Press the top of the spring down to insert the pin

particles of foreign matter. Ensure that the anti-chatter shims are a firm fit on the back of the pads.

5 Check the condition of the brake disc (see Section 4).

6 Remove all traces of corrosion from the pad pin. Inspect the pin for signs of wear and replace it with a new one if necessary. Replace the pin clip with a new one if it is corroded or sprained.

7 If you are fitting new pads, follow Steps 8 and 9. If you are refitting the same pads go to Step 10.

8 Displace the caliper (Section 3), then clean around the exposed section of each piston to remove any dirt or debris that could damage the seals. Push the pistons back into the caliper to create room for the new pads **(see illustration)** – if finger pressure is not enough BMW produces a service tool (Part Nos. 341531 and 341532), or alternatively use a commercially available piston spreading tool, a piece of wood as leverage, or fit the old pads and use a metal bar or a screwdriver inserted between them. Do not lever against the brake disc. Do not push the pistons back further than is necessary to accommodate the pads.

9 Install the caliper (Section 3).

10 Smear the shank of the pad pin with copper-based grease. Fit the pads into the caliper with the friction material facing the disc **(see illustration)**.

11 Fit the pad spring with the arrow pointing up (in the direction of normal rotation), then press it down and insert the pad pin, with the hole for the clip accessible, through both pads and over the top of the spring, then tighten it **(see illustration)**. Secure the pad pin with the spring clip **(see illustration 2.1a)**.

12 Operate the brake lever several times to bring the pads back into contact with the discs. Check the operation of the brakes before riding the bike.

Rear brake pads

13 On GS and GS Adventure models, remove the rear spray guard (see Chapter 7).

14 Pull out the R-clips, then withdraw the pad pin, using a suitable drift to push or drive it out if necessary **(see illustrations)**.

15 Withdraw the pads from the caliper **(see illustration)**.

Caution: Do not operate the rear brake pedal whilst the pads are out of the caliper.

16 Inspect the surface of each pad for contamination and check that the friction material has not worn down to the wear limit (see Chapter 1) or the minimum thickness (see Specifications).

17 Follow Steps 3 to 6 to assess the condition of the pads and to check the disc, pad pin and R-clips. If you are fitting new pads follow Steps 18, 19 and 20. If you are refitting the same pads go to Step 21.

18 Follow the procedure in Section 6 and displace the caliper, then slide the caliper and

2.14a Pull out the R-clips...

2.14b ...then remove the pad pin

2.15 Pull out the pads

2.18a Slide the caliper and bracket apart

2.18b Clean the spring and make sure it is correctly in place...

2.18c ...then do the same for the guide

bracket apart **(see illustration)**. Clean around the exposed section of both pistons to remove any dirt or debris that could damage the piston seals. Also clean the pad spring inside the caliper and the guide on the bracket, and clean all old grease off the slider pins and rubber boots **(see illustrations)**. Check the boots for cracks and splits and replace them with new ones if necessary.

19 Push the pistons back into the caliper to create room for the new pads **(see illustration)** – if finger pressure is not enough BMW produces a service tool (Part Nos. 341531 and 341532), or alternatively use a commercially available piston spreading tool, a piece of wood as leverage, or fit the old pads and use a metal bar or a screwdriver inserted between them. Do not lever against the brake disc. Do not push the pistons back further than is necessary to accommodate the pads.

20 Make sure the pad spring and guide are correctly in place **(see illustrations 2.18b and c)**. Lubricate the slider pins and rubber boots with silicone grease, then slide the caliper onto the bracket **(see illustration 2.18a)**. Install the caliper (Section 6).
21 Smear the shank of the pad pin with copper-based grease.
22 Fit the pads into the caliper with the friction material facing the disc, locating the leading edges against the guide as shown **(see illustrations)**. Press the pads against the pad spring and insert the pad pin **(see illustration)**. Fit the R-clips **(see illustration 2.14a)**.
23 On GS and GS Adventure models, install the rear spray guard (see Chapter 7).
24 Operate the brake pedal several times to bring the pads into contact with the disc. Check the operation of the brakes before riding the bike.

3 Front brake calipers

⚠️ *Warning: The dust created by the brake system is harmful to your health – never blow it out with compressed air and don't inhale any of it. An approved filtering mask should be worn when working on the brakes. Do not use petroleum-based solvents for cleaning brake system components – they will cause the seals to swell and distort. Use only clean brake fluid or dedicated brake system cleaner. Use care when working with brake fluid as it can injure your eyes and will damage painted surfaces and plastic parts*

Removal

1 It is only necessary to disconnect the brake hose if the caliper is being removed completely for overhaul (see below) – if you are just displacing the caliper for wheel removal, pad renewal or cleaning it should remain connected.
2 If poor brake action is the result of a sticking piston, or if a piston seal has failed and brake fluid is leaking from the caliper, the caliper must be overhauled. Rebuild kits are available.
3 If required remove the brake pads (see Section 2).
4 When removing the left-hand caliper unclip the wheel speed sensor wire from the brake hose **(see illustration)**. Undo the caliper

2.19 Finger pressure should be enough, but use a tool if necessary

2.22a Fit the pads...

2.22b ...making sure the leading edges locate correctly against the guide

2.22c Push the pads up to align the holes when fitting the pin

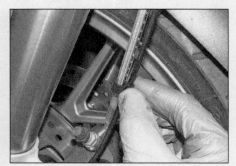

3.4a Release the wire from the hose

3.4b Unscrew the bolts…

3.4c …and slide the caliper off

3.5 Hold the pistons on one side in and pump the opposite pistons out

mounting bolts and slide the caliper off the disc **(see illustrations)** – note how the upper bolt on the left-hand caliper secures the wheel speed sensor wiring guide.

Overhaul

5 Push the pistons on one side of the caliper all the way in and hold them there, then pump the brake lever until the pistons on the opposite side are most of the way out, but not past the seals **(see illustration)**.

6 Have a container ready to catch the shower of brake fluid. Note the alignment of the hose with the caliper, then undo the banjo bolt and detach the hose **(see illustration)**. Note the sealing washers fitted to both sides of the banjo union – new ones must be used. Wrap the end of the hose in some clean rag and support it upright. Do not operate the brake lever with the hose disconnected.

7 Remove the pistons and tip the brake fluid into the container **(see illustrations)**.

8 Carefully remove the dust seals from the upper groove in each bore and the piston seal from the lower groove – use a non-metallic tool if available, and if not take care not to scratch the caliper **(see illustrations)**.

9 Lubricate the new pistons seals with new brake fluid and fit them into the lower grooves in the bores **(see illustration)**.

10 Lubricate the new dust seals with silicone grease (a sachet should be provided in the rebuild kit) and fit them into the upper grooves in the bores **(see illustration)**.

3.6 Unscrew the banjo bolt and detach the hose

3.7a Pull the pistons out…

3.7b …and drain the fluid

3.8a Remove the dust seal…

3.8b …and the piston seal from each bore

3.9 Fit the new pistons seals…

3.10 …and dust seals, making sure they seat correctly all the way round

11 Lubricate the outside of each new piston with clean brake fluid and push them squarely all the way into the bores **(see illustrations)**.

12 Repeat the procedure for the pistons and seals in the other side of the caliper – you can use compressed air or a piston removal tool to displace the pistons if available, otherwise reconnect the brake hose and pump them out as before, noting that you may have to expel the air first following the bleeding procedure in Section 10.

Installation

13 Refer to Section 2 and clean the pistons, then push them back into the caliper, all the way if new pads are being fitted, or just a little if not.

14 Slide the caliper onto the brake disc and fit the mounting bolts, securing the wheel speed sensor wiring guide with the upper bolt on the left-hand caliper, and tighten the bolts to the torque setting specified at the beginning of the Chapter **(see illustrations 3.4c and b)**.

15 Connect the brake hose to the caliper, using new sealing washers on each side of the banjo union **(see illustration)**. Align the union as shown **(see illustration)**. Tighten the banjo bolt to the specified torque setting. Clip the wheel speed sensor wire to the hose on the left-hand caliper **(see illustration 3.4a)**.

16 Install the brake pads (Section 2).

17 Top-up the master cylinder reservoir with new DOT 4 brake fluid (see *Pre-ride checks*) and bleed the brake system as described in Section 10.

18 Check for leaks and thoroughly test the operation of the brakes before riding the motorcycle.

3.11a Make sure the pistons go in straight…

3.11b …and push them all the way in

3.15a Use new sealing washers…

3.15b …and butt the hose elbow against the lug

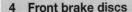

4 Front brake discs

Inspection

1 Inspect the surface of the disc for score marks and other damage. Light scratches are normal after use and won't affect brake operation, but deep grooves and heavy score marks will reduce braking efficiency and accelerate pad wear. If a disc is badly grooved it must be machined or renewed.

2 The disc must not be machined or allowed to wear down to a thickness less than the service limit listed in the specifications, and as marked on the disc itself. Check the thickness of the disc with a micrometer **(see illustration)**. If the thickness is less than the service limit, it must be replaced with a new one.

3 To check disc runout, support the bike upright so that the front wheel is raised off the ground. Mount a dial gauge to the fork leg, with the plunger on the gauge touching the surface of the disc about 10 mm (1/2 in) from the outer edge **(see illustration)**. Rotate the wheel and watch the gauge needle, then compare the reading with the limit listed in the Specifications at the beginning of this Chapter.

4 If the runout is greater than the service limit, check the wheel bearings for play (see Chapter 1). If the bearings are worn they must be replaced with new ones (Section 14). If the bearings are

good, either the disc is warped, or the rivet and washer assemblies in the floating disc mountings are damaged or worn – remove the disc to check. In both cases a new disc will have to be fitted – individual components are not available.

Removal

5 Remove the wheel (Section 12).

Caution: Do not lay the wheel down and allow it to rest on either disc – the disc could become warped. Set the wheel on wood blocks so the disc doesn't support the weight of the wheel.

6 Mark the relationship of the disc to the wheel, so it can be installed in the same position, and mark the disc itself to indicate left-or right-hand side, and which is the outer face. Undo the disc bolts, loosening them a little at a time in a criss-cross pattern, and remove the disc **(see illustration)**. Note that

4.2 Measuring the thickness of the disc with a micrometer

4.3 Set-up for checking brake disc runout with a dial gauge

4.6 Loosen the disc retaining bolts in a criss-cross pattern to avoid distorting the disc

5.3a Undo the locknut...

5.3b ...and remove the pivot bolt

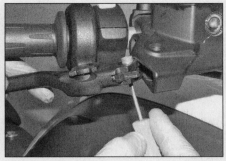

5.4 Displace the sleeve using a small screwdriver

when new, the bolts are encapsulated with a thread-locking compound, and that BMW specifies to use new bolts whenever the disc is removed, however if necessary the original bolts can be cleaned and a fresh threadlock can be applied.

Installation

7 Before fitting the disc, make sure there is no dirt or corrosion where it seats against the hub – if it does not sit flat when it is bolted down, it will appear to be warped when checked or when the brake is used.
8 Lay the disc on the wheel with the marked side facing out, aligning the previously made matchmarks if refitting the original discs.
9 Either fit new bolts or clean up the threads of the original ones and apply a suitable non-permanent thread-locking compound.
10 Tighten the bolts evenly and a little at a time in a criss-cross pattern to the torque setting specified at the beginning of the Chapter.
11 Clean the disc using acetone or brake system cleaner. If a new brake disc has been installed, remove any protective coating from its working surfaces.
12 Install the wheel (Section 12).
13 Operate the brake lever several times to bring the pads into contact with the disc. Check the operation of the brakes carefully before riding the bike.

5 Front brake master cylinder

Brake lever

1 If the brake lever feels stiff, remove and clean it as described below, and check the lever and the lever bracket for damage.
2 On GS and GS Adv models, remove the hand protector, if fitted (see Chapter 7).
3 To remove the lever undo the pivot bolt locknut on the underside, then withdraw the pivot bolt **(see illustrations)**. The nut is self-locking and BMW specifies to use a new one.
4 Displace the lever from the bracket, then push the sleeve up out of the pivot and remove the lever from the pushrod piece, noting the fitting of the small spring **(see illustration)** – the pushrod piece is part of the master cylinder.
5 Clean the contact surfaces of the lever, bracket and pivot bolt, and the sleeve and pushrod piece. If they are in good condition, lubricate the components with dry film lubricant prior to assembly.
6 Fit the spring into the lever, then fit the lever onto the pushrod piece, align the holes and insert the sleeve **(see illustrations)**. Fit the pivot bolt and thread the nut on **(see illustrations 5.3b and a)**. Counter-hold the bolt head and tighten the locknut to the torque setting specified at the beginning of the Chapter.

7 If, after cleaning and lubricating the lever, the action is still stiff, the master cylinder could be at fault.

Master cylinder

8 If there is evidence of air in the system (spongy feel to the lever), bleed the system (see Section 10).
9 If brake fluid is leaking from the master cylinder itself (as opposed to from the hose banjo union), a new master cylinder must be fitted – seal kits are not available.

Removal

Note: *If the master cylinder is just being displaced and not completely removed from the motorcycle it is not necessary to disconnect the brake hose. Secure the master cylinder to the machine with a cable-tie to avoid straining the hose and keep it upright to prevent air entering the system.*
Note: *To prevent damage to the paint from spilled brake fluid, always cover the fuel tank and bodywork when working on the master cylinder.*
10 On GS models and GS Adv models remove the hand protector, if fitted (see Chapter 7). On GS, GS Adv and R models, remove the right-hand mirror (see Chapter 7).
11 If required remove the brake lever (see above).
12 Cover the area around the end of the brake hose with clean rag to catch fluid spills. Note the alignment of the hose with the master cylinder, then undo the banjo bolt and detach the hose **(see illustration)**. Note

5.6a Fit the spring

5.6b Fit the lever onto the pushrod piece and insert the sleeve

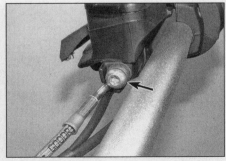

5.12 Brake hose banjo bolt (arrowed)

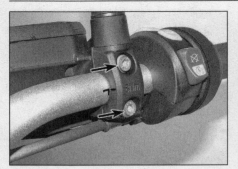

5.14 Master cylinder clamp bolts (arrowed)

6.2 Release the clip (arrowed) from the brake hose for greater freedom of movement

6.6a Undo the caliper mounting bolts...

the sealing washers fitted to both sides of the banjo union – new ones must be used.

13 Plug the master cylinder and wrap a clean rag around the end of the hose to prevent dirt entering the system – secure the hose in an upright position to minimise fluid loss.

Caution: Do not operate the brake lever (if not removed) while the hose is disconnected.

14 Support the master cylinder, undo the clamp bolts and remove it from the handlebar **(see illustration)**.

15 Undo the reservoir cover screws and remove the cover and diaphragm (see *Pre-ride checks*).

16 Empty the brake fluid into a suitable container.

17 To check the action of the master cylinder piston, temporarily install the reservoir cover and lever. Wrap some clean rag over the open end of the master cylinder hose union and operate the lever. If the lever sticks, or the action is stiff, there is a fault with the master cylinder piston. Seal kits are not available – a new master cylinder will have to be fitted.

Caution: Do not, under any circumstances, use a petroleum-based solvent to clean the master cylinder.

Installation

18 Installation is the reverse of removal, noting the following:

● On GS, GS Adv and R models align the line on the master cylinder clamp with that on the handlebar **(see illustration 5.14)**. On RT and RS models align the clamp mating

surfaces at the top with the punch mark on the handlebar. Tighten the upper bolt first to the specified torque setting, then tighten the lower bolt, so the gap is at the bottom.

● Fit new sealing washers on both sides of the banjo union.

● Align the hose as noted on removal and tighten the banjo bolt to the specified torque setting **(see illustration 5.12)**.

● Fill the fluid reservoir with new DOT 4 fluid (see *Pre-ride checks*). Bleed the air from the brake system (see Section 10).

● Check the operation of the brake before riding the motorcycle.

6 Rear brake caliper

⚠ *Warning: The dust created by the brake system could be harmful to your health – never blow it out with compressed air and don't inhale any of it. An approved filtering mask should be worn when working on the brakes. Do not use petroleum-based solvents for cleaning brake system components – they will cause the seals to swell and distort. Use only clean brake fluid or dedicated brake system cleaner. Use care when working with brake fluid as it can injure your eyes and will damage painted surfaces and plastic parts*

Removal

1 On GS and GS Adventure models, remove the rear spray guard (see Chapter 7).

2 Unclip the wheel speed sensor wiring from the brake hose **(see illustration)**.

3 It is only necessary to disconnect the brake hose if the caliper is being removed completely for overhaul (see below). If you are just displacing the caliper for pad renewal or cleaning the hose should remain connected.

4 If poor brake action is the result of a sticking piston, or if a piston seal has failed and brake fluid is leaking from the caliper, the caliper must be overhauled – rebuild kits are available.

5 If required remove the brake pads (see Section 2).

6 Undo the caliper mounting bolts, noting how they secure the wiring guide, and slide the caliper off the disc **(see illustrations)**.

7 Slide the caliper off the bracket **(see illustration 2.18a)**.

8 Clean any old grease and corrosion off the slider pins. Clean and check the condition of the rubber boots and replace them with new ones if necessary.

9 Clean the exposed sections of the pistons.

Overhaul

10 Pump the brake pedal until the pistons are most of the way out, but not past the seals **(see illustration)**.

11 Have a container ready to catch the brake fluid. Note the alignment of the hose with the caliper, then undo the banjo bolt and detach the hose **(see illustration)**. Note the sealing

6.6b ...and slide the caliper off the disc

6.10 Pump the pistons out

6.11 Unscrew the banjo bolt and detach the hose

6.12 Pull the pistons out and drain the fluid

6.13a Remove the dust seal...

6.13b ...and the piston seal from each bore

washers fitted to both sides of the banjo union – new ones must be used. Wrap the end of the hose in some clean rag and support it upright. Do not operate the brake pedal with the hose disconnected.

12 Remove the pistons and tip the brake fluid into the container **(see illustration)**.

13 Carefully remove the dust seals from the upper groove in each bore and the piston seal from the lower groove – use a non-metallic tool if available, and if not take care not to scratch the caliper **(see illustrations)**.

14 Lubricate the new pistons seals with new brake fluid and fit them into the lower grooves in the bores **(see illustration)**.

15 Lubricate the new dust seals with silicone grease (a sachet should be provided in the rebuild kit) and fit them into the upper grooves in the bores **(see illustration)**.

16 Lubricate the outside of each new piston with clean brake fluid and push them squarely all the way into the bores **(see illustrations)**.

Installation

17 Push the pistons back into the caliper, all the way if new pads are being fitted, or just a little if not **(see illustration 2.19)**.

18 Lubricate the slider pins and boot rims with a smear of silicone grease. Check that the pad spring is correctly located inside the caliper and the guide is correctly located on the bracket **(see illustrations 2.18b and c)**. Slide the caliper onto the bracket and seat the boot rims **(see illustration 2.18a)**.

19 Slide the caliper onto the brake disc and fit the mounting bolts, securing the wheel speed sensor wiring guide, and tighten the bolts to the torque setting specified at the

beginning of the Chapter **(see illustrations 6.6b and a)**.

20 Connect the brake hose to the caliper, using new sealing washers on each side of the banjo union **(see illustration)**. Butt the hose elbow against the caliper and tighten the banjo bolt to the specified torque setting **(see illustration)**.

21 Install the brake pads (Section 2).

22 Clip the speed sensor wiring to the brake hose **(see illustration 6.2)**.

23 Top-up the master cylinder reservoir with DOT 4 brake fluid (see *Pre-ride checks*) and bleed the brake system as described in Section 10.

24 On GS and GS Adventure models install the rear spray guard (see Chapter 7).

25 Check that there are no leaks and thoroughly test the operation of the brake before riding the motorcycle.

6.14 Fit the new pistons seals...

6.15 ...and dust seals, making sure they seat correctly all the way round

6.16a Make sure the pistons go in straight...

6.16b ...and push them all the way in

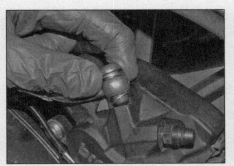

6.20a Use new sealing washers...

6.20b ...and butt the hose elbow against the caliper

7 Rear brake disc

Inspection

1 Refer to the procedure in Section 4 to check the condition of the disc. When checking disc runout, displace the brake caliper and mount the dial gauge on the final drive unit. If runout is greater than the service limit, either the disc is warped or the final drive unit bearings are worn. If the bearings need attention, have the machine checked a BMW dealer.

Removal

2 Displace the rear brake caliper (see Section 6).
3 Remove the rear wheel (see Section 13).
4 The brake disc is mounted on the inner side of the wheel mounting flange of the final drive unit (see illustration). Mark the relationship of the disc to the flange, so it can be installed in the same position, and mark the disc itself to indicate which is the outer face.
5 Undo the disc bolts, turning the disc as required to expose each bolt in turn, then applying the rear brake to lock the disc while undoing the bolt (see illustration).
6 Note that when new, the bolts are encapsulated with a thread-locking compound, and that BMW specifies to use new bolts whenever the disc is removed, however if necessary the original bolts can be cleaned and a fresh threadlock can be applied.
7 Manoeuvre the disc off the final drive unit flange.

Installation

8 Before fitting the disc, make sure there is no dirt or corrosion where it seats – if it does not sit flat when it is bolted down, it will appear to be warped when checked or when the brake is used.
9 Position the disc on the final drive flange – if the original disc is being refitted, align the previously applied matchmarks.
10 Either fit new bolts or clean up the threads of the original ones and apply a suitable non-permanent thread-locking compound.

7.4 Brake disc is mounted on the inner side of the final drive unit flange

11 Tighten the bolts evenly and a little at a time in a criss-cross pattern, rotating and locking the disc as before, to the initial torque setting specified at the beginning of the Chapter, then tighten them in the same way to the final torque setting (see illustration 7.5).
12 Clean the disc using acetone or brake system cleaner. If a new brake disc has been installed, remove any protective coating from its working surfaces.
13 Install the remaining components in the reverse order of removal.
14 Operate the brake pedal several times to bring the pads into contact with the disc. Check the operation of the brakes carefully before riding the bike.

8 Rear brake master cylinder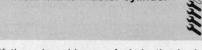

1 If there is evidence of air in the brake system (spongy feel to the pedal), bleed the system (see Section 10).
2 If brake fluid is leaking from the master cylinder, a new master cylinder must be fitted – seal kits are not available.

Removal

Note: To prevent damage to the paint from spilled brake fluid, always cover any painted parts when working on the master cylinder.
3 On RT models remove the right-hand shock absorber cover (see Chapter 7).

7.5 Access to the disc bolts is only available in one position

4 Remove the reservoir cover, diaphragm plate and diaphragm (see Pre-ride checks) and siphon the brake fluid into a suitable container, then wipe any remaining fluid out with a clean absorbent lint-free cloth. Temporarily refit the diaphragm, plate and cover.
5 On GS and GS Adventure models, undo the heel plate/master cylinder screws and remove the plate, then refit the screws to secure the master cylinder (see illustration).
6 On RT models unscrew the footrest bracket bolt from the inner side of the frame and remove the footrest assembly.
7 Straighten the ends of the split pin and remove it and the washer, then withdraw the clevis pin and separate the pushrod from the brake pedal (see illustration).
8 Release the hose clamp securing the reservoir hose to the elbow on the master cylinder and disconnect the hose, being prepared to catch any residual brake fluid (see illustration). Wrap some rag around the end of the hose.
9 Cover the area around the end of the brake hose with clean rag to catch fluid spills. Note the alignment of the hose with the master cylinder, then undo the banjo bolt and detach the hose (see illustration 8.8). Note the sealing washers fitted to both sides of the banjo union – new ones must be used.
10 Plug the master cylinder and wrap a clean plastic bag over the end of the hose to prevent dirt entering the system – secure the hose in an upright position to minimise fluid loss.

8.5 Remove the heel plate

8.7 Remove the split pin and washer (A) then withdraw the pin (B)

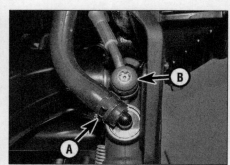

8.8 Reservoir hose clamp (A). Brake hose banjo bolt (B)

8.11 Master cylinder screws (arrowed) – R and RS models

11 Undo the screws and remove the master cylinder (see illustration).

Installation

12 Installation is the reverse of removal, noting the following:

● Tighten the master cylinder screws to the torque setting specified at the beginning of the Chapter.

● Use new sealing washers on each side of the banjo union, butt the hose elbow against the lug, and tighten the brake hose banjo bolt to the torque setting specified at the beginning of the Chapter (see illustration 8.8).

● Check the condition of the reservoir hose and replace it with a new one if there are signs of cracks or deterioration. Push the hose fully onto its union(s) and secure it with the clamp(s).

● Secure the clevis pin using a new split pin and bend its ends round to lock it (see illustration 8.7).

● On GS and GS Adventure models, if a new master cylinder has been fitted, refer to Chapter 5 Section 3 and check the gap between the brake pedal shank and the bracket is correct as described in the pedal installation sub-section, and adjust if necessary.

● Fill the reservoir with new DOT 4 fluid (see Pre-ride checks). Bleed the air from the brake system (see Section 10).

● Check the operation of the brake before riding the motorcycle.

9 Brake hoses, pipes and unions

Inspection

1 The condition of the brake hoses and pipes should be checked regularly as described in Chapter 1. For best visual access remove the fuel tank (see Chapter 4).

2 Check all hose-to-pipe joints and all the banjo unions for signs of corrosion and leakage. If leakage is found check the hose banjo bolts are tightened to the torque setting specified at the beginning of the Chapter.

Renewal

Note: *Do not operate the brake lever or pedal while a brake hose is disconnected.*

3 Remove the fuel tank and air filter housing (see Chapter 4).

4 Before loosening a hose banjo bolt, cover the surrounding area with plenty of rags to soak up any spilled brake fluid and prevent damage to painted parts.

5 Note the alignment of the banjo union on each end, then undo the banjo bolts (see illustrations 3.15b, 5.12, 6.20b, 8.8 and 17.28d). Note the sealing washers fitted on both sides of the banjo union – new ones must be used (see illustrations 3.15a, 6.20a and 17.29). Wrap some clean rag around the end of each hose and plug the master cylinder/caliper/modulator connection to catch all fluid. Make careful note of the exact routing of the hose/pipe and release it from all clips, ties and guides, then remove the hose/pipe.

6 Position the new hose/pipe exactly as noted on removal, making sure it isn't twisted or strained. Fit new sealing washers on both sides of the banjo unions and tighten the banjo bolts finger-tight only at first. Secure the hose/pipe in all its clips, ties and guides and make sure the hose is routed clear of all moving components, then tighten the banjo bolts to the torque setting specified at the beginning of this Chapter.

7 Top-up the appropriate fluid reservoir with new DOT 4 brake fluid and use the brake bleeding procedure to flush the old brake fluid from the system (see Section 10).

8 Check the operation of the brakes before riding the motorcycle.

10 Brake system bleeding and fluid change

Special tool *The brake bleeding equipment described in Step 3 will be required – ready-made bleeding kits are cheaply available from automotive stores.*

Bleeding

1 Bleeding a brake is the process of removing aerated brake fluid from the master cylinder, the hoses/pipes, modulator and the brake caliper(s).

10.5a Undo the screws…

Bleeding is necessary whenever a brake system hydraulic connection is loosened, after a component or hose is replaced with a new one, or when there is a spongy feel to the lever or pedal, and where braking force is less than it should be, and it is not due to any mechanical fault in the system (i.e. a sticking piston in the caliper, or a pad that is not moving as it should due to corrosion, for example on the pad pin). Leaks in the system may also allow air to enter, but leaking brake fluid will reveal their presence and warn you of the need for repair.

2 Brake bleeding is considered by some as a bit of a black art – seasoned professionals sometimes have trouble getting a good firm feel in the brake lever or pedal, while a first timer may have no trouble at all. One of the problems, particularly with the front brakes, is that you are working against natural principles – science dictates that air bubbles in a liquid will rise to the top, but the process entails pumping the brake fluid and any air bubbles it contains down, from the master cylinder at the top to the bleed valve in the caliper at the bottom, so while the fluid is moving down the air bubbles will want to rise. Air bubbles can also get trapped, particularly where there are high points in its path, and when there are extra components and pipes as in ABS systems.

3 To bleed the brakes using the conventional method, you will need some new DOT 4 brake fluid, a length of clear flexible hose, a small container partially filled with clean brake fluid, some rags, and a ring spanner to fit the brake caliper bleed valve. Bleeding kits that include the hose, a one-way valve and a container are available relatively cheaply from a good auto store, and simplify the task. You also need a block of wood as a support for the fluid container.

4 Cover painted components to prevent damage in the event that brake fluid is spilled. *Caution: Brake fluid attacks painted finishes and plastics – to prevent damage from spilled fluid, always cover paintwork when working on the braking system, and clean up any spills immediately using brake cleaner.*

Front brake system

5 Turn the handlebars so the reservoir is level. Undo the reservoir cover screws and remove the cover and diaphragm (see illustrations).

10.5b …and remove the cover and rubber diaphragm

10.5c Slowly pump then hold the brake lever in to force any air out of the master cylinder

10.6a Remove the dust cap

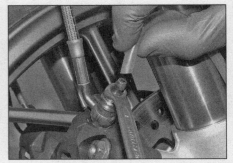

10.6b Fit the spanner over the valve then fit the hose

10.7 Keep the reservoir topped up with new brake fluid

10.8a Bleeding the front brake

10.8b Watch for air bubbles in the fluid as it comes out the valve

Slowly pump the brake lever a few times to dislodge any fine air bubbles from the holes in the bottom of the reservoir (see illustration). Now hold the lever in to force any large air bubbles out – you can tie the lever to the handlebar and leave it pressurised for a while to prevent having to hold it, then release it and slowly pump it a few times.

6 Pull the dust cap off the bleed valve on the right-hand caliper (see illustration). If using a ring spanner (which is preferable to an open-ended one) fit it onto the valve (see illustration). Attach one end of the bleeding hose to the bleed valve and, if not using a kit, submerge the other end in the clean brake fluid in the container.

7 Check the fluid level in the reservoir – keep it topped up and do not allow the level to drop below the bottom of the window during the procedure (see illustration).

8 Slowly squeeze the brake lever and open the bleed valve a quarter turn (see illustration). When the valve is opened, brake fluid will flow out of the master cylinder into the clear tubing, and the lever will move to the handlebar (see illustration). If there is air in the system there will be air bubbles in the brake fluid coming out of the caliper.

9 Tighten the bleed valve, then release the brake lever. Repeat the process until no air bubbles are visible in the brake fluid leaving the caliper, and the lever is firm when applied, topping the reservoir up when necessary. On completion tighten the bleed valve and remove the equipment, then fit the dust cap.

10 When the system has been successfully bled there should be a good and progressively firm feel as the lever is applied, and the lever should not be able to travel all the way back to the handlebar.

11 Repeat the procedure on the left-hand caliper.

12 Top-up the reservoir, then fit the diaphragm and cover. Check for spilled brake fluid and clean up as required.

13 Check there are no fluid leaks and test the operation of the brake before riding the motorcycle.

Rear brake system

14 On RT models remove the right-hand shock absorber cover (see Chapter 7).

15 Hold the reservoir and unscrew the cap, and remove the diaphragm plate and diaphragm (see illustrations). Slowly pump the brake pedal a few times to dislodge any air bubbles from the holes in the bottom of the reservoir.

16 Pull the dust cap off the bleed valve on the caliper (see illustration). If using a ring

10.15a Unscrew the cap ...

10.15b ...and remove the diaphragm plate and diaphragm

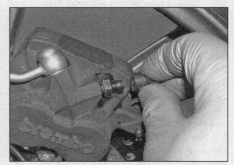

10.16a Pull the cap off the valve

10.16b Fit the spanner over the valve then fit the hose

10.17 Keep the reservoir topped up with new brake fluid

spanner (which is preferable to an open-ended one) fit it onto the valve **(see illustration)**. Attach one end of the bleeding hose to the bleed valve and, if not using a kit, submerge the other end in the clean brake fluid in the container.

17 Check the fluid level in the reservoir – keep it topped up and do not allow the level to drop below the lower level line during the procedure **(see illustration)**.

18 Slowly press the brake pedal and open the bleed valve a quarter turn **(see illustration)**. When the valve is opened, brake fluid will flow out of the master cylinder into the clear tubing, and the pedal will move down. If there is air in the system there will be air bubbles in the brake fluid coming out of the caliper **(see illustration 10.8b)**.

19 Tighten the bleed valve, then release the brake pedal. Repeat the process until no air bubbles are visible in the brake fluid leaving the caliper, and the pedal is firm when applied, topping the reservoir up when necessary.

20 When the system has been successfully bled there should be a good and progressively firm feel as the pedal is applied, and the pedal should not be able to travel all the way down to its stop.

21 On completion tighten the bleed valve and remove the equipment, then fit the dust cap.

Top-up the reservoir, then fit the diaphragm, diaphragm plate, and cap. Check for spilled brake fluid and clean up as required.

22 Check that there are no fluid leaks and test the operation of the brake before riding the motorcycle.

Both systems

23 If it is not possible to produce a firm feel to the lever or pedal, the fluid may be full of many tiny air bubbles rather than a few big ones. To remedy this apply some pressure to the system, for the front brake by tying the front brake lever lightly back to the handlebar, and for the rear by tying a weight to the brake pedal – do not apply too much pressure or the cup and seals in the master cylinder and caliper may fail. Let the fluid stabilise for a few hours, after which the tiny bubbles should either have risen to the top in the reservoir, or have formed into one or more big bubbles that can be more easily bled out by repeating the bleeding procedure.

24 If you are still having trouble look for any high point in the system in which a pocket of air may become trapped. Displace and agitate the hose or pipe so the bubble can be dislodged (but take care not to bend a pipe) – tapping it may help. If necessary displace the master cylinder and/or the caliper, and free

the brake hose from any guides and move the parts around to dislodge the air and encourage it towards a bleed valve – refer to the relevant Sections as required to displace components. It is not practical to disturb the ABS modulator as the pipes have to be detached, allowing more air to enter the system – if you cannot get the system to bleed correctly take the bike to a BMW dealer.

25 If bleeding the system using the conventional tools and methods stated does not give satisfactory results, or if otherwise preferred, you can use a commercially available vacuum-type brake bleeding tool, such as the mity-vac, following the manufacturer's instructions **(see illustration)**. This type of tool literally sucks the fluid out by creating a vacuum at the bleed valve. Users of such tools often get confused by the amount of air that appears to be in the brake fluid – more often than not this is caused by the vacuum sucking air past the bleed valve threads (air provides less resistance to the vacuum than the brake fluid) where it mixes with the fluid being drawn out. If this is the case the vacuum applied may be too great, or the bleed valve may have been loosened too much. One way to get round this is to remove the bleed valve and thread some PTFE tape around its threads, but note that doing so will be a bit messy, so have some rag to hand.

Fluid change

26 Changing the brake fluid is a similar process to bleeding the brakes and requires the same materials plus a suitable tool (such as a syringe, or alternatively lots of absorbent rag or paper) for siphoning the fluid out of the reservoir.

27 Cover painted components and fit the equipment to the relevant caliper following the appropriate Steps in the bleeding procedure given above. Remove the reservoir cover or cap, diaphragm plate (where fitted) and diaphragm **(see illustrations 10.5a and b, or 10.15a or b)**. Remove the fluid from the

10.18 Bleeding the rear brake

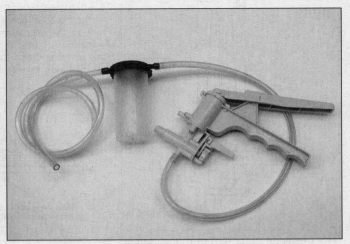

10.25 This tool creates a vacuum to suck the fluid out

reservoir into a suitable container, either by sucking it up using a tool as shown, drawing it out into a syringe, or soaking it up in some paper towel. Wipe the reservoir clean. Fill the reservoir with new brake fluid **(see illustration 10.7 or 10.17)**. Squeeze or press the brake lever or pedal and open the bleed valve **(see illustrations 10.8a and 10.18)**. When the valve is opened, brake fluid will flow out of the caliper into the clear tubing, and the lever will move toward the handlebar, or the pedal will move down.

28 Tighten the bleed valve, then slowly release the brake lever or pedal. Keep the reservoir topped-up with new fluid at all times or air may enter the system and greatly increase the length of the task. Repeat the process until new fluid can be seen emerging from the caliper bleed valve.

 HAYNES HINT *Old brake fluid is invariably much darker in colour than new fluid, making it easy to see when all old fluid has been expelled from the system*

29 On completion tighten the bleed valve and remove the equipment, then fit the dust cap. Top-up the reservoir, then fit the diaphragm, diaphragm plate (where fitted), and cover or cap. Check for spilled brake fluid and clean up as required.

30 Check that there are no fluid leaks and thoroughly test the operation of the brake before riding the motorcycle.

Draining the system for overhaul

31 Draining the brake fluid is again a similar process to bleeding the brakes. The quickest

and easiest way is to use a commercially available vacuum-type brake bleeding tool (see Step 25) – follow the manufacturer's instructions. Otherwise follow the procedure described above for changing the fluid, but quite simply do not put any new fluid into the reservoir – the system fills itself with air instead.

32 When it comes to refilling the system start by adding new fluid from a sealed container to the reservoir, then perform the bleeding procedure as described above until the fluid comes out of the bleed valve, and keep at it until you are certain there is no more air left in the system.

---

11 Wheel runout and alignment

Wheel runout

1 In order to carry out a proper inspection of the wheels, it is necessary to support the bike upright so that the wheel being inspected is raised off the ground. Position the motorcycle on its centre stand or an auxiliary stand.

2 Clean the wheels thoroughly to remove mud and dirt that may interfere with the inspection procedure or mask defects. Make a general check of the wheels (see Chapter 1, Section 13) and tyres (see *Pre-ride checks*).

3 Attach a dial gauge to the fork or the swingarm and position its tip against the side of the rim. Spin the wheel slowly and check the axial (side-to-side) runout of the rim **(see illustration)**.

4 In order to accurately check radial (out-of-round) runout with the dial gauge, the wheel will have to be removed from the machine, and the tyre from the wheel. With the axle clamped in a vice and the dial gauge positioned on the top of the rim, the wheel can be rotated to check the runout **(see illustration 11.3)**.

5 An easier, though slightly less accurate, method is to attach a stiff wire pointer to the fork or the swingarm and position the end a fraction of an inch from the wheel (where the wheel and tyre join). If the wheel is true, the distance from the pointer to the rim will

be constant as the wheel is rotated. Note: If wheel runout is excessive, check the wheel bearings (front wheel) or final drive unit bearings (rear wheel) very carefully before renewing the wheel.

Wheel alignment

6 Misalignment of the wheels can cause serious handling problems. Due to the BMW's solid engine and running gear construction, the normal problem areas for wheel misalignment (distorted frame or cocked rear wheel) do not apply. If the wheels are out of alignment, this could be due to worn or damaged Telelever components at the front, or worn swingarm bearings at the rear. If accident damage has occurred, the machine should be taken to a BMW dealer for a thorough check of the structural components.

7 To check wheel alignment you will need an assistant, a length of string or a perfectly straight length of wood or metal bar, and a ruler. A plumb bob or spirit level will also be required.

8 Support the bike in an upright position, either on its centre stand or on an auxiliary stand. Measure the width of both tyres at their widest points. Subtract the smaller measurement from the larger measurement, then divide the difference by two. The result is the amount of offset that should exist between the front and rear tyres on both sides.

9 If a string is used, have your assistant hold one end of it about halfway between the floor and the rear axle, touching the rear sidewall of the rear tyre.

10 Run the other end of the string forward and pull it tight so that it is roughly parallel to the floor. Slowly bring the string into contact with the front sidewall of the rear tyre, then turn the front wheel until it is parallel with the string **(see illustration)**. Measure the distance from the front tyre sidewall to the string.

11 Repeat the procedure on the other side of the motorcycle.

12 The distance from the front tyre sidewall to the string should be the same on both sides of the bike and equal to the tyre width offset. If the measurement differs, the wheels are out of alignment by this amount.

13 As previously mentioned, a perfectly straight length of wood or metal bar may be

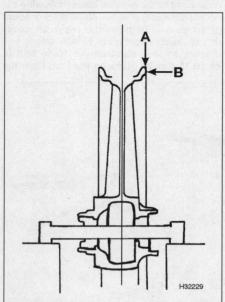

11.3 Check for radial (out-of-round) runout at point A, and axial (side-to-side) runout at point B

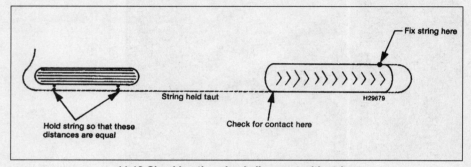

11.10 Checking the wheel alignment with string

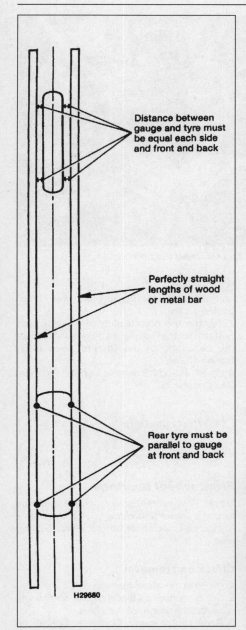

Distance between gauge and tyre must be equal each side and front and back

Perfectly straight lengths of wood or metal bar

Rear tyre must be parallel to gauge at front and back

H29680

11.13 Checking the wheel alignment with a straight-edge

substituted for the string **(see illustration)**. The procedure is the same.

14 If the wheels are out of alignment, and the fault cannot be traced to the Telelever or swingarm assemblies, the bike should be taken to a BMW dealer for verification of your findings using a track alignment gauge.

15 If the front-to-back alignment is correct, the wheels still may be out of alignment vertically.

16 Using a plumb bob or spirit level, check the rear wheel to make sure it is vertical. To do this with the plumb bob, hold the string against the tyre upper sidewall and allow the weight to settle just off the floor. When the string touches both the upper and lower tyre sidewalls and is perfectly straight, the wheel is vertical. If necessary, place thin spacers under one leg of the stand until the wheel is vertical. Using a spirit level, the level should be held against the upper and lower tyre sidewalls.

17 Once the rear wheel is vertical, check the front wheel in the same manner. If the front wheel is not perfectly vertical, the frame and/or major suspension components are bent.

12 Front wheel

Removal

1 Position the bike on its centre stand or support it securely on an auxiliary stand

so that the front wheel is off the ground. Always make sure the motorcycle is properly supported.

2 On R1200 RT models remove the front section of the front mudguard (see Chapter 7).

3 Displace the wheel speed sensor (Section 17).

4 Displace the front brake calipers (Section 3). There is no need to disconnect the hoses from the calipers. Support the calipers with a piece of wire or cable-tie so that no strain is placed on the brake hoses. **Note:** *Do not operate the front brake lever with the calipers displaced.*

5 Loosen the axle clamp bolt(s) on the bottom of each fork leg **(see illustration)**.

6 Counter-hold the head of the axle and unscrew the axle bolt from the left-hand end **(see illustrations)**. Support the wheel and withdraw the axle, then lower the wheel and draw it out from between the forks **(see illustration)**.

7 Remove the spacer from the left-hand side of the wheel **(see illustration)**.

Caution: Don't lay the wheel down and allow it to rest on either brake disc – the disc could become warped. Set the wheel on wood blocks so the tyre supports the weight of the wheel.

8 Check the axle is straight by rolling it on a flat surface such as a piece of plate glass (first wipe off all old grease and remove any corrosion using wire wool).

9 Check the condition of the wheel bearings (Section 14).

12.5 Slacken the clamp bolt(s) (arrowed) on each side

12.6a Use a hex-key tool to hold the axle…

12.6b …then unscrew the bolt

12.6c Withdraw the axle and remove the wheel

12.7 Remove the spacer

12.15 Counter-hold the head of the axle while tightening the bolt

13.3a Unscrew the bolts...

Installation

10 Make sure the brake discs and wheel speed sensor ring are clean.

11 Lubricate the axle and the inside of each bearing seal with a smear of grease, then fit the spacer into the left-hand seal, on GS, GS Adv and RT models with the grooved side facing in **(see illustration 12.7)**.

12 Manoeuvre and lift the wheel into position, then insert the axle from the right-hand side, making sure that the spacer remains in place **(see illustration 12.6c)**. Screw the axle bolt finger-tight into the left-hand end **(see illustration 12.6b)**.

13 Install the brake calipers (Section 3).

14 Temporarily take the bike off its stand and compress the front suspension several times to align the wheel and fork legs.

15 Tighten the axle bolt to the torque setting specified at the beginning of this Chapter for your model, then tighten the axle clamp bolts to the specified torque **(see illustration)**.

16 Fit the wheel speed sensor (Section 17).

17 On R1200 RT models install the front section of the front mudguard (see Chapter 7).

18 Check for correct operation of the front brake before riding the motorcycle.

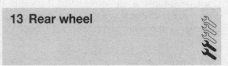

13 Rear wheel

Removal

1 Position the bike on its centre stand or support it securely on an auxiliary stand so that the rear wheel is off the ground. Always make sure the motorcycle is properly supported.

2 On RT, R and RS models remove the silencer (see Chapter 4).

3 Loosen the bolts securing the wheel to the flange on the final drive unit evenly in a criss-cross pattern, then support the wheel, withdraw the bolts and draw the wheel off the flange **(see illustrations)**.

Installation

4 Make sure the contact surfaces between the wheel hub and the final drive flange are clean.

5 Clean the threads of the wheel bolts.

6 Lift the wheel onto the flange, making sure it engages and aligns correctly,

and fit the bolts finger-tight **(see illustration 13.3b)**.

7 Tighten the bolts evenly in a criss-cross pattern to the torque setting specified at the beginning of the Chapter **(see illustration 13.3a)**.

8 On RT, R and RS models install the silencer (see Chapter 4).

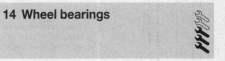

14 Wheel bearings

Front wheel bearings

Note: *Always renew the wheel bearings in pairs, never individually. Avoid using a high pressure cleaner on the wheel bearing area.*

Check and removal

1 Remove the wheel (Section 12).

2 Set the wheel on wood blocks so the tyre supports the weight of the wheel.

3 Refer to *Tools and Workshop Tips* in the Reference section and inspect the bearings for wear or damage. If the bearings do not turn smoothly or if there is freeplay between the races, they must be replaced with new ones.

4 Prise out the seal on each side of the wheel hub using a seal hook or flat-bladed screwdriver – use a piece of wood or thick card to protect the edge of the bearing housing **(see illustration)**. Discard the seals as new ones must be used.

5 To remove the bearings heat the hub around the bearing housing to 100°C and use a knife-edged bearing puller and slide-hammer arrangement to draw the first bearing out **(see illustrations)**. Lift out the bearing spacer, then heat the hub around the other bearing housing and drive the bearing out from the opposite side using a socket that bears on the

13.3b ...and draw the wheel off the flange

14.4 Lever the seal out

14.5a Locate the correct size adapter under the bearing and expand it to lock it…

14.5b …then attach the slide-hammer, hold the wheel down and jar the bearing out

inner race on an extension inserted through the centre of the hub. Note which way round the bearings are fitted.

Installation

6 Thoroughly clean the hub and bearing housings. If available use a drawbolt arrangement to fit the new bearings one at a time (see *Tools and Workshop Tips* in the Reference section). Fit the bearings with the marked or sealed side facing outwards. Make sure the drawbolt only bears on the outer race of the bearing.

7 Alternatively, use the old bearing, a bearing driver or a socket that seats on the outer race of the bearing to drive them in until they are completely seated **(see illustration)**. After fitting the first bearing, turn the wheel over and fit the bearing spacer, then drive the second bearing into place.

8 Lubricate the new seals with a smear of grease, then press them into the hub **(see illustration)**. Make sure that the seals are level with the edge of the hub by tapping them

in with a flat piece of wood **(see illustration)**.

9 Clean any grease off the brake discs using acetone or brake system cleaner, then install the wheel (Section 12).

Rear wheel bearings

10 The rear wheel bearings are part of the final drive unit. If the unit is thought to be faulty have it checked by a BMW dealer – dismantling and set-up of the final drive requires special tools and is beyond the scope of this manual. To remove the final drive unit follow the procedure in Chapter 5.

---

15 Spokes – wire spoked wheels

Caution: If a machine is ridden off-road, BMW recommend that the spoke tension should be checked on a daily basis.

1 Support the machine on its centre stand so that the wheels are free to rotate. Check each

spoke for looseness by tapping it gently with a small spanner or screwdriver and listening to the sound. The 'tone' of each spoke should sound the same.

2 If a spoke sounds dull or rattles, try to pull it backwards and forwards to confirm that it is loose. If the loose spoke is in the rear wheel and is secured to the left-hand side of the hub you need to remove the wheel to tighten it (Section 13).

3 To tighten a loose spoke, first loosen the grub screw in the spoke nipple in the hub using a 2 mm Allen key. Tighten the spoke nipple carefully to the initial, then final, torque settings specified at the beginning of this Chapter with a Torx socket and a torque wrench. Tighten the grub screw to the specified torque setting on completion.

4 If several spokes are loose it is likely that the wheel will be out of true – follow the procedure in Section 11 to check the radial and axial runout. If necessary, take the wheel to a wheel building expert for correction.

14.7 Driving a bearing in using a 33 mm socket

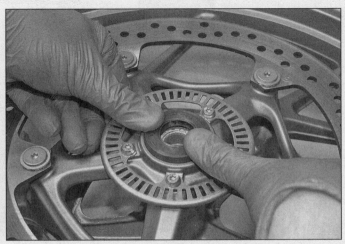

14.8 Press the seals in so they are flush with the housing

5 If a spoke is bent it must be replaced with a new one. First check the wheel runout (see Section 11). If the wheel is true, the damaged spoke can be replaced, but if the wheel is out of true, it must be taken to a wheel building expert for correction. To replace a spoke undo the grub screw and the nipple, then withdraw the spoke from the rim end – with the exception of the spokes in the left-hand side of the rear wheel hub you should be able to replace a spoke with the wheel in place, but remove the wheel if preferred. Fit the new spoke and its nipple, then tighten the nipple and the grub screw as described in Step 3.

6 If a spoke is damaged, inspect the wheel rim for damage and flat spots also.

16 Tyres – general information

General information

1 The wheels on all models, including the cross-spoke design on GS Adv models, use tubeless tyres.

2 Refer to the *Pre-ride checks* for details of tyre maintenance.

Fitting new tyres

Note: *On machines equipped with the RDC tyre pressure control system (see Section 19) special care should be taken to avoid damaging the wheel sensors.*

3 When selecting new tyres, refer to the tyre sizes given at the beginning of this chapter, the tyre options listed in rider's handbook and the tyre information label under the bike's seat. Ensure that the front and rear tyre types are compatible, and that they are of the correct size and speed rating **(see illustration)**. If necessary, seek advice from a BMW dealer or tyre fitting specialist.

4 It is recommended that tyres are fitted by a motorcycle tyre specialist rather than attempted in the home workshop. The force required to break the seal between the wheel rim and tyre bead is substantial, and is usually beyond the capabilities of an individual working with normal tyre levers. Additionally, the specialist will be able to balance the wheels after tyre fitting.

5 Note that punctured tubeless tyres can in some cases be repaired. BMW recommend that such repairs are assessed and carried out professionally.

17 ABS

System type

1 All models are equipped with BMW's Integral ABS system.

2 The system features partially integral brakes – operation of the front brake lever applies both front brakes and the rear brake, whereas operation of the rear brake pedal applies only the rear brake.

3 The ABS features an adaptive brake force distribution system that changes the proportions of front to rear brake power according to load on the wheels, thus ensuring good stability. The system also takes into account the additional loading of luggage and/or passenger.

4 The ABS prevents the wheels from locking-up under hard braking or on uneven road surfaces. A sensor on each wheel transmits wheel speed information to the ABS control unit. If the control unit senses that a wheel is about to lock, the pressure modulator releases brake pressure momentarily to that wheel, preventing a skid.

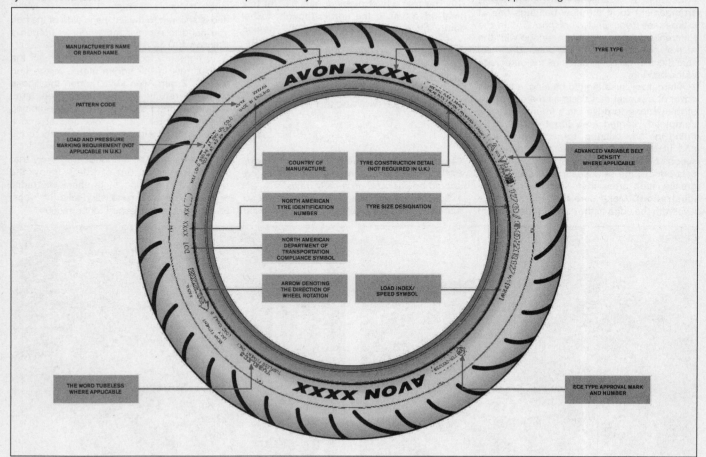

16.3 Common tyre sidewall markings

17.10 The diagnostic tester plug (arrowed) is next to the battery on all models

17.17a Undo the screw and withdraw the sensor

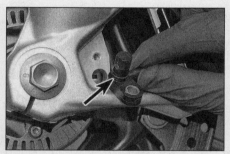

17.17b Check the condition of the O-ring (arrowed), and make sure the sensor head is clean and undamaged

5 ABS Pro is available as a factory-fit option on certain models from 2016. Using information from the angular rate (lean angle) sensor the system electronics alters ABS braking whilst cornering. Models from 2016 can also be supplied with BMW's Dynamic Brake Light. The system triggers the brake light LEDs to flash when braking at speeds above 31 mph (50 kmh), and the hazard warning lights to come on when vehicle speed drops to 7 mph (14 kmh); the hazards are switched off once road speed increases to 12 mph (20 kmh).

⚠ **Warning: If there is a fault with the ABS, extreme care must be taken when riding the motorcycle, and it should be taken immediately to a BMW dealer for analysis.**

System operation

6 The ABS is self-checking. A self-diagnosis test is performed every time the ignition is switched ON and is only completed when the machine moves forwards a few metres and the speed sensors have been checked. During the test the ABS symbol on the instrument cluster will flash. Once the test is completed satisfactorily the ABS symbol will extinguish.

7 If the symbol continues to flash the self-diagnosis test has not been completed and the ABS function will not be available, resulting in a reduced braking efficiency. Stop the machine and switch the engine OFF. Carry out the starting procedure once again.

8 If there is a fault with the ABS, the warning symbol will come on and stay illuminated. The machine may be ridden, but the ABS function

will not be available and braking efficiency will be reduced.

9 Certain operating conditions can trigger the ABS warning. Running the engine with the machine on its centre stand so that the rear wheel is free to rotate, or engaging a gear with the engine running and the machine on its centre stand. Allowing engine braking to lock the rear wheel while descending a slope with a loose or slippery surface. Under these circumstances, the ABS can be reactivated if the ignition is switched OFF and the starting procedure is carried out again.

10 The ABS control unit stores faults in its memory which can be read and cleared using the BMW dealer-only diagnostic equipment or an aftermarket tester such as the GS-911 tool with appropriate wifi interface. The tester connects into a diagnostic plug next to the battery **(see illustration)**.

11 If using a GS or GS Adventure off-road, it may be desirable to ride without the ABS functioning. To deactivate the system, stop the machine, or if already at a standstill, switch the ignition ON. Press the ASC/ABS button until the ABS symbol is displayed (the warning will alternate between the ASC symbol and ABS symbol). Release the button. The ABS symbol stays on as a reminder to the rider that ABS is turned off.

12 To reactivate ABS, again press the ASC/ABS button until the ABS symbol is displayed, then press and hold the button until the light goes out.

13 If the light continues to flash, carry-out the starting procedure (see Step 6).

14 If the light remains on, a fault is registered by the ABS system (see Steps 8 to 10).

Wheel speed sensors and sensor rings

Front wheel

15 The front wheel sensor is located on the left-hand fork leg and the sensor ring is on the left-hand side of the wheel hub. The air gap between the tip of the sensor and the surface of the ring is critical for the ABS to function correctly, and can be checked by inserting a feeler gauge between them – it should be within the range specified at the beginning of the Chapter. Check that the sensor is fitted securely and that the sensor ring is not damaged, then check that the front wheel is fitted correctly and check the wheel bearings for wear (see Chapter 1).

16 Make sure the sensor and sensor ring are clean and free of obstructions.

17 To displace the sensor undo its screw and draw it out **(see illustration)** – check the condition of the O-ring and replace it with a new one if necessary **(see illustration)**. To remove the sensor, on GS and GS Adv models remove the right-hand side panel and on RT models remove the right-hand knee support panel (see Chapter 7), and on all models remove the front wheel (Section 12). On GS, GS Adv, and RT models undo the screw securing the bottom of the mudguard to the left-hand fork **(see illustration)**. On all models undo the screw securing the wiring holder to the inside of the fork **(see illustration)**. Disconnect and release the sensor wiring and connector and feed it down to the bottom of

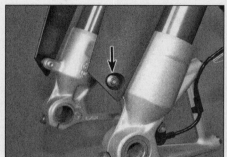

17.17c Undo the screw (arrowed) on GS and RT models...

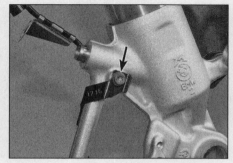

17.17d ...and the screw (arrowed) on all models

17.17e Disconnect the loom side of the wiring...

17.17f …then release the sensor side connector

17.17g On GS and RT models feed the wiring between the mudguard and the fork

17.18 Sensor ring screws

the fork, releasing it from the clips and noting its routing, and on GS, GS Adv and RT models feeding it between the bottom of the front mudguard and the fork **(see illustrations)** – on GS, GS Adv and RT models release the connector with its holder (rather than releasing the connector from the holder), and if a new sensor is being fitted you need to transfer the holder to the new connector.

18 To remove the sensor ring, remove the wheel (Section 12), then undo the screws and remove the ring **(see illustration)**.

19 Installation is the reverse of removal – on R and RS models clean the threads of the screw securing the wiring holder to the inside of the fork and apply some fresh threadlock. Fit the sensor using a new O-ring if necessary, and tighten the screw to the torque setting specified at the beginning of the Chapter. Don't forget that any fault code arising from the sensor/sensor ring damage will have to be

cleared from the control unit memory using the BMW diagnostic tester.

Rear wheel

20 The rear wheel sensor is located on the inside edge of the final drive unit, behind the drive flange. The sensor ring is an integral part of the gear assembly inside the housing.

21 To remove the sensor, on RT models remove the left-hand engine cover and shock absorber cover, and on all other models remove the frame cover from the left-hand side (see Chapter 7). On all models remove the rear wheel (Section 13).

22 Remove the rear brake hose and sensor wiring cover from the Paralever arm **(see illustrations)**. Trace the wiring and disconnect and release the sensor wiring connector, and feed the wiring back to the sensor, releasing it from all clips and guides and noting its routing.

23 Undo the sensor screw and draw the sensor out **(see illustration)** – check the condition of its O-ring and replace it with a new one if necessary **(see illustration 17.17b)**.

24 Installation is the reverse of removal. Use a new O-ring if necessary, and tighten the screw to the torque setting specified at the beginning of the Chapter. Don't forget that any fault code arising from a sensor fault will have to be cleared from the control unit memory using the BMW diagnostic tester.

ABS control unit/pressure modulator

25 The integral control unit and modulator is located under the fuel tank. Remove the fuel tank and the air filter housing (see Chapter 4).

26 The unit is not a service item – if a problem is indicated, all that can be done is to check that the multi-pin wiring connector to the unit is secure, and that the connector contacts are clean and undamaged **(see illustration 17.28f)**. Disconnect the battery (see Chapter 8) before disconnecting the modulator wiring connector.

27 Also check for leakage from the pipe banjo unions and if there is make sure the banjo bolts are tightened to the torque setting specified at the beginning of the Chapter **(see illustration 17.28d)**. If the bolts are tight either new sealing washers are needed, or a union or pipe is cracked – see below to fit new sealing washers, and to Section 9 to replace a hose/pipe.

28 To remove the modulator, drain the brake fluid from the system (Section 10). Release the CKP sensor wiring connector from the front of the modulator holder **(see illustration)**.

17.22a Undo the screw at the front of the cover…

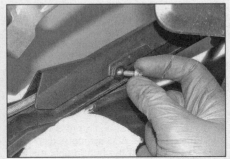

17.22b …and the screw at the back…

17.22c …and release the wire from the cover

17.23 Screw secures speed sensor

17.28a Release the connector

17.28b Release the hose joint and disconnect the wiring

17.28c Remove the tank brackets

17.28d Unscrew the hose banjo bolts (arrowed)…

Release the fuel hose joint and disconnect the pressure sensor wiring connector **(see illustration)**. Release the hoses and wiring from the fuel tank brackets, then undo the screws and remove the brackets **(see illustration)** – when removing the left-hand bracket on models with ESA refer to Chapter 5 Section 12 and remove the bracket with the rear ride height sensor attached (there is no need to detach the sensor from the bracket afterwards). Have some rag to hand. Unscrew the brake hose banjo bolts, detach the pipes and remove the sealing washers **(see illustration)**. Cover the end of each pipe in some clean rag or similar, and plug the holes in the modulator **(see illustration)**. Release and disconnect the modulator wiring connector and release the wiring clips **(see illustrations)**. Move the brake pipes aside and ease the modulator/bracket assembly out **(see illustration)**. If required release the modulator holder and undo the screws, and remove the modulator from the bracket **(see illustrations)**.

29 Installation is the reverse of removal. Use new sealing washers on the banjo unions and tighten the bolts to the torque setting specified at the beginning of the Chapter **(see illustration)**. Fill and bleed the system (Section 10). If a new modulator has been fitted the bike must be taken to a dealer for setting up on the diagnostic system.

17.28e …we cut the fingers off workshop gloves to seal the hoses and secured them with cable-ties

17.28f Note the plugs in the banjo bolt holes. Pull the catch up to release the connector…

17.28g …and pull the clips out

17.28h Draw the modulator assembly out

17.28i Release the holder…

17.28j …and undo the screws

17.29 Always use new sealing washers

Angular rate sensor

30 The sensor is fitted to models equipped with ABS Pro. On GS and Adv models remove the passenger seat to access the sensor which is retained to the mudguard by two nuts and a retaining plate. On RS and R models remove the passenger and rider's seats, then remove the seat bracket; the sensor is retained to the bracket by two screws and nuts **(see illustration)**.

18 ASC (Automatic Stability Control) system

1 ASC is a traction control system which compares the speed of both wheels and via calculation determines the amount of rear wheel slip. If the parameters are exceeded, engine torque is reduced via the ECU. The system is entirely automatic in operation, but can be deactivated by the rider if required.
2 An ASC button on the left handlebar switch unit enables the system to be deactivated, even when the motorcycle is in motion – with the ignition on press and hold the ASC button until the ASC warning symbol comes on, then release the button within 2 seconds. The ASC warning symbol will remain on to show that ASC is turned off. To reactivate the system, press the ASC button until the warning symbol goes out, then release the button within 2 seconds. The warning symbol will stay off to indicate that ASC is turned on. Alternatively the system will reactivate when the ignition is next turned off and then on again.
3 In normal use the ASC warning light will be off. Slow flashing of the warning light indicates that the system's self-diagnosis cycle has not yet completed. Quick flashing of the light occurs if ASC is in use, i.e. if the system has detected a traction problem and is reducing rear wheel torque to compensate. If the warning

17.30 Angular rate sensor is mounted inside the seat bracket on RS and R models

light comes on, and the system hasn't been deactivated by the rider, a fault is indicated in the ASC system and ASC is not working – is this instance the fault must be investigated by a BMW dealer or traced using an aftermarket diagnostic tester (see Chapter 4, Section 14).

19 RDC (tyre pressure monitoring) system

1 Sensors in the wheels, either integral with, or adjacent to, the valves relay tyre pressure values to the instrument display via a wireless link to the RDC receiver unit **(see illustrations)**.
2 Refer to your handbook for information on the display in the instrument cluster. Note that the pressure information is only transmitted once the machine has reached a road speed above 19 mph (30 kph).
3 If the pressure in either tyre is close to the edge of the permitted range the tyre pressure symbol will appear on the multi-function display panel and the appropriate tyre pressure on the display will flash.
4 If the tyre pressure becomes critical the

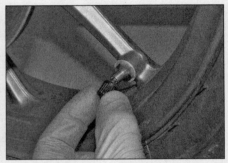

19.1 RDC sensors are either integral with or adjacent to the valves

general warning triangle will illuminate yellow.
5 If the pressure falls outside of the permitted range the warning triangle flashes red.
6 Note that the sensors transmit tyre temperature as well as pressure to the receiver unit. The pressure settings are based on a reference temperature of 20°C and the receiver unit ensures that the pressure displayed is 'temperature compensated' to take into account tyre temperature outside of this figure.
7 Be sure to advise the dealer or tyre fitter that pressure sensors are fitted as damage could be caused to the sensor if care is not taken in this area.
8 Fitting a new sensor requires the sensor to be registered with the receiver unit using the BMW diagnostic tester **(see illustrations)**.
9 The RDC receiver unit is located inside the rear bodywork – on GS and GS ADV models remove the passenger seat, on RT models remove the luggage rack, and on R and RS models remove the seat cowls, then remove the passenger seat bracket (see Chapter 7). To remove the unit undo the screws or nuts securing it to the rear mudguard, then disconnect the wiring connector **(see illustration)**.

19.8a RDC receiver on GS and Adv models

19.8b RDC receiver on the RT model

19.8c RDC receiver (arrowed) on RS and R models

Chapter 7
Bodywork

Contents

Degrees of difficulty

| Easy, suitable for novice with little experience | | Fairly easy, suitable for beginner with some experience | | Fairly difficult, suitable for competent DIY mechanic | | Difficult, suitable for experienced DIY mechanic | | Very difficult, suitable for expert DIY or professional | |

Specifications

Torque settings

Engine protection bars – R1200 GS Adventure	
M10 bolts	55 Nm
M8 bolts	19 Nm
Fuel tank protection bar bolts – R1200 GS Adventure	19 Nm
Handlebar end-weight bolts	
R1200 GS and GS Adventure	38 Nm
Luggage rack/grab-rail bolts	
R1200 GS and GS Adventure	19 Nm
R1200 RT	5 Nm
R1200 R and RS	19 Nm
Seat base bolts – R1200 GS and GS Adventure	19 Nm
Spray guard bolts – R1200 GS and GS Adventure	8 Nm

1 General information

1 This Chapter covers the procedures necessary to remove and install the bodywork. Since many service and repair operations on these motorcycles require the removal of the body parts, the procedures are grouped here and referred to from other Chapters.

2 In the case of damage to the body parts, it is usually necessary to remove the broken component and replace it with a new (or used) one. There are however some shops that specialise in 'plastic welding', so it may be worthwhile seeking the advice of one of these specialists before consigning an expensive component to the bin. Alternatively some of the DIY bodywork repair kits are ideal for small repairs.

3 When attempting to remove any body panel, first study it closely, noting any fasteners and associated fittings, to be sure of returning everything to its correct place on installation. In some cases the aid of an assistant will be required when removing panels, to help avoid the risk of damage to paintwork. Once the evident fasteners have been removed, try to withdraw the panel as described but DO NOT FORCE IT – if it will not release, check that all fasteners have been removed and try again. Where a panel engages another by means of tabs, be careful not to break the tab or its mating slot or to damage the paintwork. Remember that a few moments of patience at this stage will save you a lot of money in replacing broken fairing panels!

4 When installing a body panel, first study it closely, noting any fasteners and associated fittings removed with it, to be sure of returning everything to its correct place. If a new panel is being fitted transfer any parts necessary (such as clip-nuts, grommets, trim sections and badges) from the old panel to the new one before fitting it. Check that all fasteners are in good condition, including all trim nuts or clips and damping/rubber mounts; any of these must be replaced if faulty before the panel is reassembled. Check also that all mounting brackets are straight and repair or replace them if necessary before attempting to install the panel. Where assistance was required to remove a panel, make sure your assistant is on hand to install it.

5 Tighten the fasteners securely, but be careful not to overtighten any of them or the panel may break (not always immediately) due to the uneven stress.

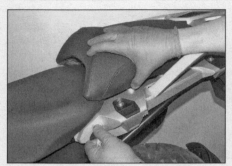

2.2a Lift the passenger's seat from the front

2.2b Note how the hooks locate, and how the lock pin locates in the catch

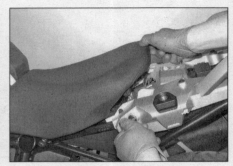

2.3a Lift the rider's seat from the rear

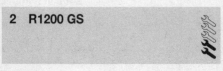

2 R1200 GS

Seats

Removal

1 Insert the ignition key into the seat lock on the left-hand side of the bike.

2 To remove the passenger seat turn the key clockwise while pressing down on the front of the seat to unlock it, then lift the front of the seat and either draw it forwards (if the rider's seat is in the high position) or push it backwards (if the rider's seat is in the low position) to release the hooks on the underside from the tabs (see illustrations).

3 To remove the rider's seat first remove the passenger seat. Turn the key anti-clockwise while pressing down on the rear of the rider's seat to unlock it, then lift the rear of the seat and draw it back to release the hooks at the front from the supports (see illustrations).

Height and tilt adjustment

4 There are two height and tilt settings for the rider's seat, giving four seat positions – the seat can be high front and rear, high at the front and low at the rear, low at the front and high at the rear, or low front and rear, as required.

5 To change the seat height from low to high or vice versa at the front, release the clip holding

2.3b Note how the hooks on the underside of the seat locate around the rubbers

2.5 Release the front clip and position the adjuster as required – this shows the low position

the adjuster to the bracket and turn it so the required letter, L for low and H for high, is facing up and at the front, then seat the trailing edge against the bracket and push the leading edge down so the clip engages (see illustration).

6 To change the seat height from low to high or vice versa at the rear, pivot the rear height adjuster up (for high) or down (for low) as required, so the corresponding letter H or L is visible (see illustration).

Installation

7 Locate the hooks on the underside of the rider's seat around the supports, then push the rear of the seat down until the lock engages (see illustration 2.3b). Check the seat is secure.

8 Position the passenger seat so the locking pin is central in the lock and the hooks are between the tabs on each side, then push down on the back of the seat and slide it backwards (if the rider's seat is in the high position) or forwards (if the rider's seat is in the low position) so the hooks engage the relevant tabs, then push the front of the seat down until the lock engages (see illustration 2.2b). Check the seat is secure.

Luggage rack and seat base

9 Remove the seats (see above).

10 Undo the luggage rack bolts and lift the rack off, noting the washers with the front bolts (see illustrations).

2.6 Pivot the adjuster to the required position – this shows the low position

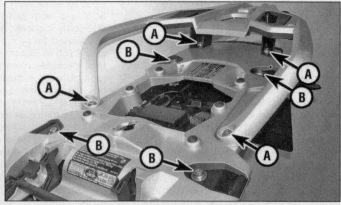

2.10 Luggage rack bolts (A), seat base bolts (B)

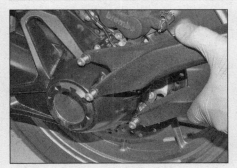

2.14 Spray guard is secured by three bolts

2.17 Disconnect the turn signal wiring connectors

2.18a Undo the screw on each side...

11 If required separate the rack from its base by undoing the four bolts.

12 Undo the seat base bolts and remove the long collars with the front bolts and the short collars with the rear bolts. Lift the seat base off.

13 Installation is the reverse of removal. Don't forget to fit the collars and washers. Clean the threads of the bolts and apply a suitable non-permanent thread locking compound. Tighten the bolts to the torque setting specified at the beginning of the Chapter.

Spray guard

14 Undo the bolts securing the spray guard to the final drive unit and lift it off **(see illustration)**.

15 Installation is the reverse of removal.

Clean the threads of the spray guard bolts and apply a suitable non-permanent thread locking compound. Tighten the bolts to the torque setting specified at the beginning of this Chapter.

Rear turn signal/number plate carrier

16 Remove the passenger seat (see above).

17 Release and disconnect the rear turn signal wiring connectors **(see illustration)**.

18 Undo the turn signal/number plate carrier screws and remove the carrier, noting how it locates at the front, and drawing the wiring out **(see illustration)**.

19 Installation is the reverse of removal. Check the operation of the turn signals before riding the motorcycle.

Side covers

20 Remove the rider's seat (see above).

21 Undo the two screws **(see illustration)**. Ease the cover to the rear to release the tab and the snap-fit studs **(see illustrations)**.

22 Installation is the reverse of removal.

Battery cover

23 Undo the screw, then carefully pull the top of the cover out to free the top peg from the grommet, then lift the bottom of the cover to free the bottom peg from the grommet **(see illustrations)**.

24 Installation is the reverse of removal.

Frame cover

25 Undo the screw, then carefully pull the top of the cover out to free the top peg from the

2.18b ...displace the carrier and draw the connectors down

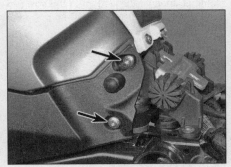

2.21a Undo the screws (arrowed)...

2.21b ...and release the tab...

2.21c ...and the studs

2.23a Undo the screw...

2.23b ...then release the pegs from the grommets

2.25a Undo the screw (arrowed)…

2.25b …pull the top peg out of the grommet…

2.25c …and lift the bottom grommet off the peg

2.27a Push the centre of the clip in, noting that it will go all the way through so take care not to lose it, then pull the clip body out of the panel

2.27b Undo the screws (arrowed) at the front…

2.27c …and on the side

2.28 Pull the peg from the grommet and release the tabs from the slots

grommet, then lift the bottom of the cover to free the bottom grommet from the peg **(see illustrations)**.

26 Installation is the reverse of removal.

Side panels

27 Release the trim clip and undo the four screws **(see illustrations)**.
28 Carefully pull the panel away to release the peg from the grommet and release the tabs **(see illustration)**.
29 If required separate the two sections of the panel by undoing the screws.

30 Installation is the reverse of removal – push the body of the trim clip into the panel, then push the pin into the body **(see illustration)**.

Fuel tank covers

Top cover

31 Remove the rider's seat (see above).
32 Undo the screws at the rear, then undo the screws at the front **(see illustrations)**.
33 Push the side cover in on each side to

2.30 Fit the body then push the pin into it

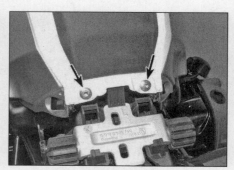

2.32a Undo the rear screws (arrowed)…

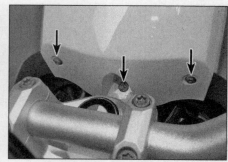

2.32b …and the front screws

2.33a Push the side covers in to release the tabs...

2.33b ...then lift the cover to release the grommets from the pegs

2.36 Side cover screws (arrowed)

2.39 Undo the screw on each side...

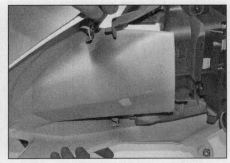

2.40 ...then draw the mudguard off the pegs

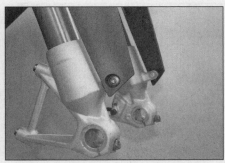

2.43a Undo the screw on each side...

release its tabs from the top cover, then carefully lift the cover to release the grommets from the pegs **(see illustrations)**.

34 Installation is the reverse of removal.

Side covers

35 Remove the top cover, the side covers and the side panels (see above).

36 Undo the five screws and remove the cover **(see illustration)**.

37 Installation is the reverse of removal.

Front mudguards

Upper mudguard

38 Remove the fuel tank covers (see above).

39 Undo the screw on each side **(see illustration)**.

40 Draw the mudguard forwards off the pegs and remove it **(see illustration)**. Check the condition of the grommets and replace them with new ones if necessary.

41 Installation is the reverse of removal.

Lower mudguard

42 Remove the front wheel (see Chapter 6).

43 Undo the four screws, then draw the mudguard forwards and off the bike **(see illustrations)**.

44 Installation is the reverse of removal.

Cockpit trim panels

45 Undo the two screws securing each side trim panel and remove the panels **(see illustration)**.

46 Ease the centre panel out from behind the windshield **(see illustrations)**.

Windshield

47 Turn the adjuster knob as required to set the windshield at maximum height.

48 Undo the screws and lift the windshield off the bracket.

49 If required undo the windshield mounting bracket screws and remove the bracket sections from both sides of the windshield. Remove the grommets and replace them with new ones.

50 Installation is the reverse of removal. Clean the threads of the screws and apply a suitable non-permanent thread locking compound, or use new screws. Take care not to over-tighten the screws.

2.43b ...and the two on the underside

2.45 Undo the screws and remove the panels

2.46 Lift the centre panel off the side panel mounts and draw it out

2.51a Unscrew the mirror using the base hex...

2.51b ...and retrieve the washer

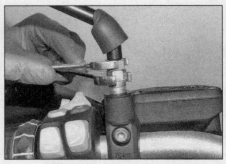

2.53 Slacken the locknut to adjust the mirror

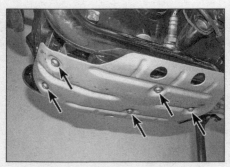

2.54 Sump guard screws (arrowed)

2.55 Remove the brackets (arrowed) if required

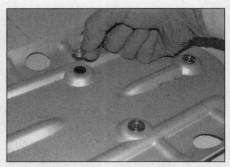

2.56 Check the grommets and collars

Mirrors

51 Lift the boot covering the base of the mirror, then slacken the mirror using the base hex and unscrew it, noting the washer **(see illustrations)**.

52 Installation is the reverse of removal.

53 To adjust the position of the mirror lift the boot covering the base, then hold the base hex and slacken the locknut above it, set and hold the mirror in the desired position, tighten the locknut and refit the boot **(see illustration)**. Final mirror position adjustment can be made by tilting the mirror head.

Sump guard

54 Undo the five screws and remove the sump guard **(see illustration)**.

55 If required, undo the screws and remove the two sump guard brackets **(see illustration)**.

56 Installation is the reverse of removal – make sure the grommets are in good condition and the collars are fitted in them **(see illustration)**.

Hand protectors

57 Refer to the Section for the GS Adventure model – the procedure is the same (Section 3).

3 R1200 GS Adventure

Seats

1 Refer to the Section for the standard GS model – the procedure is the same (Section 2).

Luggage rack and seat base

2 Refer to the Section for the standard GS model (Section 2) – the procedure is the same, but there may be differences in the collars and washers according to the type of rack, and the seat base bolts may also secure pannier racks, again according to type **(see illustration)**.

Spray guard

3 Refer to the Section for the standard GS model – the procedure is the same (Section 2).

Rear turn signal/number plate carrier

4 Refer to the Section for the standard GS model – the procedure is the same (Section 2).

Battery cover

5 Refer to the Section for the standard GS models – the procedure is the same (Section 2).

Frame cover

6 Refer to the Section for the standard GS models – the procedure is the same (Section 2).

Side panels

7 Undo the air deflector screws and remove the deflector, noting the grommets and collars **(see illustration)**.

8 Remove the fuel tank top cover and protection bar (see later).

3.2 The seat base bolts may also secure pannier racks which must be removed first

3.7 Remove the air deflector

3.9a Undo the screws (arrowed) at the front...

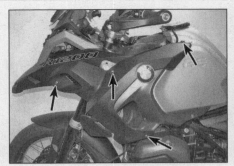

3.9b ...and on the side

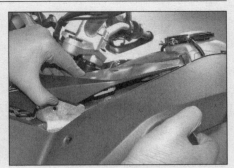

3.10a Release the tabs...

9 Undo the six screws (see illustrations).

10 Lift the upper mudguard and pull the panel away to release it from the mudguard (see illustrations).

11 Installation is the reverse of removal – make sure the air deflector grommets are in good condition and the collars are fitted in them (see illustration).

Fuel tank covers

Top cover

12 Remove the rider's seat (see above).

13 Undo the screws at the rear (see illustrations). Open the storage compartment lid and undo the screws inside, and at the front (see illustration).

14 Carefully lift the cover to release the tabs from the upper mudguard and remove it (see illustration).

15 Installation is the reverse of removal.

3.10b ...and remove the panel

Side covers

16 Remove the top cover and the side panels (see above).

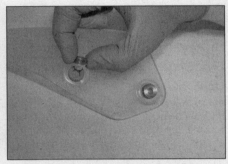

3.11 Check the grommets and collars

17 Release the trim clip and undo the three screws (see illustrations).

18 Carefully pull the peg at the top out of the

3.13a Undo the rear screws (arrowed)...

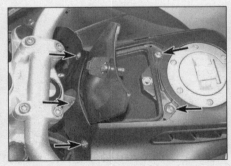

3.13b ...and the top and front screws

3.14 Release and remove the cover

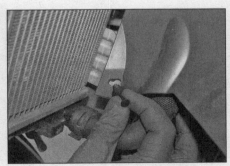

3.17a Ease the centre pin out...

3.17b ...then withdraw the body

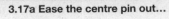

3.17c Undo the screws (arrowed)

3.18a Pull the peg out of the grommet...

3.18b ...then release the slot from the tab

grommet, then ease the cover to the rear to release its slot from the tab on the tank **(see illustrations)**.

19 Installation is the reverse of removal.

Front mudguards

Upper mudguard

20 Remove the fuel tank top cover (see above). Displace the side panel so it rests against the fuel tank protection bar (see above) – you only need to remove the protection bar if you prefer to remove the side panel rather than just displace it.

21 Undo the two upper mudguard screws **(see illustration)**. Carefully lift and spread the sides of the mudguard and draw it forwards off the bike, noting how the pegs locate in the grommets **(see illustrations)**.

22 Installation is the reverse of removal.

Lower mudguard

23 Refer to the Section for the standard GS model – the procedure is the same (Section 2).

Coolant reservoir access panel

24 Undo the screw and remove the panel (see illustration).

25 Installation is the reverse of removal.

Cockpit trim panels

26 Refer to the Section for the standard GS model – the procedure is the same (Section 2).

Windshield

27 Refer to the Section for the standard GS model – the procedure is the same (Section 2).

Mirrors

28 Refer to the Section for the standard GS model – the procedure is the same (Section 2).

Sump guard

29 Refer to the Section for the standard GS model – the procedure is the same (Section 2).

Hand protectors

30 The hand protector can be removed as a complete unit, which must be done if you are removing or displacing the brake or clutch master cylinder or lever, or the main front section can be removed leaving the mirror and bracket in place, which is all you need to do if removing a switch housing or the clutch switch.

31 To remove the complete unit remove the mirror (see Section 2). Unscrew the handlebar end-weight bolt, noting the collar, and remove the hand protector along with the end-weight that fits between it and the handlebar **(see illustration)**.

32 To remove the main front section only undo the screw securing it to the bracket, then unscrew the handlebar end-weight bolt, noting the collar, and remove the front section along with the end-weight that fits between it and the handlebar **(see illustration)**.

33 Installation is the reverse of removal – fit the handlebar end-weight components and the mirror (if removed) loosely at first to ensure correct alignment of the protector. Tighten the mirror or screw first, then hold the protector to prevent twist and tighten the end-weight bolt to the specified torque setting.

Protection bars

Engine protection bars

34 Unscrew the four bolts and remove the

3.21a Undo the screw on each side

3.21b Remove the mudguard as described...

3.21c ...noting how the pegs locate in the grommets

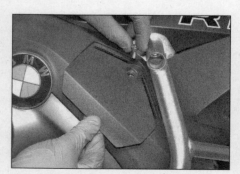

3.24 Removing the access panel

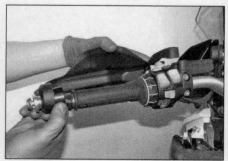

3.31 Removing the complete hand protector

3.32 Removing the front section of the hand protector

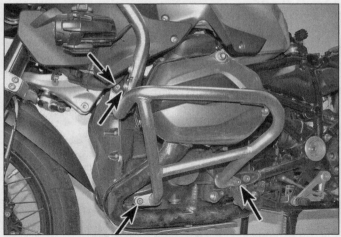

3.34 Engine protection bar bolts

3.36a Release the wiring clip (arrowed)…

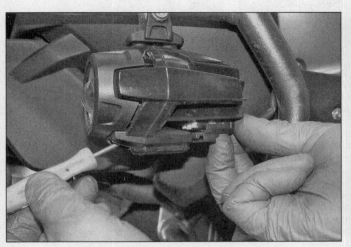

3.36b …and disconnect the connector

3.36c Hold the nut on the inside and undo the screw (arrowed) to remove the light

protection bar – note which bolt fits where **(see illustration)**. Note that if the fuel tank protection bar has already been removed there is no need to remove the bolt that secures the bar to the connecting bracket.

35 Installation is the reverse of removal. Clean the threads of the top bolt that also secures

3.37 Fuel tank protection bar bolts (arrowed)

the fuel tank protection bar and apply some fresh threadlock. Tighten all bolts finger-tight at first so the bar is correctly aligned, then tighten them to the torque settings specified at the beginning of this Chapter.

Fuel tank protection bars

36 If fog lights are fitted release the wiring from its clip and disconnect the wiring connector **(see illustrations)**. Remove the light from the bar if required **(see illustration)**.
37 Unscrew the two bolts and remove the protection bar – note which bolt fits where. Note that if the engine protection bar has already been removed there is no need to remove the bottom bolt that secures the bar to the connecting bracket.
38 Installation is the reverse of removal. Clean the threads of the bottom bolt and apply some fresh threadlock. Tighten both bolts finger-tight at first so the bar is correctly aligned, then tighten them to the torque setting specified at the beginning of this Chapter.

4 R1200 RT models

Note: *Models were available from new fitted with a range of optional electrical extras. When working on your machine, take care to ensure that all relevant electrical components are disconnected on disassembly and subsequently reconnected during the rebuild. Always take the precaution of disconnecting the battery negative (-) terminal before disconnecting an electrical wiring connector.*

Seats

Removal

1 To remove the rider's seat insert the ignition key into the seat lock on the left-hand side of the bike. Turn the key clockwise, then lift the rear of the seat and draw it back to release the hooks from the supports, and on models

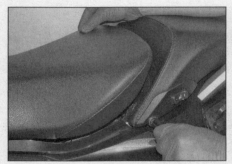

4.1a Unlock the seat and lift the rear...

4.1b ...noting how the hooks locate around the rubber supports...

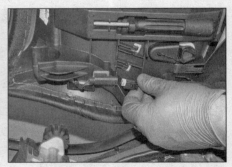

4.1c ...and disconnect the wiring

4.2a Undo the screws...

4.2b ...draw the seat forwards to release the hooks...

4.2c ...and disconnect the wiring

4.6a Undo the screws...

with heated seats disconnect the seat wiring connector (see illustrations).

2 To remove the passenger seat, first remove the rider's seat. Undo the two screws, then lift the front of the seat and draw it forwards, noting how the hooks locate, and on models with heated seats disconnect the wiring connector (see illustrations).

Height adjustment

3 To change the seat height from low to high or vice versa at the front, release the clip holding the adjuster to the bracket and turn it so the required letter, L for low and H for high, is facing up, then seat the trailing edge against the bracket and push the leading edge down so the clip engages (see illustration 2.5).

Installation

4 Install the seats in the reverse order of removal. Make sure the rider's seat is fully located on the supports, then press the rear down until the catch is heard to click. Check the seat is secure.

Luggage rack and grab-rails

5 Remove the seats (see above).

6 Undo the screws securing the top section of the rack, then release the tabs at the back and lift it off (see illustrations).

7 To remove the luggage/rack and grab-rails as an assembly unscrew the front grab-rail bolts and the four rack bolts and lift the rack/rail unit off (see illustration).

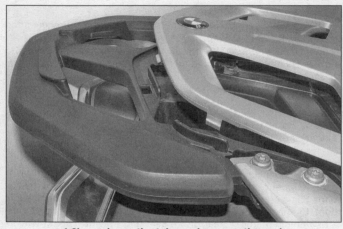

4.6b ...release the tabs and remove the rack

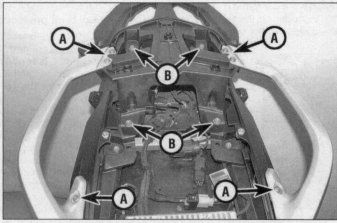

4.7 Grab-rail bolts (A), luggage rack bolts (B)

4.10 Remove the trim panels…

4.11a …then remove the windshield…

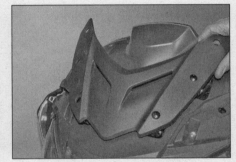

4.11b …and its support panel

4.15 Two bolts secure each mirror

4.19a Undo the screws…

4.19b …release the tabs and remove the cover

8 To remove the components separately unscrew the grab-rail bolts and detach the rails from the rack, then unscrew the rack bolts **(see illustration 4.7)**.

9 Installation is the reverse of removal. Clean the threads of the bolts and apply a suitable non-permanent thread locking compound. Tighten the bolts to the torque setting specified at the beginning of this Chapter.

Windshield

10 Undo the screws securing the windshield trim panels and lift the panels off **(see illustration)**.

11 Undo the screws securing the windshield and lift it off **(see illustration)**. Lift the support panel off the brackets **(see illustration)**.

12 For removal and installation of the windshield adjuster mechanism see Chapter 8.

13 Installation is the reverse of removal. Take care not to over-tighten the screws. Check the operation of the windshield motor.

Mirrors

14 Remove the speaker cover and where fitted the speaker, and the front fairing panel (see below).

15 Unscrew the bolts and remove the mirror **(see illustration)**.

16 If required, release the cover from the mirror and cut the retaining strap.

17 If required the glass can be replaced with a new piece – removed the glass by pulling it out at the top to release the socket from the ball head – note how the guides locate. To fit the glass align the guides and locate the head of the ball against the socket, then push the centre of the glass in to seat the ball head in the socket.

18 Installation is the reverse of removal.

Fairing panels

Speaker covers and speakers

19 Undo the two screws **(see illustration)**. Release the tabs and remove the cover **(see illustration)**.

20 To remove the speakers disconnect the wiring connector, then undo the screws and remove the speaker, noting how it locates **(see illustrations)**.

21 Installation is the reverse of removal.

Front panels

22 Remove the speaker cover, and where fitted the speaker (see above). Remove the side panel (see below).

23 On models with a stereo system, when removing the right-hand panel disconnect

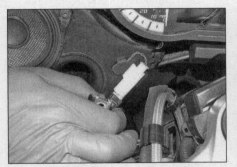

4.20a Disconnect the wiring…

4.20b …then undo the screws (arrowed)

4.20c Note how the peg locates

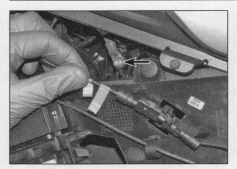

4.23 Disconnect the connector and undo the screw (arrowed)

4.24a Release the trim clip...

4.24b ...and undo the screw in the cockpit...

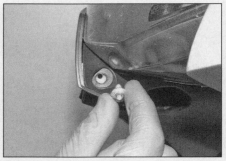

4.24c ...then undo the screw at the front...

4.24d ...and on the side

4.25a Release the tab...

the aerial connector and undo the aerial earth lead screw **(see illustration)**.

24 Release the trim clip and undo the three screws **(see illustrations)**.

25 Release the tab at the back, then carefully pull the top front away to release the peg from the grommet and remove the panel **(see**

illustrations) – note the routing of the aerial wiring where fitted on the right-hand panel **(see illustration)**.

26 Installation is the reverse of removal.

Side panels

27 Undo the screws on the inside front edge of the panel **(see illustration)**.

28 Carefully pull the bottom of the panel away to release the pegs from the grommets, then lift it so the tabs along the top release from the trim panel **(see illustrations)**.

29 If required, undo the inner trim panel screws and remove the panel, disconnecting

4.25b ...and the peg

4.25c Note the fitting of the panel...

4.25d ...and the routing of the wires

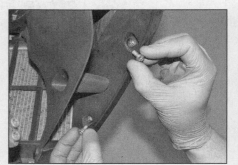

4.27 Undo the screws

4.28a Pull the pegs from the grommets...

4.28b ...then release the tabs

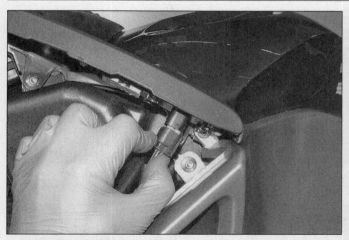

4.29a Disconnect the power socket wiring connector(s) as required

4.29b Inner panel screws (arrowed)

the wiring for the power socket and any other added extras **(see illustrations)**.

30 Installation is the reverse of removal. If the inner panel was removed make sure it locates correctly as shown **(see illustration)**. Locate the top tabs on the side panel in the trim panel, then push the pegs into the grommets, then press the top edge down into the trim panel so the tabs are heard to click into place.

Engine covers

31 To remove the right-hand cover undo the two screws, then carefully pull the panel away to release the peg from the grommet **(see illustrations)**.

32 To remove the left-hand cover undo the three screws and remove the cover **(see illustration)**.

33 Installation is the reverse of removal.

Knee support panels

34 Remove the rider's seat, the engine cover, and the side panel (see above).

35 Undo the four screws **(see illustrations)**. When removing the right-hand panel release the wiring from its guide. Release the panel from the fuel tank and remove it **(see illustrations)**.

36 Installation is the reverse of removal.

Fuel tank covers

37 Remove the knee support panels and speaker covers (see above).

4.30 Make sure inner panel locates correctly

4.31b Pull the peg from the grommet and remove the cover

4.31a Right-hand engine cover screws (arrowed)

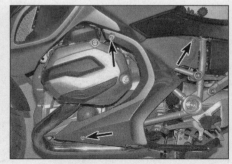

4.32 Left-hand engine cover screws (arrowed)

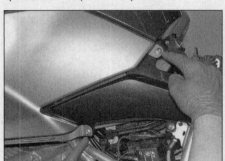

4.35a Undo the screws at the rear...

4.35b ...and at the front...

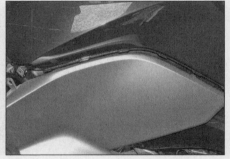

4.35c ...then release and remove the panel

4.39a Undo the screw...

4.39b ...then release and remove the compartment...

4.39c ...noting how it locates at the front

4.40a Undo the screw at the back...

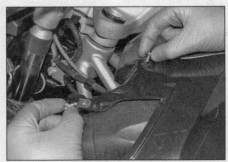

4.40b ...and the screws at the front...

4.40c ...then release and remove the cover

4.41 Top cover screws (arrowed)

38 Undo the inner trim panel screws and remove the panel, disconnecting the wiring for the power socket and any other added extras according to fitment (see illustrations 4.29a and b).

39 Remove the storage compartment from the left-hand side, and the cover or storage compartment from the right-hand side as fitted (see illustrations).

40 Undo the three screws securing the side cover, then carefully release it from the top cover (see illustrations).

41 Undo the three screws securing the top cover and lift it off (see illustration).

42 Installation is the reverse of removal.

Radiator cowls

43 Remove the fairing front panel (see above).

44 Undo the front screw for the knee support panel (see illustration 4.35b).

45 Disconnect and/or release any wiring connector(s) and/or electrical units, according to side and equipment fitted (see illustrations).

4.45a Wiring connector on left-hand radiator cowl

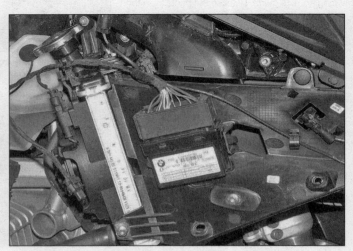

4.45b Control unit and wiring on right-hand radiator cowl

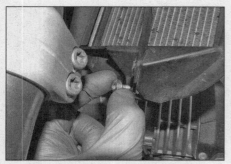

4.46a Undo the screw on the bottom...

4.46b ...and the screws at the front...

4.46c ...then release the cowl from the radiator...

46 Undo the screws, then release and remove the cowl **(see illustrations)**.
47 Installation is the reverse of removal.

Shock absorber covers

48 Carefully pull the cover away to release the pegs from the grommets **(see illustration)**.
49 Installation is the reverse of removal – make sure the grommets are in good condition and replace them with new ones if necessary. Hold the inner side of the seat cowl when pushing the top pegs into their grommets.

Seat cowlings

50 Remove the seats, the luggage rack and grab-rail assembly, and the relevant engine cover (see above). Either remove the relevant shock absorber cover (see above), or just pull its bottom peg out of the grommet and leave

4.46d ...noting how it locates at the front

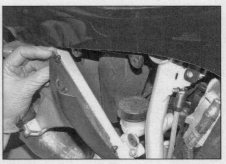

4.48 The covers are held by three pegs in grommets

the top pegs attached to the seat cowl and remove the cowl with the cover attached to it, as preferred.

51 Undo the screws securing the front of the cowling **(see illustration)**.
52 Undo the screws securing the rear of the cowling, then lift it off the pannier mount and remove it **(see illustrations)**.
53 If required unscrew the pannier carrier bolts and remove the carrier.
54 Installation is the reverse of removal. If the pannier carriers were removed clean the threads of the bolts and apply some fresh threadlock.

Rear cowl and number plate bracket

55 Remove the seat cowlings (see above).
56 Release the trim clip and undo the screw joining the rear cowls on the top **(see illustration)**. Undo the two screws securing

4.51 Undo the screws

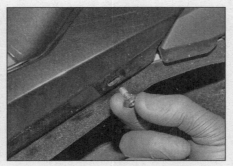

4.52a Undo the screw on the underside...

4.52b ...and on the top...

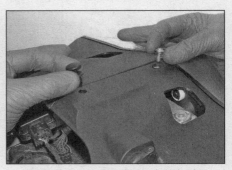

4.52c ...and lift the cowling off

4.56a Release the clip and undo the screw...

4.56b ...and the screws...

4.56c ...then lift the cowl off the pannier mount

4.60 Undo the screw (arrowed) on each side

the side of each cowl section and remove the cowls (see illustrations).

57 Remove the tail light (see Chapter 8).

58 Undo the four screws and remove the number plate bracket.

59 Installation is the reverse of removal.

Front mudguard

60 To remove the front section of the mudguard, undo the screw on each side, then draw the front section forwards and unclip it from the main mudguard (see illustration).

61 To remove the main section of the mudguard, first remove the front section, then remove the front wheel (see Chapter 6).

62 Undo the screws on the underside of the mudguard securing it to the front fork bridge, then undo the screws securing the mudguard to the front fork legs and draw the mudguard forwards and off the bike.

63 Installation is the reverse of removal.

5 R1200 R models

Seats

1 Refer to the Section for the RS model – the procedure is the same (Section 6).

Seat cowls and grab rails

2 Refer to the Section for the RS model – the procedure is the same (Section 6).

Number plate bracket

3 Refer to the Section for the RS model – the procedure is the same (Section 6).

Side covers

4 Remove the seats (see Section 6).

5 Undo the four screws, then release the peg

from the grommet and slide the cover to the rear to release the front lug, noting how the tabs locate (see illustrations).

6 Installation is the reverse of removal.

Battery cover

7 Refer to the Section for the standard GS model – the procedure is the same (Section 2).

Frame cover

8 Refer to the Section for the standard GS model – the procedure is the same (Section 2).

Fuel tank covers

9 Remove the side covers (see above).

10 Undo the five screws securing the tank side cover (see illustrations). Release it from the top cover at the front first, then at the rear (see illustration).

11 To remove the top cover first remove the tank side covers. Undo the screw securing

5.5a Side cover screws (arrowed)

5.5b Pull the peg from the grommet...

5.5c ...then slide the lug from the slot

5.10a Undo the screw at the front...

5.10b ...and the screws (arrowed) on the side...

5.10c ...then release and remove the cover

5.11a Remove the intake pipe covers...

5.11b ...then undo the two screws securing each side of the top cover

5.13 Undo the screws and remove the cowl

each air intake pipe cover and remove the covers **(see illustration)**. Undo the four screws and lift the top section off **(see illustration)**.

12 Installation is the reverse of removal.

Radiator cowls

13 Undo the two screws and remove the cowl **(see illustration)**.

14 Installation is the reverse of removal.

Engine spoilers

15 Undo the two screws and detach the spoiler from its bracket.

16 Remove the bracket if required.

17 Installation is the reverse of removal.

Front mudguard

18 Refer to the Section for the RS model – the procedure is the same (Section 6).

Mirrors

19 Refer to the Section for the GS model – the procedure is the same (Section 2).

6   R1200 RS models

Seats

1 To remove the passenger seat insert the ignition key into the seat lock located on the left-hand side of the bike. Push the front of the seat down and turn the key anti-clockwise in the lock, then lift the front and draw the seat off, noting how it locates at the back **(see illustrations)**.

2 To remove the rider's seat first remove the passenger seat. Lift the back of the seat and draw it back, noting how the hooks locate on the supports **(see illustration)**.

3 Installation is the reverse of removal. Firmly press down on the front of the passenger seat until you hear the lock engage, then check that the seat is secure.

Seat cowls and grab rails

4 Remove the seats (see above).

5 Undo the three screws, then release the tabs at the back and remove the outer section of the cowl **(see illustrations)**.

6 Undo the four screws, then release the pegs and remove the inner section of the cowl **(see illustration)**.

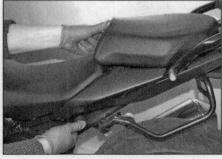

6.1a Unlock the seat and lift it off

6.1b Note how the hooks locate

6.2 Note how the hooks locate around the rubber supports

6.5a Side cover is retained by two screws (arrowed) on the top...

6.5b ...and one on the underside

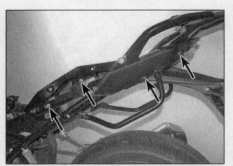

6.6 Inner section screws (arrowed)

6.7a Unscrew the bolt (arrowed) on the underside...

7 Unscrew the grab-rail bolts and remove the rail **(see illustrations)**.

8 Installation is the reverse of removal. Tighten the grab-rail bolts to the torque setting specified at the beginning of this Chapter.

Number plate bracket

9 Remove the seat cowls (see above).

10 Remove the tail light (see Chapter 8).

11 Undo the five screws and remove the cover from the underside of the bracket **(see illustrations)**.

12 Release and disconnect the rear turn signal wiring and pull the licence plate light bulbholder out of the light **(see illustrations)**.

13 Undo the screw on each side and the three at the back and remove the bracket, noting the routing of the wiring.

14 If required remove the turn signals and licence plate light (see Chapter 8).

15 Installation is the reverse of removal.

6.7b ...and the bolt (arrowed) on the top

Check the operation of the turn signals, tail light and licence plate light.

Battery cover

16 Refer to the Section for the standard GS model – the procedure is the same (see Section 2).

Frame cover

17 Refer to the section for the standard GS model – the procedure is the same (see Section 2).

Cockpit trim panels

18 Undo the two screws, release the tabs and remove the panel **(see illustrations)**.

19 Installation is the reverse of removal.

Fairing panels

Fairing upper panels and centre panel

20 Remove the cockpit trim panels (see above).

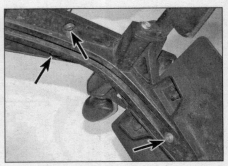

6.11a Undo the screws (arrowed) on the underside...

6.11b ...and the top and remove the cover

21 Remove the mirrors (see below).

22 Undo the air deflector screws and remove the deflectors **(see illustration)** – note the O-rings fitted around the collars.

23 Remove the windshield (see later).

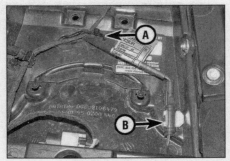

6.12a Cut the cable-tie (A) and release and disconnect the connector (B)

6.12b Cut the cable-tie (arrowed) and release and disconnect the connector

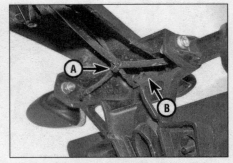

6.12c Cut the cable-tie (A) and pull the bulbholder (B) out

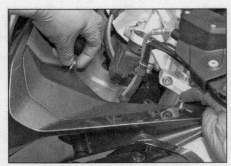

6.18a Undo the screws...

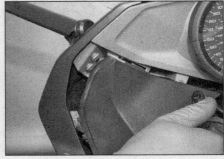

6.18b ...then release and remove the panel

6.22 Remove the air deflector

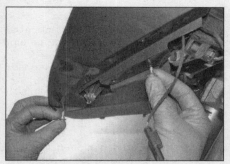

6.25a Undo the two screws on each side on the underside...

6.25b ...and on the topside

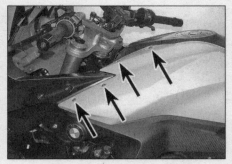

6.26 Undo the screws (arrowed)

6.27a Disconnect the wiring...

6.27b ...then undo the screws

26 Undo the four screws on the left-hand fuel tank side cover **(see illustration)**.
27 Disconnect the left-hand headlight wiring connector **(see illustration)**. Undo the two screws above the left-hand headlight **(see illustration)**.
28 Release the front of the left-hand upper panel from the centre panel, then carefully draw the upper panel forwards to release the headlight peg from the grommet, and from the tank covers **(see illustrations)**.
29 Displace the centre panel from the right-hand upper panel, then disconnect the ambient temperature sensor wiring connector and remove the panel **(see illustrations)**.
30 Undo the four screws on the right-hand fuel tank side cover **(see illustration 6.26)**.
31 Disconnect the right-hand headlight wiring connector and undo the two screws **(see illustrations)**.

24 Remove the fairing side panels and inner panels (see below).
25 Undo the four screws on the underside joining the upper panels to the centre panel,

noting which fits where **(see illustration)**. Undo the four screws on the top joining the upper panels to the centre panel **(see illustration)**.

6.28a Note how the tab on the front of the upper panel engages the slot in the centre panel...

6.28b ...and how the peg locates in the grommet

6.29a Release the panel...

6.29b ...and disconnect the wiring

6.31a Disconnect the wiring...

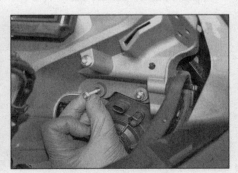

6.31b ...then undo the screws

6.32a Release the panel...

6.32b ...and draw the peg from the grommet

Fairing side panels

35 Undo the three screws, then displace the panel and release and disconnect the turn signal wiring **(see illustrations)**.
36 Remove the turn signal if required (see Chapter 8).
37 Installation is the reverse of removal. Check the operation of the turn signal.

Fairing inner panels

38 Remove the fairing side panel (see above). Remove the air deflector **(see illustration 6.22)**.
39 Release the turn signal wiring connector **(see illustration)**.
40 Undo the three screws, then release the clip from the fuel tank side cover and remove the panel, feeding the turn signal connector through the hole **(see illustrations)**.
41 Installation is the reverse of removal.

32 Release and remove the right-hand upper panel **(see illustrations)**.
33 Remove the headlights from the panels if required (see Chapter 8).
34 Installation is the reverse of removal. Make

sure the collars for the air deflector mounts are in place and are held by the O-rings **(see illustrations)**. Make sure the collars are in the upper headlight grommets (where the screws go) **(see illustration 6.32b)**.

6.34a The collars fit from the inside...

6.34b ...and the O-rings fit round them on the outside

6.35a Undo the screw on the side...

6.35b ...and the screws at the front

6.35c Release and displace the panel...

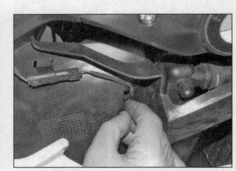

6.35d ...then free the wire from its guide...

6.35e ...and disconnect the connector

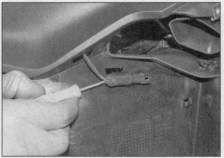

6.39 Release the connector

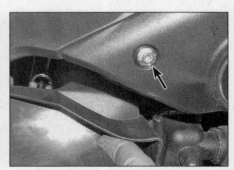

6.40a Undo the screw (arrowed) at the top...

6.40b …the screw on the bottom…

6.40c …and the screw on the inner side

6.40d Release the clip…

6.40e …and pass the connector through

Fuel tank covers

42 Remove the seats (see above).

43 Undo the air deflector screws and remove the deflector **(see illustration 6.22)**.

44 Undo the nine screws securing the upper and lower sections of the tank side cover **(see illustration)**. Pull the rear of the fairing side panel away slightly then release the lower section of the tank side cover from the inner section of the fairing side panel **(see illustration 6.40d)**. Release the upper section of the tank side cover from the top cover and remove the side cover sections together **(see illustration)**. If required separate the sections of the side cover by undoing the screws **(see illustration)**.

45 To remove the top cover first remove the side covers. Undo the four screws and lift the top cover off **(see illustration)**.

46 Installation is the reverse of removal.

Windshield

47 Undo the screws and lift the windshield off the bracket **(see illustration)**. Note the collars and grommets and remove them from the back of the windshield if required.

48 If required, release the clips securing the windshield bracket retaining pins, withdraw

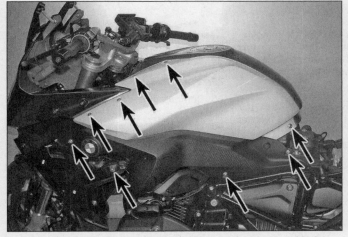

6.44a Fuel tank side cover screws (arrowed) – shown with the fairing side panel, and therefore the lowest screw, removed

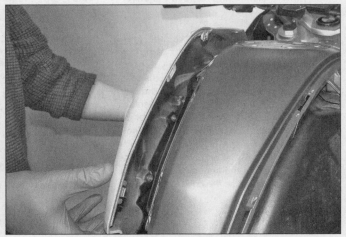

6.44b Release and remove the cover

6.44c Screws joining the sections are on the inner side

6.45 Undo the two screws on each side

6.47 Four screws secure the windshield

6.48a Release the clips (from the lower pins only if preferred)…

6.48b …then withdraw the pins and remove or displace the bracket as required

6.48c Undo the two screws on each side…

6.48d …then release and remove the cover

6.53 Front mudguard screws (arrowed)

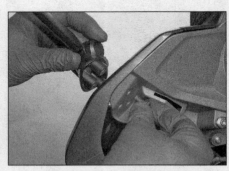

6.56 Mirror is secured by three screws

the pins and remove the bracket **(see illustrations)** – if preferred (for example if you are removing the instruments) you need only release and withdraw the lower pins then you can swing the bracket up and to the rear so it is out of the way. Undo the windshield adjuster cover screws, then slide the cover up to release the tabs and remove the cover **(see illustrations)**.

49 If required undo the adjuster mechanism screws and unhook the spring, then displace the adjuster and release the cables.

50 Installation is the reverse of removal. Position the windshield in the high or low position on the bracket as required. Take care not to over-tighten the windshield screws.

Engine spoilers

51 Undo the two screws and detach the spoiler from its bracket. Remove the bracket if required.

52 Installation is a reverse of the removal.

Front mudguard

53 Undo the screws on each side, noting the

washers, then draw the mudguard forwards **(see illustration)**.

54 Installation is the reverse of removal.

Mirrors

55 Remove the cockpit trim panel (see above).

56 Undo the the three screws and remove the mirror **(see illustration)**.

57 Installation is the reverse of removal – make sure the marks on the mirror stem and its bracket align for correct positioning of the mirror.

Chapter 8
Electrical system

Contents

Degrees of difficulty

Easy, suitable for novice with little experience	Fairly easy, suitable for beginner with some experience	Fairly difficult, suitable for competent DIY mechanic	Difficult, suitable for experienced DIY mechanic	Very difficult, suitable for expert DIY or professional

Specifications

Alternator
Type .... Three-phase AC with separate regulator/rectifier
Output .... 23 A at idle, 35 A at 6000 rpm

Battery
R1200 GS, GS Adventure, R and RS .... 12 V, 12 Ah
R1200 RT .... 12 V, 14 Ah

Bulbs
Headlights
  R1200 GS, GS Adventure, R and RS .... 55W H7 halogen x 2, or LED as OE
  R1200 RT .... 55W H1 halogen x 2 (main), 55W H7 halogen (dipped), or LED as OE
Side light .... 5W, or LED as OE
Brake/tail light .... LED
Turn signal lights
  R1200 GS, GS Adventure, R and RS .... 10W amber RY, or LED as OE
  R1200 RT .... LED
Instrument lighting and warning lights .... LED
Number plate light (R and RS models) 5W

Fuses

Circuit fuses

Fuse 1

R1200 GS and GS Adventure........................... 10 A, instruments, alarm, ignition lock, diagnostic socket

R1200 RT.. 15 A, instruments, alarm, ignition lock, diagnostic socket, top box light

R1200 R and RS...................................... 10 A, instruments, alarm, ignition lock, diagnostic socket, main relay

Fuse 2

R1200 GS and GS Adventure........................... 7.5 A – left-hand switches, tyre pressure monitors

R1200 RT.. 7.5 A – left-hand switches, tyre pressure monitors, audio system

R1200 R and RS...................................... 7.5 A – left-hand switches, tyre pressure monitors, angular rate (lean angle) sensor

Charging system fuse.................................. 50 A

On-board accessory socket

Current rating

R1200 RT.. 10 A

R1200 GS, GS Adventure, R and RS.................... 5 A

Torque settings

Alternator rotor nut

Initial setting.. 150 Nm

Final setting.. 250 Nm

Alternator stator bolts................................. 10 Nm

Alternator stator carrier bolts.......................... 12 Nm

Crankcase breather wheel bolt......................... 40 Nm

Ignition switch/steering lock bolts...................... 20 Nm

Starter motor mounting bolts........................... 12 Nm

1 General information

General information

1 All models have a 12-volt electrical system charged by a three-phase alternator and separate regulator/rectifier.

2 The rectifier converts the ac (alternating current) output of the alternator to dc (direct current), and the regulator maintains the rectified voltage output within the specified range to power the lights and other components and to charge the battery at the correct rate. The alternator rotor is mounted on the rear end of the crankshaft and the stator is bolted to the back of the crankcase.

3 The starter motor is mounted on the right-hand side of the engine. The starting system includes the starter motor, starter relay and switches. If the engine kill switch is in the RUN position and the ignition switch is ON, the starter relay allows the starter motor to operate only if the transmission is in neutral or, if the transmission is in gear, with the clutch lever pulled into the handlebar and the side stand up.

CAN/LIN-bus technology

4 All models utilise Controlled Area Network (CAN)-bus and Local Interconnect Network (LIN)-bus technology to create an electronic information network between the system control units (instrument, ABS, engine control, body control, plus others as fitted according to options selected), sensors and power-consuming components. This allows rapid and reliable data transfer around the network. It also allows comprehensive diagnosis of the entire system from one central point.

5 To reduce the amount of wiring in the network, all the components are designed to communicate via one or two wires. These wires are known as a 'data bus'. Each control unit has an integral transceiver which sends and receives data 'packets' along the bus. As the data packets travel between the units, each one examines the information and either acts upon it or ignores it, depending upon its relevance.

Note: *Keep in mind that electrical parts, once purchased, cannot be returned. To avoid unnecessary expense, make very sure the faulty component has been positively identified before buying a replacement part.*

2 Electrical system fault finding

Warning: Make sure that the ignition switch is OFF and that the battery is disconnected before any electrical components are disconnected. Failure to do so will result in fault codes being recorded in the associated system and the need to have these erased using the BMW diagnostic tester. Depending upon the system concerned, the bike's performance may be affected.

Fault finding

1 In the absence of test data, traditional probing with a multimeter should be avoided unless a specific result, as detailed in the text, is sought. The ECU and ground module are extremely sensitive to interference, and for the most part system checks should be confined to continuity tests of relevant sections of the wiring loom with the ignition switch OFF.

2 When testing for power supply to a component, always ensure that the multimeter is securely connected to the relevant wiring terminals before turning the ignition switch ON. It should be noted that in some cases, a test with the power ON may result in a fault being recorded by the ECU.

3 If at all possible, have the machine checked by a BMW dealer – recorded faults can then be analysed using the BMW diagnostic tester and remedial action taken. Fault codes should be erased from the ECU when the repair has been completed. Note that the aftermarket GS-911 tool, with appropriate wifi interface, is an alternative to the dealer-only tester.

4 Note that once a new component has been installed it will be necessary to re-instate the system programme using the diagnostic tester.

Simple wiring checks

5 Electrical problems often stem from simple causes, such as loose or corroded connections. Study the appropriate wiring diagram at the end of this Chapter to get a complete picture of what makes up that individual circuit.

6 Faults can often be tracked down by noting if other components related to that circuit are operating properly or not. If several components or circuits fail at one time, it may be that the fault lies in the earth (ground) connection, as several circuits are routed through the same earth connection.

7 Always check the condition of the wires and connections in the problem circuit. Intermittent failures can be especially frustrating, since you can't always duplicate the failure when it's convenient to test. In such situations, a good practice is to clean all connections in the affected circuit, whether or not they appear to be good. All of the connections and wires should also be wiggled to check for looseness which can cause intermittent failure.

Continuity checks

8 Continuity checks can be made with a continuity tester or a multimeter **(see illustrations)**. These testers are self-powered by a battery, therefore the checks are made with the ignition OFF. As a safety precaution, disconnect the battery negative (-) lead before making continuity checks, particularly if the ignition switch is being checked.

9 If using a multimeter, select the appropriate ohms scale and check that the meter reads infinity (∞). Touch the meter probes together and check that the meter reads zero; where necessary adjust the meter so that it reads zero. Make the test across the terminals described **(see illustrations)**. After using the meter always switch if off to conserve its battery.

10 Reconnect the machine's battery, noting the procedure in Section 3.

Voltage checks

Note: *Note the possible results of making voltage checks in Step 2.*

11 A voltage check can determine whether current is reaching a component. Tests can be made with a multimeter set to the dc volts scale or a test light **(see illustration)**.

12 Check that the multimeter leads are inserted in the correct terminals on the meter, red to positive (+) and black to negative (-). Incorrect connections could damage the meter.

13 The meter (set the dc volts scale) should always be connected in parallel (across the load). Connecting it in series will not harm the meter, but the result will not be meaningful.

14 Voltage checks are made with the ignition ON. Connect the meter's red lead to the power supply wire and the negative lead to a good earth or directly to the battery's negative terminal **(see illustration)**.

2.8a A digital multimeter can be used for all electrical tests

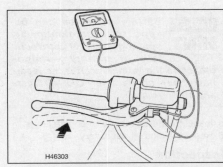

2.9a Continuity should be indicated across switch terminals when the lever is operated

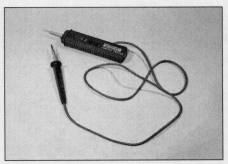

2.8b A battery powered continuity tester

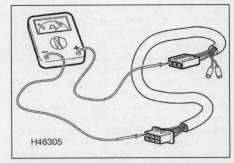

2.9b Wiring continuity check. Connect the meter probes across each end of the same wire

Earth (ground) checks

15 Earth (ground) connections are made either directly to the engine or by a separate wire into the earth circuit of the wire harness.

16 Corrosion is often the cause of a poor earth connection. If total electrical failure is experienced, check the security of the battery main earth lead at each end. If corroded, dismantle the connection and clean all surfaces back to bare metal.

17 To check the earth on a component, use an insulated jumper wire **(see illustration)** to temporarily bypass its earth connection. Connect one end of the jumper wire between the earth terminal or metal body of the component and the other end to the motorcycle's engine or frame, or if possible

directly to the earth (-) terminal on the battery.

18 If the circuit works with the jumper wire installed, the original earth circuit is faulty. Check the wiring for open-circuits or poor connections.

3 Battery

Removal and installation

1 Make sure the ignition is OFF. On GS, GS Adv, R and RS models remove the battery cover, and on RT models remove the

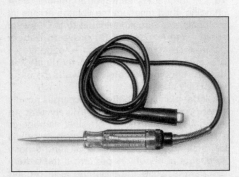

2.11 A simple test light is useful for voltage tests

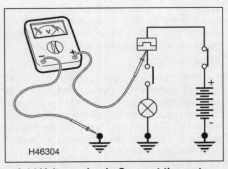

2.14 Voltage check. Connect the meter positive probe to the component and the negative probe to earth

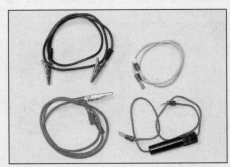

2.17 A selection of insulated jumper wires

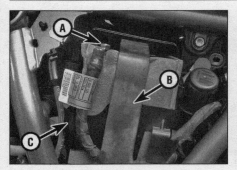

3.2 Negative (-) terminal screw (A), strap (B) and retaining plate (C)

3.3 Draw the battery out to disconnect the positive lead

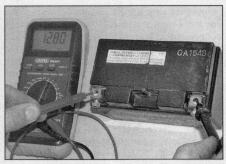

3.8 Checking the battery voltage

right-hand engine cover (see Chapter 7). If fitted, turn off the anti-theft alarm.

2 Undo the negative (-) terminal screw, noting the washer on RT models, and disconnect the lead **(see illustration)**. Unhook the rubber battery strap. Pull the retaining plate outwards then lift and remove it, noting how the side and bottom pegs locate.

3 Slide the battery out and support it, then undo the positive (+) terminal screw, noting the washer on RT models, and disconnect the lead **(see illustration)**. Remove the battery. If required lift the battery out of its insulating cover – if you are fitting a new battery fit the cover onto it on installation.

4 Installation is the reverse of removal, noting the following:

● Make sure the battery terminals and lead ends are clean.
● If removed fit the insulating cover over the battery. Make sure the battery seating pad is in the holder.
● Align the battery so that the positive (+) and negative (-) terminals are to the rear with the positive terminal going into the holder first.
● Seat the inner edge of the battery on the holder and connect the positive lead to the positive (+) terminal, not forgetting the washer on RT models, then slide the battery in and fit the retaining plate, making sure it locates correctly, then connect the negative (-) lead, routing it under the guide on the plate.
● Hook the battery strap up – the strap fits over the outside of the retaining plate and negative lead.

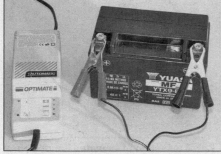

3.13 Battery connected to an after-market charger designed for motorcycles

HAYNES HINT *Battery corrosion can be kept to a minimum by applying a layer of petroleum jelly or battery terminal grease to the terminals after the leads have been connected – DO NOT use any other grease.*

5 Install the battery cover or engine cover.
6 Reset the clock if necessary.

Inspection

7 All models are fitted with a sealed MF (maintenance free) battery. All that should be done is to check that the terminals are clean and tight and that the casing is neither damaged nor leaking. Note: Do not attempt to open the battery – the resulting damage will render the battery unserviceable.

8 Check the condition of the battery by measuring the voltage at the terminals. Connect the voltmeter positive (+) probe to the battery positive (+) terminal, and the negative (-) probe to the negative (-) terminal **(see illustration)**. When fully-charged there should be approximately 12.8 volts present. If the voltage falls below 12.3 volts remove the battery and recharge it.

Charging

9 If the machine is not in regular use, either remove the battery and give it a refresher charge every four weeks as described below (bench charging), or connect a dedicated BMW float charger to the bike's electrical system via the on-board accessory socket to keep the battery charged in situ. Do not connect a battery charger to the battery terminals while the battery is on the bike.

Float charging

10 BMW produces battery chargers (different ones for different countries) that should be used for float charging – other chargers may not be suitable for the bike's electrical and electronic systems and could cause damage to them. The charger switches on and off automatically as required.

11 If the battery voltage drops below 9 V, attempting to recharge it via the accessory socket will damage the electrics. Remove the battery and bench charge it.

Bench charging

12 Whatever charger is used, ensure that it is suitable for charging a 12V battery.

13 Remove the battery from the machine (see above). Check that the charger is switched off. Connect the positive (+) charger lead to the positive (+) battery terminal and the negative (-) charger lead to the negative (-) battery terminal **(see illustration)**. Turn the charger on.

14 BMW do not specify a recommended charging rate, although the battery will be marked with a regular charge rate, plus a quick charge rate which can be used in emergencies for a short time. As a guide, a discharged battery should be charged at a low rate (approx. 1.2 amps for GS, GS Adv, R and RS models, and 1.6 amps for RT models) for 10 hours. Exceeding this figure can cause the battery to overheat, buckling the plates and rendering it useless.

15 Use of a dedicated 'intelligent' motorcycle battery charger is recommended – they are not expensive and a worthwhile investment, especially if the bike is not used over winter. These chargers assess and indicate the condition and state of charge of the battery, and regulate the charging current automatically according to the battery's need, and can also often bring heavily disharged MF batteries back to life. If a normal domestic charger is used check that after a possible initial peak, the charge rate falls to a safe level. If the battery becomes hot during charging STOP. Further charging will cause damage.

16 Let the battery settle for 30 minutes after charging, then measure the voltage across its terminals with a multimeter set to the dc volts scale – meter positive (+) prove to battery positive (+) terminal and meter negative (-) prove to battery negative (-) terminal. The battery should indicate 12.8 volts or more when fully charged.

17 If the recharged battery discharges rapidly when left disconnected it is likely that an internal short caused by physical damage or sulphation has occurred. A new battery will be required. A good battery will tend to lose its charge at about 1% per day. If the battery discharges while the machine is in regular use, either the battery is faulty or the charging system is defective. Refer to Section 23 for details of the charging system output test.

4 Fuses

1 Parts of the electrical system are protected by three fuses of different ratings (see Specifications at the beginning of the Chapter). All the fuses are under the rider's seat. The two circuit fuses are of the standard blade type and are in the holder clipped to the seat bracket. The charging system fuse is in the holder clipped to the ECU.

2 Remove the rider's seat (see Chapter 7).

3 To access the circuit fuses disconnect the connector from the holder on the seat bracket **(see illustration)**. The rating of each fuse is on the top of the fuse itself – refer to the Specifications at the beginning of the Chapter for the function of each fuse.

4 The fuses can be removed and checked visually – if you can't pull the fuse out with your fingertips, use a fuse tool or a suitable pair of pliers. A blown fuse is easily identified by a break in the element **(see illustration)**. Each fuse is clearly marked with its rating and must only be replaced by a fuse of the correct rating.

5 To access the charging system fuse displace the ECU (see Chapter 4) – there is no need to disconnect the wiring. Release the wiring from the top of the fuse holder and unclip the lid **(see illustration)**. A continuity check will determine if the fuse has blown **(see illustration)**. If it has, undo the two screws and replace the fuse with a new one.

⚠️ **Warning: Never put in a fuse of a higher rating or bridge the terminals with any other substitute, however temporary it may be. Serious damage may be done to the circuit, or a fire may start.**

6 If the new fuse blows immediately check the wiring circuit very carefully for evidence of a short-circuit. Look for bare wires and chafed, melted or burned insulation.

7 Occasionally a fuse will blow or cause an open-circuit for no obvious reason. Corrosion of the fuse ends and fusebox terminals may occur and cause poor fuse contact. If this happens, remove the corrosion with a wire brush or emery paper, then spray the fuse end and terminals with electrical contact cleaner.

5 Lighting system check

Note 1: *All models will display a warning on the instrument cluster in the event of a bulb failure.*

Note 2: *If the ignition is switched ON for any checks, remember to switch it OFF again before proceeding further or removing any electrical component from the system.*

1 The battery provides power for operation of the headlight, tail light, brake light, turn signals and instrument cluster lights. If none

4.3 Accessing the fuses

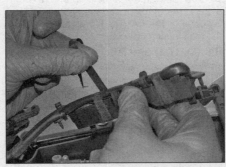
4.5a Unwrap the tape to release the wiring, then unclip the lid

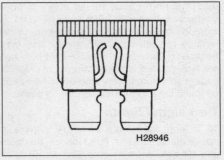
4.4 A blown fuse can be identified by a break in its element

4.5b Testing the fuse for continuity. Two screws secure the fuse

of the lights operate, always check battery condition before proceeding (Section 3).

2 When checking for a blown filament in a bulb, it is advisable to back up a visual check with a continuity test of the filament as it is not always apparent that the filament is broken. When checking continuity, remember that on turn signal bulbs it is often the metal body of the bulb that is the earth (ground).

Headlight

3 If the headlight fails to work, check the bulb and bulb terminals first (Section 6). Next disconnect the headlight wiring connector and check for battery voltage on the supply side of the wiring connector with a test light or multimeter as follows: refer to *Wiring Diagrams* at the end of this Chapter, then connect the negative probe of the multimeter to earth (ground) and the positive probe to either the high or low beam connector terminal as appropriate. Turn the ignition switch ON and select either high or low beam at the handlebar switch while conducting this test.

4 If no voltage is indicated, check the wiring between the connector and the ground module. Also check the wiring for the dimmer switch, and the switch itself (Section 19).

5 If voltage is indicated, check for continuity between the earth wire connector terminal and earth (ground). If there is no continuity, check the earth (ground) circuit for an open or poor connection.

Sidelight

6 If the sidelight fails to work, check the bulb and the bulb terminals first (Section 6). Next

disconnect the sidelight wiring connector and check for battery voltage on the supply side of the wiring connector with a test light or multimeter as follows: refer to *Wiring Diagrams* at the end of this Chapter, then connect the negative probe of the multimeter to earth (ground) and the positive probe to the sidelight connector terminal. Turn the ignition switch ON.

7 If no voltage is indicated, check the wiring between the connector and the ground module. Also check the wiring for the switch, and the switch itself (Section 19).

8 If voltage is indicated, check for continuity between the earth wire connector terminal and earth (ground). If there is no continuity, check the earth (ground) circuit for an open or poor connection.

Tail and brake lights

9 The tail and brake lights consist of a number of LEDs in a sealed unit. When a single LED fails it cannot be replaced with a new one, however the failure of one LED will not affect the function of the others. If the tail or brake light fails to work completely, check for battery voltage at the relevant terminal on the supply side of the wiring connector with a test light or multimeter as follows: connect the negative probe of the multimeter to earth (ground) and the positive probe to the tail or brake light connector terminal. If no voltage is indicated check the wiring between the connector and ground module. If voltage is indicated, check for continuity between the earth wire connector terminal and earth (ground). If there is no continuity, check the

earth (ground) circuit for an open or poor connection. If enough LEDs have failed so as to impair the safe operation of the motorcycle, replace the tail light with a new one (see Section 9). Note that the brake light switches are incorporated in the electronics of the ABS control unit/modulator – if no other faults can be found have this tested by a BMW dealer.

Turn signal lights

10 If one light fails to work, where a conventional bulb is fitted check the bulb and the bulb terminals (see Section 10). Next disconnect the turn signal wiring connector and check for battery voltage on the supply side of the connector with a test light or multimeter as follows: refer to *Wiring Diagrams* at the end of this Chapter, then connect the negative probe of the multimeter to earth (ground) and the positive probe to the signal connector terminal. Turn the ignition switch ON and select the appropriate signal (left or right) with the turn signal switch.

11 If no voltage is indicated, check the wiring between the turn signal and the ground module, and check the turn signal switch (see Section 19).

12 If voltage is indicated, check for continuity between the earth wire connector terminal and earth (ground). If there is no continuity, check the earth (ground) circuit for an open or poor connection.

13 On RT models as standard, and on other models where fitted as an optional extra, turn signals are illuminated by LEDs in a sealed unit. When a single LED fails it cannot be replaced with a new one, however the failure of one LED will not affect the function of the others. If the turn signal fails to work completely, follow the Steps above to check for battery voltage and the wiring. When sufficient LEDs have failed so as to impair the safe operation of the motorcycle, replace the turn signal unit with a new one (see Section 10).

Instrument and warning lights

14 The instrument cluster is a sealed unit. In the event of a light failure, have the instrument cluster checked by a BMW dealer.

Defective bulb warnings

15 In the event of a bulb failure, a warning appears on the instrument cluster

multifunction display (see details for individual models below). Once the fault has been corrected, the warning will be cancelled, but a fault code will be stored in the ground module which should be erased by a BMW dealer.

R1200 GS and GS Adventure

16 If a headlight, sidelight or front turn signal bulb fails, the general warning light illuminates yellow and the LAMPF warning appears on the multifunction display.

17 If a tail light, brake light or rear turn signal bulb fails, the general warning light illuminates yellow and the LAMPR warning appears on the multifunction display.

18 If a combination of the above faults occurs, the general warning light illuminates yellow and the LAMPS warning appears on the multifunction display.

R1200 RT, R and RS

19 If a headlight, sidelight or front turn signal bulb fails, the general warning light illuminates yellow and the defective bulb symbol with an arrow pointing up appears on the multifunction display.

20 If a tail light, brake light or rear turn signal bulb fails, the general warning light illuminates yellow and the defective bulb symbol with an arrow pointing down appears on the multifunction display.

21 If a combination of the above faults occurs, the general warning light illuminates yellow and the defective bulb symbol with arrows pointing up and down appear on the multifunction display.

6 Headlight and sidelight bulbs

Note: *The headlight bulb is of the quartz-halogen type. Do not touch the bulb glass as skin acids will shorten the bulb's service life. If the bulb is accidentally touched, it should be wiped carefully when cold with a rag soaked in methylated spirit and dried before fitting.*

R1200 GS and GS Adventure
Headlight

1 The high beam bulb is in the left-hand side

of the headlight and the low beam bulb is in the right-hand side.

2 Turn the bulb cover anti-clockwise and remove it **(see illustration 6.43)**. Carefully pull the wiring connector off the bulb **(see illustration 6.44)**.

3 Release the bulb retaining clip, noting how it fits, and withdraw the bulb, noting the orientation of the tab **(see illustrations 6.45a and b)**.

4 Fit the new bulb, bearing in mind the Note at the beginning of this Section, and secure it with the clip.

5 Reconnect the wiring connector.

6 Fit the bulb cover, aligning the tabs then turning it clockwise **(see illustration 6.43)**.

7 Check the operation of the headlight.

Sidelight

8 The sidelight bulbholder is in the lower left-hand side of the headlight. Turn the left-hand bulb cover anti-clockwise and remove it **(see illustration 6.43)**.

9 Carefully pull the bulbholder out of the headlight, then pull the bulb out of the holder **(see illustrations 6.51a and b)**.

10 Fit the new bulb into the holder, then fit the bulbholder into the headlight.

11 Fit the bulb cover, aligning the tabs then turning it clockwise **(see illustration 6.43)**.

12 Check the operation of the sidelight.

R1200 RT
Headlight

13 To access the high beam bulbs (in each side of the headlight), remove the left or right-hand speaker cover and speaker (if fitted) as appropriate (see Chapter 7, Section 4). To access the low beam bulb (in the centre of the headlight) reach up from under the fairing, or for better physical access and some visual access remove the left-hand fairing side and front panels (see Chapter 7), then displace the wiring connector from the radiator cowl, undo the screws and release the trim clip and remove the cowl.

14 Turn the low beam bulb cover anti-clockwise to release it **(see illustration)**.

15 Pull the high beam bulb cover off using the tab **(see illustration)**.

16 Pull the wiring connector off the bulb **(see illustrations)**.

6.14 Turn low beam bulb cover anti-clockwise

6.15 Use the tab to pull the high beam bulb cover off

6.16 Pull the wiring connector off

6.17a Low beam bulb clip – unhook at the bottom and pivot clip up

6.17b High beam bulb clip – unhook at the top and pivot clip down

6.17c Note the orientation of the bulb as you remove it – this is the low beam bulb

17 Release the bulb retaining clips, noting how they fit, and withdraw the bulb, noting the location of the tab **(see illustrations)**.

18 Fit the new bulb, bearing in mind the Note at the beginning of this Section, and secure it with the clips, which can be very tricky to relocate.

19 Reconnect the wiring connector.

20 Fit the bulb cover – for the low beam cover align the tabs then turn the cover clockwise **(see illustration 6.14)**, and for the high beam cover align the tab with the cut-out **(see illustration 6.15)**.

21 Check the operation of the headlight. Fit the speaker and its cover or the cowl and fairing panels as required.

Sidelight

Bulbs

22 Remove the relevant speaker cover, and where fitted the speaker (see Chapter 7).

23 Turn the bulb cover anti-clockwise to release it.

24 Carefully pull the bulbholder out of the headlight, then pull the bulb out of the holder **(see illustrations 6.51a and b)**.

25 Fit the new bulb into the holder, then fit the bulbholder into the headlight.

26 Fit the bulb cover, aligning the tabs then turning it clockwise.

27 Check the operation of the sidelight.

28 Fit the speaker and its cover.

LEDs

29 On models with LED sidelights new LED units can be fitted – they are only available as a pair. Remove the headlight (Section 7). Undo the screws and remove the LED units, noting the seals **(see illustration)** – new units come with new seals. Installation is the reverse of removal.

R1200 R

Headlight and sidelight

30 Remove the screws from the base of the headlight cover and ease the cover off at the top **(see illustrations)**.

31 Slacken the pivot screw on the left-hand side of the headlight two turns, and fully undo and remove the mounting screw on the right-hand side **(see illustration)**. Swivel the right-hand side of the headlight out.

6.17d Use pliers to remove the high beam bulb

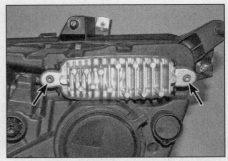

6.29 LED sidelight screws (arrowed)

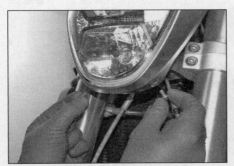

6.30a Undo the screws…

6.30b …and remove the cover, noting how it locates at the top

6.31a Slacken the pivot screw…

6.31b …and unscrew the right-hand mounting screw

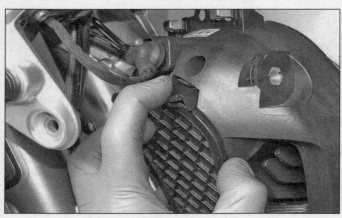

6.32a Release the tabs…

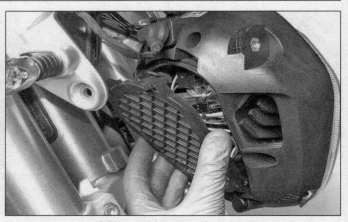

6.32b …and remove the cover

32 Press the rear cover tabs down and remove the cover **(see illustrations)**.

33 The low beam bulb is the upper bulb, the high beam bulb is the lower. The sidelight bulbs are in the middle on each side – the model shown has LED sidelights.

34 To remove the high or low beam bulb, twist the wiring connector/bulbholder anti-clockwise and draw it out of the headlight **(see illustration)**. Carefully pull the bulb off, gripping it around the base **(see illustration)**.

35 Fit the new bulb, bearing in mind the Note at the beginning of this Section. Fit the bulb into the headlight and turn the connector/holder clockwise to lock it.

36 To remove a sidelight bulb carefully pull the bulbholder out, then pull the bulb out of the holder **(see illustrations 6.51a and b)**.

37 Fit the new bulb into the holder, then fit the holder into the headlight.

38 Make sure the seal is correctly seated in its groove in the rear cover. Locate the bottom of the cover then push it in at the top to engage the tabs **(see illustration 6.32b and a)**.

39 Check the operation of the headlight and sidelight.

40 Swivel the headlight back into position, then fit the right-hand screw and tighten both screws **(see illustrations 6.31b and a)**.

41 Clip the front cover into place at the top and secure it with the screws at the bottom **(see illustrations 6.30b and a)**.

R1200 RS

42 The low beam bulb is in the right-hand headlight and the high beam is in the left. To access the headlight and sidelight bulbs, remove the left and/or right-hand cockpit trim panel as required (see Chapter 7).

Headlight

43 Turn the bulb cover anti-clockwise to release it **(see illustration)**.

44 Pull the wiring connector off the bulb **(see illustrations)**.

45 Release the bulb retaining clip, noting how it fits, and withdraw the bulb, noting the orientation of the tab **(see illustrations)**.

46 Fit the new bulb, bearing in mind the Note

6.34a Release and withdraw the bulbholder…

6.34b …and pull the bulb off

6.43 Remove the cover

6.44 Pull off the wiring connector

6.45a Release the clip…

6.45b …and remove the bulb

at the beginning of this Section, and secure it with the clip.

47 Reconnect the wiring connector.

48 Fit the bulb cover, aligning the tabs then turning it clockwise **(see illustration 6.43)**.

49 Check the operation of the headlight.

Sidelight

50 Turn the relevant bulb cover anti-clockwise to release it **(see illustration 6.43)**.

51 Carefully pull the bulbholder out of the headlight, then pull the bulb out of the holder **(see illustrations)**.

52 Fit the new bulb into the holder, then fit the bulbholder into the headlight.

53 Fit the bulb cover, aligning the tabs then turning it clockwise **(see illustration 6.43)**.

54 Check the operation of the sidelight.

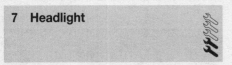

7 Headlight

Note 1: *An improperly adjusted headlight may cause problems for oncoming traffic or provide poor, unsafe illumination of the road ahead. Before adjusting the headlight aim, be sure to consult with local traffic laws and regulations – for UK models refer to MOT Test Checks in the Reference section.*

Note 2: *After removing the headlight, refer to Section 6 to remove the bulbs from the headlight if required. If a new headlight is being fitted also remove any mounting components as required according to model and transfer them to the new headlight.*

6.51a Withdraw the bulbholder, using pliers if necessary...

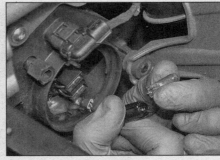

6.51b ...then carefully pull the bulb out

R1200 GS and GS Adventure

Removal

1 Remove the cockpit trim panels (see Chapter 7). For best access to the left-hand clip securing the headlight also remove the upper mudguard (see Chapter 7) – the clip is easy enough to remove with the mudguard in place, but is tricky to fit when installing the headlight.

2 Undo the screw on each side, noting the washer **(see illustration)**.

3 Remove the clips and washers from the pegs on the underside **(see illustration)**.

4 Lift the headlight so the pegs clear the grommets then draw it out and disconnect the wiring connector **(see illustrations)**.

5 Note the washers fitted in the side grommets **(see illustration)**. Check the

condition of all the mounting grommets and replace them with new ones if necessary.

Installation

6 Installation is the reverse of removal. Make sure the washers are in the side grommets **(see illustration 7.5)**. Make sure the wiring is securely connected. Make sure the clips locate correctly to secure the pegs **(see illustration)**. Check the operation of the headlight and sidelight.

7 Check the headlight aim as follows.

Adjustment

8 The headlight beam can be adjusted both horizontally and vertically. Before making any adjustment, check that the tyre pressures are correct and the suspension is adjusted as required. Make any adjustments to the headlight aim with the machine on level

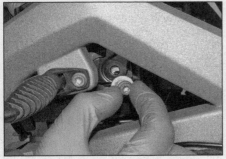

7.2 Undo the screw on each side

7.3 Pull the clips off the pegs

7.4a Manoeuvre the headlight out...

7.4b ...and disconnect the wiring

7.5 Note the washer on each side

7.6 Clips should locate under the washer and into the groove in the peg

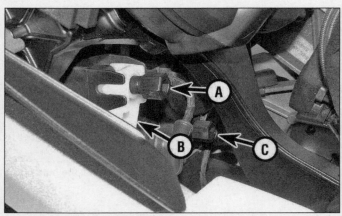

7.10 Vertical beam adjuster (A), heavy load lever (B), horizontal beam adjuster (C)

7.14a Undo the screws (arrowed) and displace the panel...

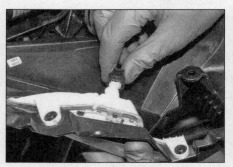

7.14b ...and disconnect the wiring

7.15a Unscrew the centre then pull the whole clip the out

7.15b Undo the screws...

ground, with the fuel tank half full and with an assistant sitting on the seat. If the bike is usually ridden with a passenger on the back, have a second assistant to do this. See Note 1 at the beginning of this Section.

9 Start the engine.

10 Vertical adjustment is made by turning the adjuster on the back of the headlight between the two bulb covers **(see illustration)**. Where fitted make sure that the heavy load lever is in the normal position (down), then turn the adjuster clockwise to raise the beam and anti-clockwise to lower it to achieve the desired setting.

11 If a heavy load is being carried, the headlight beam can be temporarily lowered without altering the standard setting by lifting the heavy load lever into the up position. Don't forget to reset the lever for normal riding.

12 Horizontal adjustment is made by turning the adjuster on the top right-hand corner of the headlight unit **(see illustration 7.10)**.

R1200 RT

Removal

13 Remove the windshield and its support panel, the fairing side and front panels, and the mirrors (see Chapter 7).

14 Undo the screw from each fairing side trim panel, displace the panel and disconnect the turn signal wiring connector **(see illustrations)**.

15 Release the trim clips and undo the screws

securing the windshield adjuster cover, then carefully lift the front of the cover to free the pegs from the grommets **(see illustrations)** – on models with the Satnav holder in the instrument cover this will come away with the adjuster cover, but rather than disconnecting the wiring lay the cover to one side, supporting or tying it up as necessary. On models without the Satnav holder remove the instrument cover.

16 Turn the ignition on and raise the windshield adjuster until the lower pivot pins in the brackets are accessible, then release the clips and withdraw the pins, noting that the spring-loaded brackets will spring up **(see illustrations)**. Turn the ignition off – the windshield adjuster will move down.

7.15c ...pull the pegs from the grommets and remove the cover

7.16a Release the clips...

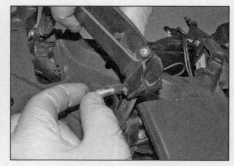

7.16b ...and withdraw the pins

7.17a Undo the screws on each side...

7.17b ...release the front of the panel...

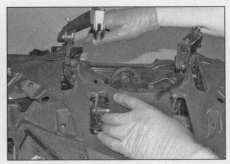

7.17c ...and remove it

17 Undo the fairing top trim panel screws, then draw the panel forwards and remove it **(see illustrations)**.
18 Cut the cable-tie on the left-hand side of the headlight, and disconnect the headlight wiring connector **(see illustration)**.
19 Remove the clips from the pegs, then undo the screws and remove the headlight **(see illustrations)**.
20 Check the condition of the grommets and replace them with new ones if necessary.

Installation

21 Installation is the reverse of removal. Make sure the clips locate correctly in their slots in the pegs **(see illustration)**. Make sure the wiring is securely connected. Check the operation of the headlight and sidelight.
22 Check the headlight aim as follows.

Adjustment

Note: *The adjuster knob on the cockpit trim panel is intended for temporary adjustment of the headlight beam when the machine is heavily loaded.*

23 The headlight beam can be adjusted both horizontally and vertically. Before making any adjustment, check that the tyre pressures are correct and the suspension is adjusted as required. Make any adjustments to the headlight aim with the machine on level ground, with the fuel tank half full and with an assistant sitting on the seat. If the bike is usually ridden with a passenger on the back, have a second assistant to do this. See Note 1 at the beginning of this Section.
24 Remove the left-hand fairing side panel (see Chapter 7).

7.18 Cut the cable-tie (arrowed) and disconnect the wiring

7.19a Pull off the three clips (arrowed) on each side...

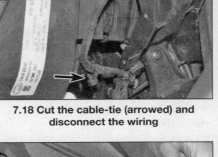

7.19b ...then undo the screw on each side...

7.19c ...and draw the headlight forwards until the pegs clear the grommets

25 Turn the heavy load adjuster lever fully anti-clockwise to the standard load position **(see illustration)**. Start the engine.
26 Vertical adjustment is made by turning

the adjuster on the left-hand side of the headlight **(see illustration)**. Turn the adjuster as required to achieve the desired setting.
27 Horizontal adjustment is made by turning

7.21 Slide the clip into the groove in the peg

7.25 Load adjuster lever (arrowed)

7.26 Vertical adjuster (arrowed)

7.27 Horizontal adjuster (arrowed)

7.28a Undo the screw on each side...

7.28b ...and disconnect the wiring connector

the adjuster on the right-hand side of the headlight unit (see illustration).

R1200 R

Removal

28 Undo the mounting screw on each side of the headlight, displace the headlight and disconnect the wiring connector (see illustrations).

Installation

29 Installation is the reverse of removal. Make sure the wiring is securely connected. Check the operation of the headlight and sidelight.
30 Before tightening the mounting bolts fully, check the headlight aim as follows.

Adjustment

31 The headlight beam can be adjusted vertically. Before making any adjustment, check that the tyre pressures are correct and the suspension is adjusted as required. Make any adjustments to the headlight aim with the machine on level ground, with the fuel tank half full and with an assistant sitting on the seat. If the bike is usually ridden with a passenger on the back, have a second assistant to do this. See Note 1 at the beginning of this Section.
32 Loosen the headlight mounting bolts so that the headlight can be pivoted up or down (see illustration). Start the engine.
33 Adjust the position of the headlight up or down as required.

34 Tighten the mounting bolts, taking care not to disturb the position of the headlight.

R1200 RS

Removal

35 The low beam and high beam headlights are separated, with the low beam headlight in the right-hand fairing upper panel and the high beam in the left – remove the relevant fairing upper panel (see Chapter 7).
36 Undo the screws and remove the headlight from the panel (see illustration).

Installation

37 Installation is the reverse of removal. Check the operation of the headlight and sidelight.
38 Check the headlight aim as follows.

Adjustment

Note: The adjuster knob on the cockpit trim panel is intended for temporary adjustment of the headlight beam when the machine is heavily loaded.
39 The headlight beams can be adjusted individually, vertically. Before making any adjustment, check that the tyre pressures are correct and the suspension is adjusted as required. Make any adjustments to the headlight aim with the machine on level ground, with the fuel tank half full and with an assistant sitting on the seat. If the bike is usually ridden with a passenger on the back, have a second assistant to do this. See Note 1 at the beginning of this Section.

40 For best access remove the cockpit trim panels (see Chapter 7). Start the engine.
41 Vertical adjustment of each beam is made by turning the adjuster above the bulb cover, next to the wiring connector (see illustration). Turn the adjuster as required to achieve the desired setting.

8	Brake/tail light LEDs and number plate light

Brake tail light

1 The tail light consists of a number of LEDs in a sealed unit. When a single LED fails it cannot be renewed, however the failure of one LED will not affect the function of the others. If the tail light fails to work completely, refer to Section 5 to check the circuit. When sufficient LEDs have failed so as to impair the safe operation of the motorcycle, renew the tail light unit (see Section 9).

Number plate light

2 On GS, GS Adv and RT models there is no separate number plate light – the plate is illuminated by the tail light via a clear lens.
3 On R and RS models, to change the bulb or remove the light, refer to Steps 27 and 28 in Section 10 and remove the cover from the underside of the tail bracket. Undo the nut and withdraw the screw, then displace the tail light

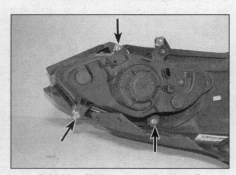

7.32 Slacken the bolt (arrowed) on each side, then pivot the headlight up or down as required

7.36 Headlight screws (arrowed)

7.41 Vertical adjuster (arrowed)

8.3a Remove the screw…

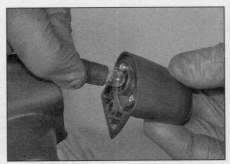

8.3b …withdraw the bulb holder…

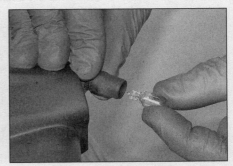

8.3c …and pull the bulb out

and pull the bulbholder out **(see illustrations)**. remove the bulb from the holder if required **(see illustration)**.

9 Tail light

R1200 GS and GS Adventure

1 Remove the rear turn signal/number plate carrier (see Chapter 7).
2 Undo the undertray screw and pull the rear of the tray down slightly **(see illustration)**.
3 Remove the retaining clips and washers from the pegs **(see illustration)**.

4 Carefully draw the tail light back to free the pegs from the grommets and disconnect the wiring connector **(see illustration)**.
5 Installation is the reverse of removal – make sure the grommets are in good condition, the wiring is securely connected, the washers are in place and the retaining clips locate correctly.
6 Check the operation of the brake/tail light.

R1200 RT

7 Remove the luggage rack and grab-rail assembly, the seat cowlings and the rear cowl (see Chapter 7).
8 Disconnect the wiring connector **(see illustration)**.

9 Remove the retaining clips from the pegs **(see illustration)**.
10 Carefully draw the tail light back to free the pegs from the grommets and disconnect the wiring connector.
11 Installation is the reverse of removal – make sure the grommets are in good condition, the wiring is securely connected, and the retaining clips locate correctly.
12 Check the operation of the brake/tail lights and turn signals.

R1200 R and RS

13 Remove the passenger seat (see Chapter 7).
14 Disconnect the wiring connector **(see illustration)**.

9.2 Undo the screw from the undertray

9.3 Pull the clip off the peg on each side and the peg at the top

9.4 Displace the light and disconnect the wiring

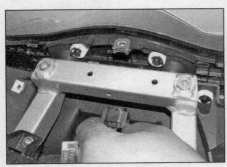

9.8 Disconnect the wiring

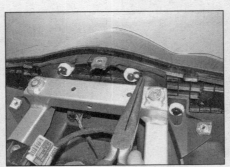

9.9 Pull the clips off the pegs

9.14 Disconnect the wiring…

15 Remove the retaining clip and washer from the peg **(see illustration)**.

16 Carefully draw the tail light back to free the outer mounting lugs from the snap-fit nuts, and the centre peg from the grommet **(see illustration)**.

17 Installation is the reverse of removal – make sure the grommet is in good condition, the wiring is securely connected, and the snap fit lugs and retaining clip locate correctly.

18 Check the operation of the brake and tail lights.

9.15 ...pull the clip off the peg...

9.16 ...and remove the light

10 Turn signals

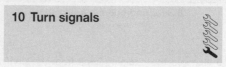

Bulb replacement

1 Most turn signal problems are the result of a burned out bulb or corroded socket. This is especially true when the turn signals function properly in one direction, but fail to flash in the other direction. Check the bulbs and the sockets as follows.

Note: *On RT models the turn signals are illuminated by LEDs in a sealed unit. On all other models optional extra (OE) turn signals*

are available illuminated by LEDs in a sealed unit. Replacement of individual LEDs is not possible – replacement of the complete turn signal unit is necessary.

2 Undo the turn signal lens screw and remove the lens, noting how the tab locates **(see illustrations)**.

3 Push the bulb into the holder and twist it anti-clockwise to remove it **(see illustration)**.

4 Check the socket and terminal for corrosion, if necessary scrape them clean and spray with electrical contact cleaner before a new bulb is fitted. Line up the pins of the new

bulb with the slots in the socket (noting that on amber bulbs the pins are offset), then push the bulb in and turn it clockwise until it locks into place.

5 Locate the tab on the lens on the inner side of the signal body and tighten the screw – do not overtighten it as it is easy to crack the lens or strip the threads.

6 Check the operation of the turn signals.

Removal and installation

R1200 GS and GS Adventure

Front turn signals

7 Remove the fuel tank covers and upper mudguard (see Chapter 7).

8 Release and disconnect the turn signal wiring and connector, noting its routing **(see illustration)**.

9 Undo the turn signal screw, then rotate the turn signal so the lens points up and draw it and the wiring out of the bracket.

10 Installation is the reverse of removal. Check the operation of the turn signals.

Rear turn signals

11 Remove the rear turn signal/number plate carrier (see Chapter 7).

12 Release the wiring from its guide. Undo the turn signal screw, then rotate the turn

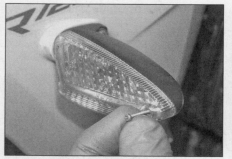

10.2a Undo the screw...

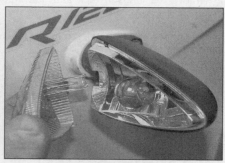

10.2b ...and lift off the lens – note how the tab locates

10.3 Push the bulb in and twist it anti-clockwise to remove it

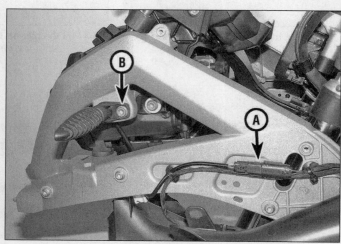

10.8 Turn signal wiring connector (A) and mounting screw (B)

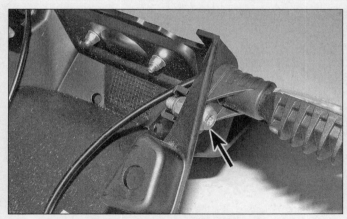

10.12 Turn signal screw (arrowed)

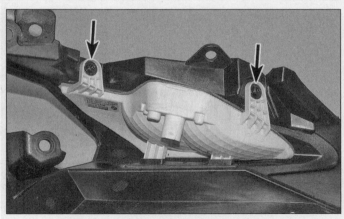

10.16 Screws (arrowed) secure turn signal unit

signal so the lens points up and draw it and the wiring out of the bracket **(see illustration)**.
13 Installation is the reverse of removal. Check the operation of the turn signals.

R1200 RT

Front turn signals

14 Remove the mirror (see Chapter 7).
15 Undo the fairing side trim panel screws, displace the panel and disconnect the turn signal wiring connector **(see illustrations 7.14a and b)**.
16 Undo the two screws then release the tabs and remove the turn signal **(see illustration)**.
17 Installation is the reverse of removal. Check the operation of the turn signals.

Rear turn signals

18 The rear turn signals are incorporated in the tail light unit – refer to Section 9.

R1200 R

Front turn signals

19 Remove the headlight (Section 7).
20 Cut the cable-tie and release and disconnect the connector **(see illustration)**.
21 Undo the turn signal screw, then rotate the turn signal so the lens points up and draw it and the wiring out of the bracket **(see illustration)**.
22 Installation is the reverse of removal. Check the operation of the turn signals.

Rear turn signals

23 Refer below to the RS model – the procedure is the same.

R1200 RS

Front turn signals

24 Remove the fairing side panel (see Chapter 7).
25 Hold the turn signal screw and undo the nut, then rotate the turn signal so the lens points up and draw it and the wiring out of the panel **(see illustrations)**.
26 Installation is the reverse of removal. Check the operation of the turn signals.

Rear turn signals

27 Remove the passenger seat (see Chapter 7).
28 Undo the five screws and remove the cover from the underside of the bracket **(see illustrations)**.

10.20 Right-hand turn signal wiring connector (arrowed)...

10.21 ...and mounting screw (arrowed)

10.25a Hold the screw (arrowed)...

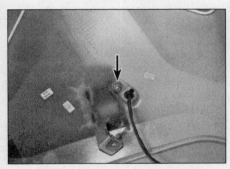

10.25b ...while unscrewing the nut (arrowed)

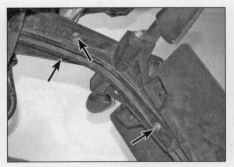

10.28a Undo the screws (arrowed)...

10.28b ...and the screws (arrowed)

10.29a Right-hand turn signal wiring connector (arrowed)

10.29b Left-hand turn signal wiring connector (arrowed)

10.30 Undo the nut and remove the screw

29 Release and disconnect the turn signal wiring and connector, noting its routing **(see illustrations)**.

30 Hold the turn signal screw and undo the nut, then rotate the turn signal so the lens points down and draw it and the wiring out of the bracket **(see illustration)**.

31 Installation is the reverse of removal. Check the operation of the turn signals.

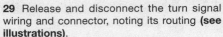

11 Instrument cluster

Note 1: *Do not disconnect the instrument wiring without first turning the ignition OFF and disconnecting the battery.*
Note 2: *In the event of an instrument failure, have the instrument cluster checked by a BMW dealer.*

Note 3: *If a new instrument cluster is being fitted, the BMW diagnostic tester must be used to register the new unit with the ground module and transfer the mileage and service data.*

R1200 GS and GS Adventure

1 Remove the cockpit trim panels (see Chapter 7).
2 Pull the retaining clip off the peg using suitable pliers, then draw the instrument cluster off to free the pegs from the grommets, then disconnect the wiring **(see illustrations)**.
3 Check the condition of the grommets and replace them with new ones if they are damaged or have deteriorated.
4 If necessary a new front cover and sealing ring can be fitted – undo the screws on the back, lift the front cover off and remove the sealing ring from its groove **(see illustration)**.

Fit the new sealing ring with the rounded side facing onto the instrument housing so the front cover sits against the flat side. Do not overtighten the screws as you could strip the threads.
5 Installation is the reverse of removal. Make sure the wiring is correctly connected and secured. Check the operation of the instrument cluster.

R1200 RT

6 Remove the windshield (see Chapter 7).
7 Release the trim clips and undo the screws securing the windshield adjuster cover, then carefully lift the front of the cover to free the pegs from the grommets **(see illustrations 7.15a, b and c)** – on models with the Satnav holder in the instrument cover this will come away with the adjuster cover, but rather than disconnecting the wiring lay the cover to one side, supporting or tying it up as necessary. On models without the Satnav holder remove the instrument cover.
8 Pull the retaining clips off the pegs using suitable pliers **(see illustration)**. Draw the instrument cluster off to free the pegs from the grommets, then disconnect the wiring **(see illustration)**.
9 Check the condition of the grommets and replace them with new ones if they are damaged or have deteriorated.
10 If necessary a new front cover and sealing ring can be fitted – undo the screws on the back, lift the front cover off and remove the sealing

11.2a Pull the clip off and displace the instruments...

11.2b ...then disconnect the wiring

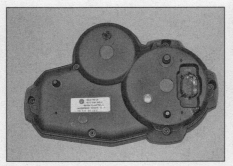

11.4 Undo the screws to release the cover

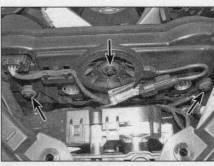

11.8a Pull off the clips (arrowed)...

11.8b ...displace the instruments and disconnect the wiring

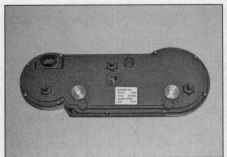

11.10 Undo the screws to release the cover

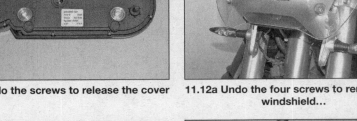

11.12a Undo the four screws to remove the windshield...

11.12b ...and the four screws to remove the bracket

ring from its groove (see illustration). Fit the new sealing ring with the rounded side facing onto the instrument housing so the front cover sits against the flat side. Do not overtighten the screws as you could strip the threads.

11 Installation is the reverse of removal. Make sure the wiring is correctly connected and secured. Check the operation of the instrument cluster.

R1200 R

12 Undo the screws securing the cover to the back of the instrument cluster and remove the cover. If a windshield is fitted, remove the windshield, then remove its bracket (see illustrations).

13 Pull the retaining clip off the peg using suitable pliers (see illustration). Draw the instrument cluster off to free the pegs from the grommets, then disconnect the wiring (see illustration).

14 Check the condition of the grommets and replace them with new ones if they are damaged or have deteriorated.

15 If necessary a new front cover and sealing ring can be fitted – undo the screws on the back, lift the front cover off and remove the sealing ring from its groove (see illustration 11.20). Fit the new sealing ring with the rounded side facing onto the instrument housing so the front cover sits against the flat side. Do not overtighten the screws as you could strip the threads.

16 Installation is the reverse of removal. Make sure the wiring is correctly connected and secured. On models with a windshield make sure the collars are fitted in the grommets (see illustration). Check the operation of the instrument cluster.

R1200 RS

17 Remove the windshield, the windshield bracket (either completely, or by pivoting it up and back so it is out of the way), and the windshield adjuster cover (see Chapter 7).

18 Pull the retaining clip off the peg using suitable pliers (see illustration). Draw the instrument cluster off to free the pegs from the grommets, then disconnect the wiring (see illustration).

19 Check the condition of the grommets and replace them with new ones if they are damaged or have deteriorated.

11.13a Disconnect the wiring connector...

11.13b ...then pull the clip off the peg

20 If necessary a new front cover and sealing ring can be fitted – undo the screws on the back, lift the front cover off and remove the sealing ring from its groove (see illustration). Fit the new sealing ring with the rounded side facing onto the instrument housing so the front cover

sits against the flat side. Do not overtighten the screws as you could strip the threads.

21 Installation is the reverse of removal. Make sure the wiring is correctly connected and secured. Check the operation of the instrument cluster.

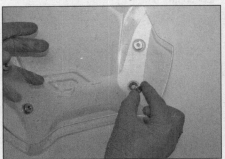

11.16 Collars fit into the back of the grommets

11.18a Pull the clip off...

11.18b ...displace the instruments and disconnect the wiring

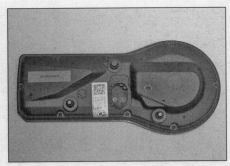

11.20 Undo the screws to release the cover

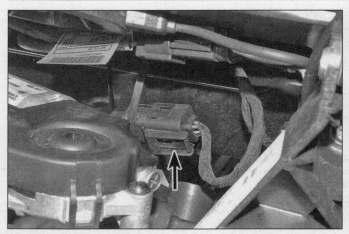

12.3 Release and disconnect the motor wiring connector (arrowed)

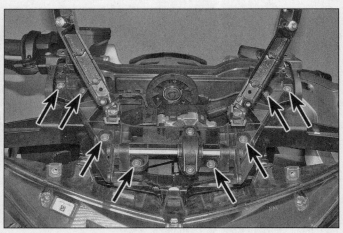

12.4 Windshield motor screws (arrowed)

12 Windshield motor (RT models)

1 Remove the windshield and the mirrors (see Chapter 7).
2 Refer to Steps 14 to 17 in Section 7 and remove the fairing side trim panels, the windshield adjuster cover, bracket pivot pins and fairing top trim panel.
3 Cut the cable-tie securing the motor wiring connector, then disconnect it (see illustration).
4 Undo the windshield motor screws and remove the motor (see illustration).

14.3 Gear position sensor wiring connector (arrowed)

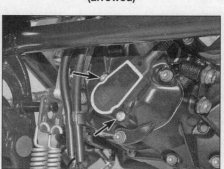

14.4 Gear position sensor screws (arrowed)

5 Installation is the reverse of removal. Make sure the wiring is correctly connected and secured. Check the operation of the windshield motor.

13 Speed sensor

1 The speedometer is activated by a speed sensor located on the inside edge of the final drive unit, behind the drive flange. The sensor ring is an integral part of the gear assembly inside the housing. Note that this sensor also supplies rear wheel speed information to the ABS control unit.
2 To remove the sensor refer to Chapter 6 Section 17.

14 Gear position sensor

1 The sensor monitors the position of the selector drum, and therefore which gear is selected. The ECU uses the information, combined with engine speed, to determine fuelling and ignition requirements.
2 Remove the starter motor (Section 22).
3 Release the cable-ties securing the sensor

15.3a Location of the air temperature sensor – RT model

wiring, then release and disconnect the connector (see illustration). Note the routing of the wire.
4 Undo the sensor screws and remove the sensor (see illustration).
5 Installation is the reverse of removal. Check the condition of the O-ring and replace it with a new one if necessary.

15 Ambient air temperature sensor

1 The ambient air temperature sensor is part of the on-board computer circuit. Note that with the machine at a standstill, engine heat can distort the reading. In these circumstances, the numerals of the temperature display are temporarily replaced by two horizontal dashes (– –).
2 If the air temperature drops below 3°C a snowflake icon appears on the multi-function display panel as a warning of the risk of black ice.
3 The ambient air temperature sensor is located under the left-hand side of the upper mudguard on GS and GS Adv models, in the right-hand radiator cowl on RT models, behind the left-hand fuel tank side cover on R models, and in the bottom of the fairing centre panel on RS models (see illustrations).

15.3b Location of the air temperature sensor – R model

15.3c Location of the air temperature sensor – RS model

16.5 Disconnect the wiring, then undo the screw (arrowed)

17 Sidestand switch

Check

1 The sidestand switch is mounted on the sidestand pivot. The switch is part of the safety circuit that allows the starter motor to operate only if the transmission is in neutral or, if the transmission is in gear, with the clutch lever pulled into the handlebar and the sidestand up.

2 Support the machine on its centrestand or on an auxiliary stand. On early GS models trace the wiring back from the switch to its connector and disconnect it. On all other models disconnect the wiring connector from the switch **(see illustration 17.8b)**.

3 Use a multimeter or continuity tester to check for continuity between the wire terminals on the switch side of the connector, first with the stand up and then with the stand down – there should be continuity with the switch in one position and not the other.

4 If the switch does not perform as described replace it with a new one.

5 If the switch is good, check the terminals in the loom side of the connector and the wiring.

6 If required, follow the procedure in Section 16 to check the operation of the safety circuit.

4 No specifications are available for testing the sensor. However, before condemning it, inspect the wiring connector and wiring for damage.

5 To remove the sensor on GS, RT and RS models, disconnect the wiring connector, then pull the sensor out. On R models cut the cable-tie to release the sensor, then disconnect the wiring.

6 Installation is the reverse of removal – make sure the sensor and its connector are securely fitted.

16 Clutch switch

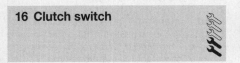

Check

1 The clutch switch is mounted in the lever bracket. The switch is part of the safety circuit that allows the starter motor to operate only if the transmission is in neutral or, if the transmission is in gear, if the clutch lever is pulled in and the sidestand is up. To check the safety circuit, follow the procedure in Steps 7 to 11.

2 Disconnect the switch wiring connector **(see illustration 16.5)**.

3 Using a multimeter or test light, check for continuity between the terminals on the switch side of the wiring connector, first with the lever at rest, then with the lever pulled in –

there should be continuity with the lever in one position only. If the switch doesn't behave as described, displace it and check the plunger as described below.

Removal and installation

4 On R1200 GS and GS Adventure models remove the main front section of the left-hand hand protector (see Chapter 7 Section 3).

5 Disconnect the wiring connector from the switch, then undo the screw and remove the switch **(see illustration)**. Check that the switch plunger is free to move – if it is stuck replace the switch with a new one.

6 Installation is the reverse of removal – fit the switch with the hole for the connector locking tab facing down.

Safety circuit check

7 Make sure that the kill switch is OFF, the sidestand is UP and the transmission is in neutral. Turn the ignition ON – neutral light N should illuminate on the instrument cluster multi-function display.

8 Select a gear – neutral light should go OFF.

9 Press the starter button – starter should not operate.

10 Extend the sidestand DOWN, pull in the clutch lever and press the starter button – starter should not operate.

11 Retract the sidestand UP and, with the clutch lever still pulled in, press the starter button – starter should operate.

Removal and installation

7 On early GS models trace the wiring back from the switch to its connector and disconnect it, then release the wiring from its ties and guide, noting its routing. Release the two circlips and remove the washer, then lift the switch off, noting how it locates.

8 On all other models undo the screw and lift the switch off, noting how it locates, then disconnect the wiring connector **(see illustrations)**.

9 Fit the sidestand switch, locating the pin on its back in the hole in the stand, and the slot in the body over the pin **(see illustration)**. On early GS models secure the switch with the washer and two new circlips, making sure each locates correctly. On all other models clean the threads of the switch screw and apply some fresh threadlock, and secure the switch with the screw.

17.8a Displace the switch...

17.8b ...then disconnect the wiring

17.9 Locate the pin in the hole

10 On early GS models secure the wiring in its guide and with new cable-ties, making sure it is correctly routed. On all models connect the wiring connector – on all except early GS models push the connector in until two clicks have been heard, indicating both catches have secured.

18 Ignition switch

18.2 The bolt heads must be drilled off

19.3 Disconnect the throttle unit wiring

Removal

1 Follow the relevant steps in the procedure of Chapter 5 Section 8 (GS, GS Adv and RT models) or Chapter 5 Section 9 (R and RS models) to remove the top yoke.

2 Special security bolts are used to mount the ignition switch/steering lock assembly on the underside of the top yoke **(see illustration)**. Drill the heads off the bolts and draw the assembly off. Use a stud extractor to unscrew the remains of the security bolts (see *Tools and Workshop Tips* in the Reference section).

Installation

3 Fit the switch/lock assembly onto the fork bridge and secure it with new security bolts – the bolts require a service tool (No. 510531) to engage their heads; tighten the bolts to the torque setting specified at the beginning of this Chapter.

4 Follow the relevant procedure in Chapter 5 and install the fork top yoke. Make sure

wiring is securely connected and check the operation of the ignition switch.

19 Handlebar switches

1 Generally speaking, the switches are reliable and trouble-free. Most problems, when they do occur, are caused by dirty or corroded contacts, but wear and breakage of internal parts is a possibility that should not be overlooked. If breakage does occur, the entire switch assembly will have to be replaced with a new one – individual parts are not available.

2 The switches can be checked for continuity using an ohmmeter or a continuity test light (see Section 2).

Right-hand switch

3 Disconnect the throttle unit wiring connector **(see illustration)**.

4 Undo the screw on the rear of the housing **(see illustration)**.

5 Lower the cover at the back, then push it forwards to unclip the front edge **(see illustration)**.

6 Undo the screw and displace the switch housing, then disconnect the wiring connectors **(see illustrations)**.

Left-hand switch

Caution: Do not undo the screws on the back of the switch housing.

7 On GS and GS Adventure models, where fitted remove the hand protectors (see Chapter 7 Section 3). On all other models undo the handlebar end-weight screw and remove the weight **(see illustration)**.

19.4 Undo the screw at the rear

19.5 Release and remove the cover

19.6a Undo the screw...

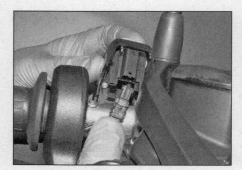

19.6b ...and disconnect the wiring connector at the front...

19.6c ...and at the back

19.7 End-weight screw (arrowed)

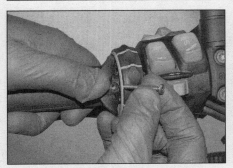
19.8 Hold back the flange and undo the screw

19.10a Release the clips...

19.10b ...and remove the cover

8 Hold back the flange of the handlebar grip and undo the screw **(see illustration)**.

9 Disconnect the clutch switch wiring connector **(see illustration 16.5)**. Release the handlebar switch wiring from its clips and ties.

10 Release the clips and remove the cover, then slide the handlebar grip/switch assembly off the handlebar **(see illustrations)**.

11 Either remove the blanked connector and disconnect the wired connector, or disconnect the two wired connectors, according to equipment level **(see illustration)**.

12 Carefully lift the retainer tab inside the housing and draw the grip out **(see illustrations)**.

13 Where fitted, and if required, undo the three screws securing the multi-control ring, then release the connector for the heated grip and remove the multi-control ring, noting how it aligns and locates.

Installation

14 Installation is the reverse of removal. Check the operation of the switches.

20 Horn

1 To access the horn on GS and GS Adv models remove the right-hand side panel (see Chapter 7) **(see illustration)**.

2 On RT models the horn is on the right-hand side **(see illustration)**.

3 To access the horn on R models remove the

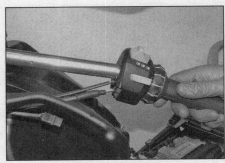
19.10c Slide the assembly off

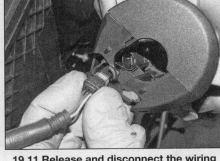
19.11 Release and disconnect the wiring

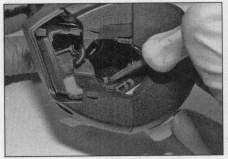
19.12a Lift the tab...

19.12b ...to release the grip from the housing

fuel tank and air filter housing (see Chapter 4).

4 To access the horn on RS models, for best access remove the fairing centre panel, though it is accessible by just removing the

cockpit trim panels (see Chapter 7) **(see illustration)**.

5 Disconnect the wiring connector, then undo the screw and remove the horn.

20.1 Horn – GS Adv model

20.2 Horn – RT model

20.4 Horn – RS model

6 To check the horn use a fully charged 12 volt battery and two insulated jumper wires, and apply voltage directly to the terminals on the horn.

7 If the horn sounds, check the switch (see Section 19) and the wiring between the switch and the horn (see Wiring Diagrams at the end of this Chapter).

8 If the horn doesn't sound, replace it with a new one.

9 Installation is the reverse of removal. Check the operation of the horn.

21 Relays

Main relay

1 Make sure the ignition is OFF. On GS, GS Adv, R and RS models remove the battery cover, and on RT models remove the right-hand engine cover (see Chapter 7).

2 Release the diagnostic plug from its clip **(see illustration)**.

3 Release the relay holder from the battery housing, then press the catch and pull the relay off its socket **(see illustrations)**. Check the sockets and terminals are clean and free of corrosion **(see illustration)**.

4 To test the relay connect a multi-meter set to the ohms x 1 scale or a continuity tester to terminals 3 and 4 on the relay – there should be no continuity (infinite resistance). Connect a 12 V battery to terminals 1 and 2 using suitable leads – the relay should click and there should now be continuity (zero resistance) between terminals 3 and 4. If the relay does not test as described replace it with a new one.

Starter relay

5 If the starter circuit is faulty, first check that the battery is fully charged. Check that the engine kill switch is in the RUN position, that the sidestand is up and that the transmission is in neutral. If the starter motor still fails to operate, turn the ignition OFF and disconnect the battery negative (-) lead (see Section 3).

6 On GS, GS Adv, R and RS models remove the frame cover from the left-hand side of the bike, and on RT models remove the left-hand engine cover (see Chapter 7).

21.2 Release the diagnostic plug

21.3b …then remove the relay

7 Disconnect the relay wiring connector, then unscrew the nuts and detach the battery and starter motor leads, noting which fits where **(see illustrations)**.

8 Release the wiring connector from the top of the relay **(see illustration)**. Lift the relay out from its holder, noting how it locates **(see illustration)**.

9 To test the relay connect a multimeter set to the ohms x 1 scale or a continuity tester to the relay's battery and starter motor lead terminals – there should be no continuity (infinite resistance). Connect a 12 V battery to the terminals in the wiring connector socket using suitable leads – the relay should click and there should now be continuity (zero resistance) between the battery and starter lead terminals. If the relay does not test as described replace it with a new one.

10 If the relay and its wiring are good,

21.3a Release the holder…

21.3c Check the terminals and sockets – terminal numbers marked

check the other components in the starter circuit (clutch switch, sidestand switch, gear position sensor, starter button and kill switch) as described in the relevant sections of this Chapter. If all components are good, check the wiring between the various components in the starter circuit (see Wiring Diagrams at the end of this Chapter).

11 If all components in the starter circuit are proved good, the fault could be due to a faulty starter motor (see Section 22).

22 Starter motor

Removal

1 The starter motor is on the right-hand side of the engine.

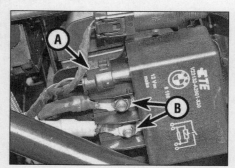

21.7 Relay wiring connector (A) and battery and starter motor leads (B)

21.8a Release the connector…

21.8b …and remove the relay

22.4a Release the connector...

22.4b ...then disconnect it

22.4c Disconnect the servo connector...

2 On R1200 RT models remove the right-hand engine cover, and on all other models remove the battery cover (see Chapter 7).

3 Disconnect the battery negative (-) lead (see Section 3).

4 Release and disconnect the right-hand exhaust downpipe oxygen sensor wiring connector **(see illustrations)**. Disconnect the exhaust flow control valve servo wiring connector **(see illustration)**. Undo the servo mounting screw and remove the washer, then draw the servo out of the grommets and allow it to hang by the cables **(see illustrations)**.

5 Release and remove the starter motor terminal cover **(see illustration)**. Unscrew the nut and detach the main lead **(see illustration)**. Undo the screw and detach the earth lead **(see illustration)**.

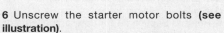
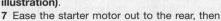

22.4d ...then undo the screw...

22.4e ...and displace the servo

6 Unscrew the starter motor bolts **(see illustration)**.

7 Ease the starter motor out to the rear, then swing the front end out and remove the motor, releasing the cable-tie from the top mounting lug **(see illustrations)**.

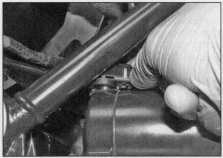

22.5a Remove the cover...

22.5b ...then unscrew the nut (arrowed) and detach the main lead

22.5c Detach the earth lead

22.6 Starter motor bolts (arrowed)

22.7a Draw the starter back...

22.7b ...then out

22.8 Check the O-ring (arrowed)

8 Check the condition of the O-ring and replace it with a new one if necessary **(see illustration)**.

9 No internal components are available for the starter motor – if it is faulty it must be replaced with a new one.

Installation

10 Installation is the reverse of removal. Lubricate the O-ring with a smear of oil.

11 Check the operation of the starter motor.

23 Charging system check

Note: *If the general warning light and the battery symbol come on while the bike is being ridden, before assuming there is a charging*

system fault check the charging system fuse (Section 4) – there have been instances of the fuse mounting bolts coming loose, causing a poor or open circuit.

1 Accurate assessment of alternator output should be undertaken by a BMW dealer. However, a charging voltage output test can be undertaken as follows.

2 Release and displace the battery, leaving its leads connected, and position it so both terminals are exposed, making sure it is adequately supported (Section 3). Check the voltage of the battery (Section 3).

3 Start the engine and let it idle. Using a multimeter set to the 0 to 20 volts DC scale, connect the positive (+) meter lead to the battery positive (+) terminal and the negative (-) lead to the negative (-) terminal. The meter should indicate 13 to 15 volts – increase engine speed a bit to determine the maximum voltage.

4 Now select high beam – the voltage may drop momentarily, but should then return to the original indicated 13 to 15 volts.

5 If the output test indicates a voltage either lower or higher than the suggested range, or if there is no change from the battery voltage measured before and there is no variation with engine speed, it is likely that the alternator stator or the regulator/rectifier is faulty – have the charging system checked by a BMW dealer.

6 Refer to Section 24 for details of alternator removal and installation, and to Section 25 for the regulator/rectifier.

24 Alternator

1 Refer to Section 23 to check the alternator output. If the alternator is faulty, a new one must be fitted. Note that if it is faulty it is most likely that it is the stator that is at fault and not the rotor, but unfortunately they are supplied as a pair and are not available individually (though it is worth checking with a dealer). As removal of the rotor requires a special tool and can be difficult you may wish to consider only replacing the stator with the new one, leaving the old rotor in place. The only reason to renew the rotor is if it is physically damaged, or if it has lost its magnetism, and in either case this will be obvious when you remove the stator.

2 The alternator is mounted inside the engine on the back of the crankcase. Remove the engine from the frame, then remove the gearbox (see Chapter 2).

Stator

Removal

3 Unscrew the crankcase breather bolt and remove the breather **(see illustration)**.

4 Unscrew the stator carrier bolts **(see illustration)**. Release the wiring grommet from its cut-out **(see illustration)**.

5 Grasp the carrier and pull the stator out of the rotor, noting that it is held by the force of the magnets **(see illustration)** – if necessary have an assistant use flat-bladed screwdrivers or suitable pry bars on each side (just below the bolt hole in the 3 o'clock position and just above the bolt hole in the 9 o'clock position) to displace the carrier far enough to get a good grip. Note how the carrier locates on two dowels.

6 To remove the stator from its carrier cut the cable-tie, then unscrew the bolts and lift the stator off **(see illustration)**.

7 Check the condition of the crankshaft bearing in the carrier and replace it with

24.3 Remove the breather wheel

24.4a Unscrew the bolts...

24.4b ...and free the grommet

24.5 Draw the stator out of the rotor

24.6 The stator is secured by three bolts

24.7 Check the bearing

24.19a Fit the puller and counter-hold the rotor using a socket drive as shown...

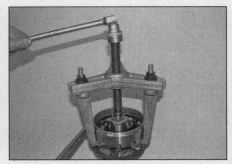

24.19b ...then pull the rotor off the shaft

a new one if necessary (see illustration) – remove the stator from the carrier, then remove the circlip, and drive the bearing out from the outer (rear) side of the carrier, using a suitable driver or socket. Fit the new bearing with its marked side facing into the rear side of the carrier, and drive it in using a driver or socket that bears on the outer race only. Secure the bearing with a new circlip.

Installation

8 Installation is the reverse of removal, noting the following:

- If removed clean the threads of the stator bolts and apply some fresh threadlock, and tighten them to the torque setting specified at the beginning of this Chapter. Secure the wiring with a new cable tie.
- Apply a suitable sealant to the groove in the curved side of the wiring grommet.
- Make sure the carrier locating dowels are in place. When fitting the carrier note that the stator will be forcibly drawn into the rotor by the magnets, so make sure it is correctly aligned to locate on the dowels.
- Tighten the stator carrier bolts to the specified torque. Make sure the wiring grommet is correctly seated in its cut-out.
- Tighten the breather wheel bolt to the specified torque.

9 Install the gearbox and engine (see Chapter 2).

Rotor

Removal

Note: *To remove the rotor you need the BMW puller (tool No. 120531). The rotor can be removed using a three-legged puller, but to do this you need to separate the crankcases and remove the crankshaft (see Chapter 2).*

Using the BMW puller

10 Remove the stator (see above).
11 Turn the engine to TDC and fit the crankshaft locking tool.
12 Heat the rotor nut and the bearing race on the end of the crankshaft to 120°C using a hot air gun. Fully unscrew the nut so that it is clear of its threads and up against the race – use an air ratchet gun to loosen the nut if available, or if not hold the engine using a strong bar in the rear mounting bolt hole as shown in illustration 24.26b, but on the opposite side.
13 Release the crankshaft locking tool.
14 Fit the puller onto the rotor and turn its centre bolt until the rotor is displaced from the shaft, bringing the bearing race and nut with it.
15 If required remove the starter clutch from the rotor (see Chapter 2).

Using a three-legged puller

16 Remove the stator (see above).
17 Heat the rotor nut and the bearing race on the end of the crankshaft to 120°C using a hot air gun. Fully unscrew the nut so that it is clear of its threads and up against the race – use an

air ratchet gun to loosen the nut if available, or if not hold the engine using a strong bar in the rear mounting bolt hole as shown in illustration 24.26b, but on the opposite side.
18 Remove the crankshaft (see Chapter 2).
19 Fit the puller onto the rotor, making sure its legs are fully seated under it. Use a half inch socket drive on a long handle fitting into one of the cut-outs in the rotor to counter-hold it, and turn the puller centre bolt until the rotor is displaced from the shaft, bringing the bearing race and nut with it **(see illustrations)**.
20 If required remove the starter clutch from the rotor (see Chapter 2).

Installation

21 If the crankshaft was removed to enable a three-legged puller to be used to remove the rotor, refit the crankshaft and assemble the crankcases before fitting the rotor (see Chapter 2).
22 If removed fit the starter clutch onto the back of the rotor (see Chapter 2).
23 Clean the tapered section of the crankshaft and the bore of the rotor with solvent. Make sure the Woodruff key is in its slot in the crankshaft **(see illustration)**.
24 Align the slot in the rotor with the key and slide the rotor onto the crankshaft, turning the starter driven gear anti-clockwise as you do to allow its hub to enter the starter clutch **(see illustration)**.

24.23 Check the key (arrowed) is in place

24.24 Turn the driven gear anti-clockwise as you slide the rotor on

24.26a Fit the washer and the nut…

24.26b …and tighten the nut as described, holding the engine as shown

24.27a Heat the race…

24.27b …seat it on the shaft…

24.27c …and drive it on using a socket

torque setting specified at the beginning of the Chapter, then fully slacken the nut and tighten it to the final torque setting specified **(see illustrations)**.

27 Turn the engine onto its front. Heat the bearing race using a hot air gun, place it onto the end of the crankshaft and drive it onto its seat using a 26 mm socket **(see illustrations)**.

28 Install the stator (see above).

25 Regulator/rectifier

1 The regulator/rectifier is mounted on the underside of the rear undertray. On RT models remove the shock absorber left-hand cover (see Chapter 7).

2 Disconnect the wiring connectors from the regulator/rectifier **(see illustration)**.

3 Undo the two screws and remove the regulator/rectifier **(see illustration)**.

4 Installation is the reverse of removal.

25 Make sure the engine is at TDC and fit the crankshaft locking tool.

26 Clean the threads of the crankshaft and the rotor nut and apply some high strength threadlock. Insert a strong bar through the engine rear mounting bolt hole to counter-hold the engine while tightening the nut. Fit the nut with its washer and tighten it to the initial

26 Wiring Diagrams

1 Wiring diagrams are provided as separate circuits e.g. Engine DME (ECU) and Headlight circuit.

2 Connector plug terminal number details are given to aid testing and terminal identification. The DME (ECU) has two connector blocks numbered 1 and 2 **(see illustration)** and the terminals pins are numbered within the blocks; the wiring diagrams show a circled 1 or 2 to identify the connector.

3 Note that components are not always shown complete, only the terminals relating to the circuit are shown.

4 Internal connections within the wiring harness are represented by full points.

5 Engine cylinders are referred to as Cyl 1 for the left-hand cylinder and Cyl 2 for the right-hand cylinder.

25.2 Disconnect the wiring…

25.3 …then undo the screws (arrowed)

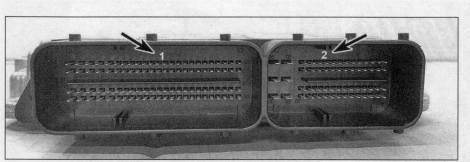

26.2 DME (ECU) connectors are labelled 1 and 2. Pin numbers can be established from detail at the end of each line of pins

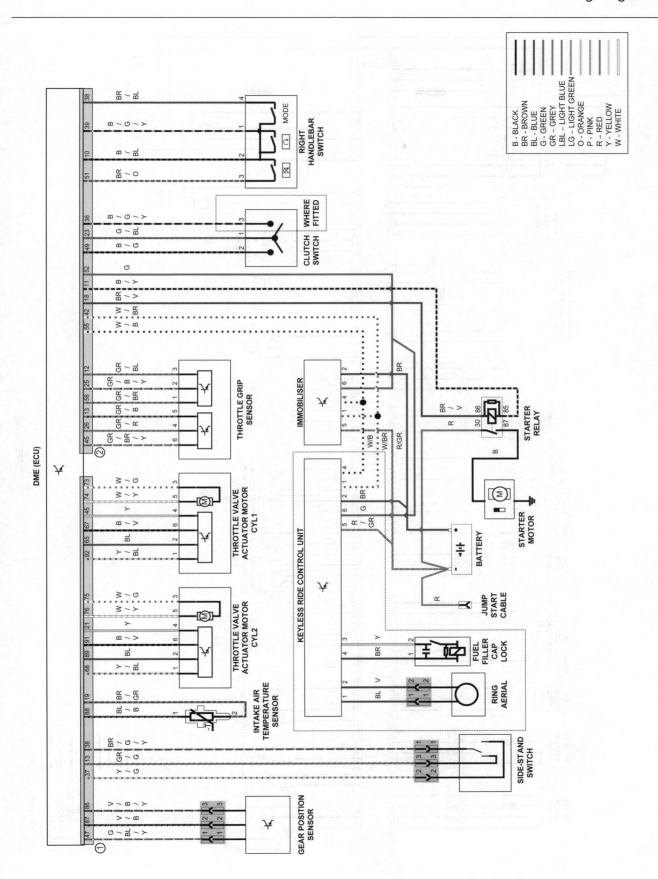

Starter circuit, Keyless ride and DME (ECU) (R1200GS shown)

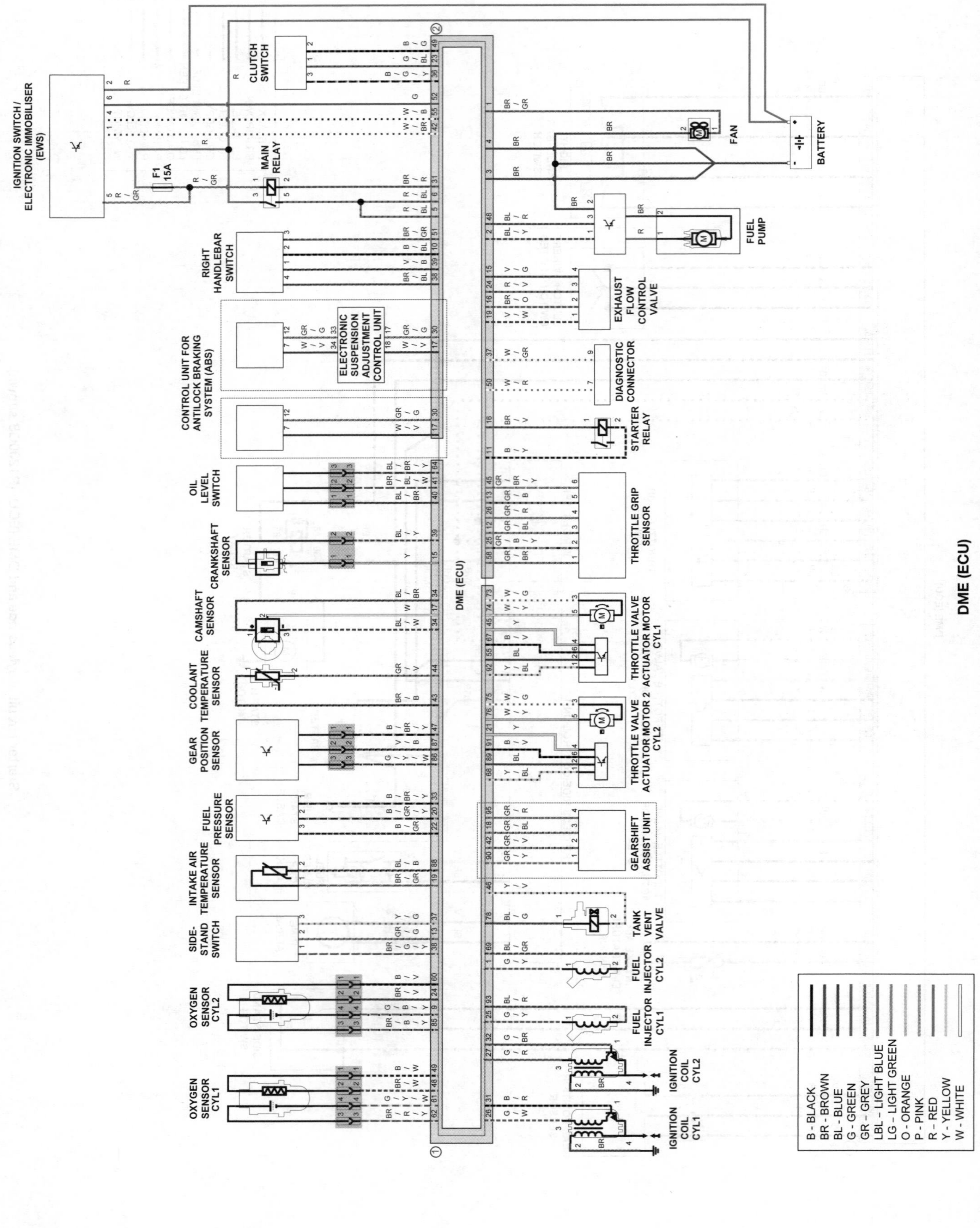
IGNITION SWITCH / ELECTRONIC IMMOBILISER (EWS)
F1 15A
MAIN RELAY
CLUTCH SWITCH
RIGHT HANDLEBAR SWITCH
CONTROL UNIT FOR ANTILOCK BRAKING SYSTEM (ABS)
ELECTRONIC SUSPENSION ADJUSTMENT CONTROL UNIT
OIL LEVEL SWITCH
CRANKSHAFT SENSOR
CAMSHAFT SENSOR
COOLANT TEMPERATURE SENSOR
GEAR POSITION SENSOR
FUEL PRESSURE SENSOR
INTAKE AIR TEMPERATURE SENSOR
SIDE-STAND SWITCH
OXYGEN SENSOR CYL2
OXYGEN SENSOR CYL1
DME (ECU)
FAN
BATTERY
FUEL PUMP
EXHAUST FLOW CONTROL VALVE
DIAGNOSTIC CONNECTOR
STARTER RELAY
THROTTLE GRIP SENSOR
THROTTLE VALVE ACTUATOR MOTOR CYL1
THROTTLE VALVE ACTUATOR MOTOR 2 CYL2
GEARSHIFT ASSIST UNIT
TANK VENT VALVE
FUEL INJECTOR CYL2
FUEL INJECTOR CYL1
IGNITION COIL CYL2
IGNITION COIL CYL1
B - BLACK
BR - BROWN
BL - BLUE
G - GREEN
GR - GREY
LBL - LIGHT BLUE
LG - LIGHT GREEN
O - ORANGE
P - PINK
R - RED
Y - YELLOW
W - WHITE
DME (ECU)

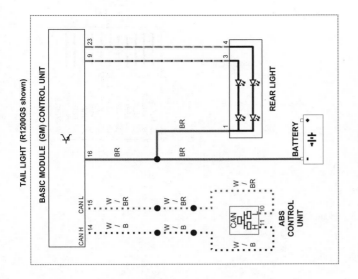

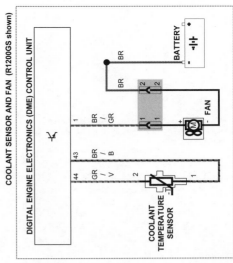

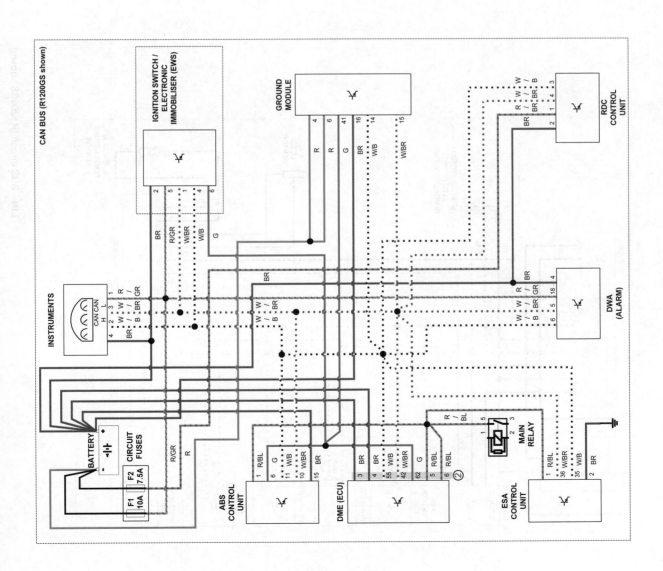

CAN - BUS circuit components, tail light, coolant sensor

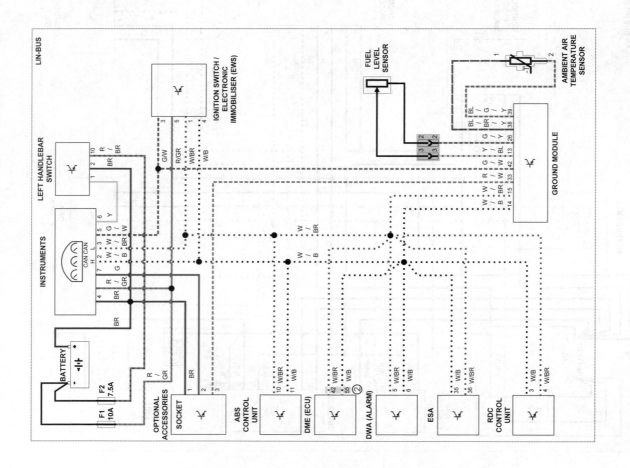

LIN - BUS circuit (R1200GS shown)

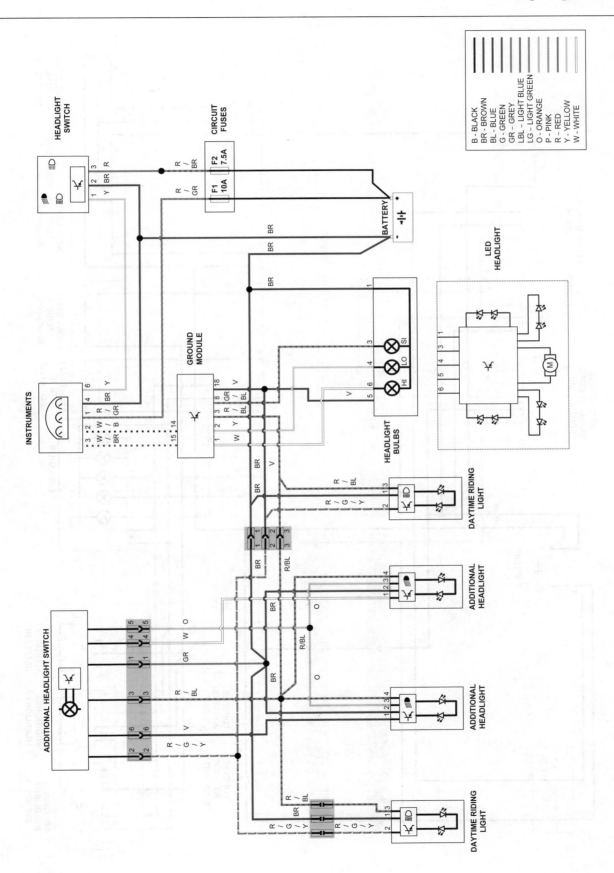

Headlight circuit (R1200GS shown)

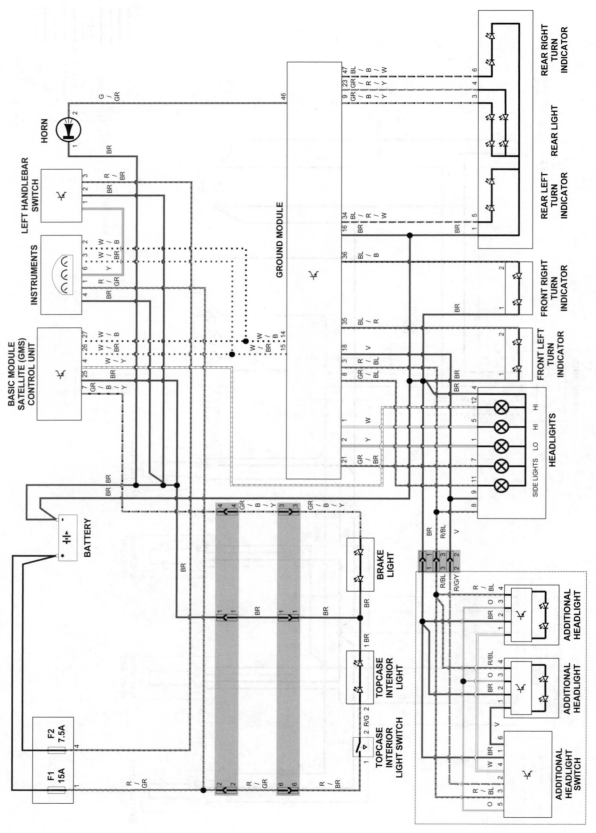

Lighting circuit, horn and turn signals (R1200RT)

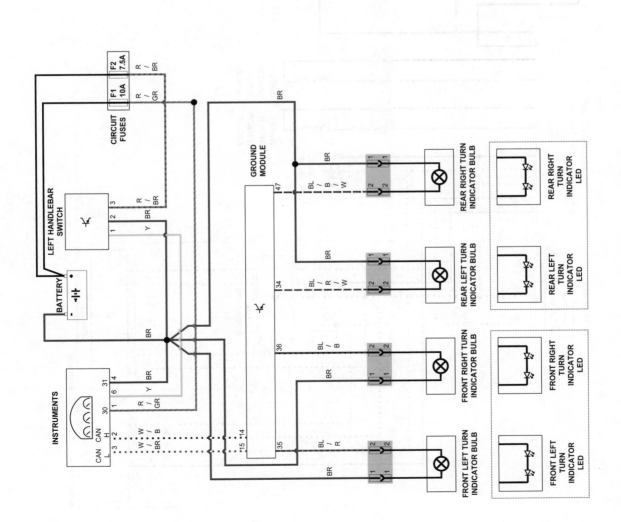

Turn signal circuit (R1200GS shown)

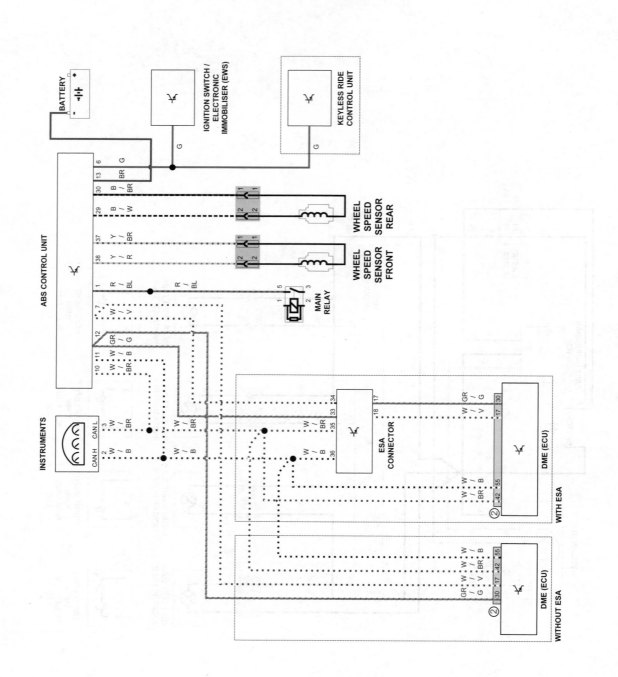

ABS circuit (R1200GS shown)

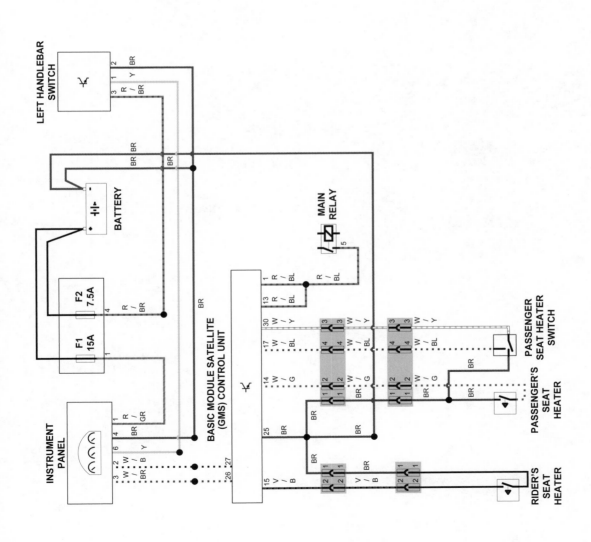

Heated seat circuit (R1200RT)

Notes

Reference

Tools and Workshop Tips

● Building up a tool kit and equipping your workshop ● Using tools ● Understanding bearing, seal, fastener and chain sizes and markings ● Repair techniques

Security

● Locks and chains ● U-locks ● Disc locks ● Alarms and immobilisers ● Security marking systems ● Tips on how to prevent bike theft

Lubricants and fluids

● Engine oils ● Transmission (gear) oils ● Coolant/anti-freeze ● Fork oils and suspension fluids ● Brake/clutch fluids ● Spray lubes, degreasers and solvents

MOT Test Checks

● A guide to the UK MOT test ● Which items are tested ● How to prepare your motorcycle for the test and perform a pre-test check

Storage

● How to prepare your motorcycle for going into storage and protect essential systems ● How to get the motorcycle back on the road

Conversion Factors

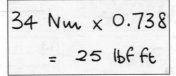

34 Nm x 0.738 = 25 lbf ft

● Formulae for conversion of the metric (SI) units used throughout the manual into Imperial measures

Fault Finding

● Common faults and their likely causes ● Links to main chapters for testing and repair procedures

Technical Terms Explained

● Component names, technical terms and common abbreviations explained

Index

Buying tools

A toolkit is a fundamental requirement for servicing and repairing a motorcycle. Although there will be an initial expense in building up enough tools for servicing, this will soon be offset by the savings made by doing the job yourself. As experience and confidence grow, additional tools can be added to enable the repair and overhaul of the motorcycle. Many of the specialist tools are expensive and not often used so it may be preferable to hire them, or for a group of friends or motorcycle club to join in the purchase.

As a rule, it is better to buy more expensive, good quality tools. Cheaper tools are likely to wear out faster and need to be renewed more often, nullifying the original saving.

> ⚠ **Warning: To avoid the risk of a poor quality tool breaking in use, causing injury or damage to the component being worked on, always aim to purchase tools which meet the relevant national safety standards.**

The following lists of tools do not represent the manufacturer's service tools, but serve as a guide to help the owner decide which tools are needed for this level of work. In addition, items such as an electric drill, hacksaw, files, soldering iron and a workbench equipped with a vice, may be needed. Although not classed as tools, a selection of bolts, screws, nuts, washers and pieces of tubing always come in useful.

For more information about tools, refer to the Haynes *Motorcycle Workshop Practice Techbook* (Bk. No. 3470).

Manufacturer's service tools

Inevitably certain tasks require the use of a service tool. Where possible an alternative tool or method of approach is recommended, but sometimes there is no option if personal injury or damage to the component is to be avoided. Where required, service tools are referred to in the relevant procedure.

Service tools can usually only be purchased from a motorcycle dealer and are identified by a part number. Some of the commonly-used tools, such as rotor pullers, are available in aftermarket form from mail-order motorcycle tool and accessory suppliers.

Maintenance and minor repair tools

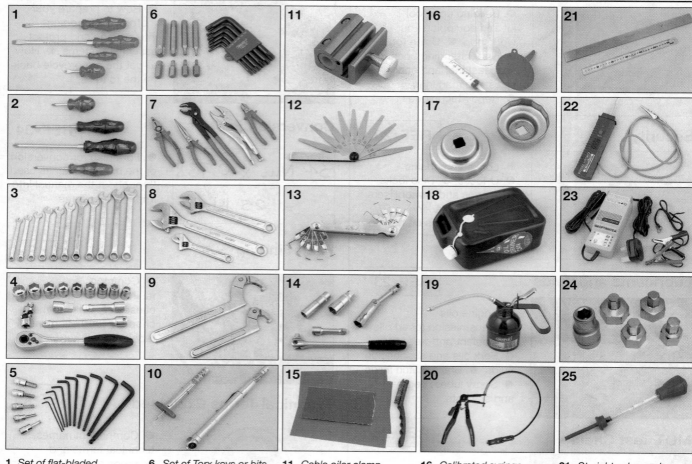

1 Set of flat-bladed screwdrivers	**6** Set of Torx keys or bits
2 Set of Phillips head screwdrivers	**7** Pliers, cutters and self-locking grips (Mole grips)
3 Combination open-end and ring spanners	**8** Adjustable spanners
4 Socket set (3/8 inch or 1/2 inch drive)	**9** C-spanners
5 Set of Allen keys or bits	**10** Tread depth gauge and tyre pressure gauge

11 Cable oiler clamp	**16** Calibrated syringe, measuring vessel and funnel
12 Feeler gauges	**17** Oil filter adapters
13 Spark plug gap measuring tool	**18** Oil drainer can or tray
14 Spark plug spanner or deep plug sockets	**19** Pump type oil can
15 Wire brush and emery paper	**20** Hose clamp pliers

21 Straight-edge and steel rule
22 Continuity tester
23 Battery charger
24 Large hex-bit set
25 Anti-freeze tester (for liquid-cooled engines)

Repair and overhaul tools

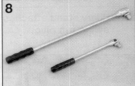

1 Torque wrench
  (small and mid-ranges)
2 Conventional, plastic or
  soft-faced hammers
3 Impact driver set

4 Vernier gauge
5 Circlip pliers (internal and
  external, or combination)
6 Set of cold chisels
  and punches

7 Selection of pullers
8 Breaker bars
9 Freeze spray and heat
  gun

10 Wire stripper and
   crimper tool
11 Multimeter (measures
   amps, volts and ohms)
12 Angle gauge

13 Strap wrench
14 Clutch holding tool
15 One-man brake/clutch
   bleeder kit

Specialist tools

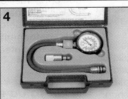
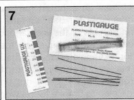

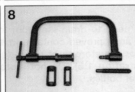

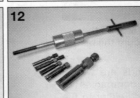
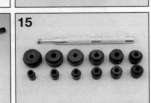

1 Micrometers
  (external type)
2 Telescoping gauges
3 Dial gauge

4 Cylinder
  compression gauge
5 Piston ring clamp
6 Oil pressure gauge

7 Plastigauge kit
8 Valve spring compressor
9 Two-piece seal driver –
  ideal for fork seals

10 Piston ring removal and
   installation tool
11 Tap and die set
12 Slide-hammer with knife-
   edged bearing pullers

13 Stud extractor
14 Screw extractor set
15 Bearing driver set

1 Workshop equipment and facilities

The workbench

● Work is made much easier by raising the bike up on a ramp - components are much more accessible if raised to waist level. The hydraulic or pneumatic types seen in the dealer's workshop are a sound investment if you undertake a lot of repairs or overhauls (see illustration 1.1).

1.1 Hydraulic motorcycle ramp

● If raised off ground level, the bike must be supported on the ramp to avoid it falling. Most ramps incorporate a front wheel locating clamp which can be adjusted to suit different diameter wheels. When tightening the clamp, take care not to mark the wheel rim or damage the tyre - use wood blocks on each side to prevent this.

● Secure the bike to the ramp using tie-downs (see illustration 1.2). If the bike has only a sidestand, and hence leans at a dangerous angle when raised, support the bike on an auxiliary stand.

1.2 Tie-downs are used around the passenger footrests to secure the bike

● Auxiliary (paddock) stands are widely available from mail order companies or motorcycle dealers and attach either to the wheel axle or swingarm pivot (see illustration 1.3). If the motorcycle has a centrestand, you can support it under the crankcase to prevent it toppling whilst either wheel is removed (see illustration 1.4).

1.3 This auxiliary stand attaches to the swingarm pivot

1.4 Always use a block of wood between the engine and jack head when supporting the engine in this way

Fumes and fire

● Refer to the Safety first! page at the beginning of the manual for full details. Make sure your workshop is equipped with a fire extinguisher suitable for fuel-related fires (Class B fire - flammable liquids) - it is not sufficient to have a water-filled extinguisher.

● Always ensure adequate ventilation is available. Unless an exhaust gas extraction system is available for use, ensure that the engine is run outside of the workshop.

● If working on the fuel system, make sure the workshop is ventilated to avoid a build-up of fumes. This applies equally to fume build-up when charging a battery. Do not smoke or allow anyone else to smoke in the workshop.

Fluids

● If you need to drain fuel from the tank, store it in an approved container marked as suitable for the storage of petrol (gasoline) (see illustration 1.5). Do not store fuel in glass jars or bottles.

1.5 Use an approved can only for storing petrol (gasoline)

● Use proprietary engine degreasers or solvents which have a high flash-point, such as paraffin (kerosene), for cleaning off oil, grease and dirt - never use petrol (gasoline) for cleaning. Wear rubber gloves when handling solvent and engine degreaser. The fumes from certain solvents can be dangerous - always work in a well-ventilated area.

Dust, eye and hand protection

● Protect your lungs from inhalation of dust particles by wearing a filtering mask over the nose and mouth. Many frictional materials still contain asbestos which is dangerous to your health. Protect your eyes from spouts of liquid and sprung components by wearing a pair of protective goggles (see illustration 1.6).

1.6 A fire extinguisher, goggles, mask and protective gloves should be at hand in the workshop

● Protect your hands from contact with solvents, fuel and oils by wearing rubber gloves. Alternatively apply a barrier cream to your hands before starting work. If handling hot components or fluids, wear suitable gloves to protect your hands from scalding and burns.

What to do with old fluids

● Old cleaning solvent, fuel, coolant and oils should not be poured down domestic drains or onto the ground. Package the fluid up in old oil containers, label it accordingly, and take it to a garage or disposal facility. Contact your local authority for location of such sites or ring the oil care hotline.

OIL CARE FOLLOW THE CODE

Note: It is antisocial and illegal to dump oil down the drain. To find the location of your local oil recycling bank in the UK, call 03708 506 506 or visit www.oilbankline.org.uk

In the USA, note that any oil supplier must accept used oil for recycling.

2 Fasteners - screws, bolts and nuts

Fastener types and applications

Bolts and screws

● Fastener head types are either of hexagonal, Torx or splined design, with internal and external versions of each type **(see illustrations 2.1 and 2.2)**; splined head fasteners are not in common use on motorcycles. The conventional slotted or Phillips head design is used for certain screws. Bolt or screw length is always measured from the underside of the head to the end of the item **(see illustration 2.11)**.

2.1 Internal hexagon/Allen (A), Torx (B) and splined (C) fasteners, with corresponding bits

2.2 External Torx (A), splined (B) and hexagon (C) fasteners, with corresponding sockets

● Certain fasteners on the motorcycle have a tensile marking on their heads, the higher the marking the stronger the fastener. High tensile fasteners generally carry a 10 or higher marking. Never replace a high tensile fastener with one of a lower tensile strength.

Washers (see illustration 2.3)

● Plain washers are used between a fastener head and a component to prevent damage to the component or to spread the load when torque is applied. Plain washers can also be used as spacers or shims in certain assemblies. Copper or aluminium plain washers are often used as sealing washers on drain plugs.

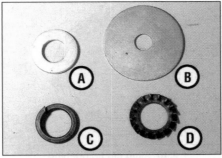

2.3 Plain washer (A), penny washer (B), spring washer (C) and serrated washer (D)

● The split-ring spring washer works by applying axial tension between the fastener head and component. If flattened, it is fatigued and must be renewed. If a plain (flat) washer is used on the fastener, position the spring washer between the fastener and the plain washer.

● Serrated star type washers dig into the fastener and component faces, preventing loosening. They are often used on electrical earth (ground) connections to the frame.

● Cone type washers (sometimes called Belleville) are conical and when tightened apply axial tension between the fastener head and component. They must be installed with the dished side against the component and often carry an OUTSIDE marking on their outer face. If flattened, they are fatigued and must be renewed.

● Tab washers are used to lock plain nuts or bolts on a shaft. A portion of the tab washer is bent up hard against one flat of the nut or bolt to prevent it loosening. Due to the tab washer being deformed in use, a new tab washer should be used every time it is disturbed.

● Wave washers are used to take up endfloat on a shaft. They provide light springing and prevent excessive side-to-side play of a component. Can be found on rocker arm shafts.

Nuts and split pins

● Conventional plain nuts are usually six-sided **(see illustration 2.4)**. They are sized by thread diameter and pitch. High tensile nuts carry a number on one end to denote their tensile strength.

2.4 Plain nut (A), shouldered locknut (B), nylon insert nut (C) and castellated nut (D)

● Self-locking nuts either have a nylon insert, or two spring metal tabs, or a shoulder which is staked into a groove in the shaft - their advantage over conventional plain nuts is a resistance to loosening due to vibration. The nylon insert type can be used a number of times, but must be renewed when the friction of the nylon insert is reduced, ie when the nut spins freely on the shaft. The spring tab type can be reused unless the tabs are damaged. The shouldered type must be renewed every time it is disturbed.

● Split pins (cotter pins) are used to lock a castellated nut to a shaft or to prevent slackening of a plain nut. Common applications are wheel axles and brake torque arms. Because the split pin arms are deformed to lock around the nut a new split pin must always be used on installation - always fit the correct size split pin which will fit snugly in the shaft hole. Make sure the split pin arms are correctly located around the nut **(see illustrations 2.5 and 2.6)**.

2.5 Bend split pin (cotter pin) arms as shown (arrows) to secure a castellated nut

2.6 Bend split pin (cotter pin) arms as shown to secure a plain nut

Caution: If the castellated nut slots do not align with the shaft hole after tightening to the torque setting, tighten the nut until the next slot aligns with the hole - never slacken the nut to align its slot.

● R-pins (shaped like the letter R), or slip pins as they are sometimes called, are sprung and can be reused if they are otherwise in good condition. Always install R-pins with their closed end facing forwards **(see illustration 2.7)**.

2.7 Correct fitting of R-pin. Arrow indicates forward direction

Circlips (see illustration 2.8)

● Circlips (sometimes called snap-rings) are used to retain components on a shaft or in a housing and have corresponding external or internal ears to permit removal. Parallel-sided (machined) circlips can be installed either way round in their groove, whereas stamped circlips (which have a chamfered edge on one face) must be installed with the chamfer facing away from the direction of thrust load (see illustration 2.9).

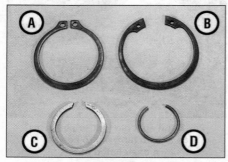

2.8 External stamped circlip (A), internal stamped circlip (B), machined circlip (C) and wire circlip (D)

● Always use circlip pliers to remove and install circlips; expand or compress them just enough to remove them. After installation, rotate the circlip in its groove to ensure it is securely seated. If installing a circlip on a splined shaft, always align its opening with a shaft channel to ensure the circlip ends are well supported and unlikely to catch (see illustration 2.10).

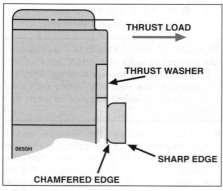

2.9 Correct fitting of a stamped circlip

THRUST LOAD

THRUST WASHER

SHARP EDGE

CHAMFERED EDGE

0650H

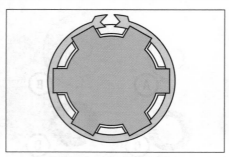

2.10 Align circlip opening with shaft channel

● Circlips can wear due to the thrust of components and become loose in their grooves, with the subsequent danger of becoming dislodged in operation. For this reason, renewal is advised every time a circlip is disturbed.

● Wire circlips are commonly used as piston pin retaining clips. If a removal tang is provided, long-nosed pliers can be used to dislodge them, otherwise careful use of a small flat-bladed screwdriver is necessary. Wire circlips should be renewed every time they are disturbed.

Thread diameter and pitch

● Diameter of a male thread (screw, bolt or stud) is the outside diameter of the threaded portion (see illustration 2.11). Most motorcycle manufacturers use the ISO (International Standards Organisation) metric system expressed in millimetres, eg M6 refers to a 6 mm diameter thread. Sizing is the same for nuts, except that the thread diameter is measured across the valleys of the nut.

● Pitch is the distance between the peaks of the thread (see illustration 2.11). It is expressed in millimetres, thus a common bolt size may be expressed as 6.0 x 1.0 mm (6 mm thread diameter and 1 mm pitch). Generally pitch increases in proportion to thread diameter, although there are always exceptions.

● Thread diameter and pitch are related for conventional fastener applications and the accompanying table can be used as a guide. Additionally, the AF (Across Flats), spanner or socket size dimension of the bolt or nut (see illustration 2.11) is linked to thread and pitch specification. Thread pitch can be measured with a thread gauge (see illustration 2.12).

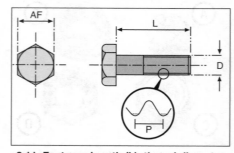

2.11 Fastener length (L), thread diameter (D), thread pitch (P) and head size (AF)

AF

L

D

P

2.12 Using a thread gauge to measure pitch

AF size	Thread diameter x pitch (mm)
8 mm	M5 x 0.8
8 mm	M6 x 1.0
10 mm	M6 x 1.0
12 mm	M8 x 1.25
14 mm	M10 x 1.25
17 mm	M12 x 1.25

● The threads of most fasteners are of the right-hand type, ie they are turned clockwise to tighten and anti-clockwise to loosen. The reverse situation applies to left-hand thread fasteners, which are turned anti-clockwise to tighten and clockwise to loosen. Left-hand threads are used where rotation of a component might loosen a conventional right-hand thread fastener.

Seized fasteners

● Corrosion of external fasteners due to water or reaction between two dissimilar metals can occur over a period of time. It will build up sooner in wet conditions or in countries where salt is used on the roads during the winter. If a fastener is severely corroded it is likely that normal methods of removal will fail and result in its head being ruined. When you attempt removal, the fastener thread should be heard to crack free and unscrew easily - if it doesn't, stop there before damaging something.

● A smart tap on the head of the fastener will often succeed in breaking free corrosion which has occurred in the threads (see illustration 2.13).

● An aerosol penetrating fluid (such as WD-40) applied the night beforehand may work its way down into the thread and ease removal. Depending on the location, you may be able to make up a Plasticine well around the fastener head and fill it with penetrating fluid.

2.13 A sharp tap on the head of a fastener will often break free a corroded thread

● If you are working on an engine internal component, corrosion will most likely not be a problem due to the well lubricated environment. However, components can be very tight and an impact driver is a useful tool in freeing them **(see illustration 2.14)**.

2.14 Using an impact driver to free a fastener

● Where corrosion has occurred between dissimilar metals (eg steel and aluminium alloy), the application of heat to the fastener head will create a disproportionate expansion rate between the two metals and break the seizure caused by the corrosion. Whether heat can be applied depends on the location of the fastener - any surrounding components likely to be damaged must first be removed **(see illustration 2.15)**. Heat can be applied using a paint stripper heat gun or clothes iron, or by immersing the component in boiling water - wear protective gloves to prevent scalding or burns to the hands.

2.15 Using heat to free a seized fastener

● As a last resort, it is possible to use a hammer and cold chisel to work the fastener head unscrewed **(see illustration 2.16)**. This will damage the fastener, but more importantly extreme care must be taken not to damage the surrounding component.

Caution: Remember that the component being secured is generally of more value than the bolt, nut or screw - when the fastener is freed, do not unscrew it with force, instead work the fastener back and forth when resistance is felt to prevent thread damage.

2.16 Using a hammer and chisel to free a seized fastener

Broken fasteners and damaged heads

● If the shank of a broken bolt or screw is accessible you can grip it with self-locking grips. The knurled wheel type stud extractor tool or self-gripping stud puller tool is particularly useful for removing the long studs which screw into the cylinder mouth surface of the crankcase or bolts and screws from which the head has broken off **(see illustration 2.17)**. Studs can also be removed by locking two nuts together on the threaded end of the stud and using a spanner on the lower nut **(see illustration 2.18)**.

2.17 Using a stud extractor tool to remove a broken crankcase stud

2.18 Two nuts can be locked together to unscrew a stud from a component

● A bolt or screw which has broken off below or level with the casing must be extracted using a screw extractor set. Centre punch the fastener to centralise the drill bit, then drill a hole in the fastener **(see illustration 2.19)**. Select a drill bit which is approximately half to three-quarters the diameter of the fastener

2.19 When using a screw extractor, first drill a hole in the fastener . . .

and drill to a depth which will accommodate the extractor. Use the largest size extractor possible, but avoid leaving too small a wall thickness otherwise the extractor will merely force the fastener walls outwards wedging it in the casing thread.

● If a spiral type extractor is used, thread it anti-clockwise into the fastener. As it is screwed in, it will grip the fastener and unscrew it from the casing **(see illustration 2.20)**.

2.20 . . . then thread the extractor anti-clockwise into the fastener

● If a taper type extractor is used, tap it into the fastener so that it is firmly wedged in place. Unscrew the extractor (anti-clockwise) to draw the fastener out.

⚠️ *Warning: Stud extractors are very hard and may break off in the fastener if care is not taken - ask an engineer about spark erosion if this happens.*

● Alternatively, the broken bolt/screw can be drilled out and the hole retapped for an oversize bolt/screw or a diamond-section thread insert. It is essential that the drilling is carried out squarely and to the correct depth, otherwise the casing may be ruined - if in doubt, entrust the work to an engineer.

● Bolts and nuts with rounded corners cause the correct size spanner or socket to slip when force is applied. Of the types of spanner/socket available always use a six-point type rather than an eight or twelve-point type - better grip

2.21 Comparison of surface drive ring spanner (left) with 12-point type (right)

is obtained. Surface drive spanners grip the middle of the hex flats, rather than the corners, and are thus good in cases of damaged heads **(see illustration 2.21)**.

● Slotted-head or Phillips-head screws are often damaged by the use of the wrong size screwdriver. Allen-head and Torx-head screws are much less likely to sustain damage. If enough of the screw head is exposed you can use a hacksaw to cut a slot in its head and then use a conventional flat-bladed screwdriver to remove it. Alternatively use a hammer and cold chisel to tap the head of the fastener around to slacken it. Always replace damaged fasteners with new ones, preferably Torx or Allen-head type.

HAYNES HINT

A dab of valve grinding compound between the screw head and screw-driver tip will often give a good grip.

Thread repair

● Threads (particularly those in aluminium alloy components) can be damaged by overtightening, being assembled with dirt in the threads, or from a component working loose and vibrating. Eventually the thread will fail completely, and it will be impossible to tighten the fastener.

● If a thread is damaged or clogged with old locking compound it can be renovated with a thread repair tool (thread chaser) **(see illustrations 2.22 and 2.23)**; special thread

2.22 A thread repair tool being used to correct an internal thread

2.23 A thread repair tool being used to correct an external thread

chasers are available for spark plug hole threads. The tool will not cut a new thread, but clean and true the original thread. Make sure that you use the correct diameter and pitch tool. Similarly, external threads can be cleaned up with a die or a thread restorer file **(see illustration 2.24)**.

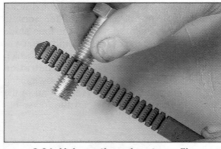

2.24 Using a thread restorer file

● It is possible to drill out the old thread and retap the component to the next thread size. This will work where there is enough surrounding material and a new bolt or screw can be obtained. Sometimes, however, this is not possible - such as where the bolt/screw passes through another component which must also be suitably modified, also in cases where a spark plug or oil drain plug cannot be obtained in a larger diameter thread size.

● The diamond-section thread insert (often known by its popular trade name of Heli-Coil) is a simple and effective method of renewing the thread and retaining the original size. A kit can be purchased which contains the tap, insert and installing tool **(see illustration 2.25)**. Drill out the damaged thread with the size drill specified **(see illustration 2.26)**. Carefully retap the thread **(see illustration 2.27)**. Install the

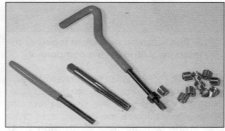

2.25 Obtain a thread insert kit to suit the thread diameter and pitch required

2.26 To install a thread insert, first drill out the original thread . . .

2.27 . . . tap a new thread . . .

2.28 . . . fit insert on the installing tool . . .

2.29 . . . and thread into the component . . .

2.30 . . . break off the tang when complete

insert on the installing tool and thread it slowly into place using a light downward pressure **(see illustrations 2.28 and 2.29)**. When positioned between a 1/4 and 1/2 turn below the surface withdraw the installing tool and use the break-off tool to press down on the tang, breaking it off **(see illustration 2.30)**.

● There are epoxy thread repair kits on the market which can rebuild stripped internal threads, although this repair should not be used on high load-bearing components.

Thread locking and sealing compounds

● Locking compounds are used in locations where the fastener is prone to loosening due to vibration or on important safety-related items which might cause loss of control of the motorcycle if they fail. It is also used where important fasteners cannot be secured by other means such as lockwashers or split pins.

● Before applying locking compound, make sure that the threads (internal and external) are clean and dry with all old compound removed. Select a compound to suit the component being secured - a non-permanent general locking and sealing type is suitable for most applications, but a high strength type is needed for permanent fixing of studs in castings. Apply a drop or two of the compound to the first few threads of the fastener, then thread it into place and tighten to the specified torque. Do not apply excessive thread locking compound otherwise the thread may be damaged on subsequent removal.

● Certain fasteners are impregnated with a dry film type coating of locking compound on their threads. Always renew this type of fastener if disturbed.

● Anti-seize compounds, such as copper-based greases, can be applied to protect threads from seizure due to extreme heat and corrosion. A common instance is spark plug threads and exhaust system fasteners.

---

3 Measuring tools and gauges

Feeler gauges

● Feeler gauges (or blades) are used for measuring small gaps and clearances (see illustration 3.1). They can also be used to measure endfloat (sideplay) of a component on a shaft where access is not possible with a dial gauge.

● Feeler gauge sets should be treated with care and not bent or damaged. They are etched with their size on one face. Keep them clean and very lightly oiled to prevent corrosion build-up.

3.1 Feeler gauges are used for measuring small gaps and clearances - thickness is marked on one face of gauge

---

● When measuring a clearance, select a gauge which is a light sliding fit between the two components. You may need to use two gauges together to measure the clearance accurately.

Micrometers

● A micrometer is a precision tool capable of measuring to 0.01 or 0.001 of a millimetre. It should always be stored in its case and not in the general toolbox. It must be kept clean and never dropped, otherwise its frame or measuring anvils could be distorted resulting in inaccurate readings.

● External micrometers are used for measuring outside diameters of components and have many more applications than internal micrometers. Micrometers are available in different size ranges, eg 0 to 25 mm, 25 to 50 mm, and upwards in 25 mm steps; some large micrometers have interchangeable anvils to allow a range of measurements to be taken. Generally the largest precision measurement you are likely to take on a motorcycle is the piston diameter.

● Internal micrometers (or bore micrometers) are used for measuring inside diameters, such as valve guides and cylinder bores. Telescoping gauges and small hole gauges are used in conjunction with an external micrometer, whereas the more expensive internal micrometers have their own measuring device.

External micrometer

Note: *The conventional analogue type instrument is described. Although much easier to read, digital micrometers are considerably more expensive.*

● Always check the calibration of the micrometer before use. With the anvils closed (0 to 25 mm type) or set over a test gauge

---

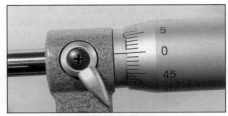

3.2 Check micrometer calibration before use

(for the larger types) the scale should read zero (see illustration 3.2); make sure that the anvils (and test piece) are clean first. Any discrepancy can be adjusted by referring to the instructions supplied with the tool. Remember that the micrometer is a precision measuring tool - don't force the anvils closed, use the ratchet (4) on the end of the micrometer to close it. In this way, a measured force is always applied.

● To use, first make sure that the item being measured is clean. Place the anvil of the micrometer (1) against the item and use the thimble (2) to bring the spindle (3) lightly into contact with the other side of the item (see illustration 3.3). Don't tighten the thimble down because this will damage the micrometer - instead use the ratchet (4) on the end of the micrometer. The ratchet mechanism applies a measured force preventing damage to the instrument.

● The micrometer is read by referring to the linear scale on the sleeve and the annular scale on the thimble. Read off the sleeve first to obtain the base measurement, then add the fine measurement from the thimble to obtain the overall reading. The linear scale on the sleeve represents the measuring range of the micrometer (eg 0 to 25 mm). The annular scale

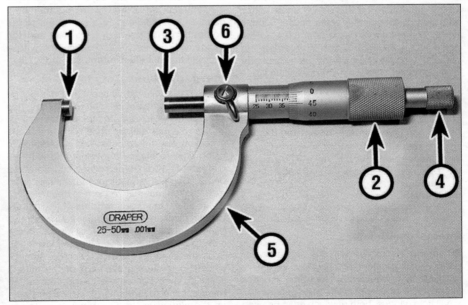

3.3 Micrometer component parts

1	Anvil	3	Spindle	5	Frame
2	Thimble	4	Ratchet	6	Locking lever

on the thimble will be in graduations of 0.01 mm (or as marked on the frame) - one full revolution of the thimble will move 0.5 mm on the linear scale. Take the reading where the datum line on the sleeve intersects the thimble's scale. Always position the eye directly above the scale otherwise an inaccurate reading will result.

In the example shown the item measures 2.95 mm **(see illustration 3.4)**:

Linear scale	2.00 mm
Linear scale	0.50 mm
Annular scale	0.45 mm
Total figure	2.95 mm

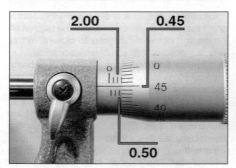

3.4 **Micrometer reading of 2.95 mm**

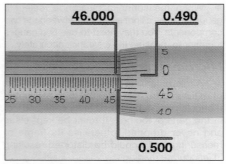

3.5 **Micrometer reading of 46.99 mm on linear and annular scales . . .**

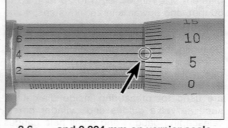

3.6 **. . . and 0.004 mm on vernier scale**

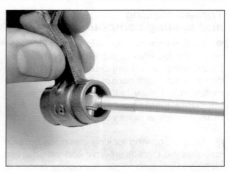

3.7 **Expand the telescoping gauge in the bore, lock its position . . .**

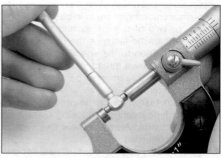

3.8 **. . . then measure the gauge with a micrometer**

3.9 **Expand the small hole gauge in the bore, lock its position . . .**

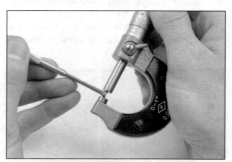

3.10 **. . . then measure the gauge with a micrometer**

Most micrometers have a locking lever (6) on the frame to hold the setting in place, allowing the item to be removed from the micrometer.
● Some micrometers have a vernier scale on their sleeve, providing an even finer measurement to be taken, in 0.001 increments of a millimetre. Take the sleeve and thimble measurement as described above, then check which graduation on the vernier scale aligns with that of the annular scale on the thimble. **Note:** *The eye must be perpendicular to the scale when taking the vernier reading - if necessary rotate the body of the micrometer to ensure this.* Multiply the vernier scale figure by 0.001 and add it to the base and fine measurement figures.

In the example shown the item measures 46.994 mm **(see illustrations 3.5 and 3.6)**:

Linear scale (base)	46.000 mm
Linear scale (base)	00.500 mm
Annular scale (fine)	00.490 mm
Vernier scale	00.004 mm
Total figure	46.994 mm

Internal micrometer

● Internal micrometers are available for measuring bore diameters, but are expensive and unlikely to be available for home use. It is suggested that a set of telescoping gauges and small hole gauges, both of which must be used with an external micrometer, will suffice for taking internal measurements on a motorcycle.
● Telescoping gauges can be used to measure internal diameters of components. Select a gauge with the correct size range, make sure its ends are clean and insert it into the bore. Expand the gauge, then lock its position and withdraw it from the bore **(see illustration 3.7)**. Measure across the gauge ends with a micrometer **(see illustration 3.8)**.
● Very small diameter bores (such as valve guides) are measured with a small hole gauge. Once adjusted to a slip-fit inside the component, its position is locked and the gauge withdrawn for measurement with a micrometer **(see illustrations 3.9 and 3.10)**.

Vernier caliper

Note: *The conventional linear and dial gauge type instruments are described. Digital types are easier to read, but are far more expensive.*
● The vernier caliper does not provide the precision of a micrometer, but is versatile in being able to measure internal and external diameters. Some types also incorporate a depth gauge. It is ideal for measuring clutch plate friction material and spring free lengths.
● To use the conventional linear scale vernier, slacken off the vernier clamp screws (1) and set its jaws over (2), or inside (3), the item to be measured **(see illustration 3.11)**. Slide the jaw into contact, using the thumb-wheel (4) for fine movement of the sliding scale (5) then tighten the clamp screws (1). Read off the main scale (6) where the zero on the sliding scale (5) intersects it, taking the whole number to the left of the zero; this provides the base measurement. View along the sliding scale and select the division which lines up exactly with any of the divisions on the main scale, noting that the divisions usually represents 0.02 of a millimetre. Add this fine measurement to the base measurement to obtain the total reading.

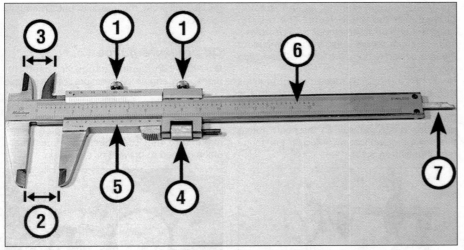

3.11 Vernier component parts (linear gauge)

1 Clamp screws	3 Internal jaws	5 Sliding scale	7 Depth gauge
2 External jaws	4 Thumbwheel	6 Main scale	

In the example shown the item measures 55.92 mm **(see illustration 3.12)**:

Base measurement	55.00 mm
Fine measurement	00.92 mm
Total figure	55.92 mm

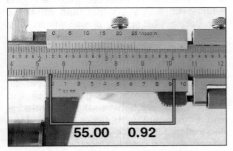

3.12 Vernier gauge reading of 55.92 mm

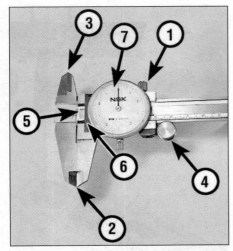

3.13 Vernier component parts (dial gauge)

1 Clamp screw	5 Main scale
2 External jaws	6 Sliding scale
3 Internal jaws	7 Dial gauge
4 Thumbwheel	

● Some vernier calipers are equipped with a dial gauge for fine measurement. Before use, check that the jaws are clean, then close them fully and check that the dial gauge reads zero. If necessary adjust the gauge ring accordingly. Slacken the vernier clamp screw (1) and set its jaws over (2), or inside (3), the item to be measured **(see illustration 3.13)**. Slide the jaws into contact, using the thumbwheel (4) for fine movement. Read off the main scale (5) where the edge of the sliding scale (6) intersects it, taking the whole number to the left of the zero; this provides the base measurement. Read off the needle position on the dial gauge (7) scale to provide the fine measurement; each division represents 0.05 of a millimetre. Add this fine measurement to the base measurement to obtain the total reading.

In the example shown the item measures 55.95 mm **(see illustration 3.14)**:

Base measurement	55.00 mm
Fine measurement	00.95 mm
Total figure	55.95 mm

3.14 Vernier gauge reading of 55.95 mm

Plastigauge

● Plastigauge is a plastic material which can be compressed between two surfaces to measure the oil clearance between them. The width of the compressed Plastigauge is measured against a calibrated scale to determine the clearance.

● Common uses of Plastigauge are for measuring the clearance between crankshaft journal and main bearing inserts, between crankshaft journal and big-end bearing inserts, and between camshaft and bearing surfaces. The following example describes big-end oil clearance measurement.

● Handle the Plastigauge material carefully to prevent distortion. Using a sharp knife, cut a length which corresponds with the width of the bearing being measured and place it carefully across the journal so that it is parallel with the shaft **(see illustration 3.15)**. Carefully install both bearing shells and the connecting rod. Without rotating the rod on the journal tighten its bolts or nuts (as applicable) to the specified torque. The connecting rod and bearings are then disassembled and the crushed Plastigauge examined.

3.15 Plastigauge placed across shaft journal

● Using the scale provided in the Plastigauge kit, measure the width of the material to determine the oil clearance **(see illustration 3.16)**. Always remove all traces of Plastigauge after use using your fingernails.

Caution: Arriving at the correct clearance demands that the assembly is torqued correctly, according to the settings and sequence (where applicable) provided by the motorcycle manufacturer.

3.16 Measuring the width of the crushed Plastigauge

Dial gauge or DTI (Dial Test Indicator)

● A dial gauge can be used to accurately measure small amounts of movement. Typical uses are measuring shaft runout or shaft endfloat (sideplay) and setting piston position for ignition timing on two-strokes. A dial gauge set usually comes with a range of different probes and adapters and mounting equipment.

● The gauge needle must point to zero when at rest. Rotate the ring around its periphery to zero the gauge.

● Check that the gauge is capable of reading the extent of movement in the work. Most gauges have a small dial set in the face which records whole millimetres of movement as well as the fine scale around the face periphery which is calibrated in 0.01 mm divisions. Read off the small dial first to obtain the base measurement, then add the measurement from the fine scale to obtain the total reading.

In the example shown the gauge reads 1.48 mm **(see illustration 3.17)**:

Base measurement	1.00 mm
Fine measurement	0.48 mm
Total figure	1.48 mm

3.17 Dial gauge reading of 1.48 mm

● If measuring shaft runout, the shaft must be supported in vee-blocks and the gauge mounted on a stand perpendicular to the shaft. Rest the tip of the gauge against the centre of the shaft and rotate the shaft slowly whilst watching the gauge reading **(see illustration 3.18)**. Take several measurements along the length of the shaft and record the

3.18 Using a dial gauge to measure shaft runout

maximum gauge reading as the amount of runout in the shaft. **Note:** *The reading obtained will be total runout at that point - some manufacturers specify that the runout figure is halved to compare with their specified runout limit.*

● Endfloat (sideplay) measurement requires that the gauge is mounted securely to the surrounding component with its probe touching the end of the shaft. Using hand pressure, push and pull on the shaft noting the maximum endfloat recorded on the gauge **(see illustration 3.19)**.

3.19 Using a dial gauge to measure shaft endfloat

● A dial gauge with suitable adapters can be used to determine piston position BTDC on two-stroke engines for the purposes of ignition timing. The gauge, adapter and suitable length probe are installed in the place of the spark plug and the gauge zeroed at TDC. If the piston position is specified as 1.14 mm BTDC, rotate the engine back to 2.00 mm BTDC, then slowly forwards to 1.14 mm BTDC.

Cylinder compression gauges

● A compression gauge is used for measuring cylinder compression. Either the rubber-cone type or the threaded adapter type can be used. The latter is preferred to ensure a perfect seal against the cylinder head. A 0 to 300 psi (0 to 20 Bar) type gauge (for petrol/gasoline engines) will be suitable for motorcycles.

● The spark plug is removed and the gauge either held hard against the cylinder head (cone type) or the gauge adapter screwed into the cylinder head (threaded type) **(see illustration 3.20)**. Cylinder compression is measured with the engine turning over, but not running. The

3.20 Using a rubber-cone type cylinder compression gauge

gauge will hold the reading until manually released.

Oil pressure gauge

● An oil pressure gauge is used for measuring engine oil pressure. Most gauges come with a set of adapters to fit the thread of the take-off point **(see illustration 3.21)**. If the take-off point specified by the motorcycle manufacturer is an external oil pipe union, make sure that the specified replacement union is used to prevent oil starvation.

3.21 Oil pressure gauge and take-off point adapter (arrow)

● Oil pressure is measured with the engine running (at a specific rpm) and often the manufacturer will specify pressure limits for a cold and hot engine.

Straight-edge and surface plate

● If checking the gasket face of a component for warpage, place a steel rule or precision straight-edge across the gasket face and measure any gap between the straight-edge and component with feeler gauges **(see illustration 3.22)**. Check diagonally across the component and between mounting holes **(see illustration 3.23)**.

3.22 Use a straight-edge and feeler gauges to check for warpage

3.23 Check for warpage in these directions

● Checking individual components for warpage, such as clutch plain (metal) plates, requires a perfectly flat plate or piece or plate glass and feeler gauges.

4 Torque and leverage

What is torque?

● Torque describes the twisting force about a shaft. The amount of torque applied is determined by the distance from the centre of the shaft to the end of the lever and the amount of force being applied to the end of the lever; distance multiplied by force equals torque.

● The manufacturer applies a measured torque to a bolt or nut to ensure that it will not slacken in use and to hold two components securely together without movement in the joint. The actual torque setting depends on the thread size, bolt or nut material and the composition of the components being held.

● Too little torque may cause the fastener to loosen due to vibration, whereas too much torque will distort the joint faces of the component or cause the fastener to shear off. Always stick to the specified torque setting.

Using a torque wrench

● Check the calibration of the torque wrench and make sure it has a suitable range for the job. Torque wrenches are available in Nm (Newton-metres), kgf m (kilograms-force metre), lbf ft (pounds-feet), lbf in (inch-pounds). Do not confuse lbf ft with lbf in.

● Adjust the tool to the desired torque on the scale (see illustration 4.1). If your torque wrench is not calibrated in the units specified, carefully convert the figure (see Conversion Factors). A manufacturer sometimes gives a torque setting as a range (8 to 10 Nm) rather than a single figure - in this case set the tool midway between the two settings. The same torque may be expressed as 9 Nm ± 1 Nm. Some torque wrenches have a method of locking the setting so that it isn't inadvertently altered during use.

4.1 Set the torque wrench index mark to the setting required, in this case 12 Nm

● Install the bolts/nuts in their correct location and secure them lightly. Their threads must be clean and free of any old locking compound. Unless specified the threads and flange should be dry - oiled threads are necessary in certain circumstances and the manufacturer will take this into account in the specified torque figure. Similarly, the manufacturer may also specify the application of thread-locking compound.

● Tighten the fasteners in the specified sequence until the torque wrench clicks, indicating that the torque setting has been reached. Apply the torque again to double-check the setting. Where different thread diameter fasteners secure the component, as a rule tighten the larger diameter ones first.

● When the torque wrench has been finished with, release the lock (where applicable) and fully back off its setting to zero - do not leave the torque wrench tensioned. Also, do not use a torque wrench for slackening a fastener.

Angle-tightening

● Manufacturers often specify a figure in degrees for final tightening of a fastener. This usually follows tightening to a specific torque setting.

● A degree disc can be set and attached to the socket (see illustration 4.2) or a protractor can be used to mark the angle of movement on the bolt/nut head and the surrounding casting (see illustration 4.3).

4.2 Angle tightening can be accomplished with a torque-angle gauge . . .

4.3 . . . or by marking the angle on the surrounding component

Loosening sequences

● Where more than one bolt/nut secures a component, loosen each fastener evenly a little at a time. In this way, not all the stress of the joint is held by one fastener and the components are not likely to distort.

● If a tightening sequence is provided, work in the REVERSE of this, but if not, work from the outside in, in a criss-cross sequence (see illustration 4.4).

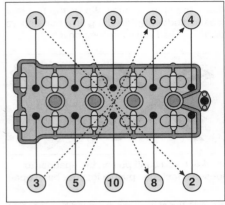

4.4 When slackening, work from the outside inwards

Tightening sequences

● If a component is held by more than one fastener it is important that the retaining bolts/nuts are tightened evenly to prevent uneven stress build-up and distortion of sealing faces. This is especially important on high-compression joints such as the cylinder head.

● A sequence is usually provided by the manufacturer, either in a diagram or actually marked in the casting. If not, always start in the centre and work outwards in a criss-cross pattern (see illustration 4.5). Start off by securing all bolts/nuts finger-tight, then set the torque wrench and tighten each fastener by a small amount in sequence until the final torque is reached. By following this practice,

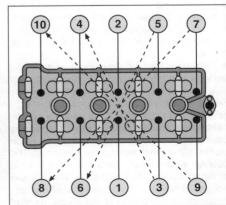

4.5 When tightening, work from the inside outwards

the joint will be held evenly and will not be distorted. Important joints, such as the cylinder head and big-end fasteners often have two- or three-stage torque settings.

Applying leverage

● Use tools at the correct angle. Position a socket wrench or spanner on the bolt/nut so that you pull it towards you when loosening. If this can't be done, push the spanner without curling your fingers around it **(see illustration 4.6)** - the spanner may slip or the fastener loosen suddenly, resulting in your fingers being crushed against a component.

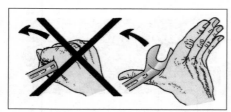

4.6 If you can't pull on the spanner to loosen a fastener, push with your hand open

● Additional leverage is gained by extending the length of the lever. The best way to do this is to use a breaker bar instead of the regular length tool, or to slip a length of tubing over the end of the spanner or socket wrench.
● If additional leverage will not work, the fastener head is either damaged or firmly corroded in place (see Fasteners).

5 Bearings

Bearing removal and installation

Drivers and sockets

● Before removing a bearing, always inspect the casing to see which way it must be driven out - some casings will have retaining plates or a cast step. Also check for any identifying markings on the bearing and if installed to a certain depth, measure this at this stage. Some roller bearings are sealed on one side - take note of the original fitted position.
● Bearings can be driven out of a casing using a bearing driver tool (with the correct size head) or a socket of the correct diameter. Select the driver head or socket so that it contacts the outer race of the bearing, not the balls/rollers or inner race. Always support the casing around the bearing housing with wood blocks, otherwise there is a risk of fracture. The bearing is driven out with a few blows on the driver or socket from a heavy mallet. Unless access is severely restricted (as with wheel bearings), a pin-punch is not recommended unless it is moved around the bearing to keep it square in its housing.

● The same equipment can be used to install bearings. Make sure the bearing housing is supported on wood blocks and line up the bearing in its housing. Fit the bearing as noted on removal - generally they are installed with their marked side facing outwards. Tap the bearing squarely into its housing using a driver or socket which bears only on the bearing's outer race - contact with the bearing balls/rollers or inner race will destroy it **(see illustrations 5.1 and 5.2)**.
● Check that the bearing inner race and balls/rollers rotate freely.

5.1 Using a bearing driver against the bearing's outer race

5.2 Using a large socket against the bearing's outer race

Pullers and slide-hammers

● Where a bearing is pressed on a shaft a puller will be required to extract it **(see illustration 5.3)**. Make sure that the puller clamp or legs fit securely behind the bearing and are unlikely to slip out. If pulling a bearing

5.3 This bearing puller clamps behind the bearing and pressure is applied to the shaft end to draw the bearing off

off a gear shaft for example, you may have to locate the puller behind a gear pinion if there is no access to the race and draw the gear pinion off the shaft as well **(see illustration 5.4)**.

Caution: Ensure that the puller's centre bolt locates securely against the end of the shaft and will not slip when pressure is applied. Also ensure that puller does not damage the shaft end.

5.4 Where no access is available to the rear of the bearing, it is sometimes possible to draw off the adjacent component

● Operate the puller so that its centre bolt exerts pressure on the shaft end and draws the bearing off the shaft.
● When installing the bearing on the shaft, tap only on the bearing's inner race - contact with the balls/rollers or outer race with destroy the bearing. Use a socket or length of tubing as a drift which fits over the shaft end **(see illustration 5.5)**.

5.5 When installing a bearing on a shaft use a piece of tubing which bears only on the bearing's inner race

● Where a bearing locates in a blind hole in a casing, it cannot be driven or pulled out as described above. A slide-hammer with knife-edged bearing puller attachment will be required. The puller attachment passes through the bearing and when tightened expands to fit firmly behind the bearing **(see illustration 5.6)**. By operating the slide-hammer part of the tool the bearing is jarred out of its housing **(see illustration 5.7)**.
● It is possible, if the bearing is of reasonable weight, for it to drop out of its housing if the casing is heated as described opposite.

5.6 Expand the bearing puller so that it locks behind the bearing . . .

5.7 . . . attach the slide hammer to the bearing puller

If this method is attempted, first prepare a work surface which will enable the casing to be tapped face down to help dislodge the bearing - a wood surface is ideal since it will not damage the casing's gasket surface. Wearing protective gloves, tap the heated casing several times against the work surface to dislodge the bearing under its own weight **(see illustration 5.8).**

5.8 Tapping a casing face down on wood blocks can often dislodge a bearing

● Bearings can be installed in blind holes using the driver or socket method described above.

Drawbolts

● Where a bearing or bush is set in the eye of a component, such as a suspension linkage arm or connecting rod small-end, removal by drift may damage the component. Furthermore, a rubber bushing in a shock absorber eye cannot successfully be driven out of position. If access is available to a engineering press, the task is straightforward. If not, a drawbolt can be fabricated to extract the bearing or bush.

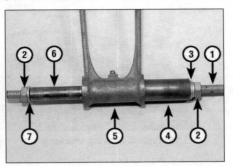

5.9 Drawbolt component parts assembled on a suspension arm

1 Bolt or length of threaded bar
2 Nuts
3 Washer (external diameter greater than tubing internal diameter)
4 Tubing (internal diameter sufficient to accommodate bearing)
5 Suspension arm with bearing
6 Tubing (external diameter slightly smaller than bearing)
7 Washer (external diameter slightly smaller than bearing)

5.10 Drawing the bearing out of the suspension arm

● To extract the bearing/bush you will need a long bolt with nut (or piece of threaded bar with two nuts), a piece of tubing which has an internal diameter larger than the bearing/bush, another piece of tubing which has an external diameter slightly smaller than the bearing/bush, and a selection of washers **(see illustrations 5.9 and 5.10)**. Note that the pieces of tubing must be of the same length, or longer, than the bearing/bush.
● The same kit (without the pieces of tubing) can be used to draw the new bearing/bush back into place **(see illustration 5.11)**.

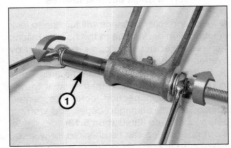

5.11 Installing a new bearing (1) in the suspension arm

Temperature change

● If the bearing's outer race is a tight fit in the casing, the aluminium casing can be heated to release its grip on the bearing. Aluminium will expand at a greater rate than the steel bearing outer race. There are several ways to do this, but avoid any localised extreme heat (such as a blow torch) - aluminium alloy has a low melting point.
● Approved methods of heating a casing are using a domestic oven (heated to 100°C) or immersing the casing in boiling water **(see illustration 5.12)**. Low temperature range localised heat sources such as a paint stripper heat gun or clothes iron can also be used **(see illustration 5.13)**. Alternatively, soak a rag in boiling water, wring it out and wrap it around the bearing housing.

> ⚠️ **Warning: All of these methods require care in use to prevent scalding and burns to the hands. Wear protective gloves when handling hot components.**

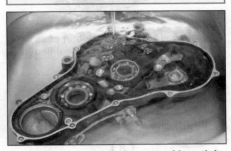

5.12 A casing can be immersed in a sink of boiling water to aid bearing removal

5.13 Using a localised heat source to aid bearing removal

● If heating the whole casing note that plastic components, such as the neutral switch, may suffer - remove them beforehand.
● After heating, remove the bearing as described above. You may find that the expansion is sufficient for the bearing to fall out of the casing under its own weight or with a light tap on the driver or socket.
● If necessary, the casing can be heated to aid bearing installation, and this is sometimes the recommended procedure if the motorcycle manufacturer has designed the housing and bearing fit with this intention.

● Installation of bearings can be eased by placing them in a freezer the night before installation. The steel bearing will contract slightly, allowing easy insertion in its housing. This is often useful when installing steering head outer races in the frame.

Bearing types and markings

● Plain shell bearings, ball bearings, needle roller bearings and tapered roller bearings will all be found on motorcycles (see illustrations 5.14 and 5.15). The ball and roller types are usually caged between an inner and outer race, but uncaged variations may be found.

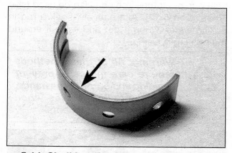

5.14 Shell bearings are either plain or grooved. They are usually identified by colour code (arrow)

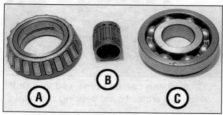

5.15 Tapered roller bearing (A), needle roller bearing (B) and ball journal bearing (C)

● Shell bearings (often called inserts) are usually found at the crankshaft main and connecting rod big-end where they are good at coping with high loads. They are made of a phosphor-bronze material and are impregnated with self-lubricating properties.

● Ball bearings and needle roller bearings consist of a steel inner and outer race with the balls or rollers between the races. They require constant lubrication by oil or grease and are good at coping with axial loads. Taper roller bearings consist of rollers set in a tapered cage set on the inner race; the outer race is separate. They are good at coping with axial loads and prevent movement along the shaft - a typical application is in the steering head.

● Bearing manufacturers produce bearings to ISO size standards and stamp one face of the bearing to indicate its internal and external diameter, load capacity and type (see illustration 5.16).

● Metal bushes are usually of phosphor-bronze material. Rubber bushes are used in suspension mounting eyes. Fibre bushes have also been used in suspension pivots.

5.16 Typical bearing marking

Bearing fault finding

● If a bearing outer race has spun in its housing, the housing material will be damaged. You can use a bearing locking compound to bond the outer race in place if damage is not too severe.

● Shell bearings will fail due to damage of their working surface, as a result of lack of lubrication, corrosion or abrasive particles in the oil (see illustration 5.17). Small particles of dirt in the oil may embed in the bearing material whereas larger particles will score the bearing and shaft journal. If a number of short journeys are made, insufficient heat will be generated to drive off condensation which has built up on the bearings.

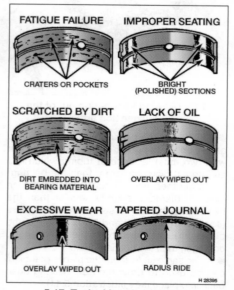

5.17 Typical bearing failures

● Ball and roller bearings will fail due to lack of lubrication or damage to the balls or rollers. Tapered-roller bearings can be damaged by overloading them. Unless the bearing is sealed on both sides, wash it in paraffin (kerosene) to remove all old grease then allow it to dry. Make a visual inspection looking to dented balls or rollers, damaged cages and worn or pitted races (see illustration 5.18).

● A ball bearing can be checked for wear by listening to it when spun. Apply a film of light oil to the bearing and hold it close to the ear - hold the outer race with one hand and spin the

5.18 Example of ball journal bearing with damaged balls and cages

5.19 Hold outer race and listen to inner race when spun

inner race with the other hand (see illustration 5.19). The bearing should be almost silent when spun; if it grates or rattles it is worn.

6 Oil seals

Oil seal removal and installation

● Oil seals should be renewed every time a component is dismantled. This is because the seal lips will become set to the sealing surface and will not necessarily reseal.

● Oil seals can be prised out of position using a large flat-bladed screwdriver (see illustration 6.1). In the case of crankcase seals, check first that the seal is not lipped on the inside, preventing its removal with the crankcases joined.

6.1 Prise out oil seals with a large flat-bladed screwdriver

● New seals are usually installed with their marked face (containing the seal reference code) outwards and the spring side towards the fluid being retained. In certain cases, such as a two-stroke engine crankshaft seal, a double lipped seal may be used due to there being fluid or gas on each side of the joint.

● Use a bearing driver or socket which bears only on the outer hard edge of the seal to install it in the casing - tapping on the inner edge will damage the sealing lip.

Oil seal types and markings

● Oil seals are usually of the single-lipped type. Double-lipped seals are found where a liquid or gas is on both sides of the joint.

● Oil seals can harden and lose their sealing ability if the motorcycle has been in storage for a long period - renewal is the only solution.

● Oil seal manufacturers also conform to the ISO markings for seal size - these are moulded into the outer face of the seal **(see illustration 6.2)**.

6.2 These oil seal markings indicate inside diameter, outside diameter and seal thickness

7 Gaskets and sealants

Types of gasket and sealant

● Gaskets are used to seal the mating surfaces between components and keep lubricants, fluids, vacuum or pressure contained within the assembly. Aluminium gaskets are sometimes found at the cylinder joints, but most gaskets are paper-based. If the mating surfaces of the components being joined are undamaged the gasket can be installed dry, although a dab of sealant or grease will be useful to hold it in place during assembly.

● RTV (Room Temperature Vulcanising) silicone rubber sealants cure when exposed to moisture in the atmosphere. These sealants are good at filling pits or irregular gasket faces, but will tend to be forced out of the joint under very high torque. They can be used to replace a paper gasket, but first make sure that the width of the paper gasket is not essential to the shimming of internal components. RTV sealants should not be used on components containing petrol (gasoline).

● Non-hardening, semi-hardening and hard setting liquid gasket compounds can be used with a gasket or between a metal-to-metal joint. Select the sealant to suit the application: universal non-hardening sealant can be used on virtually all joints; semi-hardening on joint faces which are rough or damaged; hard setting sealant on joints which require a permanent bond and are subjected to high temperature and pressure. **Note:** *Check first if the paper gasket has a bead of sealant*

impregnated in its surface before applying additional sealant.

● When choosing a sealant, make sure it is suitable for the application, particularly if being applied in a high-temperature area or in the vicinity of fuel. Certain manufacturers produce sealants in either clear, silver or black colours to match the finish of the engine. This has a particular application on motorcycles where much of the engine is exposed.

● Do not over-apply sealant. That which is squeezed out on the outside of the joint can be wiped off, whereas an excess of sealant on the inside can break off and clog oilways.

Breaking a sealed joint

● Age, heat, pressure and the use of hard setting sealant can cause two components to stick together so tightly that they are difficult to separate using finger pressure alone. Do not resort to using levers unless there is a pry point provided for this purpose **(see illustration 7.1)** or else the gasket surfaces will be damaged.

● Use a soft-faced hammer **(see illustration 7.2)** or a wood block and conventional hammer to strike the component near the mating surface. Avoid hammering against cast extremities since they may break off. If this method fails, try using a wood wedge between the two components.

Caution: If the joint will not separate, double-check that you have removed all the fasteners.

7.1 If a pry point is provided, apply gently pressure with a flat-bladed screwdriver

7.2 Tap around the joint with a soft-faced mallet if necessary - don't strike cooling fins

Removal of old gasket and sealant

● Paper gaskets will most likely come away complete, leaving only a few traces stuck

Most components have one or two hollow locating dowels between the two gasket faces. If a dowel cannot be removed, do not resort to gripping it with pliers - it will almost certainly be distorted. Install a close-fitting socket or Phillips screwdriver into the dowel and then grip the outer edge of the dowel to free it.

on the sealing faces of the components. It is imperative that all traces are removed to ensure correct sealing of the new gasket.

● Very carefully scrape all traces of gasket away making sure that the sealing surfaces are not gouged or scored by the scraper **(see illustrations 7.3, 7.4 and 7.5)**. Stubborn deposits can be removed by spraying with an aerosol gasket remover. Final preparation of

7.3 Paper gaskets can be scraped off with a gasket scraper tool . . .

7.4 . . . a knife blade . . .

7.5 . . . or a household scraper

7.6 Fine abrasive paper is wrapped around a flat file to clean up the gasket face

7.7 A kitchen scourer can be used on stubborn deposits

the gasket surface can be made with very fine abrasive paper or a plastic kitchen scourer **(see illustrations 7.6 and 7.7).**

● Old sealant can be scraped or peeled off components, depending on the type originally used. Note that gasket removal compounds are available to avoid scraping the components clean; make sure the gasket remover suits the type of sealant used.

8 Chains

Breaking and joining final drive chains

● Drive chains for all but small bikes are continuous and do not have a clip-type connecting link. The chain must be broken using a chain breaker tool and the new chain securely riveted together using a new soft rivet-type link. Never use a clip-type connecting link instead of a rivet-type link, except in an emergency. Various chain breaking and riveting tools are available, either as separate tools or combined as illustrated in the accompanying photographs - read the instructions supplied with the tool carefully.

> ⚠ **Warning: The need to rivet the new link pins correctly cannot be overstressed - loss of control of the motorcycle is very likely to result if the chain breaks in use.**

● Rotate the chain and look for the soft link. The soft link pins look like they have been

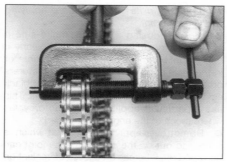

8.1 Tighten the chain breaker to push the pin out of the link . . .

8.2 . . . withdraw the pin, remove the tool . . .

8.3 . . . and separate the chain link

deeply centre-punched instead of peened over like all the other pins **(see illustration 8.9)** and its sideplate may be a different colour. Position the soft link midway between the sprockets and assemble the chain breaker tool over one of the soft link pins **(see illustration 8.1).** Operate the tool to push the pin out through the chain **(see illustration 8.2).** On an O-ring chain, remove the O-rings **(see illustration 8.3).** Carry out the same procedure on the other soft link pin.

> **Caution: Certain soft link pins (particularly on the larger chains) may require their ends to be filed or ground off before they can be pressed out using the tool.**

● Check that you have the correct size and strength (standard or heavy duty) new soft link - do not reuse the old link. Look for the size marking on the chain sideplates **(see illustration 8.10).**

● Position the chain ends so that they are engaged over the rear sprocket. On an O-ring

8.4 Insert the new soft link, with O-rings, through the chain ends . . .

8.5 . . . install the O-rings over the pin ends . . .

8.6 . . . followed by the sideplate

chain, install a new O-ring over each pin of the link and insert the link through the two chain ends **(see illustration 8.4).** Install a new O-ring over the end of each pin, followed by the sideplate (with the chain manufacturer's marking facing outwards) **(see illustrations 8.5 and 8.6).** On an unsealed chain, insert the link through the two chain ends, then install the sideplate with the chain manufacturer's marking facing outwards.

● Note that it may not be possible to install the sideplate using finger pressure alone. If using a joining tool, assemble it so that the plates of the tool clamp the link and press the sideplate over the pins **(see illustration 8.7).** Otherwise, use two small sockets placed over

8.7 Push the sideplate into position using a clamp

8.8 Assemble the chain riveting tool over one pin at a time and tighten it fully

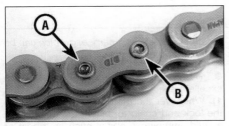

8.9 Pin end correctly riveted (A), pin end unriveted (B)

the rivet ends and two pieces of the wood between a G-clamp. Operate the clamp to press the sideplate over the pins.

● Assemble the joining tool over one pin (following the maker's instructions) and tighten the tool down to spread the pin end securely **(see illustrations 8.8 and 8.9)**. Do the same on the other pin.

 Warning: Check that the pin ends are secure and that there is no danger of the sideplate coming loose. If the pin ends are cracked the soft link must be renewed.

Final drive chain sizing

● Chains are sized using a three digit number, followed by a suffix to denote the chain type **(see illustration 8.10)**. Chain type is either standard or heavy duty (thicker sideplates), and also unsealed or O-ring/X-ring type.

● The first digit of the number relates to the pitch of the chain, ie the distance from the centre of one pin to the centre of the next pin **(see illustration 8.11)**. Pitch is expressed in eighths of an inch, as follows:

8.10 Typical chain size and type marking

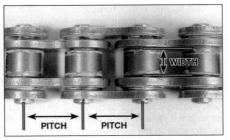

8.11 Chain dimensions

| Sizes commencing with a 4 (eg 428) have a pitch of 1/2 inch (12.7 mm) |
| Sizes commencing with a 5 (eg 520) have a pitch of 5/8 inch (15.9 mm) |
| Sizes commencing with a 6 (eg 630) have a pitch of 3/4 inch (19.1 mm) |

● The second and third digits of the chain size relate to the width of the rollers, again in imperial units, eg the 525 shown has 5/16 inch (7.94 mm) rollers **(see illustration 8.11)**.

9 Hoses

Clamping to prevent flow

● Small-bore flexible hoses can be clamped to prevent fluid flow whilst a component is worked on. Whichever method is used, ensure that the hose material is not permanently distorted or damaged by the clamp.

a) A brake hose clamp available from auto accessory shops **(see illustration 9.1)**.
b) A wingnut type hose clamp **(see illustration 9.2)**.

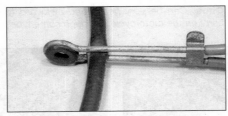

9.1 Hoses can be clamped with an automotive brake hose clamp . . .

9.2 . . . a wingnut type hose clamp . . .

c) Two sockets placed each side of the hose and held with straight-jawed self-locking grips **(see illustration 9.3)**.
d) Thick card each side of the hose held between straight-jawed self-locking grips **(see illustration 9.4)**.

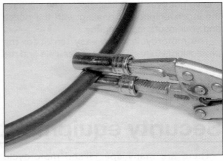

9.3 . . . two sockets and a pair of self-locking grips . . .

9.4 . . . or thick card and self-locking grips

Freeing and fitting hoses

● Always make sure the hose clamp is moved well clear of the hose end. Grip the hose with your hand and rotate it whilst pulling it off the union. If the hose has hardened due to age and will not move, slit it with a sharp knife and peel its ends off the union **(see illustration 9.5)**.

● Resist the temptation to use grease or soap on the unions to aid installation; although it helps the hose slip over the union it will equally aid the escape of fluid from the joint. It is preferable to soften the hose ends in hot water and wet the inside surface of the hose with water or a fluid which will evaporate.

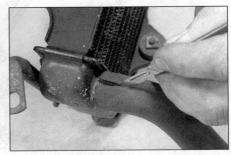

9.5 Cutting a coolant hose free with a sharp knife

Introduction

In less time than it takes to read this introduction, a thief could steal your motorcycle. Returning only to find your bike has gone is one of the worst feelings in the world. Even if the motorcycle is insured against theft, once you've got over the initial shock, you will have the inconvenience of dealing with the police and your insurance company.

The motorcycle is an easy target for the professional thief and the joyrider alike and the official figures on motorcycle theft make for depressing reading; on average a motor-cycle is stolen every 16 minutes in the UK!

Motorcycle thefts fall into two categories, those stolen 'to order' and those taken by opportunists. The thief stealing to order will be on the look out for a specific make and model and will go to extraordinary lengths to obtain that motorcycle. The opportunist thief on the other hand will look for easy targets which can be stolen with the minimum of effort and risk.

Whilst it is never going to be possible to make your machine 100% secure, it is estimated that around half of all stolen motorcycles are taken by opportunist thieves. Remember that the opportunist thief is always on the look out for the easy option: if there are two similar motorcycles parked side-by-side, they will target the one with the lowest level of security. By taking a few precautions, you can reduce the chances of your motorcycle being stolen.

Security equipment

There are many specialised motorcycle security devices available and the following text summarises their applications and their good and bad points.

Once you have decided on the type of security equipment which best suits your needs, we recommended that you read one of the many equipment tests regularly carried out by the motorcycle press. These tests compare the products from all the major manufacturers and give impartial ratings on their effectiveness, value-for-money and ease of use.

No one item of security equipment can provide complete protection. It is highly recommended that two or more of the items described below are combined to increase the security of your motorcycle (a lock and chain plus an alarm system is just about ideal). The more security measures fitted to the bike, the less likely it is to be stolen.

Lock and chain

Pros: *Very flexible to use; can be used to secure the motorcycle to almost any immovable object. On some locks and chains, the lock can be used on its own as a disc lock (see below).*

Cons: *Can be very heavy and awkward to carry on the motorcycle, although some types will be supplied with a carry bag which can be strapped to the pillion seat.*

● Heavy-duty chains and locks are an excellent security measure **(see illustration 1)**. Whenever the motorcycle is parked, use the lock and chain to secure the machine to a solid, immovable object such as a post or railings. This will prevent the machine from being ridden away or being lifted into the back of a van.

● When fitting the chain, always ensure the chain is routed around the motorcycle frame or swingarm **(see illustrations 2 and 3)**. Never merely pass the chain around one of the wheel rims; a thief may unbolt the wheel and lift the rest of the machine into a van, leaving you with just the wheel! Try to avoid having excess chain free, thus making it difficult to use cutting tools, and keep the chain and lock off the ground to prevent thieves attacking it with a cold chisel. Position the lock so that its lock barrel is facing downwards; this will make it harder for the thief to attack the lock mechanism.

Ensure the lock and chain you buy is of good quality and long enough to shackle your bike to a solid object

Pass the chain through the bike's frame, rather than just through a wheel . . .

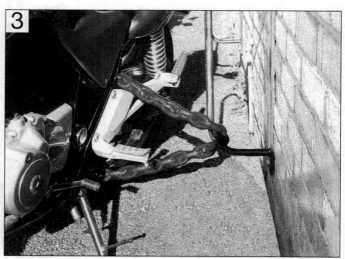

. . . and loop it around a solid object

U-locks

Pros: *Highly effective deterrent which can be used to secure the bike to a post or railings. Most U-locks come with a carrier which allows the lock to be easily carried on the bike.*

Cons: *Not as flexible to use as a lock and chain.*

● These are solid locks which are similar in use to a lock and chain. U-locks are lighter than a lock and chain but not so flexible to use. The length and shape of the lock shackle limit the objects to which the bike can be secured **(see illustration 4)**.

Disc locks

Pros: *Small, light and very easy to carry; most can be stored underneath the seat.*

Cons: *Does not prevent the motorcycle being lifted into a van. Can be very embarrassing if*

4

U-locks can be used to secure the bike to a solid object – ensure you purchase one which is long enough

you forget to remove the lock before attempting to ride off!

● Disc locks are designed to be attached to the front brake disc. The lock passes through one of the holes in the disc and prevents the wheel rotating by jamming against the fork/brake caliper **(see illustration 5)**. Some are equipped with an alarm siren which sounds if the disc lock is moved; this not only acts as a theft deterrent but also as a handy reminder if you try to move the bike with the lock still fitted.

● Combining the disc lock with a length of cable which can be looped around a post or railings provides an additional measure of security **(see illustration 6)**.

Alarms and immobilisers

Pros: *Once installed it is completely hassle-free to use. If the system is 'Thatcham' or 'Sold Secure-approved', insurance companies may give you a discount.*

Cons: *Can be expensive to buy and complex to install. No system will prevent the motorcycle from being lifted into a van and taken away.*

● Electronic alarms and immobilisers are available to suit a variety of budgets. There are three different types of system available: pure alarms, pure immobilisers, and the more expensive systems which are combined alarm/immobilisers **(see illustration 7)**.
● An alarm system is designed to emit an audible warning if the motorcycle is being tampered with.
● An immobiliser prevents the motorcycle being started and ridden away by disabling its electrical systems.
● When purchasing an alarm/immobiliser system, check the cost of installing the system unless you are able to do it yourself. If the motorcycle is not used regularly, another consideration is the current drain of the system. All alarm/immobiliser systems are powered by the motorcycle's battery; purchasing a system with a very low current drain could prevent the battery losing its charge whilst the motorcycle is not being used.

5

A typical disc lock attached through one of the holes in the disc

6

A disc lock combined with a security cable provides additional protection

7

A typical alarm/immobiliser system

Indelible markings can be applied to most areas of the bike – always apply the manufacturer's sticker to warn off thieves

Chemically-etched code numbers can be applied to main body panels . . .

. . . again, always ensure that the kit manufacturer's sticker is applied in a prominent position

Security marking kits

Pros: *Very cheap and effective deterrent. Many insurance companies will give you a discount on your insurance premium if a recognised security marking kit is used on your motorcycle.*

Cons: *Does not prevent the motorcycle being stolen by joyriders.*

● There are many different types of security marking kits available. The idea is to mark as many parts of the motorcycle as possible with a unique security number **(see illustrations 8, 9 and 10)**. A form will be included with the kit to register your personal details and those of the motorcycle with the kit manufacturer. This register is made available to the police to help them trace the rightful owner of any motorcycle or components which they recover should all other forms of identification have been removed. Always apply the warning stickers provided with the kit to deter thieves.

Ground anchors, wheel clamps and security posts

Pros: *An excellent form of security which will deter all but the most determined of thieves.*

Cons: *Awkward to install and can be expensive.*

● Whilst the motorcycle is at home, it is a good idea to attach it securely to the floor or a solid wall, even if it is kept in a securely locked garage. Various types of ground anchors, security posts and wheel clamps are available for this purpose **(see illustration 11)**. These security devices are either bolted to a solid concrete or brick structure or can be cemented into the ground.

Permanent ground anchors provide an excellent level of security when the bike is at home

Security at home

A high percentage of motorcycle thefts are from the owner's home. Here are some things to consider whenever your motorcycle is at home:

● Where possible, always keep the motorcycle in a securely locked garage. Never rely solely on the standard lock on the garage door, these are usual hopelessly inadequate. Fit an additional locking mechanism to the door and consider having the garage alarmed. A security light, activated by a movement sensor, is also a good investment.

● Always secure the motorcycle to the ground or a wall, even if it is inside a securely locked garage.

● Do not regularly leave the motorcycle outside your home, try to keep it out of sight wherever possible. If a garage is not available, fit a motorcycle cover over the bike to disguise its true identity.

● It is not uncommon for thieves to follow a motorcyclist home to find out where the bike is kept. They will then return at a later date. Be aware of this whenever you are returning home on your motorcycle. If you suspect you are being followed, do not return home, instead ride to a garage or shop and stop as a precaution.

● When selling a motorcycle, do not provide your home address or the location where the bike is normally kept. Arrange to meet the buyer at a location away from your home. Thieves have been known to pose as potential buyers to find out where motorcycles are kept and then return later to steal them.

Security away from the home

As well as fitting security equipment to your motorcycle here are a few general rules to follow whenever you park your motorcycle.
● Park in a busy, public place.
● Use car parks which incorporate security features, such as CCTV.

● At night, park in a well-lit area, preferably directly underneath a street light.
● Engage the steering lock.
● Secure the motorcycle to a solid, immovable object such as a post or railings with an additional lock. If this is not possible, secure the bike to a friend's motorcycle. Some public parking places provide security loops for motorcycles.

● Never leave your helmet or luggage attached to the motorcycle. Take them with you at all times.

Lubricants and fluids

A wide range of lubricants, fluids and cleaning agents is available for motor-cycles. This is a guide as to what is available, its applications and properties.

Four-stroke engine oil

● Engine oil is without doubt the most important component of any four-stroke engine. Modern motorcycle engines place a lot of demands on their oil and choosing the right type is essential. Using an unsuitable oil will lead to an increased rate of engine wear and could result in serious engine damage. Before purchasing oil, always check the recommended oil specification given by the manufacturer. The manufacturer will state a recommended 'type or classification' and also a specific 'viscosity' range for engine oil.

● The oil 'type or classification' is identified by its API (American Petroleum Institute) rating. The API rating will be in the form of two letters, e.g. SG. The S identifies the oil as being suitable for use in a petrol (gasoline) engine (S stands for spark ignition) and the second letter, ranging from A to J, identifies the oil's performance rating. The later this letter, the higher the specification of the oil; for example API SG oil exceeds the requirements of API SF oil. **Note:** *On some oils there may also be a second rating consisting of another two letters, the first letter being C, e.g. API SF/CD. This rating indicates the oil is also suitable for use in a diesel engines (the C stands for compression ignition) and is thus of no relevance for motorcycle use.*

● The 'viscosity' of the oil is identified by its SAE (Society of Automotive Engineers) rating. All modern engines require multigrade oils and the SAE rating will consist of two numbers, the first followed by a W, e.g. 10W/40. The first number indicates the viscosity rating of the oil at low temperatures (W stands for winter – tested at –20°C) and the second number represents the viscosity of the oil at high temperatures (tested at 100°C). The lower the number, the thinner the oil. For example an oil with an SAE 10W/40 rating will give better cold starting and running than an SAE 15W/40 oil.

● As well as ensuring the 'type' and 'viscosity' of the oil match the recommendations, another consideration to make when buying engine oil is whether to purchase a standard mineral-based oil, a semi-synthetic oil (also known as a synthetic blend or synthetic-based oil) or a fully-synthetic oil. Although all oils will have a similar rating and viscosity, their cost will vary considerably; mineral-based oils are the cheapest, the fully-synthetic oils the most expensive with the semi-synthetic oils falling somewhere in-between. This decision is very much up to the owner, but it should be noted that modern synthetic oils have far better lubricating and cleaning qualities than traditional mineral-based oils and tend to retain these properties for far longer. Bearing in mind the operating conditions inside a modern, high-revving motorcycle engine it is highly recommended that a fully synthetic oil is used. The extra expense at each service could save you money in the long term by preventing premature engine wear.

● As a final note always ensure that the oil is specifically designed for use in motorcycle engines. Engine oils designed primarily for use in car engines sometimes contain additives or friction modifiers which could cause clutch slip on a motorcycle fitted with a wet-clutch.

Two-stroke engine oil

● Modern two-stroke engines, with their high power outputs, place high demands on their oil. If engine seizure is to be avoided it is essential that a high-quality oil is used. Two-stroke oils differ hugely from four-stroke oils. The oil lubricates only the crankshaft and piston(s) (the transmission has its own lubricating oil) and is used on a total-loss basis where it is burnt completely during the combustion process.

● The Japanese have recently introduced a classification system for two-stroke oils, the JASO rating. This rating is in the form of two letters, either FA, FB or FC – FA is the lowest classification and FC the highest. Ensure the oil being used meets or exceeds the recommended rating specified by the manufacturer.

● As well as ensuring the oil rating matches the recommendation, another consideration to make when buying engine oil is whether to purchase a standard mineral-based oil, a semi-synthetic oil (also known as a synthetic blend or synthetic-based oil) or a fully-synthetic oil. The cost of each type of oil varies considerably; mineral-based oils are the cheapest, the fully-synthetic oils the most expensive with the semi-synthetic oils falling somewhere in-between. This decision is very much up to the owner, but it should be noted that modern synthetic oils have far better lubricating properties and burn cleaner than traditional mineral-based oils. It is therefore recommended that a fully synthetic oil is used. The extra expense could save you money in the long term by preventing premature engine wear, engine performance will be improved, carbon deposits and exhaust smoke will be reduced.

● Always ensure that the oil is specifically designed for use in an injector system. Many high quality two-stroke oils are designed for competition use and need to be pre-mixed with fuel. These oils are of a much higher viscosity and are not designed to flow through the injector pumps used on road-going two-stroke motorcycles.

Transmission (gear) oil

● On a two-stroke engine, the transmission and clutch are lubricated by their own separate oil bath which must be changed in accordance with the Maintenance Schedule.
● Although the engine and transmission units of most four-strokes use a common lubrication supply, there are some exceptions where the engine and gearbox have separate oil reservoirs and a dry clutch is used.
● Motorcycle manufacturers will either recommend a monograde transmission oil or a four-stroke multigrade engine oil to lubricate the transmission.
● Transmission oils, or gear oils as they are often called, are designed specifically for use in transmission systems. The viscosity of these oils is represented by an SAE number, but the scale of measurement applied is different to that used to grade engine oils. As a rough guide a SAE90 gear oil will be of the same viscosity as an SAE50 engine oil.

Shaft drive oil

● On models equipped with shaft final drive, the shaft drive gears are will have their own oil supply. The manufacturer will state a recommended 'type or classification' and also a specific 'viscosity' range in the same manner as for four-stroke engine oil.
● Gear oil classification is given by the number which follows the API GL (GL standing for gear lubricant) rating, the higher the number, the higher the specification of the oil, e.g. API GL5 oil is a higher specification than API GL4 oil. Ensure the oil meets or

exceeds the classification specified and is of the correct viscosity. The viscosity of gear oils is also represented by an SAE number but the scale of measurement used is different to that used to grade engine oils. As a rough guide an SAE90 gear oil will be of the same viscosity as an SAE50 engine oil.
● If the use of an EP (Extreme Pressure) gear oil is specified, ensure the oil purchased is suitable.

Fork oil and suspension fluid

● Conventional telescopic front forks are hydraulic and require fork oil to work. To ensure the forks function correctly, the fork oil must be changed in accordance with the Maintenance Schedule.
● Fork oil is available in a variety of viscosities, identified by their SAE rating; fork oil ratings vary from light (SAE 5) to heavy (SAE 30). When purchasing fork oil, ensure the viscosity rating matches that specified by the manufacturer.
● Some lubricant manufacturers also produce a range of high-quality suspension fluids which are very similar to fork oil but are designed mainly for competition use. These fluids may have a different viscosity rating system which is not to be confused with the SAE rating of normal fork oil. Refer to the manufacturer's instructions if in any doubt.

Brake and clutch fluid

● All disc brake systems and some clutch systems are hydraulically operated. To ensure correct operation, the hydraulic fluid must be changed in accordance with the Maintenance Schedule.
● Brake and clutch fluid is classified by its DOT rating with most motorcycle manufacturers specifying DOT 3 or 4 fluid. Both fluid types are glycol-based and can be mixed together without adverse effect; DOT 4 fluid exceeds the requirements of DOT 3

fluid. Although it is safe to use DOT 4 fluid in a system designed for use with DOT 3 fluid, never use DOT 3 fluid in a system which specifies the use of DOT 4 as this will adversely affect the system's performance. The type required for the system will be marked on the fluid reservoir cap.
● Some manufacturers also produce a DOT 5 hydraulic fluid. DOT 5 hydraulic fluid is silicone-based and is not compatible with the glycol-based DOT 3 and 4 fluids. Never mix DOT 5 fluid with DOT 3 or 4 fluid as this will seriously affect the performance of the hydraulic system.

Coolant/antifreeze

● When purchasing coolant/antifreeze, always ensure it is suitable for use in an aluminium engine and contains corrosion inhibitors to prevent possible blockages of the internal coolant passages of the system. As a general rule, most coolants are designed to be used neat and should not be diluted whereas antifreeze can be mixed with distilled water to provide a coolant solution of the required strength. Refer to the manufacturer's instructions on the bottle.
● Ensure the coolant is changed in accordance with the Maintenance Schedule.

Chain lube

● Chain lube is an aerosol-type spray lubricant specifically designed for use on motorcycle final drive chains. Chain lube has two functions, to minimise friction between the final drive chain and sprockets and to prevent corrosion of the chain. Regular use of a good-quality chain lube will extend the life of the drive chain and sprockets and thus maximise the power being transmitted from the transmission to the rear wheel.
● When using chain lube, always allow some time for the solvents in the lube to evaporate before riding the motorcycle. This will minimise the amount of lube which will

'fling' off from the chain when the motorcycle is used. If the motorcycle is equipped with an 'O-ring' chain, ensure the chain lube is labelled as being suitable for use on 'O-ring' chains.

Degreasers and solvents

● There are many different types of solvents and degreasers available to remove the grime and grease which accumulate around the motorcycle during normal use. Degreasers and solvents are usually available as an aerosol-type spray or as a liquid which you apply with a brush. Always closely follow the manufacturer's instructions and wear eye protection during use. Be aware that many solvents are flammable and may give off noxious fumes; take adequate precautions when using them (see Safety First!).
● For general cleaning, use one of the many solvents or degreasers available from most motorcycle accessory shops. These solvents are usually applied then left for a certain time before being washed off with water.

Brake cleaner is a solvent specifically designed to remove all traces of oil, grease and dust from braking system components. Brake cleaner is designed to evaporate quickly and leaves behind no residue.

Carburettor cleaner is an aerosol-type solvent specifically designed to clear carburettor blockages and break down the hard deposits and gum often found inside carburettors during overhaul.

Contact cleaner is an aerosol-type solvent designed for cleaning electrical components. The cleaner will remove all traces of oil and dirt from components such as switch contacts or fouled spark plugs and then dry, leaving behind no residue.

Gasket remover is an aerosol-type solvent designed for removing stubborn gaskets from engine components during overhaul. Gasket remover will minimise the amount of scraping required to remove the gasket and therefore reduce the risk of damage to the mating surface.

Spray lubricants

● Aerosol-based spray lubricants are widely available and are excellent for lubricating lever pivots and exposed cables and switches. Try to use a lubricant which is of the dry-film type as the fluid evaporates, leaving behind a dry-film of lubricant. Lubricants which leave behind an oily residue will attract dust and dirt which will increase the rate of wear of the cable/lever.

● Most lubricants also act as a moisture dispersant and a penetrating fluid. This means they can also be used to 'dry out' electrical components such as wiring connectors or switches as well as helping to free seized fasteners.

Greases

● Grease is used to lubricate many of the pivot-points. A good-quality multi-purpose grease is suitable for most applications but some manufacturers will specify the use of specialist greases for use on components such as swingarm and suspension linkage bushes. These specialist greases can be purchased from most motorcycle (or car) accessory shops; commonly specified types include molybdenum disulphide grease, lithium-based grease, graphite-based grease, silicone-based grease and high-temperature copper-based grease.

Gasket sealing compounds

● Gasket sealing compounds can be used in conjunction with gaskets, to improve their sealing capabilities, or on their own to seal metal-to-metal joints. Depending on their type, sealing compounds either set hard or stay relatively soft and pliable.

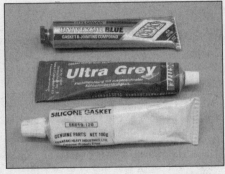

● When purchasing a gasket sealing compound, ensure that it is designed specifically for use on an internal combustion engine. General multi-purpose sealants available from DIY stores may appear visibly similar but they are not designed to withstand the extreme heat or contact with fuel and oil encountered when used on an engine (see 'Tools and Workshop Tips' for further information).

Thread locking compound

● Thread locking compounds are used to secure certain threaded fasteners in position to prevent them from loosening due to vibration. Thread locking compounds can be purchased from most motorcycle (and car) accessory shops. Ensure the threads of the both components are completely clean and dry before sparingly applying the locking compound (see 'Tools and Workshop Tips' for further information).

Fuel additives

● Fuel additives which protect and clean the fuel system components are widely available. These additives are designed to remove all traces of deposits that build up on the carburettors/injectors and prevent wear, helping the fuel system to operate more efficiently. If a fuel additive is being used, check that it is suitable for use with your motorcycle, especially if your motorcycle is equipped with a catalytic converter.

● Octane boosters are also available. These additives are designed to improve the performance of highly-tuned engines being run on normal pump-fuel and are of no real use on standard motorcycles.

About the MOT Test

In the UK, all vehicles more than three years old are subject to an annual test to ensure that they meet minimum safety requirements. A current test certificate must be issued before a machine can be used on public roads, and is required before a road fund licence can be issued. Riding without a current test certificate will also invalidate your insurance.

For most owners, the MOT test is an annual cause for anxiety, and this is largely due to owners not being sure what needs to be checked prior to submitting the motorcycle for testing. The simple answer is that a fully roadworthy motorcycle will have no difficulty in passing the test.

This is a guide to getting your motorcycle through the MOT test. Obviously it will not be possible to examine the motorcycle to the same standard as the professional MOT tester, particularly in view of the equipment required for some of the checks. However, working through the following procedures will enable you to identify any problem areas before submitting the motorcycle for the test.

It has only been possible to summarise the test requirements here, based on the regulations in force at the time of printing. Test standards are becoming increasingly stringent, although there are some exemptions for older vehicles. More information about the test can be obtained from the MOT Inspection Manual for Motor Bicycle and Side Car Testing at www.gov.uk

Many of the checks require that one of the wheels is raised off the ground. If the motorcycle doesn't have a centre stand, note that an auxiliary stand will be required. Additionally, the help of an assistant may prove useful.

Certain exceptions apply to machines under 50 cc, machines without a lighting system, and Classic bikes - if in doubt about any of the requirements listed below seek confirmation from an MOT tester prior to submitting the motorcycle for the test.

Check that the frame number is clearly visible.

Electrical System

Lights, turn signals, horn and reflector

● With the ignition on, check the operation of the following electrical components. **Note:** *The electrical components on certain small-capacity machines are powered by the generator, requiring that the engine is run for this check.*

a) *Headlight and tail light. Check that both illuminate in the low and high beam switch positions.*

b) *Position lights. Check that the front position (or sidelight) and tail light illuminate in this switch position.*

c) *Turn signals. Check that all flash at the correct rate, and that the warning light(s) function correctly. Check that the turn signal switch works correctly.*

d) *Hazard warning system (where fitted). Check that all four turn signals flash in this switch position.*

e) *Brake stop light. Check that the light comes on when the front and rear brakes are independently applied. Models first used on or after 1st April 1986 must have a brake light switch on each brake.*

f) *Horn. Check that the sound is continuous and of reasonable volume.*

● Check that there is a red reflector on the rear of the machine, either mounted separately or as part of the tail light lens.

● Check the condition of the headlight, tail light and turn signal lenses.

Headlight beam height

● The MOT tester will perform a headlight beam height check using specialised beam setting equipment **(see illustration 1)**. This equipment will not be available to the home mechanic, but if you suspect that the headlight is incorrectly set or may have been maladjusted in the past, you can perform a rough test as follows.

● Position the bike in a straight line facing a brick wall. The bike must be off its stand, upright and with a rider seated. Measure the height from the ground to the centre of the headlight and mark a horizontal line on the wall at this height. Position the motorcycle 3.8 metres from the wall and draw a vertical

Headlight beam height checking equipment

line up the wall central to the centreline of the motorcycle. Switch to dipped beam and check that the beam pattern falls slightly lower than the horizontal line and to the left of the vertical line **(see illustration 2)**.

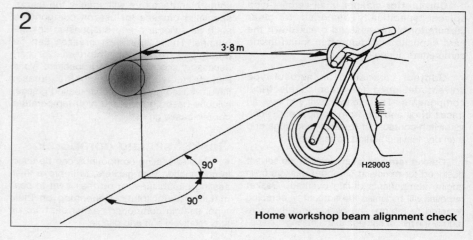

3·8 m

90°

90°

H29003

Home workshop beam alignment check

Exhaust System and Final Drive

Exhaust

● Check that the exhaust mountings are secure and that the system does not foul any of the rear suspension components.
● Start the motorcycle. When the revs are increased, check that the exhaust is neither holed nor leaking from any of its joints. On a linked system, check that the collector box is not leaking due to corrosion.

● Note that the exhaust decibel level ("loudness" of the exhaust) is assessed at the discretion of the tester. If the motorcycle was first used on or after 1st January 1985 the silencer must carry the BSAU 193 stamp, or a marking relating to its make and model, or be of OE (original equipment) manufacture. If the silencer is marked NOT FOR ROAD USE, RACING USE ONLY or similar, it will fail the MOT.

Final drive

● On chain or belt drive machines, check that the chain/belt is in good condition and does not have excessive slack. Also check that the sprocket is securely mounted on the rear wheel hub. Check that the chain/belt guard is in place.
● On shaft drive bikes, check for oil leaking from the drive unit and fouling the rear tyre.

Steering and Suspension

Steering

● With the front wheel raised off the ground, rotate the steering from lock to lock. The handlebar or switches must not contact the fuel tank or be close enough to trap the rider's hand. Problems can be caused by damaged lock stops on the lower yoke and frame, or by the fitting of non-standard handlebars.
● When performing the lock to lock check, also ensure that the steering moves freely without drag or notchiness. Steering movement can be impaired by poorly routed cables, or by overtight head bearings or worn bvearings. The tester will perform a check of the steering head bearing lower race by mounting the front wheel on a surface plate, then performing a lock to

lock check with the weight of the machine on the lower bearing (see illustration 3).
● Grasp the fork sliders (lower legs) and attempt to push and pull on the forks

Front wheel mounted on a surface plate for steering head bearing lower race check

(see illustration 4). Any play in the steering head bearings will be felt. Note that in extreme cases, wear of the front fork bushes can be misinterpreted for head bearing play.
● Check that the handlebars are securely mounted.
● Check that the handlebar grip rubbers are secure. They should by bonded to the bar left end and to the throttle cable pulley on the right end.

Front suspension

● With the motorcycle off the stand, hold the front brake on and pump the front forks up and down (see illustration 5). Check that they are adequately damped.

Checking the steering head bearings for freeplay

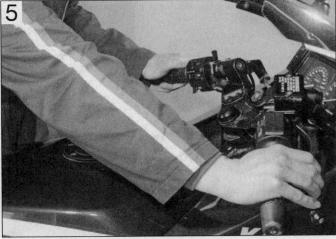

Hold the front brake on and pump the front forks up and down to check operation

Inspect the area around the fork dust seal for oil leakage (arrow)

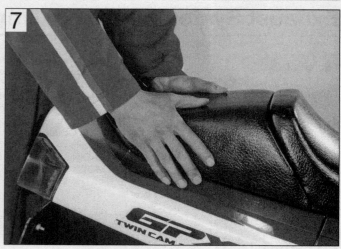

Bounce the rear of the motorcycle to check rear suspension operation

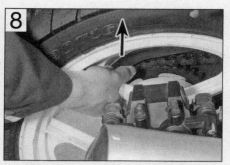

Checking for rear suspension linkage play

● Inspect the area above and around the front fork oil seals **(see illustration 6)**. There should be no sign of oil on the fork tube (stanchion) nor leaking down the slider (lower leg). On models so equipped, check that there is no oil leaking from the anti-dive units.

● On models with swingarm front suspension, check that there is no freeplay in the linkage when moved from side to side.

Rear suspension

● With the motorcycle off the stand and an assistant supporting the motorcycle by its handlebars, bounce the rear suspension **(see illustration 7)**. Check that the suspension components do not foul on any of the cycle parts and check that the shock absorber(s) provide adequate damping.

● Visually inspect the shock absorber(s) and check that there is no sign of oil leakage from its damper. This is somewhat restricted on certain single shock models due to the location of the shock absorber.

● With the rear wheel raised off the ground, grasp the wheel at the highest point and attempt to pull it up **(see illustration 8)**. Any play in the swingarm pivot or suspension linkage bearings will be felt as movement. **Note:** *Do not confuse play with actual suspension movement.* Failure to lubricate suspension linkage bearings can lead to bearing failure **(see illustration 9)**.

● With the rear wheel raised off the ground, grasp the swingarm ends and attempt to move the swingarm from side to side and forwards and backwards - any play indicates wear of the swingarm pivot bearings **(see illustration 10)**.

Worn suspension linkage pivots (arrows) are usually the cause of play in the rear suspension

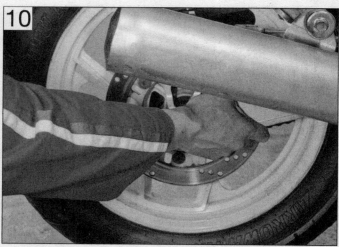

Grasp the swingarm at the ends to check for play in its pivot bearings

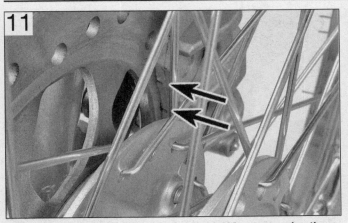

Brake pad wear can usually be viewed without removing the caliper. Most pads have wear indicator grooves (arrowed) and some also have indicator tangs or cut-outs.

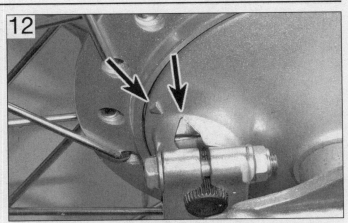

On drum brakes, check the angle of the operating lever with the brake fully applied. Most drum brakes have a wear indicator pointer or scale.

Brakes, Wheels and Tyres

Brakes

● With the wheel raised off the ground, apply the brake then free it off, and check that the wheel is about to revolve freely without brake drag.

● On disc brakes, examine the disc itself. Check that it is securely mounted and not cracked.

● On disc brakes, view the pad material through the caliper mouth and check that the pads are not worn down beyond the limit **(see illustration 11)**.

● On drum brakes, check that when the brake is applied the angle between the operating lever and cable or rod is not too great **(see illustration 12)**. Check also that the operating lever doesn't foul any other components.

● On disc brakes, examine the flexible hoses from top to bottom. Have an assistant hold the brake on so that the fluid in the hose is under pressure, and check that there is no sign of fluid leakage, bulges or cracking. If there are any metal brake pipes or unions, check that these are free from corrosion and damage. Where a brake-linked anti-dive system is fitted, check the hoses to the anti-dive in a similar manner.

● Check that the rear brake torque arm is secure and that its fasteners are secured by self-locking nuts or castellated nuts with split-pins or R-pins **(see illustration 13)**.

● On models with ABS, check that the self-check warning light in the instrument panel works.

● The MOT tester will perform a test of the motorcycle's braking efficiency based on a calculation of rider and motorcycle weight. Although this cannot be carried out at home, you can at least ensure that the braking systems are properly maintained. For hydraulic disc brakes, check the fluid level, lever/pedal feel (bleed of air if its spongy) and pad material. For drum brakes, check adjustment, cable or rod operation and shoe lining thickness.

Wheels and tyres

● Check the wheel condition. Cast wheels should be free from cracks and if of the built-up design, all fasteners should be secure. Spoked wheels should be checked for broken, corroded, loose or bent spokes.

● With the wheel raised off the ground, spin the wheel and visually check that the tyre and wheel run true. Check that the tyre does not foul the suspension or mudguards.

● With the wheel raised off the ground, grasp the wheel and attempt to move it about the axle (spindle) **(see illustration 14)**. Any play felt here indicates wheel bearing failure.

Brake torque arm must be properly secured at both ends

Check for wheel bearing play by trying to move the wheel about the axle (spindle)

Checking the tyre tread depth

Tyre direction of rotation arrow can be found on tyre sidewall

Castellated type wheel axle (spindle) nut must be secured by a split pin or R-pin

Two straightedges are used to check wheel alignment

● Check the tyre tread depth, tread condition and sidewall condition **(see illustration 15)**.
● Check the tyre type. Front and rear tyre types must be compatible and be suitable for road use. Tyres marked NOT FOR ROAD USE, COMPETITION USE ONLY or similar, will fail the MOT.

● If the tyre sidewall carries a direction of rotation arrow, this must be pointing in the direction of normal wheel rotation **(see illustration 16)**.
● Check that the wheel axle (spindle) nuts (where applicable) are properly secured. A self-locking nut or castellated nut with a split-pin or R-pin can be used **(see illustration 17)**.
● Wheel alignment is checked with the motorcycle off the stand and a rider seated. With the front wheel pointing straight ahead, two perfectly straight lengths of metal or wood and placed against the sidewalls of both tyres **(see illustration 18)**. The gap each side of the front tyre must be equidistant on both sides. Incorrect wheel alignment may be due to a cocked rear wheel (often as the result of poor chain adjustment) or in extreme cases, a bent frame.

General checks and condition

● Check the security of all major fasteners, bodypanels, seat, fairings (where fitted) and mudguards.

● Check that the rider and pillion footrests, handlebar levers and brake pedal are securely mounted.

● Check for corrosion on the frame or any load-bearing components. If severe, this may affect the structure, particularly under stress.

Sidecars

A motorcycle fitted with a sidecar requires additional checks relating to the stability of the machine and security of attachment and swivel joints, plus specific wheel alignment (toe-in) requirements. Additionally, tyre and lighting requirements differ from conventional motorcycle use. Owners are advised to check MOT test requirements with an official test centre.

Preparing for storage

Before you start

If repairs or an overhaul is needed, see that this is carried out now rather than left until you want to ride the bike again.

Give the bike a good wash and scrub all dirt from its underside. Make sure the bike dries completely before preparing for storage.

Engine

● Remove the spark plug(s) and lubricate the cylinder bores with approximately a teaspoon of motor oil using a spout-type oil can (see illustration 1). Reinstall the spark plug(s). Crank the engine over a couple of times to coat the piston rings and bores with oil. If the bike has a kickstart, use this to turn the engine over. If not, flick the kill switch to OFF position and crank the engine over on the starter (see illustration 2). If the nature on the ignition system prevents the starter operating with the kill switch in the OFF position, remove

the spark plugs and fit them back in their caps; ensure that the plugs are earthed (grounded) against the cylinder head when the starter is operated (see illustration 3).

⚠️ Warning: It is important that the plugs are earthed (grounded) away from the spark plug holes otherwise there is a risk of atomised fuel from the cylinders igniting.

HAYNES HINT *On a single cylinder four-stroke engine, you can seal the combustion chamber completely by positioning the piston at TDC on the compression stroke.*

● Drain the carburettor(s) otherwise there is a risk of jets becoming blocked by gum deposits from the fuel (see illustration 4).

● If the bike is going into long-term storage, consider adding a fuel stabiliser to the fuel in the tank. If the tank is drained completely, corrosion of its internal surfaces may occur if left unprotected for a long period. The tank can be treated with a rust preventative especially for this purpose. Alternatively, remove the tank and pour half a litre of motor oil into it, install the filler cap and shake the tank to coat its internals with oil before draining off the excess. The same effect can also be achieved by spraying WD40 or a similar water-dispersant around the inside of the tank via its flexible nozzle.

● Make sure the cooling system contains the correct mix of antifreeze. Antifreeze also contains important corrosion inhibitors.

● The air intakes and exhaust can be sealed off by covering or plugging the openings. Ensure that you do not seal in any condensation; run the engine until it is hot,

Squirt a drop of motor oil into each cylinder

Flick the kill switch to OFF . . .

. . . and ensure that the metal bodies of the plugs (arrows) are earthed against the cylinder head

Connect a hose to the carburettor float chamber drain stub (arrow) and unscrew the drain screw

Exhausts can be sealed off with a plastic bag

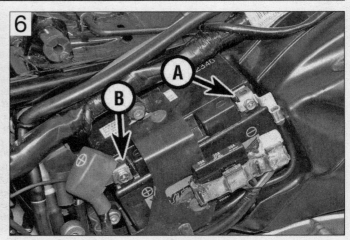

Disconnect the negative lead (A) first, followed by the positive lead (B)

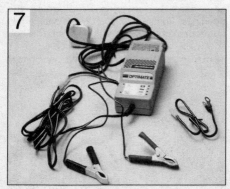

Use a suitable battery charger - this kit also assess battery condition

then switch off and allow to cool. Tape a piece of thick plastic over the silencer end(s) **(see illustration 5)**. Note that some advocate pouring a tablespoon of motor oil into the silencer(s) before sealing them off.

Battery

● Remove it from the bike - in extreme cases of cold the battery may freeze and crack its case **(see illustration 6)**.

● Check the electrolyte level and top up if necessary (conventional refillable batteries). Clean the terminals.
● Store the battery off the motorcycle and away from any sources of fire. Position a wooden block under the battery if it is to sit on the ground.
● Give the battery a trickle charge for a few hours every month **(see illustration 7)**.

Tyres

● Place the bike on its centrestand or an auxiliary stand which will support the motorcycle in an upright position. Position wood blocks under the tyres to keep them off the ground and to provide insulation from damp. If the bike is being put into long-term storage, ideally both tyres should be off the ground; not only will this protect the tyres, but will also ensure that no load is placed on the steering head or wheel bearings.
● Deflate each tyre by 5 to 10 psi, no more or the beads may unseat from the rim, making subsequent inflation difficult on tubeless tyres.

Pivots and controls

● Lubricate all lever, pedal, stand and footrest

pivot points. If grease nipples are fitted to the rear suspension components, apply lubricant to the pivots.
● Lubricate all control cables.

Cycle components

● Apply a wax protectant to all painted and plastic components. Wipe off any excess, but don't polish to a shine. Where fitted, clean the screen with soap and water.
● Coat metal parts with Vaseline (petroleum jelly). When applying this to the fork tubes, do not compress the forks otherwise the seals will rot from contact with the Vaseline.
● Apply a vinyl cleaner to the seat.

Storage conditions

● Aim to store the bike in a shed or garage which does not leak and is free from damp.
● Drape an old blanket or bedspread over the bike to protect it from dust and direct contact with sunlight (which will fade paint). This also hides the bike from prying eyes. Beware of tight-fitting plastic covers which may allow condensation to form and settle on the bike.

Getting back on the road

Engine and transmission

● Change the oil and replace the oil filter. If this was done prior to storage, check that the oil hasn't emulsified - a thick whitish substance which occurs through condensation.
● Remove the spark plugs. Using a spout-type oil can, squirt a few drops of oil into the cylinder(s). This will provide initial lubrication as the piston rings and bores comes back into contact. Service the spark plugs, or fit new ones, and install them in the engine.

● Check that the clutch isn't stuck on. The plates can stick together if left standing for some time, preventing clutch operation. Engage a gear and try rocking the bike back and forth with the clutch lever held against the handlebar. If this doesn't work on cable-operated clutches, hold the clutch lever back against the handlebar with a strong elastic band or cable tie for a couple of hours **(see illustration 8)**.
● If the air intakes or silencer end(s) were blocked off, remove the bung or cover used.
● If the fuel tank was coated with a rust

Hold clutch lever back against the handlebar with elastic bands or a cable tie

preventative, oil or a stabiliser added to the fuel, drain and flush the tank and dispose of the fuel sensibly. If no action was taken with the fuel tank prior to storage, it is advised that the old fuel is disposed of since it will go off over a period of time. Refill the fuel tank with fresh fuel.

Frame and running gear

● Oil all pivot points and cables.
● Check the tyre pressures. They will definitely need inflating if pressures were reduced for storage.
● Lubricate the final drive chain (where applicable).
● Remove any protective coating applied to the fork tubes (stanchions) since this may well destroy the fork seals. If the fork tubes weren't protected and have picked up rust spots, remove them with very fine abrasive paper and refinish with metal polish.
● Check that both brakes operate correctly. Apply each brake hard and check that it's not possible to move the motorcycle forwards, then check that the brake frees off again once released. Brake caliper pistons can stick due to corrosion around the piston head, or on the sliding caliper types, due to corrosion of the slider pins. If the brake doesn't free after repeated operation, take the caliper off for examination. Similarly drum brakes can stick due to a seized operating cam, cable or rod linkage.
● If the motorcycle has been in long-term storage, renew the brake fluid and clutch fluid (where applicable).
● Depending on where the bike has been stored, the wiring, cables and hoses may have been nibbled by rodents. Make a visual check and investigate disturbed wiring loom tape.

Battery

● If the battery has been previously removal and given top up charges it can simply be reconnected. Remember to connect the positive cable first and the negative cable last.
● On conventional refillable batteries, if the battery has not received any attention, remove it from the motorcycle and check its electrolyte level. Top up if necessary then charge the battery. If the battery fails to hold a charge and a visual checks show heavy white sulphation of the plates, the battery is probably defective and must be renewed. This is particularly likely if the battery is old. Confirm battery condition with a specific gravity check.
● On sealed (MF) batteries, if the battery has not received any attention, remove it from the motorcycle and charge it according to the information on the battery case - if the battery fails to hold a charge it must be renewed.

Starting procedure

● If a kickstart is fitted, turn the engine over a couple of times with the ignition OFF to distribute oil around the engine. If no kickstart is fitted, flick the engine kill switch OFF and the ignition ON and crank the engine over a couple of times to work oil around the upper cylinder components. If the nature of the ignition system is such that the starter won't work with the kill switch OFF, remove the spark plugs, fit them back into their caps and earth (ground) their bodies on the cylinder head. Reinstall the spark plugs afterwards.
● Switch the kill switch to RUN, operate the choke and start the engine. If the engine won't start don't continue cranking the engine - not only will this flatten the battery, but the starter motor will overheat. Switch the ignition off and try again later. If the engine refuses to start, go through the fault finding procedures in this manual. **Note:** *If the bike has been in storage for a long time, old fuel or a carburettor blockage may be the problem. Gum deposits in carburettors can block jets - if a carburettor cleaner doesn't prove successful the carburettors must be dismantled for cleaning.*
● Once the engine has started, check that the lights, turn signals and horn work properly.
● Treat the bike gently for the first ride and check all fluid levels on completion. Settle the bike back into the maintenance schedule.

Conversion factors

Length (distance)

Inches (in)	x 25.4	= Millimetres (mm)	x 0.0394	= Inches (in)
Feet (ft)	x 0.305	= Metres (m)	x 3.281	= Feet (ft)
Miles	x 1.609	= Kilometres (km)	x 0.621	= Miles

Volume (capacity)

Cubic inches (cu in; in³)	x 16.387	= Cubic centimetres (cc; cm³)	x 0.061	= Cubic inches (cu in; in³)
Imperial pints (Imp pt)	x 0.568	= Litres (l)	x 1.76	= Imperial pints (Imp pt)
Imperial quarts (Imp qt)	x 1.137	= Litres (l)	x 0.88	= Imperial quarts (Imp qt)
Imperial quarts (Imp qt)	x 1.201	= US quarts (US qt)	x 0.833	= Imperial quarts (Imp qt)
US quarts (US qt)	x 0.946	= Litres (l)	x 1.057	= US quarts (US qt)
Imperial gallons (Imp gal)	x 4.546	= Litres (l)	x 0.22	= Imperial gallons (Imp gal)
Imperial gallons (Imp gal)	x 1.201	= US gallons (US gal)	x 0.833	= Imperial gallons (Imp gal)
US gallons (US gal)	x 3.785	= Litres (l)	x 0.264	= US gallons (US gal)

Mass (weight)

Ounces (oz)	x 28.35	= Grams (g)	x 0.035	= Ounces (oz)
Pounds (lb)	x 0.454	= Kilograms (kg)	x 2.205	= Pounds (lb)

Force

Ounces-force (ozf; oz)	x 0.278	= Newtons (N)	x 3.6	= Ounces-force (ozf; oz)
Pounds-force (lbf; lb)	x 4.448	= Newtons (N)	x 0.225	= Pounds-force (lbf; lb)
Newtons (N)	x 0.1	= Kilograms-force (kgf; kg)	x 9.81	= Newtons (N)

Pressure

Pounds-force per square inch (psi; lbf/in²; lb/in²)	x 0.070	= Kilograms-force per square centimetre (kgf/cm²; kg/cm²)	x 14.223	= Pounds-force per square inch (psi; lbf/in²; lb/in²)
Pounds-force per square inch (psi; lbf/in²; lb/in²)	x 0.068	= Atmospheres (atm)	x 14.696	= Pounds-force per square inch (psi; lbf/in²; lb/in²)
Pounds-force per square inch (psi; lbf/in²; lb/in²)	x 0.069	= Bars	x 14.5	= Pounds-force per square inch (psi; lbf/in²; lb/in²)
Pounds-force per square inch (psi; lbf/in²; lb/in²)	x 6.895	= Kilopascals (kPa)	x 0.145	= Pounds-force per square inch (psi; lbf/in²; lb/in²)
Kilopascals (kPa)	x 0.01	= Kilograms-force per square centimetre (kgf/cm²; kg/cm²)	x 98.1	= Kilopascals (kPa)
Millibar (mbar)	x 100	= Pascals (Pa)	x 0.01	= Millibar (mbar)
Millibar (mbar)	x 0.0145	= Pounds-force per square inch (psi; lbf/in²; lb/in²)	x 68.947	= Millibar (mbar)
Millibar (mbar)	x 0.75	= Millimetres of mercury (mmHg)	x 1.333	= Millibar (mbar)
Millibar (mbar)	x 0.401	= Inches of water (inH₂O)	x 2.491	= Millibar (mbar)
Millimetres of mercury (mmHg)	x 0.535	= Inches of water (inH₂O)	x 1.868	= Millimetres of mercury (mmHg)
Inches of water (inH₂O)	x 0.036	= Pounds-force per square inch (psi; lbf/in²; lb/in²)	x 27.68	= Inches of water (inH₂O)

Torque (moment of force)

Pounds-force inches (lbf in; lb in)	x 1.152	= Kilograms-force centimetre (kgf cm; kg cm)	x 0.868	= Pounds-force inches (lbf in; lb in)
Pounds-force inches (lbf in; lb in)	x 0.113	= Newton metres (Nm)	x 8.85	= Pounds-force inches (lbf in; lb in)
Pounds-force inches (lbf in; lb in)	x 0.083	= Pounds-force feet (lbf ft; lb ft)	x 12	= Pounds-force inches (lbf in; lb in)
Pounds-force feet (lbf ft; lb ft)	x 0.138	= Kilograms-force metres (kgf m; kg m)	x 7.233	= Pounds-force feet (lbf ft; lb ft)
Pounds-force feet (lbf ft; lb ft)	x 1.356	= Newton metres (Nm)	x 0.738	= Pounds-force feet (lbf ft; lb ft)
Newton metres (Nm)	x 0.102	= Kilograms-force metres (kgf m; kg m)	x 9.804	= Newton metres (Nm)

Power

Horsepower (hp)	x 745.7	= Watts (W)	x 0.0013	= Horsepower (hp)

Velocity (speed)

Miles per hour (miles/hr; mph)	x 1.609	= Kilometres per hour (km/hr; kph)	x 0.621	= Miles per hour (miles/hr; mph)

Fuel consumption*

Miles per gallon, Imperial (mpg)	x 0.354	= Kilometres per litre (km/l)	x 2.825	= Miles per gallon, Imperial (mpg)
Miles per gallon, US (mpg)	x 0.425	= Kilometres per litre (km/l)	x 2.352	= Miles per gallon, US (mpg)

Temperature

Degrees Fahrenheit = (°C x 1.8) + 32   Degrees Celsius (Degrees Centigrade; °C) = (°F - 32) x 0.56

It is common practice to convert from miles per gallon (mpg) to litres/100 kilometres (l/100km), where mpg x l/100 km = 282

This Section provides an easy reference-guide to the more common faults that are likely to afflict your machine. Obviously, the opportunities are almost limitless for faults to occur as a result of obscure failures, and to try and cover all eventualities would require a separate book. Indeed, a number have been written on the subject.

Successful fault finding is not a mysterious 'black art' but the application of a bit of knowledge combined with a systematic and logical approach to the problem. Begin by first accurately identifying the symptom and then checking through the list of possible causes, starting with the simplest or most obvious and progressing in stages to the most complex.

Take nothing for granted, but above all apply liberal quantities of common sense.

The main symptom of a fault is given in the text as a major heading below which are listed the various systems or areas which may contain the fault. Details of each possible cause for a fault and the remedial action to be taken are given, in brief, in the paragraphs below each heading. Further information should be sought in the relevant Chapter.

Engine doesn't start or is difficult to start

- ☐ Starter motor doesn't rotate
- ☐ Starter motor rotates but engine does not turn over
- ☐ Starter works but engine won't turn over (seized)
- ☐ No fuel flow
- ☐ Engine flooded
- ☐ No spark or weak spark
- ☐ Compression low
- ☐ Stalls after starting
- ☐ Rough idle

Poor running at low speeds

- ☐ Spark weak
- ☐ Fuel/air mixture incorrect
- ☐ Compression low
- ☐ Poor acceleration

Poor running or no power at high speed

- ☐ Firing incorrect
- ☐ Fuel/air mixture incorrect
- ☐ Compression low
- ☐ Knocking or pinking
- ☐ Miscellaneous causes

Overheating

- ☐ Engine overheats
- ☐ Firing incorrect
- ☐ Fuel/air mixture incorrect
- ☐ Compression too high
- ☐ Engine load excessive
- ☐ Lubrication inadequate
- ☐ Miscellaneous causes

Clutch problems

- ☐ Clutch slipping
- ☐ Clutch not disengaging completely (drag)

Gearchange problems

- ☐ Doesn't go into gear or lever doesn't return
- ☐ Jumps out of gear
- ☐ Overshifts

Abnormal engine noise

- ☐ Knocking or pinking
- ☐ Piston slap or rattling
- ☐ Valve noise
- ☐ Other noise

Abnormal driveline noise

- ☐ Clutch noise
- ☐ Gearbox noise
- ☐ Final drive noise

Abnormal frame and suspension noise

- ☐ Front end noise
- ☐ Rear end noise
- ☐ Shock absorber noise
- ☐ Brake noise

Excessive exhaust smoke

- ☐ White smoke
- ☐ Black smoke
- ☐ Brown smoke

Poor handling or stability

- ☐ Handlebars hard to turn
- ☐ Handlebar shakes or vibrates excessively
- ☐ Handlebar pulls to one side
- ☐ Poor shock absorbing qualities

Braking problems

- ☐ Brakes are spongy, don't hold
- ☐ Brake lever or pedal pulsates
- ☐ Brakes drag

Electrical problems

- ☐ Battery dead or weak
- ☐ Battery overcharged

Engine doesn't start or is difficult to start

Starter motor doesn't rotate

- ☐ Engine kill switch OFF.
- ☐ Engine kill switch defective. Check for wet, dirty or corroded contacts. Clean or renew the switch as necessary (Chapter 8).
- ☐ Faulty gear position sensor, side stand or clutch switch. Check starter safety circuit (Chapter 4). Check the operation of each switch according to the procedures in Chapter 8.
- ☐ Battery voltage low. Check and recharge battery (Chapter 8).
- ☐ Starter relay faulty. Check it according to the procedure in Chapter 8.
- ☐ Starter motor defective. Make sure the wiring to the starter is secure. Make sure the starter relay clicks when the start button is pushed. If the relay clicks, then the fault is in the wiring or motor.
- ☐ Starter switch not contacting. The contacts could be wet, corroded or dirty. Disassemble and clean the switch (Chapter 8).
- ☐ Wiring open or shorted. Check all wiring connections and harnesses to make sure that they are dry, tight and not corroded. Also check for broken or frayed wires that can cause a short to earth (see *Wiring Diagrams*).
- ☐ Ignition switch defective. Check the switch according to the procedure in Chapter 8. Renew the switch if it is defective.

Starter motor rotates but engine does not turn over

- ☐ Starter clutch fault (Chapter 8).
- ☐ Starter idle and/or reduction gears damaged (Chapters 2 and 8).

Starter works but engine won't turn over (seized)

- ☐ Seized engine caused by one or more internally damaged components. Failure due to wear, abuse or lack of lubrication. Damage can include seized valves, camshafts, pistons, crankshaft, connecting rod bearings, or transmission gears or bearings. Refer to Chapter 2 for engine disassembly.

No fuel flow

- ☐ No fuel in tank.
- ☐ Fuel pump failure or filter/strainer blocked (Chapter 4).
- ☐ Fuel tank breather hose obstructed.
- ☐ Injector clogged. For the injectors to be clogged, either a very bad batch of fuel with an unusual additive has been used, or some other foreign material has entered the system. Sometimes, after a machine has been stored for many months without running, the fuel turns to a varnish-like liquid and forms deposits in the injectors.

Engine flooded

- ☐ Starting technique incorrect. Under normal circumstances the machine should start with no throttle. When the ambient temperature is very low, and the engine is cold, open the throttle slightly and pull the clutch lever in after switching the ignition ON. If the engine floods i.e. fuel is injected but not ignited by the spark plugs, check the ignition system (Chapter 4).

No spark or weak spark

- ☐ Engine kill switch OFF.
- ☐ Battery voltage low. Check and recharge the battery (Chapter 8).
- ☐ Spark plugs dirty, defective or worn out (Chapter 1).
- ☐ Ignition coils not making good contact. Make sure that the coils fit snugly over the plug ends. Check the coil wiring (Chapter 4).
- ☐ Ignition HT coils defective. Check the coils (Chapter 4).
- ☐ Engine control unit (ECU) or ignition system component faulty (Chapter 4). Refer to a BMW dealer equipped with the diagnostic tester.
- ☐ Wiring shorted or broken between:
  - *a)* Ignition or kill switch shorted. This is usually caused by water, corrosion, damage or excessive wear. Check the operation of the switches and renew if necessary (Chapter 8).
  - *b)* Ignition switch and engine kill switch
  - *c)* ECU and engine kill switch
  - *d)* ECU and ignition HT coils
  - *e)* Ignition system sensors
  Make sure that all wiring connections are clean, dry and tight. Look for chafed and broken wires (Chapters 4 and 8).

Compression low

- ☐ Spark plugs loose. Remove the plugs and inspect their threads. Reinstall and tighten to the specified torque (Chapter 1).
- ☐ Cylinder head not sufficiently tightened down. If the cylinder head is suspected of being loose, then there's a chance that the gasket or head is damaged if the problem has persisted for any length of time. The head nuts should be tightened to the specified torque in the correct sequence (Chapter 2).
- ☐ Improper valve clearance. This means that the valve is not closing completely and compression pressure is leaking past the valve. Check and adjust the valve clearances (Chapter 1).
- ☐ Cylinder and/or piston worn. Excessive wear will cause compression pressure to leak past the rings. This is usually accompanied by worn rings as well. A top-end overhaul is necessary (Chapter 2).
- ☐ Piston rings worn, weak, broken, or sticking. Broken or sticking piston rings usually indicate a lubrication or fuel problem that causes excess carbon deposits to form on the pistons and rings. Top-end overhaul is necessary (Chapter 2).
- ☐ Piston ring-to-groove clearance excessive. This is caused by excessive wear of the piston ring lands. Piston renewal is necessary (Chapter 2).
- ☐ Cylinder head gasket damaged. If the head is allowed to become loose, or if excessive carbon build-up on the piston crown and combustion chamber causes extremely high compression, the head gasket may leak. A new gasket is necessary (Chapter 2).
- ☐ Cylinder head warped. This is caused by overheating or improperly tightened head nuts. Machine shop resurfacing or head renewal is necessary (Chapter 2).
- ☐ Valve spring broken or weak. Caused by component failure or wear, the springs must be renewed (Chapter 2).
- ☐ Valve not seating properly. This is caused by a bent valve (from over-revving or improper valve adjustment), burned valve or seat or an accumulation of carbon deposits on the seat. The valves must be cleaned and/or renewed and the seats serviced (Chapter 2).

Engine doesn't start or is difficult to start (continued)

Stalls after starting

- [ ] Ignition malfunction (Chapter 4).
- [ ] Injector malfunction (Chapter 4).
- [ ] Fuel pump failure or filter/strainer blocked (Chapter 4).
- [ ] Fuel contaminated. The fuel can be contaminated with either dirt or water, or can change chemically if the machine has been stored for many months without running. Drain the tank and fuel hoses (Chapter 4).
- [ ] Intake air leak. Check for loose throttle body-to-intake manifold and air duct connections (Chapter 4), or loose injectors.

Rough idle

- [ ] Ignition malfunction (Chapter 4).
- [ ] Injector malfunction (Chapter 4).
- [ ] Fuel contaminated. The fuel can be contaminated with either dirt or water, or can change chemically if the machine has been stored for many months without running. Drain the tank and fuel hoses (Chapter 4).
- [ ] Intake air leak. Check for loose throttle body-to-intake manifold and air duct connections (Chapter 4), or loose injectors.
- [ ] Air filter clogged – renew the filter element (Chapter 1).

Poor running at low speeds

Spark weak

- [ ] Battery voltage low – check and recharge battery (Chapter 8).
- [ ] Spark plugs dirty, defective or worn out (Chapter 1). Locate reason for fouled plugs using spark plug condition chart at the end of this manual.
- [ ] Incorrect spark plugs. Wrong type or heat range. Check and install correct plugs (Chapter 1).
- [ ] HT coil not making good contact over spark plug.
- [ ] HT coil or HT wiring defective (Chapter 4).
- [ ] Engine control unit (ECU) or ignition system component faulty (Chapter 4). Refer to a BMW dealer equipped with the diagnostic tester.

Fuel/air mixture incorrect

- [ ] Air filter clogged, poorly sealed or missing (Chapter 1).
- [ ] Air intake duct blocked or disconnected (Chapter 1).
- [ ] Intake air leak. Check for loose throttle body-to-intake manifold and air duct connections (Chapter 4), or loose injectors.
- [ ] Fuel pump failure or filter/strainer blocked (Chapter 4).
- [ ] Fuel tank breather hose obstructed.
- [ ] Injector clogged. Dirt, water or other contaminants can clog the injectors. Clean the injectors (Chapter 4).

Compression low

- [ ] Spark plugs loose. Remove the plugs and inspect their threads. Reinstall and tighten to the specified torque (Chapter 1).
- [ ] Cylinder head not sufficiently tightened down. If the cylinder head is suspected of being loose, then there's a chance that the gasket and head are damaged if the problem has persisted for any length of time. The head nuts should be tightened to the specified torque in the correct sequence (Chapter 2).
- [ ] Improper valve clearance. This means that the valve is not closing completely and compression pressure is leaking past the valve. Check and adjust the valve clearances (Chapter 1).

- [ ] Cylinder and/or piston worn. Excessive wear will cause compression pressure to leak past the rings. This is usually accompanied by worn rings as well. A top-end overhaul is necessary (Chapter 2).
- [ ] Piston rings worn, weak, broken, or sticking. Broken or sticking piston rings usually indicate a lubrication or mixture problem that causes excess carbon deposits or seizures to form on the pistons and rings. Top-end overhaul is necessary (Chapter 2).
- [ ] Piston ring-to-groove clearance excessive. This is caused by excessive wear of the piston ring lands. Piston renewal is necessary (Chapter 2).
- [ ] Cylinder head gasket damaged. If the head is allowed to become loose, or if excessive carbon build-up on the piston crown and combustion chamber causes extremely high compression, the head gasket may leak. A new gasket is necessary (Chapter 2).
- [ ] Cylinder head warped. This is caused by overheating or improperly tightened head nuts. Machine shop resurfacing or head renewal is necessary (Chapter 2).
- [ ] Valve spring broken or weak. Caused by component failure or wear, the springs must be renewed (Chapter 2).
- [ ] Valve not seating properly. This is caused by a bent valve (from over-revving or improper valve adjustment), burned valve or seat or an accumulation of carbon deposits on the seat. The valves must be cleaned and/or renewed and the seats serviced (Chapter 2).

Poor acceleration

- [ ] Timing not advancing. Refer to a BMW dealer equipped with the diagnostic tester.
- [ ] Engine oil viscosity too high. Using a heavier oil than that recommended in *Pre-ride checks* can damage the oil pump or lubrication system and cause drag on the engine.
- [ ] Brakes dragging. Usually caused by debris which has entered the brake piston seals, or from a warped disc or bent axle (Chapter 6).

Poor running or no power at high speed

Firing incorrect

- [ ] Air filter clogged – renew the filter element (Chapter 1).
- [ ] Spark plugs dirty, defective or worn out (Chapter 1). Incorrect spark plugs. Wrong type or heat range. Check and install correct plugs (Chapter 1).
- [ ] HT coil not in good contact over spark plug.
- [ ] HT coil or HT wiring defective (Chapter 4).
- [ ] Engine control unit (ECU) or ignition system component faulty (Chapter 4). Refer to a BMW dealer equipped with the diagnostic tester.

Fuel/air mixture incorrect

- [ ] Air filter clogged, poorly sealed or missing (Chapter 1).
- [ ] Air intake duct blocked or disconnected (Chapter 1).
- [ ] Intake air leak. Check for loose throttle body-to-intake manifold and air duct connections (Chapter 4), or loose injectors.
- [ ] Fuel pump failure or filter/strainer blocked (Chapter 4).
- [ ] Fuel tank breather hose obstructed.
- [ ] Injector clogged. Dirt, water or other contaminants can clog the injectors. Clean the injectors (Chapter 4).

Compression low

- [ ] Spark plugs loose. Remove the plugs and inspect their threads. Reinstall and tighten to the specified torque (Chapter 1).
- [ ] Cylinder head not sufficiently tightened down. If the cylinder head is suspected of being loose, then there's a chance that the gasket and head are damaged if the problem has persisted for any length of time. The head nuts should be tightened to the specified torque in the correct sequence (Chapter 2).
- [ ] Improper valve clearance. This means that the valve is not closing completely and compression pressure is leaking past the valve. Check and adjust the valve clearances (Chapter 1).
- [ ] Cylinder and/or piston worn. Excessive wear will cause compression pressure to leak past the rings. This is usually accompanied by worn rings as well. A top-end overhaul is necessary (Chapter 2).
- [ ] Piston rings worn, weak, broken, or sticking. Broken or sticking piston rings usually indicate a lubrication or mixture problem that causes excess carbon deposits or seizures to form on the pistons and rings. Top-end overhaul is necessary (Chapter 2).
- [ ] Piston ring-to-groove clearance excessive. This is caused by excessive wear of the piston ring lands. Piston renewal is necessary (Chapter 2).
- [ ] Cylinder head gasket damaged. If the head is allowed to become loose, or if excessive carbon build-up on the piston crown and combustion chamber causes extremely high compression, the head gasket may leak. A new gasket is necessary (Chapter 2).
- [ ] Cylinder head warped. This is caused by overheating or improperly tightened head nuts. Machine shop resurfacing or head renewal is necessary (Chapter 2).
- [ ] Valve spring broken or weak. Caused by component failure or wear, the springs must be renewed (Chapter 2).
- [ ] Valve not seating properly. This is caused by a bent valve (from over-revving or improper valve adjustment), burned valve or seat or an accumulation of carbon deposits on the seat. The valves must be cleaned and/or renewed and the seats serviced (Chapter 2).

Knocking or pinking

- [ ] Incorrect or poor quality fuel. Old or improper grades of fuel can cause detonation. This causes the piston to rattle, thus the knocking or pinking sound. Drain old fuel and refill with the recommended fuel grade.
- [ ] Carbon build-up in combustion chamber. Use of a fuel additive that will dissolve the adhesive bonding the carbon particles to the crown and chamber is the easiest way to remove the build-up. Otherwise, the cylinder heads will have to be removed and decarbonised (Chapter 2).
- [ ] Spark plug heat range incorrect. Uncontrolled detonation indicates the plug heat range is too hot. The plug in effect becomes a glow plug, raising cylinder temperatures. Install the specified plugs (Chapter 1).
- [ ] Improper air/fuel mixture. This will cause the cylinder to run hot, which leads to detonation. Refer to a BMW dealer equipped with the diagnostic tester.

Miscellaneous causes

- [ ] Faulty or incorrectly installed side stand switch causing the safety interlock circuit to cut ignition. Check the installation and function of the switch, and its wiring and connectors (see Chapter 8).
- [ ] Clutch slipping. May be caused by loose or worn clutch components. Refer to Chapter 2 for clutch overhaul procedures.
- [ ] Timing not advancing – refer to a BMW dealer equipped with the diagnostic tester.
- [ ] Engine oil viscosity too high. Using a heavier oil than the one recommended in *Pre-ride checks* can damage the oil pump or lubrication system and cause drag on the engine.
- [ ] Brakes dragging. Usually caused by debris which has entered the brake piston seals, or from a warped disc or bent axle (Chapter 6).

Overheating

Engine overheats

- [ ] Coolant level low. Check the level in the reservoir (*Pre-ride checks*).
- [ ] Leak in cooling system. Check entire system for evidence of leakage (Chapter 1)
- [ ] Faulty radiator cap. If the cap does not keep the system pressurised it will overheat. Fit a new cap (Chapter 1).
- [ ] Faulty thermostat (Chapter 3).
- [ ] Radiator fins clogged preventing flow of air over them. Check and clean (Chapter 1).
- [ ] Radiator or coolant passage clogged. Drain and flush the system (Chapter 1).
- [ ] Cooling fan not cutting in. Fan motor or wiring defective, or faulty ECT sensor (Chapter 3).
- [ ] Water pump damaged (Chapter 3).

Firing incorrect

- [ ] Spark plugs dirty, defective or worn out (Chapter 1). Locate reason for fouled plugs using spark plug condition chart at the end of this manual.
- [ ] Incorrect spark plugs. Wrong type or heat range. Check and install correct plugs (Chapter 1).
- [ ] Engine control unit (ECU) or ignition system component faulty (Chapter 4). Refer to a BMW dealer equipped with the diagnostic tester.
- [ ] Ignition HT coils defective (Chapter 4).

Fuel/air mixture incorrect

- [ ] Air filter clogged, poorly sealed or missing (Chapter 1).
- [ ] Air intake duct blocked or disconnected (Chapter 1).
- [ ] Intake air leak. Check for loose throttle body-to-intake manifold and air duct connections (Chapter 4), or loose injectors.
- [ ] Fuel pump failure or filter/strainer blocked (Chapter 4).
- [ ] Fuel tank breather hose obstructed.
- [ ] Injector clogged. Dirt, water or other contaminants can clog the injectors. Clean the injectors (Chapter 4).

Compression too high

- [ ] Carbon build-up in combustion chamber. Use of a fuel additive that will dissolve the adhesive bonding the carbon particles to the piston crown and chamber is the easiest way to remove the build-up. Otherwise, the cylinder heads will have to be removed and decarbonised (Chapter 2).

Engine load excessive

- [ ] Clutch slipping. Can be caused by damaged, loose or worn clutch components. Refer to Chapter 2 for overhaul procedures.
- [ ] Engine oil level too high. The addition of too much oil will cause pressurisation of the crankcase and inefficient engine operation. Drain to proper level (Chapter 1 and *Pre-ride checks*).
- [ ] Engine oil viscosity too high. Using a heavier oil than the one recommended in *Pre-ride checks* can damage the oil pump or lubrication system as well as cause drag on the engine.
- [ ] Brakes dragging. Usually caused by debris which has entered the brake piston seals, or from a warped disc or bent axle (Chapter 6).

Lubrication inadequate

- [ ] Engine oil level too low. Friction caused by intermittent lack of lubrication or from oil that is overworked can cause overheating. The oil provides a definite cooling function in the engine. Check the oil level (*Pre-ride checks*).
- [ ] Poor quality engine oil or incorrect viscosity or type. Oil is rated not only according to viscosity but also according to type. Some oils are not rated high enough for use in this engine. Check the Specifications (*Pre-ride checks*) and drain and refill with the correct oil if necessary (Chapter 1).

Miscellaneous causes

- [ ] Modification to exhaust system. Most aftermarket exhaust systems cause the engine to run leaner, which make them run hotter.

Clutch problems

Clutch slipping

- [ ] Clutch friction plates worn (Chapter 2).
- [ ] Clutch springs broken or weak (Chapter 2).
- [ ] Clutch release mechanism faulty (Chapter 2).
- [ ] Incorrect oil used in engine. Oils designed for car engines often contain friction modifiers which if used in an engine with a wet clutch can promote clutch slip. Always use an oil designed for motorcycle engines (*Pre-ride checks*).
- [ ] Wear in clutch housing and/or clutch centre preventing correct engagement and disengagement of plates (Chapter 2).

Clutch not disengaging completely (drag)

Note: *Poor clutch disengagement and clunky gear changes in GS models up to engine No. 122EN36130280 may be caused by a clutch component that has since been upgraded – refer to your BMW dealer for details.*

- [ ] Clutch release mechanism faulty (Chapter 2). This will cause clutch drag, which in turn will cause the machine to creep.
- [ ] Clutch plates warped or damaged (Chapter 2).
- [ ] Engine oil viscosity high, or oil very old. Change the oil and filter (Chapter 1).

Gearchange problems

Doesn't go into gear or lever doesn't return

- [ ] Clutch not disengaging – check the clutch release mechanism (Chapter 2).
- [ ] Selector fork(s) bent or seized – check the gearchange mechanism (Chapter 2).
- [ ] Gear(s) stuck on shaft. Most often caused by a lack of lubrication or excessive wear in transmission bearings. Fit new gearbox (Chapter 2).
- [ ] Selector drum binding. Caused by lubrication failure or excessive wear. Check the drum and bearing (Chapter 2).
- [ ] Gearchange lever return spring weak or broken (Chapter 2).
- [ ] Gearchange lever broken. Splines stripped out of lever or shaft, caused by allowing the lever to get loose. Renew necessary parts (Chapter 2).

- [ ] Stopper arm broken or worn. Poor gear engagement and rotary movement of selector drum results. Check the mechanism (Chapter 2).
- [ ] Stopper arm spring broken. Allows arm to float, causing sporadic shift operation. Check the spring (Chapter 2).

Jumps out of gear

- [ ] Selector fork(s) worn – fit new gearbox (Chapter 2).
- [ ] Gear groove(s) worn – fit new gearbox (Chapter 2).
- [ ] Gear dogs or dog slots worn or damaged – fit new gearbox (Chapter 2).

Overshifts

- [ ] Stopper arm spring weak or broken (Chapter 2).
- [ ] Gearchange shaft return spring post broken or distorted (Chapter 2).

Abnormal engine noise

Knocking or pinking

- [ ] Incorrect or poor quality fuel. Old or improper grades of fuel can cause detonation. This causes the piston to rattle, thus the knocking or pinking sound. Drain old fuel and refill with the recommended fuel grade.
- [ ] Carbon build-up in combustion chamber. Use of a fuel additive that will dissolve the adhesive bonding the carbon particles to the crown and chamber is the easiest way to remove the build-up. Otherwise, the cylinder heads will have to be removed and decarbonised (Chapter 2).
- [ ] Spark plug heat range incorrect. Uncontrolled detonation indicates the plug heat range is too hot. The plug in effect becomes a glow plug, raising cylinder temperatures. Install the specified plugs (Chapter 1).
- [ ] Improper air/fuel mixture. This will cause the cylinder to run hot, which leads to detonation. Refer to a BMW dealer equipped with the diagnostic tester.

Piston slap or rattling

- [ ] Cylinder-to-piston clearance excessive, caused by wear or improper assembly (Chapter 2).
- [ ] Connecting rod bent. Caused by over-revving, trying to start a badly flooded engine or from ingesting a foreign object into the combustion chamber (Chapter 2).
- [ ] Piston pin or piston pin bore worn or seized from wear or lack of lubrication (Chapter 2).

- [ ] Piston rings worn, broken or sticking in their grooves (Chapter 2).
- [ ] Piston seizure damage. Usually from lack of lubrication or overheating. Renew the pistons and cylinders, as a pair (Chapter 2).
- [ ] Connecting rod small-end or big-end bearing clearance excessive. Caused by excessive wear or lack of lubrication (Chapter 2).

Valve noise

- [ ] Incorrect valve clearances (Chapter 1).
- [ ] Valve spring broken or weak (Chapter 2).
- [ ] Camshafts or intermediate shaft worn, gears damaged or their bearing surfaces worn (Chapter 2).

Other noise

- [ ] Cylinder head gasket leaking (Chapter 2).
- [ ] Exhaust pipe leaking at cylinder head connection. Caused by improper fit of pipe(s) or loose exhaust flange. All exhaust fasteners should be tightened evenly and carefully (Chapter 4).
- [ ] Crankshaft runout excessive. Caused by a bent crankshaft (from over-revving) or damage from an upper cylinder component failure (Chapter 2).
- [ ] Crankshaft main bearings worn (Chapter 2).
- [ ] Cam chain tensioner defective (Chapter 2).
- [ ] Cam chain, sprockets or guides worn (Chapter 2).

Abnormal driveline noise

Clutch noise

☐ Loose or damaged clutch components (Chapter 2).

Gearbox noise

☐ Bearings worn. Also includes the possibility that the shafts are worn (Chapter 2).
☐ Gears worn or chipped (Chapter 2).
☐ Metal chips jammed in gear teeth. Probably pieces from a broken gear or selector mechanism that were picked up by the gears. This will cause early bearing failure (Chapter 2).

☐ Gearbox oil level too low. Causes a howl from gearbox (Chapter 1).

Final drive noise

☐ Final drive oil level too low (Chapter 1).
☐ Worn or damaged gears or final drive bearings. Refer to a BMW dealer.
☐ Driveshaft splines or universal joint worn (Chapter 5).

Abnormal frame and suspension noise

Front end noise

☐ Telelever ball joint loose or worn (Chapter 5).
☐ Telelever mountings loose or bearings worn (Chapter 5).
☐ Worn fork bushes (Chapter 5).
☐ Steering head bearing worn or damaged – clicks when braking (Chapter 5).
☐ Fork bridge or top yoke loose – ensure that all bolts are tight (Chapter 5).
☐ Fork tube bent – possibility if machine has crashed. Renew both fork tubes (Chapter 5).
☐ Front axle or axle clamp bolt loose. Tighten to the specified torque settings (Chapter 6).
☐ Loose or worn wheel bearings (Chapter 6).
☐ Shock absorber faulty (see below).

Rear end noise

☐ Swingarm mountings loose or bearings worn (Chapter 5).
☐ Final drive unit mountings loose or bearings worn (Chapter 5).
☐ Paralever arm mountings loose (Chapter 5).
☐ Shock absorber faulty.

Shock absorber noise

☐ Loose or worn mounting bolts, or worn bushes (Chapter 5).
☐ Fluid level low due to leak caused by defective seal (Chapter 5).
☐ Defective shock absorber with internal damage (Chapter 5).
☐ Bent damper rod or damaged shock body (Chapter 5).

Brake noise

☐ Squeal caused by dust on brake pads – usually found in combination with glazed pads (Chapter 6).
☐ Contamination of brake pads – oil or brake fluid causing brake to chatter or squeal (Chapter 6).
☐ Pads glazed caused by excessive heat from prolonged use or from contamination (Chapter 6).
☐ Disc warped – can cause a chattering, clicking or intermittent squeal, usually accompanied by a pulsating lever and uneven braking (Chapter 6).

Excessive exhaust smoke

White smoke

- [ ] Piston oil ring worn or broken, causing oil from the crankcase to be pulled past the piston into the combustion chamber. Renew the rings (Chapter 2).
- [ ] Cylinders worn or scored, caused by overheating or oil starvation. Measure cylinder diameter and renew if necessary (Chapter 2).
- [ ] Valve oil seals damaged or worn – renew oil seals (Chapter 2).
- [ ] Valve guides worn – complete valve job required (Chapter 2).
- [ ] Engine oil level too high, which causes the oil to be forced past the rings. Drain oil to the proper level (Chapter 1 and *Pre-ride checks*).
- [ ] Head gasket broken between oil return and cylinder. Causes oil to be pulled into the combustion chamber. Renew the head gasket and check the head for warpage (Chapter 2).
- [ ] Abnormal crankcase pressurisation, which forces oil past the rings. Damaged or dirty vent valve or clogged breather hose is usually the cause (Chapter 2).

Black smoke

- [ ] Air filter clogged – renew the filter element (Chapter 1).
- [ ] Engine control unit (ECU) defective. Refer to a BMW dealer equipped with the diagnostic tester.

Brown smoke

- [ ] Fuel filter or strainer clogged (Chapter 4).
- [ ] Fuel flow insufficient. Have a BMW dealer perform a fuel pressure check.
- [ ] Intake air leak. Check for loose throttle body-to-intake manifold and air duct connections (Chapter 4), or loose injectors.
- [ ] Air filter poorly sealed or not installed (Chapter 1).

Poor handling or stability

Handlebars hard to turn

- [ ] Steering head bearing defective (Chapter 5).
- [ ] Front tyre air pressure too low (*Pre-ride checks*).

Handlebar shakes or vibrates excessively

- [ ] Tyres worn or out of balance. Inspect for wear (*Pre-ride checks*). Have a tyre specialist balance the wheels.
- [ ] Swingarm or Telelever bearings worn (Chapter 5).
- [ ] Wheel rim(s) warped or damaged – check wheel runout (Chapter 6).
- [ ] Wheel bearings worn (Chapter 1).
- [ ] Handlebar mounting bolts loose (Chapter 5).
- [ ] Fork bridge or top yoke bolts loose (Chapter 5).

Handlebar pulls to one side

- [ ] Wheels out of alignment (Chapter 6).
- [ ] Front or rear suspension components worn or damaged caused by accident. Have the machine checked thoroughly by a BMW dealer or frame specialist.
- [ ] Fork tube bent – renew both fork tubes (Chapter 5).

Poor shock absorbing qualities

- [ ] Incorrect adjustment of suspension (Chapter 5).
- [ ] Tyre pressures incorrect (*Pre-ride checks*).
- [ ] Front or rear shock absorber damage (Chapter 5).

Braking problems

Brakes are spongy, don't hold

- [ ] Air in brake line. Caused by inattention to master cylinder fluid level or by leakage. Locate problem and bleed brakes (Chapter 6).
- [ ] Brake fluid leak.
- [ ] Brake fluid deteriorated through age or contaminated. Change brake fluid (Chapter 6).
- [ ] Master cylinder internal parts worn or damaged causing fluid to bypass. Fit a new master cylinder (Chapter 6).
- [ ] Pads or disc worn (Chapter 6).
- [ ] Brake pads contaminated with oil, grease or brake fluid. Renew pads and clean disc thoroughly with brake cleaner (Chapter 6).
- [ ] Disc warped (Chapter 6).
- [ ] ABS system faulty (Chapter 6).

Brake lever or pedal pulsates

- [ ] Disc warped (Chapter 6).
- [ ] Axle bent (Chapter 6).

- [ ] Brake caliper mounting bolts loose (Chapter 6).
- [ ] Rear brake caliper sliders damaged or sticking, causing caliper to bind. Clean and lubricate the sliders (Chapter 6).
- [ ] Wheel warped or otherwise damaged (Chapter 6).
- [ ] Wheel bearings worn (Chapter 1).
- [ ] ABS system faulty (Chapter 6).

Brakes drag

- [ ] Master cylinder piston seized (Chapter 6).
- [ ] Lever balky or stuck (Chapter 1).
- [ ] Rear brake caliper binds – caused by inadequate lubrication or damage to caliper slider pins (Chapter 6).
- [ ] Brake caliper piston seized in bore (Chapter 6).
- [ ] Brake pad damaged. Pad material separated from backing plate, usually caused by faulty manufacturing process or from contact with chemicals. Renew pads (Chapter 6).
- [ ] Pads improperly installed (Chapter 6).

Electrical problems

Battery dead or weak

- [ ] Battery faulty due to lack of maintenance or internal damage (Chapter 8).
- [ ] Battery leads making poor contact (Chapter 8).
- [ ] Load excessive. Caused by addition of high wattage lights or other electrical accessories.
- [ ] Ignition switch defective. Switch either earths (grounds) internally or fails to shut off system (Chapter 8).
- [ ] Charging system defective (Chapter 8).
- [ ] Wiring faulty. Wiring earthed (grounded) or connections loose in ignition, charging or lighting circuits (Chapter 8).

Battery overcharged

- [ ] Alternator defective. Overcharging is noticed when battery gets excessively warm (Chapter 8).
- [ ] Battery has internal fault (Chapter 8).
- [ ] Battery amperage too low, wrong type or size. Install manufacturer's specified amp-hour battery to handle charging load (Chapter 8).

A

ABS (Anti-lock braking system) A system, usually electronically controlled, that senses incipient wheel lockup during braking and relieves hydraulic pressure at wheel which is about to skid.

Aftermarket Components suitable for the motorcycle, but not produced by the motorcycle manufacturer.

Allen key A hexagonal wrench which fits into a recessed hexagonal hole.

Alternating current (ac) Current produced by an alternator. Requires converting to direct current by a rectifier for charging purposes.

Alternator Converts mechanical energy from the engine into electrical energy to charge the battery and power the electrical system.

Ampere (amp) A unit of measurement for the flow of electrical current. Current = Volts ÷ Ohms.

Ampere-hour (Ah) Measure of battery capacity.

Angle-tightening A torque expressed in degrees. Often follows a conventional tightening torque for cylinder head or main bearing fasteners **(see illustration)**.

Angle-tightening con-rod bolts

Antifreeze A substance (usually ethylene glycol) mixed with water, and added to the cooling system, to prevent freezing of the coolant in winter. Antifreeze also contains chemicals to inhibit corrosion and the formation of rust and other deposits that would tend to clog the radiator and coolant passages and reduce cooling efficiency.

Anti-dive System attached to the fork lower leg (slider) to prevent fork dive when braking hard.

Anti-seize compound A coating that reduces the risk of seizing on fasteners that are subjected to high temperatures, such as exhaust clamp bolts and nuts.

API American Petroleum Institute. A quality standard for 4-stroke motor oils.

Asbestos A natural fibrous mineral with great heat resistance, commonly used in the composition of brake friction materials. Asbestos is a health hazard and the dust created by brake systems should never be inhaled or ingested.

ATF Automatic Transmission Fluid. Often used in front forks.

ATU Automatic Timing Unit. Mechanical device for advancing the ignition timing on early engines.

ATV All Terrain Vehicle. Often called a Quad.

Axial play Side-to-side movement.

Axle A shaft on which a wheel revolves. Also known as a spindle.

B

Backlash The amount of movement between meshed components when one component is held still. Usually applies to gear teeth.

Ball bearing A bearing consisting of a hardened inner and outer race with hardened steel balls between the two races.

Bearings Used between two working surfaces to prevent wear of the components and a build-up of heat. Four types of bearing are commonly used on motorcycles: plain shell bearings, ball bearings, tapered roller bearings and needle roller bearings.

Bevel gears Used to turn the drive through 90°. Typical applications are shaft final drive and camshaft drive **(see illustration)**.

Bevel gears are used to turn the drive through 90°

BHP Brake Horsepower. The British measurement for engine power output. Power output is now usually expressed in kilowatts (kW).

Bias-belted tyre Similar construction to radial tyre, but with outer belt running at an angle to the wheel rim.

Big-end bearing The bearing in the end of the connecting rod that's attached to the crankshaft.

Bleeding The process of removing air from an hydraulic system via a bleed nipple or bleed screw.

Bottom-end A description of an engine's crankcase components and all components contained there-in.

BTDC Before Top Dead Centre in terms of piston position. Ignition timing is often expressed in terms of degrees or millimetres BTDC.

Bush A cylindrical metal or rubber component used between two moving parts.

Burr Rough edge left on a component after machining or as a result of excessive wear.

C

Cam chain The chain which takes drive from the crankshaft to the camshaft(s).

Canister The main component in an evaporative emission control system (California market only); contains activated charcoal granules to trap vapours from the fuel system rather than allowing them to vent to the atmosphere.

Castellated Resembling the parapets along the top of a castle wall. For example, a castellated wheel axle or spindle nut.

Catalytic converter A device in the exhaust system of some machines which converts certain pollutants in the exhaust gases into less harmful substances.

Charging system Description of the components which charge the battery, ie the alternator, rectifier and regulator.

Circlip A ring-shaped clip used to prevent endwise movement of cylindrical parts and shafts. An internal circlip is installed in a groove in a housing; an external circlip fits into a groove on the outside of a cylindrical piece such as a shaft. Also known as a snap-ring.

Clearance The amount of space between two parts. For example, between a piston and a cylinder, between a bearing and a journal, etc.

Coil spring A spiral of elastic steel found in various sizes throughout a vehicle, for example as a springing medium in the suspension and in the valve train.

Compression Reduction in volume, and increase in pressure and temperature, of a gas, caused by squeezing it into a smaller space.

Compression damping Controls the speed the suspension compresses when hitting a bump.

Compression ratio The relationship between cylinder volume when the piston is at top dead centre and cylinder volume when the piston is at bottom dead centre.

Continuity The uninterrupted path in the flow of electricity. Little or no measurable resistance.

Continuity tester Self-powered bleeper or test light which indicates continuity.

Cp Candlepower. Bulb rating commonly found on US motorcycles.

Crossply tyre Tyre plies arranged in a criss-cross pattern. Usually four or six plies used, hence 4PR or 6PR in tyre size codes.

Cush drive Rubber damper segments fitted between the rear wheel and final drive sprocket to absorb transmission shocks **(see illustration)**.

Cush drive rubbers dampen out transmission shocks

D

Decarbonisation The process of removing carbon deposits - typically from the combustion chamber, valves and exhaust port/system.

Degree disc Calibrated disc for measuring piston position. Expressed in degrees.

Detonation Destructive and damaging explosion of fuel/air mixture in combustion chamber instead of controlled burning.

Dial gauge Clock-type gauge with adapters for measuring runout and piston position. Expressed in mm or inches.

Diaphragm The rubber membrane in a master cylinder or carburettor which seals the upper chamber.

Diaphragm spring A single sprung plate often used in clutches.

Direct current (dc) Current produced by a dc generator.

Diode An electrical valve which only allows current to flow in one direction. Commonly used in rectifiers and starter interlock systems.

Disc valve (or rotary valve) A induction system used on some two-stroke engines.

Double-overhead camshaft (DOHC) An engine that uses two overhead camshafts, one for the intake valves and one for the exhaust valves.

Drivebelt A toothed belt used to transmit drive to the rear wheel on some motorcycles. A drivebelt has also been used to drive the camshafts. Drivebelts are usually made of Kevlar.

Driveshaft Any shaft used to transmit motion. Commonly used when referring to the final driveshaft on shaft drive motorcycles.

E

Earth return The return path of an electrical circuit, utilising the motorcycle's frame.

ECU (Electronic Control Unit) A computer which controls (for instance) an ignition system, or an anti-lock braking system.

EGO Exhaust Gas Oxygen sensor. Sometimes called a Lambda sensor.

Electrolyte The fluid in a lead-acid battery.

EMS (Engine Management System) A computer controlled system which manages the fuel injection and the ignition systems in an integrated fashion.

Endfloat The amount of lengthways movement between two parts. As applied to a crankshaft, the distance that the crankshaft can move side-to-side in the crankcase.

Endless chain A chain having no joining link. Common use for cam chains and final drive chains.

EP (Extreme Pressure) Oil type used in locations where high loads are applied, such as between gear teeth.

Evaporative emission control system Describes a charcoal filled canister which stores fuel vapours from the tank rather than allowing them to vent to the atmosphere. Usually only fitted to California models and referred to as an EVAP system.

Expansion chamber Section of two-stroke engine exhaust system so designed to improve engine efficiency and boost power.

F

Feeler blade or gauge A thin strip or blade of hardened steel, ground to an exact thickness, used to check or measure clearances between parts.

Final drive Description of the drive from the transmission to the rear wheel. Usually by chain or shaft, but sometimes by belt.

Firing order The order in which the engine cylinders fire, or deliver their power strokes, beginning with the number one cylinder.

Flooding Term used to describe a high fuel level in the carburettor float chambers, leading to fuel overflow. Also refers to excess fuel in the combustion chamber due to incorrect starting technique.

Free length The no-load state of a component when measured. Clutch, valve and fork spring lengths are measured at rest, without any preload.

Freeplay The amount of travel before any action takes place. The looseness in a linkage, or an assembly of parts, between the initial application of force and actual movement. For example, the distance the rear brake pedal moves before the rear brake is actuated.

Fuel injection The fuel/air mixture is metered electronically and directed into the engine intake ports (indirect injection) or into the cylinders (direct injection). Sensors supply information on engine speed and conditions.

Fuel/air mixture The charge of fuel and air going into the engine. See Stoichiometric ratio.

Fuse An electrical device which protects a circuit against accidental overload. The typical fuse contains a soft piece of metal which is calibrated to melt at a predetermined current flow (expressed as amps) and break the circuit.

G

Gap The distance the spark must travel in jumping from the centre electrode to the side electrode in a spark plug. Also refers to the distance between the ignition rotor and the pickup coil in an electronic ignition system.

Gasket Any thin, soft material - usually cork, cardboard, asbestos or soft metal - installed between two metal surfaces to ensure a good seal. For instance, the cylinder head gasket seals the joint between the block and the cylinder head.

Gauge An instrument panel display used to monitor engine conditions. A gauge with a movable pointer on a dial or a fixed scale is an analogue gauge. A gauge with a numerical readout is called a digital gauge.

Gear ratios The drive ratio of a pair of gears in a gearbox, calculated on their number of teeth.

Glaze-busting see **Honing**

Grinding Process for renovating the valve face and valve seat contact area in the cylinder head.

Gudgeon pin The shaft which connects the connecting rod small-end with the piston. Often called a piston pin or wrist pin.

H

Helical gears Gear teeth are slightly curved and produce less gear noise that straight-cut gears. Often used for primary drives.

Helicoil A thread insert repair system. Commonly used as a repair for stripped spark plug threads **(see illustration)**.

Installing a Helicoil thread insert

Honing A process used to break down the glaze on a cylinder bore (also called glaze-busting). Can also be carried out to roughen a rebored cylinder to aid ring bedding-in.

HT (High Tension) Description of the electrical circuit from the secondary winding of the ignition coil to the spark plug.

Hydraulic A liquid filled system used to transmit pressure from one component to another. Common uses on motorcycles are brakes and clutches.

Hydrometer An instrument for measuring the specific gravity of a lead-acid battery.

Hygroscopic Water absorbing. In motorcycle applications, braking efficiency will be reduced if DOT 3 or 4 hydraulic fluid absorbs water from the air - care must be taken to keep new brake fluid in tightly sealed containers.

I

lbf ft Pounds-force feet. An imperial unit of torque. Sometimes written as ft-lbs.

lbf in Pound-force inch. An imperial unit of torque, applied to components where a very low torque is required. Sometimes written as in-lbs.

IC Abbreviation for Integrated Circuit.

Ignition advance Means of increasing the timing of the spark at higher engine speeds. Done by mechanical means (ATU) on early engines or electronically by the ignition control unit on later engines.

Ignition timing The moment at which the spark plug fires, expressed in the number of crankshaft degrees before the piston reaches the top of its stroke, or in the number of millimetres before the piston reaches the top of its stroke.

Infinity (∞) Description of an open-circuit electrical state, where no continuity exists.

Inverted forks (upside down forks) The sliders or lower legs are held in the yokes and the fork tubes or stanchions are connected to the wheel axle (spindle). Less unsprung weight and stiffer construction than conventional forks.

J

JASO Quality standard for 2-stroke oils.

Joule The unit of electrical energy.

Journal The bearing surface of a shaft.

K

Kickstart Mechanical means of turning the engine over for starting purposes. Only usually fitted to mopeds, small capacity motorcycles and off-road motorcycles.

Kill switch Handebar-mounted switch for emergency ignition cut-out. Cuts the ignition circuit on all models, and additionally prevent starter motor operation on others.

km Symbol for kilometre.

kmh Abbreviation for kilometres per hour.

L

Lambda (λ) sensor A sensor fitted in the exhaust system to measure the exhaust gas oxygen content (excess air factor).

Lapping see Grinding.

LCD Abbreviation for Liquid Crystal Display.

LED Abbreviation for Light Emitting Diode.

Liner A steel cylinder liner inserted in a aluminium alloy cylinder block.

Locknut A nut used to lock an adjustment nut, or other threaded component, in place.

Lockstops The lugs on the lower triple clamp (yoke) which abut those on the frame, preventing handlebar-to-fuel tank contact.

Lockwasher A form of washer designed to prevent an attaching nut from working loose.

LT Low Tension Description of the electrical circuit from the power supply to the primary winding of the ignition coil.

M

Main bearings The bearings between the crankshaft and crankcase.

Maintenance-free (MF) battery A sealed battery which cannot be topped up.

Manometer Mercury-filled calibrated tubes used to measure intake tract vacuum. Used to synchronise carburettors on multi-cylinder engines.

Micrometer A precision measuring instrument that measures component outside diameters **(see illustration)**.

Tappet shims are measured with a micrometer

MON (Motor Octane Number) A measure of a fuel's resistance to knock.

Monograde oil An oil with a single viscosity, eg SAE80W.

Monoshock A single suspension unit linking the swingarm or suspension linkage to the frame.

mph Abbreviation for miles per hour.

Multigrade oil Having a wide viscosity range (eg 10W40). The W stands for Winter, thus the viscosity ranges from SAE10 when cold to SAE40 when hot.

Multimeter An electrical test instrument with the capability to measure voltage, current and resistance. Some meters also incorporate a continuity tester and buzzer.

N

Needle roller bearing Inner race of caged needle rollers and hardened outer race. Examples of uncaged needle rollers can be found on some engines. Commonly used in rear suspension applications and in two-stroke engines.

Nm Newton metres.

NOx Oxides of Nitrogen. A common toxic pollutant emitted by petrol engines at higher temperatures.

O

Octane The measure of a fuel's resistance to knock.

OE (Original Equipment) Relates to components fitted to a motorcycle as standard or replacement parts supplied by the motorcycle manufacturer.

Ohm The unit of electrical resistance. Ohms = Volts ÷ Current.

Ohmmeter An instrument for measuring electrical resistance.

Oil cooler System for diverting engine oil outside of the engine to a radiator for cooling purposes.

Oil injection A system of two-stroke engine lubrication where oil is pump-fed to the engine in accordance with throttle position.

Open-circuit An electrical condition where there is a break in the flow of electricity - no continuity (high resistance).

O-ring A type of sealing ring made of a special rubber-like material; in use, the O-ring is compressed into a groove to provide the sealing action.

Oversize (OS) Term used for piston and ring size options fitted to a rebored cylinder.

Overhead cam (sohc) engine An engine with single camshaft located on top of the cylinder head.

Overhead valve (ohv) engine An engine with the valves located in the cylinder head, but with the camshaft located in the engine block or crankcase.

Oxygen sensor A device installed in the exhaust system which senses the oxygen content in the exhaust and converts this information into an electric current. Also called a Lambda sensor.

P

Plastigauge A thin strip of plastic thread, available in different sizes, used for measuring clearances. For example, a strip of Plastigauge is laid across a bearing journal. The parts are assembled and dismantled; the width of the crushed strip indicates the clearance between journal and bearing.

Polarity Either negative or positive earth (ground), determined by which battery lead is connected to the frame (earth return). Modern motorcycles are usually negative earth.

Pre-ignition A situation where the fuel/air mixture ignites before the spark plug fires. Often due to a hot spot in the combustion chamber caused by carbon build-up. Engine has a tendency to 'run-on'.

Pre-load (suspension) The amount a spring is compressed when in the unloaded state. Preload can be applied by gas, spacer or mechanical adjuster.

Premix The method of engine lubrication on older two-stroke engines. Engine oil is mixed with the petrol in the fuel tank in a specific ratio. The fuel/oil mix is sometimes referred to as "petroil".

Primary drive Description of the drive from the crankshaft to the clutch. Usually by gear or chain.

PS Pfedestärke - a German interpretation of BHP.

PSI Pounds-force per square inch. Imperial measurement of tyre pressure and cylinder pressure measurement.

PTFE Polytetrafluroethylene. A low friction substance.

Pulse secondary air injection system A process of promoting the burning of excess fuel present in the exhaust gases by routing fresh air into the exhaust ports.

Q

Quartz halogen bulb Tungsten filament surrounded by a halogen gas. Typically used for the headlight **(see illustration)**.

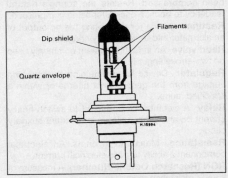

Quartz halogen headlight bulb construction

R

Rack-and-pinion A pinion gear on the end of a shaft that mates with a rack (think of a geared wheel opened up and laid flat). Sometimes used in clutch operating systems.

Radial play Up and down movement about a shaft.

Radial ply tyres Tyre plies run across the tyre (from bead to bead) and around the circumference of the tyre. Less resistant to tread distortion than other tyre types.

Radiator A liquid-to-air heat transfer device designed to reduce the temperature of the coolant in a liquid cooled engine.

Rake A feature of steering geometry - the angle of the steering head in relation to the vertical **(see illustration)**.

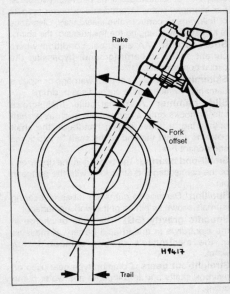

Steering geometry

Rebore Providing a new working surface to the cylinder bore by boring out the old surface. Necessitates the use of oversize piston and rings.

Rebound damping A means of controlling the oscillation of a suspension unit spring after it has been compressed. Resists the spring's natural tendency to bounce back after being compressed.

Rectifier Device for converting the ac output of an alternator into dc for battery charging.

Reed valve An induction system commonly used on two-stroke engines.

Regulator Device for maintaining the charging voltage from the generator or alternator within a specified range.

Relay A electrical device used to switch heavy current on and off by using a low current auxiliary circuit.

Resistance Measured in ohms. An electrical component's ability to pass electrical current.

RON (Research Octane Number) A measure of a fuel's resistance to knock.

rpm revolutions per minute.

Runout The amount of wobble (in-and-out movement) of a wheel or shaft as it's rotated. The amount a shaft rotates `out-of-true'. The out-of-round condition of a rotating part.

S

SAE (Society of Automotive Engineers) A standard for the viscosity of a fluid.

Sealant A liquid or paste used to prevent leakage at a joint. Sometimes used in conjunction with a gasket.

Service limit Term for the point where a component is no longer useable and must be renewed.

Shaft drive A method of transmitting drive from the transmission to the rear wheel.

Shell bearings Plain bearings consisting of two shell halves. Most often used as big-end and main bearings in a four-stroke engine. Often called bearing inserts.

Shim Thin spacer, commonly used to adjust the clearance or relative positions between two parts. For example, shims inserted into or under tappets or followers to control valve clearances. Clearance is adjusted by changing the thickness of the shim.

Short-circuit An electrical condition where current shorts to earth (ground) bypassing the circuit components.

Skimming Process to correct warpage or repair a damaged surface, eg on brake discs or drums.

Slide-hammer A special puller that screws into or hooks onto a component such as a shaft or bearing; a heavy sliding handle on the shaft bottoms against the end of the shaft to knock the component free.

Small-end bearing The bearing in the upper end of the connecting rod at its joint with the gudgeon pin.

Spalling Damage to camshaft lobes or bearing journals shown as pitting of the working surface.

Specific gravity (SG) The state of charge of the electrolyte in a lead-acid battery. A measure of the electrolyte's density compared with water.

Straight-cut gears Common type gear used on gearbox shafts and for oil pump and water pump drives.

Stanchion The inner sliding part of the front forks, held by the yokes. Often called a fork tube.

Stoichiometric ratio The optimum chemical air/fuel ratio for a petrol engine, said to be 14.7 parts of air to 1 part of fuel.

Sulphuric acid The liquid (electrolyte) used in a lead-acid battery. Poisonous and extremely corrosive.

Surface grinding (lapping) Process to correct a warped gasket face, commonly used on cylinder heads.

T

Tapered-roller bearing Tapered inner race of caged needle rollers and separate tapered outer race. Examples of taper roller bearings can be found on steering heads.

Tappet A cylindrical component which transmits motion from the cam to the valve stem, either directly or via a pushrod and rocker arm. Also called a cam follower.

TCS Traction Control System. An electronically-controlled system which senses wheel spin and reduces engine speed accordingly.

TDC Top Dead Centre denotes that the piston is at its highest point in the cylinder.

Thread-locking compound Solution applied to fastener threads to prevent slackening. Select type to suit application.

Thrust washer A washer positioned between two moving components on a shaft. For example, between gear pinions on gearshaft.

Timing chain See **Cam Chain**.

Timing light Stroboscopic lamp for carrying out ignition timing checks with the engine running.

Top-end A description of an engine's cylinder block, head and valve gear components.

Torque Turning or twisting force about a shaft.

Torque setting A prescribed tightness specified by the motorcycle manufacturer to ensure that the bolt or nut is secured correctly. Undertightening can result in the bolt or nut coming loose or a surface not being sealed. Overtightening can result in stripped threads, distortion or damage to the component being retained.

Torx key A six-point wrench.

Tracer A stripe of a second colour applied to a wire insulator to distinguish that wire from another one with the same colour insulator. For example, Br/W is often used to denote a brown insulator with a white tracer.

Trail A feature of steering geometry. Distance from the steering head axis to the tyre's central contact point.

Triple clamps The cast components which extend from the steering head and support the fork stanchions or tubes. Often called fork yokes.

Turbocharger A centrifugal device, driven by exhaust gases, that pressurises the intake air. Normally used to increase the power output from a given engine displacement.

TWI Abbreviation for Tyre Wear Indicator. Indicates the location of the tread depth indicator bars on tyres.

U

Universal joint or U-joint (UJ) A double-pivoted connection for transmitting power from a driving to a driven shaft through an angle. Typically found in shaft drive assemblies.

Unsprung weight Anything not supported by the bike's suspension (ie the wheel, tyres, brakes, final drive and bottom (moving) part of the suspension).

V

Vacuum gauges Clock-type gauges for measuring intake tract vacuum. Used for carburettor synchronisation on multi-cylinder engines.

Valve A device through which the flow of liquid, gas or vacuum may be stopped, started or regulated by a moveable part that opens, shuts or partially obstructs one or more ports or passageways. The intake and exhaust valves in the cylinder head are of the poppet type.

Valve clearance The clearance between the valve tip (the end of the valve stem) and the rocker arm or tappet/follower. The valve clearance is measured when the valve is closed. The correct clearance is important - if too small the valve won't close fully and will burn out, whereas if too large noisy operation will result.

Valve lift The amount a valve is lifted off its seat by the camshaft lobe.

Valve timing The exact setting for the opening and closing of the valves in relation to piston position.

Vernier caliper A precision measuring instrument that measures inside and outside dimensions. Not quite as accurate as a micrometer, but more convenient.

Wet liner arrangement

VIN Vehicle Identification Number. Term for the bike's engine and frame numbers.

Viscosity The thickness of a liquid or its resistance to flow.

Volt A unit for expressing electrical "pressure" in a circuit. Volts = current x ohms.

W

Water pump A mechanically-driven device for moving coolant around the engine.

Watt A unit for expressing electrical power. Watts = volts x current.

Wear limit see **Service limit**

Wet liner A liquid-cooled engine design where the pistons run in liners which are directly surrounded by coolant **(see illustration)**.

Wheelbase Distance from the centre of the front wheel to the centre of the rear wheel.

Wiring harness or loom Describes the electrical wires running the length of the motorcycle and enclosed in tape or plastic sheathing. Wiring coming off the main harness is usually referred to as a sub harness.

Woodruff key A key of semi-circular or square section used to locate a gear to a shaft. Often used to locate the alternator rotor on the crankshaft.

Wrist pin Another name for gudgeon or piston pin.

Note: *References throughout this index are in the form - "Chapter number" • "Page number"*

Note: *References throughout this index are in the form - "Chapter number" • "Page number"*

Preserving Our Motoring Heritage

< The Model J Duesenberg Derham Tourster. Only eight of these magnificent cars were ever built – this is the only example to be found outside the United States of America

Almost every car you've ever loved, loathed or desired is gathered under one roof at the Haynes Motor Museum. Over 300 immaculately presented cars and motorbikes represent every aspect of our motoring heritage, from elegant reminders of bygone days, such as the superb Model J Duesenberg to curiosities like the bug-eyed BMW Isetta. There are also many old friends and flames. Perhaps you remember the 1959 Ford Popular that you did your courting in? The magnificent 'Red Collection' is a spectacle of classic sports cars including AC, Alfa Romeo, Austin Healey, Ferrari, Lamborghini, Maserati, MG, Riley, Porsche and Triumph.

A Perfect Day Out

Each and every vehicle at the Haynes Motor Museum has played its part in the history and culture of Motoring. Today, they make a wonderful spectacle and a great day out for all the family. Bring the kids, bring Mum and Dad, but above all bring your camera to capture those golden memories for ever. You will also find an impressive array of motoring memorabilia, a comfortable 70 seat video cinema and one of the most extensive transport book shops in Britain. The Pit Stop Cafe serves everything from a cup of tea to wholesome, home-made meals or, if you prefer, you can enjoy the large picnic area nestled in the beautiful rural surroundings of Somerset.

John Haynes O.B.E., Founder and Chairman of the museum at the wheel of a Haynes Light 12.

< The 1936 490cc sohc-engined International Norton – well known for its racing success

The Museum is situated on the A359 Yeovil to Frome road at Sparkford, just off the A303 in Somerset. It is about 40 miles south of Bristol, and 25 minutes drive from the M5 intersection at Taunton.
Open 9.30am - 5.30pm (10.00am - 4.00pm Winter) 7 days a week, *except Christmas Day, Boxing Day and New Years Day*
Special rates available for schools, coach parties and outings Charitable Trust No. 292048